ANDREW FURUSETH

Andrew Furuseth

PUBLICATIONS OF THE
INSTITUTE OF INDUSTRIAL RELATIONS
UNIVERSITY OF CALIFORNIA

ANDREW FURUSETH
Emancipator of the Seamen

By
HYMAN WEINTRAUB

UNIVERSITY OF CALIFORNIA PRESS
BERKELEY AND LOS ANGELES
1959

UNIVERSITY OF CALIFORNIA PRESS
BERKELEY AND LOS ANGELES
CALIFORNIA

◇

CAMBRIDGE UNIVERSITY PRESS
LONDON, ENGLAND

© 1959 BY THE REGENTS OF THE UNIVERSITY
OF CALIFORNIA

LIBRARY OF CONGRESS CATALOG CARD NO. 59-5747

TO
MY PARENTS
whose pride in their son
I have tried to justify

FOREWORD

THE HISTORY of the American labor movement has been enriched by forceful leaders, men whose lives and contributions deserve biography. Among the most interesting and important is Andrew Furuseth, the stern seafaring Norwegian, who came to San Francisco in 1880 and was to devote his life to the organization and welfare of the seamen. The union he built—the Sailors' Union of the Pacific—was to prove enduring; it is, in fact, still in existence and thriving. In Furuseth's lifetime the SUP played a central role in the unfolding drama of American labor history. The story of Furuseth and the SUP throws light upon many aspects of the labor movement: the problems of leadership within an organization, the importance of inter- and intraunion rivalries, the emergence and the troubles of the philosophy of business unionism, the part played by labor in politics in California and the nation, the development of protective labor legislation, and the role of unions in international affairs.

The unfortunate fact that no proper life of Furuseth has existed until now is remedied with the publication of this study by Dr. Hyman Weintraub. He came to this task with two notable assets: direct knowledge of the labor movement combined with professional training as a historian. He gained the former from personal experience as well as family connections, and the latter from doctoral work at the University of California, Los Angeles. Each will be evident to the reader of this volume.

The Institute of Industrial Relations, Southern Division, presents this work as part of its continuing research program in American labor history. The Institute has already published Dr. Grace Heilman Stimson's *Rise of the Labor Movement in Los Angeles*, carrying that story to 1912, with a second volume dealing with more recent times now under way. In addition, there is in preparation a general history of American labor between the 1920's and the outbreak of World War II.

GEORGE H. HILDEBRAND, *Director*
Institute of Industrial Relations
University of California, Los Angeles

PREFACE

WHEN THE RESEARCH for this book began, I expected to enshrine in labor's temple a forgotten saint. After several years of collecting evidence, I found that Andrew Furuseth was in truth a forgotten man, but not a saint. He was very much of this world. He possessed human shortcomings. He made mistakes. He made enemies. And he made history.

There is no saint and there are no miracles in this biography, because the truth did not uncover them. Instead, a more dramatic story unfolded—the seamen's struggle to raise their economic and social level and the tragedy of the lonely man who led them. It became more important to use Andrew Furuseth as a symbol for the thousands of labor leaders who have led their people out of bondage, than to prove that labor has had its share of saints.

Unfortunately for Furuseth, his historical fate lies within these pages. Aside from being a trained historian with some firsthand knowledge of trade unions, I make no pretense of any special qualifications for undertaking this biography. Paul Scharrenberg, a close associate of Andrew Furuseth, frankly told me that since I had not sailed before the mast, I would fail to understand men like Furuseth. I have been around the labor movement long enough to know the universal opinion that one must have calluses to understand labor.

I hope that the skeptics will be pleasantly disappointed. I have tried to make up for my inadequacies by diligent and exhaustive research, and by writing in a manner that will meet the best academic standards. It is not the scholar, however, for whom this book is primarily intended, but the men in the sailors' union and the leaders in many unions who have a lesson to learn from the story of Andrew Furuseth.

An author who gives proper credit to all those who have contributed toward making his book possible must conclude by taking credit for nothing except the mistakes. I readily admit that, but for the help of many individuals, this volume would never have appeared.

For example, without permission to use the files of the Sailors' Union of the Pacific, this would have been a superficial biography. The late Harry Lundeberg gave me unlimited access to the files. The sailors have had high regard for the judgment of history and their files are amazingly complete. To all the unnamed secretaries who kept such careful records, I am deeply grateful.

Librarians throughout the country were coöperative in describing their holdings on Andrew Furuseth, but special thanks are extended to the librarians at the University of California, Los Angeles; the Institute of Industrial Relations Library at UCLA; and the Bancroft Library in Berkeley, who did not spare themselves in complying with any fantastic request I made.

In the course of gathering material for this biography, I talked to dozens of people who knew Furuseth. Some of these people are listed in the bibliography, but to all those whose names are not mentioned, I extend my apologies. There were also a number of individuals like Silas B. Axtell to whom thanks are due for making available their private collections of materials on Furuseth.

Many hardy individuals have waded through the rough draft of this manuscript. Lou Goldowitz, my brother-in-law, made many valuable editorial changes in my first draft. My sister-in-law, Victoria Margolin, then retyped the manuscript. At this point I had the courage to take it outside my family. Anne P. Cook, editor for the Institute of Industrial Relations at UCLA, reviewed every page to eliminate clumsy errors. Archie Green of San Francisco, a human bibliography of the labor movement, made extensive notes on and criticisms of the original manuscript. Two "real" sailors who were intimately acquainted with Furuseth, Selim Silver and Paul Scharrenberg, read the document to check its seaworthiness. Harry Lang, labor editor of the *Jewish Daily Forward*, reviewed it carefully to see that the book caught the spirit of Gompers' labor movement. Among many others who read the manuscript, I am grateful for the comments made by Dr. Ruth Baugh, Dr. Robert Burke, Dr. Irving Bernstein, Dr. John W. Caughey, and Francis Gates.

I have taxed the patience of many people. Dr. Irving Bernstein listened for hours to my problems. Dr. John W. Caughey, my teacher for more than ten years, patiently prodded me toward completion of the book and was always on hand for advice and encouragement. But the most patient and understanding of all was my wife, who gave up her husband and her social life, and substituted as the father of our three children—all for "the cause."

My most sincere appreciation goes to the Institute of Industrial Relations at UCLA and its former director, the late Edgar L. Warren, for the financial aid that enabled me to devote all my spare time to research and writing. Association with the staff of the Institute was an additional personal reward which I shall long cherish.

H. W.

CONTENTS

I. Sailor	1
II. Union Man	11
III. Lobbyist for Seamen	28
IV. Labor Theorist	45
V. Fighter	57
VI. Labor Leader	85
VII. The Seamen's Act	108
VIII. Using the Seamen's Act	133
IX. World War I	143
X. Changing Fortunes	155
XI. Defender of the Seamen's Act	164
XII. Lonely Warrior	177
Notes	203
Bibliography	239
Index	263

I. SAILOR

IN FRONT of Sailors' Union headquarters in San Francisco is a bronze bust of a man with a stern face and a long beaklike nose. Most of the seamen who pass the statue daily hardly recognize the name of Andrew Furuseth.[1] The unfamiliar features might remind them of the American eagle or of Cruikshank's caricature of Scrooge in *A Christmas Carol*. But observers would be aware of something basically wrong in that impression. The forehead and the eyes—did they not belie the stern, uncompromising features? Surely the man was too much of a philosopher to fit the picture of the eagle or of Scrooge.

The bust is no enigma to those who knew and admired Andrew Furuseth. Furuseth was a tough fighter. His features, like those of his Viking ancestors, were carved by the harsh struggle with the sea and the land. His face was stern because one did not wrest life from the ocean or sustenance from the land with laughter. It was kindly and philosophic because Furuseth's struggles were never undertaken in his own behalf; he devoted his life to advancing the interests of the lowest, the most scorned section of society—the seamen.

Fanciful stories have been told to explain Furuseth's lifelong devotion to the cause of the seamen. According to one of these tales, Furuseth was stricken with a fever while sailing on the Indian Ocean in 1874. An unmerciful first mate demanded that he continue his regular duties, despite his illness. Furuseth, filled with anger and resentment against the mate, determined to kill him. But no opportunity presented itself, and when the fever had passed, Furuseth had time for a sober second thought. He realized that killing the mate would have been no solution for himself or for other seamen who were driven like slaves. Organization by the seamen, and organization alone, could improve their status; and so the young sailor vowed to devote his life to this work. He deliberately set his course for the United States, whose principles of freedom offered all the sailors of the world the best opportunity for emancipation.[2]

This story could certainly have been true. Any sailor in the 1870's could have had such an experience. That Furuseth was the victim of harsh treatment or that he saw others being victimized during his years as a sailor can hardly be doubted. But it is unlikely that he made his resolve to free the seamen of the world when he was only twenty years old and had been at sea less than a year. It was to be another eleven years before he joined with other sailors in the Coast Seamen's Union. Moreover, in 1874 Furuseth knew no country but Norway, and at that time his native land had no examples of workingmen organizing to improve their conditions.[3]

Furuseth's background was like that of many Norwegians who followed the sea for a livelihood.[4] His father, Andreas Nielsen, who worked in the peat bogs, married Marthe Jensdatter on April 17, 1846. The young couple lived in Graaberget until 1852, when they moved to a cottage in Furuseth, a village southeast of the town of Romedal, about fifty miles north of Oslo. Here Anders, the fifth child, was born on March 12, 1854.[5] In accordance with Scandinavian custom, the boy was known by the name of the village in which he was born—Andrew Furuseth. In 1855 the family moved to Damstuen, where five more children were born. Nielsen's job there was to look after the locks of a dam.[6] His income was too small to support such a large family, and the Nielsens suffered continuous poverty. Meals often consisted of potatoes dipped in herring sauce and bread made of tree bark and flour. To supplement this starchy diet, the father would hunt and fish. Although the diet was not appetizing, it did not impair the longevity of the family; the father lived more than ninety years, and six of the children more than eighty.[7]

When Andrew was eight years old, he was sent to Romedal to live and work with Jonas S. Schjotz, a farmer, in order to relieve the family budget. The choice was fortunate, for Schjotz, noticing the boy's keen interest in learning, arranged for his admission to the private parish school. When Andrew was confirmed in 1869, at the age of fifteen, the church register recorded, "knowledge good, fairly good condition." On June 2, 1870, he left the Schjotz farm and went to Oslo,[8] where he remained for three years. For a time he clerked in a grocery store, and then entered a training school for noncommissioned officers in the hope that he might be admitted to the Norwegian equivalent of America's West Point. Despite coaching by his friends, he was rejected. But his keen interest in languages, developed while he was a student, enabled him to supplement his earnings by translating English, German, Dutch, and French.

In 1873 Furuseth joined the crew of the bark *Marie* out of Draman. It is easy to understand why a young man of nineteen, blocked in his ambition to become an officer, seeing no future in working as a clerk, and with only the slimmest of family ties, would turn to the sea. There he would find a life of adventure; he could see the world about which he had been reading; he could dream of commanding a vessel. From

1873 until August, 1880, when Furuseth arrived in California,[9] he sailed on Norwegian, Swedish, British, French, and American vessels. He may have spent part of his time fishing on the Newfoundland banks.[10] Although there is no record of Furuseth's experiences during those seven years, his familiarity with ports throughout the world suggests that he sailed most of the seven seas.

It is unlikely that Furuseth had any experience aboard a steamship. His attitude toward steamship sailors was typical of the old-time sailor who thought of them as second-class citizens of the sea. Long after the sailing ship had, for all practical purposes, disappeared as a commercial rival to the steamship, Furuseth still held that a sailor could get his best training on board a sailing vessel.

Sailor's Life

There are many accounts of life aboard a sailing ship, depicting it as either a floating heaven or a floating hell. The truth is that it was neither heaven nor hell, but a purgatory of unending monotony. Occasionally a storm, a shipwreck, or a rescue punctuated the tedium and called forth the best in each man; or perhaps a beating or a fight occurred, demonstrating the depraved depths to which these same men could sink. Most days at sea, however, followed one another in monotonous regularity. The sailor's adventurous life, in fact, was more myth than reality.[11]

Although the seaman's daily tasks were not unlike those of workers on land, there were important differences in his situation. Primarily, his ship was not just a place to work; it was his home. The men with whom he worked were not merely fellow employees, but his social companions and his family. The second important difference was the relationship of the sailor to the master of the vessel. Other workers, when conditions became unbearable, could quit, either singly or in unison. Seamen had no such choice. As Richard Henry Dana put it,

... what is there for the sailors to do? If they resist it is mutiny, if they succeed, and take the vessel, it is piracy. If they ever yield again, their punishment must come; and if they do not yield, they are pirates for life. If a sailor resists his commander, he resists the law, and piracy and submission are his only alternatives.[12]

Such absolute power led to abuses. Seamen were whipped, beaten, kicked, clubbed for minor offenses or no offenses at all. It is true that such treatment was the exception, but so was the whipping of slaves. The fact remains that both the slave and the sailor were subject to beatings at the will of the master, who could administer them with almost complete immunity. This unlimited authority presented those who possessed it with a strong temptation to use it. The captain was a lonely man; except for the mate, he had no one to talk to on long voyages. He was a virtual prisoner in solitary confinement on his own ship. Sometimes a captain would take out his own bitterness on his men.

A favorite method was to get a man when he was at the wheel. While both the sailor's hands were occupied, the master or his mate would taunt the poor devil until he answered back. This provided the excuse and the opportunity to strike him. If the wheelsman was a big fellow, a belaying pin was used instead of fists. The victim was expected to clean up his own blood.

If a sailor was killed, the captain or officer was not convicted. The record of the official log was carefully worded to justify any unusual act on the part of the authorities. Testimony was quickly suppressed or manufactured. Witnesses were easily disposed of in foreign ports. Sailors whose testimony was feared were promptly turned over to the boarding house keepers. After a short debauch, they were put on some vessel about to sail for another part of the world. It was always assumed that the punishment, or even death, of a sailor was caused by his rebellion against his authorities. In many cases this was so, but it would be useless to deny that seamen were occasionally, if not frequently, brutally treated, and sometimes murdered on the high seas.[13]

Although watch followed watch in uninterrupted monotony, the seaman knew that this apparent serenity was enforced by the brass "knuck," the bare fist, the boot, and the belaying pin. These weapons might never be used, but their threatening presence was always part of the sailor's consciousness.

THE CRIMPING SYSTEM

If such cruelties were practiced, or even if the sailor suffered the mental indignity of being in an inferior social position, why then did he not leave the sea? It is difficult for the free man to comprehend the status of the slave. It seems so easy, so simple a solution, to get another job. But even when the sailor went ashore, he did not escape from bondage; he fell victim to another kind of tyranny—the system of hiring through boardinghouses and "crimps." Caught in the toils of this system, the average sailor was virtually penniless, with no place to stay except the boardinghouse that enticed him, and with only a seaman's skills to earn his living.[14]

In essence, the system was an economic arrangement whereby a ship's captain, instead of hiring sailors individually, relied on a seamen's boardinghouse to furnish his crew. Since the boardinghouse master agreed to supply men when needed and since competition was keen, he often resorted to unfair tactics to get and keep seamen in his clutches. Obviously, the time to catch the sailor was when his vessel entered the harbor, and so the boardinghouse employed runners who went out in small boats to meet the ships. They climbed aboard and tried to convince the sailors to patronize their particular establishment. They were free in handing out drinks. They made promises of fabulous jobs ashore or of much higher paying jobs on other vessels. They compared the paradise of the city with the hell on board ship, with the prospect of days and perhaps weeks of tedious loading and unloading of cargo in port. They handed out a few more drinks. They spotted the leader of the crew and made him a special offer. When they were ready to go ashore, they had usually convinced some of the men to come with them. Each sailor who went forfeited his wages and whatever clothes and equipment he left behind, because he had deserted the vessel.

At the boardinghouse the sailor was provided with a bed, food and drink, cigars, and even clothes and supplies. If he ran out of money, the boardinghouse keeper extended credit; if he went on a binge, the keeper sobered him up; if he got into trouble with the police, the keeper had connections to "spring him from the brig." Most important, the boarding master always managed to find him a berth on some vessel.

For all these services the sailor paid dearly. When he came ashore, he was charged five dollars by the runner, a dollar for the boat, and another dollar for the wagon that took him to the house. There he paid five dollars per week whether he stayed one night or all week. He had to buy supplies for his next trip: five dollars for oils, some more for cigars, a tin plate, a pot, a bundle of matches, a plug of tobacco, and a straw bed. It was no secret that the sailor was overcharged for everything he bought, but the boardinghouse keeper and the clothier felt that they were justified because they sold on credit. The seaman dared not buy for cash at some other establishment since that might jeopardize his chance of getting a job.

To prevent a sailor from leaving without paying his bill, the boarding master had worked out a foolproof system. When the sailor shipped out, the captain gave the boarding master an advance on the sailor's wages to pay the debts he had run up at the house; or the sailor authorized an allotment to the boarding master, which was a lien on his future earnings. Maritime law provided that he could not sign over more than one month's earnings, but somehow he seldom owed more than that amount. On the other hand, he rarely got a ship until he had run up a bill equal to one month's pay. In fact, the seaman soon learned that the faster he got into debt, the more quickly another job would be found for him. The sailor who did not drink or squander his money, who dreamed of saving enough to buy himself a little farm, soon discovered that there were no jobs for him. The boardinghouse could keep him without any risk and there was no hurry to find him a ship.

Into this picture there entered a broker known on the water front as the "crimp."[15] He was a middleman, analogous to an employment agent. Instead of dealing directly with the vessels, the boardinghouse often made arrangements with a crimp to ship its men. The crimp contacted the captains and obtained crews for them; he also employed runners to bring sailors to the house. He charged each sailor five dollars for a "chance"—the fee of the employment agent. In addition, the crimp made money by charging the boardinghouse for shipping its men when there was an abundance of sailors. In time of scarcity, he demanded "blood money" from the captain and a commission on everything the sailor spent at the clothier's and at the house. He made loans to seamen and collected advances both for himself and for the boardinghouse. The crimp might also be a boarding master, a clothier, or even a runner; what distinguished him was his middleman function. Of all the links in the system, the sailor hated the crimp most. From the boardinghouse he got food and drink; from the captain, wages; but from the broker he got nothing.

No matter how much they hated the crimps, most sailors could not escape from the system. Only when seamen were unusually scarce could a man get a job on his own initiative, even with a captain who knew him and had been pleased with his work.[16] A few found their avenue of escape in advancing from able seaman to boatswain, then to third mate, and up the ladder to captain of the vessel. But for the great majority there was no alternative but starvation.

The system became so firmly entrenched because it had advantages for everyone—even for the seamen. Many sailors preferred to let the boardinghouse keeper find them jobs rather than to tramp the docks themselves in search of work. Relying on the system, the sailor had no worries. The boarding master was content with an arrangement that enabled him to keep his house full. His best means of attracting customers was to promise them jobs and to extend them credit.

The captain and the owner of the vessel were also satisfied with the system. A captain could not spend his limited time in port rounding up a crew, for he had many other things to do. It was more convenient to let the boarding master know how many men he needed. This arrangement, moreover, eliminated haggling over wages with individual seamen; the boarding master knew what would be paid and which men could be obtained for that figure. When sailors were scarce, he somehow knew where additional men could be picked up. Except for the few occasions when seamen were in such short supply that the boardinghouse keeper demanded a bonus, his services cost the captain nothing. In fact, a boarding master might even pay a captain for an agreement to take sailors from his particular house.[17]

Under this arrangement a captain was not concerned about losing some of his crew. The same runner who took the men off had others waiting at the boardinghouse to take their places. If the ship was to be in port for any length of time, the captain would have to feed and pay a crew that he did not really need. Even if sailors were in high demand and he was later held up for "blood money," the expense would be more than offset by forfeited wages and by the savings made while in port. On a long voyage the amount of wages forfeited might be so substantial that captains were known to "work the men ashore." This was notoriously true of British captains.[18] Before a vessel put into a harbor, discipline would become especially strict, the amount of work would increase, petty annoyances would be invented, and the food would become bad. If the sailors still stayed aboard, the captain would refuse to grant shore leave while working the crew long hours in port. It was an unusual sailor who could, under such circumstances, resist the blandishments of the runner.[19]

A Coasting Sailor

The crimping system was of necessity a part of the experience of seaman Andy Furuseth. When Furuseth left his ship in San Francisco in 1880, at the age of twenty-six, he went to a boardinghouse. For four years, as long as he stayed at the house, he had no difficulty in shipping.[20] Then, motivated by a desire for greater privacy or the wish to break away from the clutches of the boarding master, Furuseth moved to a rooming house occupied by other Scandinavian sailors at 26 Steuart Street. When seamen were in great demand, he could still get a job, but in 1885 he walked the beach for six weeks without work. Furuseth, who had been sailing along the Pacific Coast for five years and was probably known to most of the captains, was hard put to find a berth without the aid of a boarding master. Imagine, then, the fate of a sailor who was a stranger to San Francisco.

During this period Furuseth changed from a deepwater sailor—one who voyaged to foreign lands—to a coasting sailor and a fisherman. The sea was a means of earning a living. Since coastal sailors were paid more than deepwater sailors, and the chances of making a big catch of fish in the Columbia River promised greater returns than shipping to China or around the Horn, Furuseth settled down to what amounted, for a sailor, to a domestic life.

On the San Francisco water front, Furuseth found congenial company. He did not seek companionship in the sense of looking for a confidant or a bosom pal, but he liked to talk and he needed men with whom he could talk. In San Francisco he found these men, for fully 90 per cent of the seamen in the coastwise trade were Scandinavians. Although Furuseth knew French, German, and English, there is little doubt that he felt more comfortable speaking his native tongue. He could have found the same concentration of Scandinavians in the coastal trade on the Atlantic or on the Great Lakes,[11] but San Francisco had the further advantage of paying the highest wages.

Like most Scandinavian seamen, Furuseth probably sailed in the large, square-rigged vessels that hauled lumber from the forests of Washington and Oregon to the booming community in the south, Los Angeles. Sailors on these ships not only were expected to be excellent seamen, but they also had to be adept at loading and unloading lumber. For, unlike most seamen, the West Coast sailor did the work of the longshoreman. This important peculiarity explains the ferocity of Furuseth's later attacks on longshoremen on the Pacific Coast and throughout the world. The nature of the California seacoast and the type of products shipped made it necessary for the sailor to handle cargo. In the days of the hide and tallow trade, seamen were expected to take the vessel to a point close to a ranch where they could pick up the bundles of hides and transport them to the ship. Men on shore could not be hired to do the loading because it was not a year-round job, but would take only a few hours or, at most, a few weeks. The same situation existed in the lumber trade. Longshoremen were not waiting at each lumber camp at which the vessel stopped, and the sailors were expected to load the cargo. Although most sailors considered longshore work beneath their station, the Scandinavians on the West Coast realized the advantages it gave them: they were better paid; they were not laid off every time a vessel came into port because the captain had no use for them; and they developed skill in handling and stowing lumber which made them difficult to replace.

To make voyages profitable, it was necessary to carry a heavy load since little of value was shipped north. It was customary to fill the holds with lumber and then to load the deck until the water reached the deck line. Skilled men were needed to secure the load so that it would not shift at sea and cause the loss of both ship and cargo. Skilled seamen were needed to maneuver the vessel safely into port in San Pedro, San Diego, or Wilmington.

Quite often the men preferred to go fishing in Washington or British Columbia. The work was harder and the hours were longer, but there was always the possibility of returning with a "nest egg." The sailor who turned to fishing left San Francisco with the fishing fleet in March or April. He signed an agreement providing for a minimum monthly wage, but in addition he was either entitled to a share in the total catch or was paid extra for every fish caught. If he were fortunate, he might be back in San Francisco in two or three months with enough money to last until the next fishing season. More often he would return in September or October, complain about his poor luck, and receive about the same pay as if he had been working in the coastwise trade.[22]

Andrew Furuseth made several such fishing expeditions during his years as a coastal sailor. His last long voyage took him to Alaska, where a new salmon-canning industry was developing. Early in April, 1889, when he was thirty-five years old, he joined a crew of some 250 fishermen who were going to Nashagak to establish a cannery. At the time Furuseth reported that his trip "was as uneventful as a sea voyage generally is,"[23] but almost thirty years later he described a dramatic incident that occurred just before the vessel reached its destination.[24] In the Bering Sea, the sailors noticed clouds of black smoke coming from one of the holds, which was loaded with highly flammable materials needed for the cannery. As the vessel pitched and rolled in the rough sea, the sailors opened the hatches and began digging through the cargo; fanned by the wind, the fire could have turned into a holocaust. Fortunately, the experienced seamen discovered the source and extinguished a conflagration that might have sent them all to the bottom of the sea. Perhaps Furuseth could characterize such a voyage as uneventful because, like most seamen, he had already experienced similar fires.

Furuseth was not particularly impressed with Alaska. In a letter home he wrote:

> When we arrived here [probably early in May] the snow was just getting off the ground, and it has been keeping on getting off ever since. This is a strange country. It would be warm if the sun would but shine; dry weather if the rain would but cease; and money to be made if the salmon would but come in, but thus far—and the season is about over—the salmon have been scarce, at least, where we are. Should other places turn out the same, the salmon fishing must, I think, be considered a failure.[25]

Furuseth probably sailed for short periods after his return from Alaska in September; he spent almost two months on the Columbia River in 1892. But in 1885 he had joined the newly formed Coast Seamen's Union and had soon become so involved in its affairs that he could not have spent much time on ships after 1889. Furuseth had long been outraged by the seaman's virtual slavery under the crimping system. He saw that sailors were victimized by everyone on shore with whom they were forced to come in contact. Everyone profited at their expense, and worst of all, there was little chance to escape. It was in character for Furuseth to turn to organization as a means of achieving freedom. Even if he had been concerned only with his own welfare, it is unlikely that he himself could have escaped from the system by rising to officer status. Although he may have served as boatswain occasionally, he fell short of the qualifications necessary for advancement in the sailing ship era. A boatswain had to be big and strong, and willing to use his fists and boots to drive the men to work. Furuseth was tall, broad-shouldered, muscular, and capable of handling himself in any contest of strength, but he lacked the willingness to use his physical prowess to drive men to work. Moreover, he must already have exhibited some of the characteristics that marked him in later life as a recluse devoted to reading and meditation. If he were working today on a road gang, his fellow workers would probably call him "professor"—if they dared. Captains looking for boatswains did not ordinarily pick the intellectual type. Men on shipboard were ruled, not by reason, but by force or the fear of force.

Andrew Furuseth always regarded himself as a sailor. Everyone who ever met him thought of him as a sailor. He looked and dressed, walked and talked like a sailor. He thought like a sailor. But from September, 1889, until he died in 1938, Furuseth earned his living principally on land.

II. UNION MAN

ON JUNE 3, 1885, Andrew Furuseth made application for membership in the Coast Seamen's Union.[1] This simple act changed the course of his entire life and eventually affected the lives of hundreds of thousands of seamen throughout the world.

ORGANIZATION OF COAST SEAMEN'S UNION, 1885

The Coast Seamen's Union had been organized in San Francisco while Furuseth was absent from the city. In 1885 the shipping industry was in the doldrums. Jobs were scarce, and wages low. On March 4 it was announced that monthly wages would be further cut to $20 and $25 for inside and outside ports, respectively.[2] The seamen refused to accept the reduction: they milled around the water front, held informal "gripe" sessions on the docks, and induced crews to desert their vessels.

Among the most outspoken was Sigismund Danielwicz, a coasting sailor who was a member of the socialist International Workingmen's Association.[3] Urging organization, and promising support from the IWA, he persuaded the men to meet on the Folsom Street Wharf on the evening of March 6, 1885. Several hundred sailors gathered near the lumber piles on the wharf to hear the IWA speakers whom Danielwicz had procured. Again the theme of organization was pounded home. The men contributed enough money to hire the Irish-American Hall for the following night, and there they laid plans for the Coast Seamen's Union.[4] Two days later, 456 members accepted a constitution and bylaws submitted by Burnette G. Haskell, leader of the IWA in San Francisco. They further decided to boycott any boardinghouse that shipped nonunion men. On March 11, the sailors met again to elect officers. George Thompson, who had been chairman of the original meeting on the wharf, was chosen president, and Rasmus Nielsen secretary. Real control of the union was lodged in the Advisory Committee which, according to the constitution, was to be composed of members of the International Workingmen's Association. The first Advisory Committee consisted of Sigismund Danielwicz, Burnette G. Haskell, James J. Martin, P. Ross Martin, and Martin Schneider. The IWA donated the use of its offices at 6 Eddy Street for the headquarters of the union.

For two months the newly formed organization skirmished with the shipowners in attempts to prevent them from shipping nonunion men at the reduced scale of wages. By July 1 the Coast Seamen's Union had 2,200 members out of the 3,000 to 3,500 coasting sailors. This was not a high enough proportion effectively to control all shipping on the coast. It was fortuitous, however, that the union was organized at the time of year when many coasting sailors left San Francisco for the fishing grounds in the north. Thus the relative scarcity of seamen and the degree of organization served to keep wages up on most of the vessels. Another aspect of the struggle was to wrest control of shipping from the boarding masters and crimps. Less than a month after it had been organized, the union opened its own shipping office at 7 Spear Street, and Edward Crangle became the first shipping master chosen by seamen themselves anywhere in the world. In May the union opened its own boardinghouse at 217 Broadway. Neither the shipping office nor the house, however, was able to secure control of water-front jobs. A third objective was to prevent nonunion men from sailing at any wage. From March to the middle of May the water front reverberated with sluggings and beatings. The crimps and boarding masters on the one hand, and the union on the other, recognized that they were in a life-and-death struggle. The situation was not conducive to sweet reasonableness.[5]

During these tumultuous days Furuseth was fishing on the Columbia River.[6] As soon as he returned, he joined the union. Aside from any intellectual conviction he might have formed on the need for organization, he had the same reasons for joining as most sailors had: solidarity with his fellow workers, opposition to wage reductions, freedom from the crimp's control, and the promise of greater self-respect.

A union in the process of organization, and engaged in bitter conflict with employers, presents many opportunities for leadership. Direction of the union, which had fallen to members of the Workingmen's Association, had necessarily to be placed in the hands of the seamen themselves. Furuseth was active in the union while this change was taking place, and to him eventually fell the role of the seamen's leader.

STRIKE OF 1886

For a year the union consolidated its forces. By the spring of 1886 it was strong enough to enforce a higher scale of wages on all coasting vessels—$35 to inside and $40 to outside ports. In June an event occurred which was to test the mettle of the infant union.[7] The firemen of the Oceanic Steamship Company, owned by John D. Spreckles, went on strike in a dispute over the number of firemen one vessel was to carry. At the request of the Federated Trades, the central labor body of San Francisco, about a hundred sailors walked out in sympathy with the firemen. There is little doubt that if Oceanic had been forced to face the organized seamen alone, it would have had to capitulate. But the shipowners foresaw the danger of having to surrender one at a time to the demands of their workers, and on June 7 they formed an association.[8] They issued orders to their captains that all men were to be hired through a shipping office established by the association. No one could ship through the office unless he surrendered his union book and obtained a "grade book." The captain would record a seaman's service in his grade book, noting the dates of the voyage, the grade and capacity in which the seaman had served, and a comment on the quality of his work. Without the book a man could not get a position on any vessel belonging to a member of the association. With the book, anyone who complained about the food, refused to kowtow to the officers, or quit because he could no longer endure the conditions under which he worked, would receive an unsatisfactory mark. This would effectively prevent a "troublemaker" from securing future employment.

As long as the union had been able to increase wages and control jobs, a large number of men had switched from the crimps to the union. When there was a fight, however, these men did not make dependable members. When they saw the shipowners bringing in deepwater sailors, "pier-head" loafers, and farm hands to take their places, they became panicky and began surrendering their union books for grade books. The situation called for action. At a meeting of all water-front unions on August 26, Haskell urged the necessity for answering the employers' challenge with a general strike, but his proposal was defeated. After the meeting the sailors decided that their alternatives were to submit to the grade-book system and disband the union, or to strike against the combined power of the Shipowners' Association. They chose to call out their 3,000 members from all coastwise vessels.

During the entire month of September blood flowed freely on the water front as union pickets tried to prevent crimps from shipping men through the association office. Several men were killed. Off the water front, union officials tried to negotiate with the shipowners, but despite several meetings and compromise proposals made by the union, the owners insisted upon complete surrender. The union, without funds and with many deserters, gave up the fight on September 30, 1886. Many of those who had not left the union while the fight was in progress now saw no reason to remain with it. They either sailed as nonunion men or took jobs ashore. It was this organization that Furuseth was to take over four months after its disastrous defeat.

Furuseth Becomes Secretary

In those days Furuseth was a rarity—a literate seaman. Even before the strike, his knowledge of financial matters had been recognized by his appointment to the Finance Committee. His work on the committee and his participation in the strike won for him a reputation that made him the logical choice to succeed Rasmus Nielsen as secretary when Nielsen died in January, 1887.[9] This was the most important position in the union, for the office of president had been abolished and a chairman was elected at each meeting instead. The only other full-time paid employees were the patrolmen in San Francisco, whose tasks were analogous to those of a business agent in any other union, and the agents in the ports of Eureka, San Pedro, San Diego, and Seattle, where the union maintained branch offices. The secretary had to take minutes of the meetings, keep all financial records, take care of correspondence, collect dues, supervise the activities of the branches, examine applicants for membership, and handle a host of other miscellaneous duties. Furuseth devoted fourteen to sixteen hours a day to this job. Without a family and with no special interests except reading to distract him, he gave every moment of his time to the union.

A typical day in the office, now located at 513½ East Street, would start at seven in the morning.[10] The patrolmen climb the narrow, muddy staircase to ask for any last-minute news or instructions before they go out to the docks. The secretary opens the mail. There may be several requests as to the whereabouts of boys who have left home and are believed to be sailing along the Pacific Coast. There may be a request for shipwreck benefits from a union member whose vessel was smashed in the Bering Sea. An agent may send additional news not included in his weekly report. A sick member in the hospital writes for his monthly benefit of one dollar. The secretary answers as many of these letters as time allows, but he must spend at least several hours this morning in preparing the minutes of the previous night's meeting and in making neat, legible copies to send to the branches. This work takes longer than it should because he is interrupted by visitors. Some men come in briefly to pay their dues, others just to "shoot the bull." One man comes to bring charges against another member for having shipped below the union scale. A mate complains about a union member who reported for duty drunk.

The morning goes by with most of the work yet to be done. The meeting has authorized the payment of a number of bills and has instructed the secretary to ask the landlord of the building to fix the plumbing. These matters need immediate attention. Invariably, someone from the Cigar Makers' Union, the Brewery Workers' Union, or one of the many other unions that belong to the Federated Trades Council visits the secretary to ask for help. Perhaps it is only to use the seamen's hall for a meeting, or the brewery workers may ask Furuseth to urge the proprietor of a water-front saloon to cease buying "scab" beer. A patrolman brings in three men who have just come into port and would like to join the union. Furuseth examines them to make sure they are qualified seamen, and then helps them fill out the application blanks. A destitute sailor, still a little wobbly from last night's binge, comes in for a handout.

By five o'clock, many of the sailors who have been loading or unloading in the port begin drifting into the office. Some come to complain that the patrolmen have not handled their grievances properly; one accuses a patrolman of having been drunk; another says that he was not properly credited with having paid his dues in San Pedro; others come with "scuttlebutt" which they think the secretary should know. Later, when the office has cleared out somewhat, the Trial Committee meets to hear charges against the janitor for neglect of his duties. The secretary is not on the committee, but because his knowledge is indispensable to the conduct of the hearing, he remains to help in any way he can. When the meeting is over and everyone has gone home, there is still unfinished business to be cleared up, because the next day will be as busy as this one has been.

In return for this grinding schedule, the union paid its secretary and the other full-time officials—patrolmen and agents—from $10 to $15 a week.[11] When many men were out of work, or if the union was on strike, this salary was cut in half or canceled entirely. Usually it was slightly higher than the wages of an able seaman, but because the officials had to pay for their own food and lodging, they actually received less than they could have made by sailing. But it is not difficult to understand why they worked longer hours at less pay. Many men have given up better-paid jobs to accept ones with less drudgery, more dignity, greater prestige, or more social value.

A lesser man than Furuseth would have been overwhelmed by the enormity of the task that he faced upon taking office. Union membership had dwindled to slightly more than a thousand, and even these members were being forced to sail under grade books issued by the shipowners. Morale was low. Nevertheless, several factors favored a revival of the union's strength. Perhaps most important was the low scale of wages imposed upon the seamen by the triumphant shipowners. This was an object lesson in the advantages of unionism. Furthermore, there had been an upturn in trade, and the increasing demand for seamen put the union in a favorable bargaining position. These factors alone, however, would not have rebuilt the union unless there had been men capable of utilizing the situation.

Instead of retrenching, Furuseth worked for an expanding union with a dynamic program. In January, 1887, the same month he was elected, he urged upon the union a plan to retaliate against the shipowners.[12] Several months later he was among those most actively supporting the establishment of a union newspaper, and he was on the committee that made this dream a reality in the *Coast Seamen's Journal*.[13] In June Furuseth tried to put the shipowners on the defensive by requesting the California Bureau of Labor Statistics to investigate the water-front situation. Such action, he was certain, would reveal "evidence of the most startling character ... [and] show how the sailor has been kept purposely in his present acknowledged degraded condition, to render him a will-less commodity in the hands of unscrupulous speculators with which they could 'bear' and 'bull' the market."[14] Union finances were put on a businesslike basis. Wages gradually rose to the prestrike level, members began to return to the union, the treasury was rebuilt, and morale was restored. Proud of their newspaper and their union, the men began to discuss moving from their crowded office on East Street to quarters more befitting a stable, wealthy union.[15] Of the many unions in San Francisco, few had their own headquarters or meeting hall, and no other union had its own newspaper.

After two years as secretary, Furuseth decided to return to the sea, for he did not then believe in long tenure in office for union officials. When he told the union on November 19, 1888, that he would under no circumstances be a candidate for reëlection, he could take pride in his accomplishments. His last financial report early in 1889 showed more than 2,000 members and a treasury of more than $22,000.[16] Instead of the confused jumble of papers he had inherited when he took office, Furuseth handed over the union records in perfect condition. At the birthday celebration of the union on March 6, 1888, Furuseth had been spontaneously awarded three cheers by the assembled sailors. There is no doubt that he could have been elected again with practically no opposition.

Conflict with Burnette G. Haskell

While Furuseth was secretary and during the period when he held no official position, two internal union matters were of particular interest to him. One was the fight to rid the union of the influence of Haskell and his Socialist followers. The other was the matter of reaching some agreement with the Steamship Sailors' Protective Union. Furuseth's conflict with Haskell may have been on ideological grounds, but it was expressed only in the practical, day-to-day problems of the union. Even before Furuseth became secretary there had been dissatisfaction over the close relationship between the International Workingmen's Association and the Coast Seamen's Union, which had resulted in the union's move to its own office on East Street. Furuseth, in auditing the books, found fault with the way in which Haskell had kept the financial records.

To undermine Haskell and his fellow Socialists took more than showing that they were bad bookkeepers. The sailors knew that these men were the most devoted and most active members of the union. They were dedicated to the building of the union and received no financial rewards for their work. Most of the sailors saw nothing wrong in the provision of the union constitution that the Advisory Committee should consist only of members of the International Workingmen's Association. But even if there had been widespread opposition to the Socialists, it would have been difficult to get rid of them, because most of them had given up sailing and were now employed on shore. These men could come to every meeting; the others seldom attended because they were at sea.[17]

With the gentle prodding and political maneuvering of Furuseth and other leaders who shared his views, Burnette G. Haskell undermined himself. Haskell was a strange man—especially strange in the labor movement.[18] He was a native Californian who had attended the University of California, the University of Illinois, and Oberlin College, though he had not been graduated from any of them. In 1879 he passed the California Bar examination, and for a time, on his own admission, was employed by the railroad interests in California to pay off the local and state legislators when their votes were needed. In January, 1882, he inherited a newspaper from an uncle and decided that publishing was much more to his taste than the legal profession. Haskell had never given much thought to social problems; he had bribed legislators without a qualm.[19] But he realized that a paper had to have a cause, and he found it in the labor movement. He organized a study group which he called "The Invisible Republic" for the purpose of studying socialism. Later he organized the International Workingmen's Association, a semi-secret revolutionary group patterned after Karl Marx's First International. An elaborate secret code was worked out and plans were made for taking over the government of California by seizing the mint, the armories, the customhouses, Alcatraz, the Presidio, and the newspapers. The membership of this revolutionary society has been estimated to have been as high as 2,000 in California, but according to Frank Roney, a labor leader who attended some of the society's meetings, the number of members was closer to 100 and most of those were in the Coast Seamen's Union.[20]

Many of Haskell's followers became important figures in the San Francisco labor movement. Alfred Fuhrman, for example, became a leader of the brewery workers, and Edward Anderson was long the treasurer of the Seamen's Union. Whereas such men were to influence the California labor movement for many years, Haskell's career was short-lived.[21] He had a knack for making enemies and for being caught in political intrigues. Though he helped to organize many unions, he was soon shoved aside. When he died destitute and alone in 1907, a few old comrades in the sailors' union saved him from a pauper's burial by inducing the union to donate a plot of ground for the man who had been its founder.[22]

Furuseth saw in Haskell's leadership of the sailors a threat to the well-being of the union. Haskell had recklessly proposed that the seamen enter a revolutionary float in the first official Labor Day parade in San Francisco on May 11, 1886. Word had already reached the city of the Haymarket Riot in Chicago. In the charged atmosphere of those days, Haskell planned a float depicting armed sailors storming the Bastille. Nothing would have proved more conclusively to the enemies of labor the revolutionary designs of the labor movement in general and of the sailors' union in particular. Only the firm refusal of Frank Roney, then president of the Federated Trades Council, to enter such a float saved the union from untold embarrassment.[23]

As the leader of the sailors' strike in 1886, Haskell could be saddled with the blame for its failure. He had made extravagant promises of support from the rest of the labor movement which never materialized. The failure of a coöperative society which he had founded, and in which many sailors had invested money and labor, also alienated the seamen.

The final fight that eliminated Haskell as an influence in the union occurred while Furuseth was in Alaska, but the groundwork had been laid while the latter was secretary. Haskell tried to organize the "elite" of the Coast Seamen's Union into a legion of honor, and this was interpreted by his opponents as an attempt to bolster his waning control. Members were told either to drop out of the legion of honor or to leave the union. Haskell's right to use the union hall for educational meetings

Union Man

was withdrawn. The Advisory Committee was first opened up to any member of the union, and later was abolished. By these means the control of the International Workingmen's Association over the union was broken. This was Furuseth's first experience with fighting Marxists, and one of many internal struggles that he was to wage as a leader of the union.[24]

AMALGAMATION WITH STEAMSHIP SAILORS

The second sore point which Furuseth worked assiduously to clear up concerned the rival union of steamship sailors.[25] Shipowners on the West Coast were slowly being converted to the use of steam vessels which made up for their expensive fuel by more regular sailing schedules. Not trusting entirely to the new motive power, the early vessels carried sails as well as engines. In January, 1886, the firemen, cooks, and waiters on the steamships formed the Steamshipmen's Protective Union, but as yet the sailors—the deck hands—on these vessels had no union. The Coast Seamen's Union, which was composed of men who manned sailing ships, regarded steamship sailors with contempt and made no effort to organize them. Accordingly the steamshipmen, also under the leadership of Burnette Haskell, started their own organization in May, 1886.

Conflict between the two unions began almost immediately. Whenever a sailing vessel was modified for steam, both organizations claimed jurisdiction. If a shipowner who had been getting his men from the Coast Seamen's Union decided to buy a steamship, the CSU asserted its right to man that vessel also. At first Furuseth and his sailors tried to destroy the new union. Outnumbering the steamship sailors at least three to one, they succeeded in having their rivals thrown out of the Federated Trades Council on October 14, 1887. They charged that the shipowners had established the Steamship Sailors' Union in order to forestall a combined organization of all sailors. They intimated that its secretary, Dave McDonald, was in the employ of the owners; otherwise, how could his repeated refusal to work jointly with the Coast Seamen's Union be explained? The crowning charge was the steamship union's alleged offer to man the steamship *Navarro* for monthly wages ten dollars less than CSU rates.[26]

Expulsion of the steamship sailors from the Federated Trades Council did not halt the jurisdictional fights between their union and the CSU. Furuseth, soon realizing the futility of attempting to destroy the Steamship Sailors' Union, advocated an agreement providing for an exchange of books, which would allow members of both unions to work on either sail or steam vessels. Several times Furuseth served on a committee to negotiate with the steamship sailors. Problems concerning the jurisdiction of particular vessels could be solved, but, despite repeated efforts, no satisfactory compromise could be worked out to eliminate conflict between the two groups. Finally, on July 29, 1891, Furuseth signed his name to a formal agreement which provided for the amalgamation of both organizations into the Sailors' Union of the Pacific.[27]

An Episode in International Unionism

The union faced another competitive group of seamen in the deepwater sailors. Although the coasting sailors possessed the advantage of familiarity with the vessels and ports of the Pacific Coast, their wages and conditions would not be secure so long as the British deepwater seamen's wages averaged $15 per month less than their own. To eliminate this source of competition, the coasting sailors placed their hopes in the National Amalgamated Sailors' and Firemen's Union of Great Britain and Ireland, which was endeavoring to organize the British seamen.

The *Coast Seamen's Journal* followed with great interest every development of the British union.[28] Correspondence between the British and West Coast unions became increasingly frequent during 1888, and in May, 1890, the Coast Seamen's Union accepted an invitation of the British union to attend the International Conference of Seamen to be held in Glasgow, Scotland, in October of that year. Andrew Furuseth, Frank Waterhouse, and Edward Crangle were elected as delegates by the members, who had been advised to select brainy men, well versed in the labor movement. It is not certain that this was the basis upon which the sailors made their choice, but Furuseth, for one, had evinced great interest in the problem of eliminating the competition of British seamen by raising their wages through organization.[29]

The delegates were instructed to ask the British union to use every effort to man all vessels coming to the Pacific Coast with union crews, and to make plans to organize the seamen in those countries where they were not yet organized. In Scotland, they were disappointed to find that they were actually attending a convention of the British seamen's union at which they were treated like visitors. Their proposal for a mutual exchange of membership cards among all unions was ruled out of order on a technicality. Privately they concluded that their British brothers were dictatorially ruled by their president, J. Havelock Wilson,[30] and predicted that the British shipowners would "hammer the exclusiveness out of them or hammer them to pieces." Furuseth and his fellow delegates disgustedly walked out of the convention and returned to America.[31]

Union Man

Before the delegates returned to California, they stopped at the principal ports of the Atlantic, the Great Lakes, and the Gulf of Mexico to examine firsthand the sailors' organizing activities in these ports. What they saw convinced them that both a need and a desire existed for a nationwide organization of seamen.[32] Although the international mission was a failure, the contacts made in the United States were to result in the formation of the National Seamen's Union within a short time.

A SEAFARER BECOMES A UNION OFFICIAL

Another problem that confronted the union, dishonesty on the part of some of its officials, was responsible for Furuseth's return to the position of secretary. Union officers are no different from other people, and some of them occasionally succumb to the temptation of using union funds for their own purposes. The final blow to the Seamen's Protective Association, an organization that preceded the Coast Seamen's Union, was the treasurer's theft of all its funds. In the early days of the Coast Seamen's Union, the chest in which the union monies were kept was rifled. From time to time union agents or patrolmen were accused of improperly using the organization's funds or of charging sailors for a "chance" to ship.[33]

Such dishonesty had been comparatively rare in the Coast Seamen's Union. Moreover, a system of receipts and vouchers, weekly financial reports, and deposit of funds in the bank, all instituted when Furuseth was secretary, made dishonesty difficult to conceal. Nevertheless, early in 1891 the union was bedeviled with a veritable siege of defalcations of union funds. Among the most serious was that of the treasurer, W. A. Bushnell, who failed to turn over several hundred dollars to his successor.[34] After a few weeks Bushnell scraped together most of the money, which he had been using temporarily, and returned it to the union. Even more serious was the sudden disappearance of Henry Ark, secretary of the union, on April 1. A quick investigation disclosed that almost $2,000 in union funds had also vanished. Ark was arrested, tried, and sentenced to San Quentin, where he died in 1894. "The story is briefly told," said the *Coast Seamen's Journal*, "an unscrupulous woman, an infatuated weak man."[35]

Putting Ark behind prison bars did not restore the confidence of the members in their officials, and the union faced a difficult problem. Members who believed their officers were interested only in personal gain would see no distinction between the union and the crimps except in the methods they used to fleece the sailor of his money. To command loyalty, officers had to prove their dedication to the men's welfare. Members might complain about their leaders and outwardly take the attitude that no officer is honest, but if they genuinely believed that the officials could not be trusted, there would be no union. Only one man had won the complete confidence of the membership. Despite some reluctance to resume the position of secretary, Furuseth probably realized that the fate of the union depended upon him, and he was prevailed upon to run for the office in April, 1891. The extent of his popularity is indicated by his victory over all other candidates by a vote of 219 to 62.[36]

Less than a year later, on February 8, 1892, Furuseth submitted his resignation as secretary. When the union took no action, he insisted that his resignation be accepted on the grounds that many people felt he had "grown fast in his seat" and "he himself thought that some other work would be better for himself and the union both."[37] As soon as arrangements were made to replace him, Furuseth shipped out on a fishing boat. But within two months the union asked him to return. He agreed on condition that he be paid as much as he would make fishing,[38] and by the middle of June he was back in the post that he was to hold until 1936.[39]

STRIKE OF 1893

After Henry Ark's arrest, Furuseth's main job was to restore faith in the union officials. In other respects, the union was in a healthy condition. It could boast of a whopping treasury of more than $37,000 and a membership in good standing of 2,317.[40] In the five years since its crushing defeat in 1886, the union had raised wages to $40 per month for inside ports by pressing every advantage that the economic situation presented. The sailors felt so confident that early in 1891 they decided once more to open their own shipping office, or hiring hall. In negotiations with vessel owners during the spring, they were assured that there would be no objection to hiring through the union; since a large majority of the coasting sailors belonged to the union, there would not have been much point in objecting. The formal opening of the shipping office on March 19 was greeted with much rejoicing and was regarded as the final victory of the organized seamen over the shipowners. Edward Crangle was again chosen shipping master, and a system of rotary hiring was approved.[41]

Many years later Furuseth opposed the principle of a union hiring hall and the rotation system, but at this time he was enthusiastic over the union's victory. The hiring hall effectively undercut the crimp because the union took over his function, and it gave the union control of virtually all the jobs in the coasting trade. The rotation system seemed eminently fair. Sailors who wanted work deposited their union books with the shipping master. When there was a call for men in the hiring hall, those who had been waiting the longest had first chance at the jobs.

The union was now charged with the responsibility of supplying shipowners with good crews. Furuseth took this responsibility very seriously. He felt that a sailor who reported for work drunk, or failed to show up for work, or lacked adequate skill, was a reflection upon the union. At meeting after meeting he admonished the members that their new shipping office entailed responsibilities as well as rights. The sailors did not respond to these noble sentiments. Charges of favoritism in shipping and of bribery were voiced openly at the meetings,[42] and the resentment once reserved for the crimp was vented upon the hiring hall.

The high hopes of early 1891 were soon dashed. Internal dissension, an increase in the number of nonunion sailors in the city, and the decline in shipping that preceded the general business depression of 1893 led to renewed conflict with the shipowners which once more almost annihilated the union. When the owners first asked for a $10 reduction in wages, in November, 1891, the union successfully resisted.[43] But, realizing the unfavorable economic situation, Furuseth sought to prevent any strife. When the branch in San Diego tried to hold up a vessel for wages higher than those agreed to by the union, Furuseth sent a crew from San Francisco to take the place of the union men who had walked out. Defending his strikebreaking action before the membership, he explained, "The union gave an inch in order to get a fathom," and argued that if the union wanted to do business with employers, it had to operate on business principles.[44]

Furuseth understood the necessity for creating a favorable climate of opinion for the union. At the first sign of trouble, he warned the members to exercise extreme caution so that the responsibility for any conflict would not rest upon the union. Mindful of the large army of unemployed, he opposed raising the initiation fee, because this would be the surest way to keep men out of the union and drive them into the camp of potential scabs. At a mass meeting called by the Federated Trades Council in the Metropolitan Temple on June 27, 1892, Furuseth stressed the high moral principles of the trade-union movement. Answering the employers' charges of racketeering and hoodlumism, he said, "The labor movement received its charter on Mount Sinai when God, through Moses, handed down the law in which we read, 'Thou shalt not steal,' to which Thomas Carlyle, the truth speaker of the nineteenth century, adds, 'Thou shalt not be stolen from.' "[45]

The conflict between the union and the owners in 1892 was neither a strike nor a lockout. The owners tried to hire men who would sail their ships for less than union rates. They enlisted the aid of crimps to find among the unemployed and the deepwater sailors enough men to man their vessels. If they could not get a nonunion crew, they paid the union scale, but they tried not to hire through the union office. The main objective of the Sailors' Union was to prevent anyone from sailing below the union scale. It was aided by the fact that San Francisco was a "union town," where many employees would not think of working for less than the scale, and others could be shamed into refusing to take the jobs of union men.

Nevertheless, the union had a hard fight on its hands and resorted to a variety of tactics. It took nonunion sailors out of the boardinghouses where they would be at the mercy of the crimps and sent them, at union expense, to live in the country. It shipped union sailors in the deepwater trade, thus encroaching on a field of employment which the crimps had exclusively controlled. To harass shipowners, the union brought suit in court for the recovery of advances made to crimps above the amount allowed by law. "Dummies" were sent aboard ship for the purpose of deserting the vessel at the very last moment, thus delaying the sailing.[46] When these methods failed, union patrolmen used force to prevent scabbing. Blood flowed freely on the water front in 1892 as the crimps fought the union for control of shipping.

In January, 1893, Furuseth confidently reported to members that many of the shipowners were ready to give up, but he warned that the San Francisco Employers' Association was urging a lockout. Although the owners were divided on the question of continuing the struggle, most of them were finally brought into line, and the conflict assumed a fiercer aspect under the leadership of G. C. Williams. Williams had been a member of a trade union in the East and a newspaper reporter in San Francisco. He was hired by the Employers' Association and lent to the shipowners, who gave him the title, "Secretary of the Shipowners' Association."[47] It was later learned that the name Williams was actually an alias for Walthew. "Criminal Walthew," as the *Journal* thereafter referred to him, was wanted by the Michigan police on a charge of bribing state legislators. Since he had testified before the California Labor Commissioner under his assumed name, he was also guilty of perjury. His advice to the Seattle agent of the Shipowners' Association indicates the methods he intended to use to break the union. "A dose of cold lead," he wrote, "has a wonderful effect in quieting disorders...."[48]

The association reopened its own shipping office and issued instructions that all hiring must be done through it. The union countered with a circular asking men to stay away from the association's office and offering to provide room and board until the men could be shipped out. It rented a house in the country for this purpose. More than a fifth of the union treasury, $10,000, was withdrawn from the bank to finance the fight.[49]

The economic depression of 1893 proved to be the shipowners' greatest ally. A relative scarcity of men in January was suddenly converted into a surplus when thousands of men lost their jobs and were willing to take any work. The association shipping office was able to get as many men as it needed. The violence of 1892 was surpassed in 1893. Two nonunion men on the schooner *Emily* were assaulted and brutally beaten when they were in a drunken sleep. The cables on the nonunion schooner *Tacoma* were sawed and the vessel allowed to drift out to sea. Twelve sticks of dynamite were found on the British tramp steamer *Bawnmore*. Dynamite was discovered on the tugs *Ethel* and *Marian*. The union denied all knowledge of such incidents and claimed that the crimps and the shipowners, the "Association of Desperate Discontents," had probably manufactured most of them in order to blame them on the union.[50]

The sailors appealed for public sympathy. At a mass meeting on the union's birthday, Furuseth declared that the seamen were asking only for justice. "American seamen are the worst fed and the worst treated.... Conditions have so degenerated that no native American nor self-respecting men of any flag will sail in [American ships]...."[51] Furuseth warned that the seamen would go elsewhere to earn a living if shipowners continued to degrade them. He tried to instill a fighting spirit in the union by making optimistic reports and by ridiculing the caliber of the men hired by the owners. Urging the sailors to greater efforts, he decried their apathy.[52]

In May the situation became even worse for the union. All shipowners who had thus far refused to work with the association now joined the combination. The union increased the size of the patrols guarding the water front and drew out the balance of its funds from the bank.[53] But by the end of July it was evident that the union had lost the fight. It ceased to patrol the water front and began to seek a basis for settlement. In September, 1893, it decided to lower its wage scale. This was not done because the union was defeated, ran the statement, but because the economic situation had changed. The depression was no longer local or even national, but "universal."[54]

The sailors had merely retreated. Several days later they were to be in a complete rout. At midnight on Sunday, September 24, six sailors were returning to Johnny Curtin's boardinghouse on Main Street after an evening of carousing. Curtin was a well-known boarding master and crimp who controlled the jobs on the coaling vessels that sailed from San Francisco to British Columbia. These vessels were manned almost exclusively by British sailors. One of the six sailors returning to the house was Curtin's son, and as they approached the entrance, he noticed a small black valise. He picked it up, then quickly dropped it and ran across the street, shouting, "It's dynamite." The other sailors were more curious than frightened. As they stooped over to examine the valise, a tremendous explosion shook the entire neighborhood. Four of the sailors were instantly killed and the other was badly mutilated.[55]

The following evening the Sailors' Union of the Pacific held its regular Monday night meeting, and Furuseth announced what everyone already knew—that "the most dastardly crime ever committed on the waterfront" had taken place the previous evening.[56] He had already been questioned by the police, who assumed, as did the newspapers and the public, that this was the work of the union. He argued that the union had nothing to gain from such a crime. The only parties who might benefit were the shipowners, the crimps, and the boarding masters, and Furuseth demanded that the chief of police turn his investigation to them. The union offered a reward of $1,000 for any information leading to the arrest of the criminals.[57]

But it was no use protesting. Almost without exception the newspapers and the citizens of San Francisco had already condemned the sailors. Even when subsequent arrests and trials failed to show any connection between the union and the bombing, the press and the public stood firm in their conviction that the Sailors' Union was guilty. Whatever sympathy had existed for "Poor Jack" in his fight against the powerful and unpopular Employers' Association disappeared when the bomb exploded. The sailors knew they were licked. A week after the bombing they decided to close the union shipping office and to permit members to find work on whatever conditions the employers set.[58]

With an empty treasury, with members rushing to accept any job, with public opinion which had been nurtured for eight years suddenly turned against the union, the situation looked bleak indeed. In this darkest hour, Furuseth wrote a message of courage and hope to the membership. His words were not merely the proper sentiments to be expressed on such an occasion; they had the ring of sincerity which made their central theme, "Tomorrow is also a day," the watchword of the union to this day. After reviewing the events from 1891 to the decision to reduce wages in September, 1893, Furuseth wrote:

> [L]ike a clap of thunder from the clear sky came the dynamite outrage setting the whole city against us. We are innocent... but it is there and must be reckoned with in all our dealings for the future. Hence peace, even the Christian peace of turning the other cheek, must be our policy in the future....
> [S]ince we do submit we do so without grumbling or crying... that is our lot at present and trough [through] it we shall yet come up to our old standard, but we shall reach there through the mind.... Let us comrades take our medicine like stoics and from our trouble shall we rise again enobled [sic] and purified.... They [cannot] prevent us from staying with the union, paying our dues and joining other willing sailors into our ranks. Our money is our own—our soul also—and while we are true to ourselves time is passing and we remember that tomorrow is also a day.... Like the bird sucking sweets from the poisoned flower let us from our troubles suck straight [strength] and devotion to our cause.[59]

In the eight years since Furuseth had joined the Sailors' Union, this was the second time it had abjectly surrendered to the shipowners. In 1886 the union had been defeated, but it had survived and regained its strength. Furuseth confidently expected that the union would survive the defeat of 1893. In eight years, he had become wise in the labor movement, he had served for four years as secretary of one of the most important unions on the West Coast, he had attended an international conference of seamen. He had also begun to establish himself as an intellectual leader in San Francisco and to make his mark in the national labor movement, where he was influential in starting a national seamen's organization and launching a legislative program for seamen.

III. LOBBYIST FOR SEAMEN

ALTHOUGH FURUSETH'S EFFORTS to organize the seamen met with reversals during the 1890's, his legislative efforts brought about revolutionary changes in their status.[1] It is not known when Furuseth first became interested in legal questions, but it was quite common for sailors to have some knowledge of the rudimentary rules of maritime law. The more literate sailor often became an authority on legal matters, or was so regarded by other sailors. Life aboard ship gave the "sea lawyer" ample opportunity to practice his unpaid profession. Under what circumstances was the crew entitled to a share of the salvage of a wrecked vessel? What were the limits of a consul's authority? How leaky did a vessel have to be before it could be declared unseaworthy? Such questions were propounded day after day in the "foc'sle."

That Furuseth should have been acquainted with maritime law was not unusual, but the extent of his information was phenomenal. One of his favorite expressions before congressional committees was, "I will stake my reputation of twenty [or thirty] years for veracity and truth...," and then he would quote the maritime law of England, Germany, or Panama, or cite court cases to make his point. He was never found to be in error, though, like any lawyer, he marshaled the laws and cases that best supported his argument. It is not surprising that he knew more about maritime law and custom than the members of Congress who made the laws, even though some of them were shipowners. But he also demonstrated in hearings that he had a wider knowledge than the commissioner of navigation, charged with execution of the laws, and the attorneys whom the shipowners hired to argue against him.

Familiarity with the law would not have been enough to bring about the changes that Furuseth effected. He also knew how to appeal to the hearts of the legislators and how to discredit his opponents so that their testimony seemed hardly credible. Furuseth could speak as a humanitarian, opposed to cruelty to seamen and in favor of manning vessels with American seamen and of putting the safety of passengers above profits, but shipowners had to defend themselves against charges that they beat defenseless seamen, hired foreigners instead of Americans, and were more concerned with dividends than with lives.

Lobbyist for Seamen

First Legislative Program

When the Coast Seamen's Union suffered its first industrial defeat in 1886, it turned to legislative reform. The sailors believed that their chief enemy was the crimp and that, once free of his strangle hold, they could deal with the shipowners. Congress had already tried twice, unsuccessfully, to deal with the evils of the crimping system. The Shipping Commissioners Act of 1872 provided that seamen must sign their shipping articles, or articles of agreement, before the shipping commissioner in a sober condition. It was thought that this would abolish the shanghaiing[2] practiced by crimps, but the law was easily evaded by having a sober man sign the name of a doped derelict who was later delivered to the captain. Another attempt was made in 1884 with the passage of the Dingley Act, which forbade allotment of wages to anyone except a wife or a close relative.[3] So complete was the control of the crimp over the shipping of seamen that scarcely a man sailed except in violation of the law. After two years the Dingley Act was modified to permit allotment to "original creditors"—crimps and boarding masters.

In 1887 the union considered a brief legislative program outlined by Volney Hoffmeyer, who later became an attorney in San Francisco.[4] He suggested that, in addition to abolishing allotment again, no one be allowed to be present when the seaman signed his shipping articles. If a seaman could appear before the shipping commissioner without a boardinghouse keeper or a crimp, he could sign without allotting a share of his earnings to these parasites, who would thus die for want of sustenance.

The union did not push this legislative program because in January, 1887, Furuseth had suggested a better remedy. In studying contemporary court decisions, he discovered that seamen in the coasting trade were not subject to the penalties for desertion and other offenses provided for in the Shipping Commissioners Act of 1872. This had come about because shipowners had objected to the inconvenience of signing men on and off before a commissioner when the total distance traveled might be less than ten miles. Congress in 1874 obligingly exempted the coasting trade from the provisions of the act of 1872. When the courts began to interpret the act of 1874, they read it literally and decided that if owners in the coasting trade were exempt from signing their crews on before a commissioner, the coasting sailors were exempt from the penalties provided for in the earlier act.

By long custom the seaman had come to occupy the relationship of a serf to the vessel. The earliest American law dealing with seamen, in

1790, provided for the arrest of deserters. All maritime nations had similar laws. Furuseth realized that the courts' interpretation of the act of 1874 had suddenly made the coasting sailor a free man. He could now quit his vessel just as any worker could quit his job without fear of being imprisoned. After the 1886 strike, the shipowners had lowered wages and imposed the grade-book system. Following Furuseth's advice, the union men accepted the grade book and went aboard the vessels, but just before the ship was to sail, they would throw their belongings on the dock and jump overboard. The captain was then obliged to delay his sailing until he could get a new crew. Often the same procedure would be repeated several times, and a vessel could be held up for days or weeks. Profits were made by keeping the vessels moving freight; delays meant financial losses. Under the old laws sailors could have been arrested and brought back to the vessel, but now they had the right to quit whenever they wished. Within a short time grade books were abolished and wages began to rise.

Now dissatisfied with the law that had been passed in their behalf, the shipowners went to Congress. On August 19, 1890, despite letters and telegrams of protest from West Coast seamen, they secured passage of a law making the coasting seaman subject to the penalties of the 1872 act, provided he signed articles before the shipping commissioner. For a time the union conducted a vigorous campaign urging seamen to keep their freedom by refusing to sign before the commissioner.[5] If a majority of the sailors had taken the union's advice, there would have been no need for legislative reform. But in the early 1890's the union was unable to maintain a solid front and was losing its fight with the crimps and the shipowners. If a sailor wanted to work, he had to allot wages to the crimp and give up his freedom by signing before the shipping commissioner.[6]

Without freedom, there could be no union. Without a union, wages could not be increased, conditions could not be improved, and the men who would be attracted to the sailor's occupation would be the misfits, the derelicts of society. Such men would further depress the standards of the industry. If reform could not be achieved in the industrial field, it might be achieved in the legislative field. The Scandinavian seamen who manned American vessels believed that their adopted country could not deny them the liberty that it extended to all other citizens.

MAGUIRE ACT, 1895

In January, 1892, the union elected a committee to plan a legislative program. The committee consisted of some of the union's most vocal members: George Bolton, Ed Crangle, Nicholas Jortall, George M. Lynch, and Frank Waterhouse. Furuseth was secretary at the time, and the general practice was not to give the secretary extra work by putting him on committees. However, the group met in the union hall and it is probable that Furuseth, with his interest in legal matters, took part in the deliberations.

The committee members read articles in the *Coast Seamen's Journal* about maritime law,[7] and studied court decisions. But primarily they relied upon their own personal knowledge to draw up "An Appeal to Congress" in which they suggested almost thirty needed reforms. Most of these recommended amendments to the Shipping Commissioners Act of 1872 were restrictions upon shipowners. Vessels would be required to carry a full crew at all times and to replace any men who deserted. Owners would be required to provide transportation back to the United States for seamen discharged in foreign ports. This would apply to men who became ill, were forced to sign off because of cruelty, or left the vessel after it was legally declared unseaworthy. Shipowners would be prohibited from paying an advance on wages. It was proposed that the forecastle space be enlarged from the legal minimum of 70 cubic feet per man to 120 cubic feet, that the scale of provisions be improved, that the deck crew be divided into two watches, that no unnecessary work be done on Sundays and holidays, that the vessel be made liable for any cruelties inflicted upon the men by its officers, and that the punishments for desertion, absence without leave, and willful disobedience to commands be slightly reduced.

Another proposed change was elimination of the "master's option." Under the act of 1872, the master was required to pay a seaman one third of his earned wages in any port unless the shipping articles specified otherwise. It soon became common practice, however, to insert in the articles a "master's option" to pay the seaman only when the captain wished. Without his pay, a sailor in port was easily victimized by a crimp, who was always ready to make him a loan. Another amendment would have given a majority of the crew, exclusive of the officers, the right to demand a survey of the seaworthiness of a vessel. The existing law made it necessary to have the consent of one of the officers. Since officers feared to incur the displeasure of the owners, they would seldom consent, and the crew was forced to sail even when a majority of the men considered the vessel unsafe. To counteract the shipowners' grade book, the union suggested that the government provide each seaman with a discharge book, but give him the option of keeping or discarding his individual discharges, much as a worker may offer only those references that are favorable.[8]

The union offered to send a representative to Congress to explain the needed changes in the law. Senator William P. Frye replied that this was unnecessary and that the commissioner of navigation was considering the seamen's bill. Furuseth wrote to Samuel Gompers, T. V. Powderly, and other national labor leaders urging their support, and a committee was elected to see Senator Leland Stanford.[9]

Although Furuseth would never admit it, the next step in support of the seamen's proposals was a complete about-face of the Sailors' Union policy of staying out of politics. A few months before, the *Journal* had printed an editorial commending the Federated Trades Council for refusing to take political action to fight employers.[10] Experience had shown, it said, that workers were satisfied with the old parties and would not vote for a labor candidate. Now, on September 12, 1892, the union decided to endorse James G. Maguire, Democratic candidate for Congress from the Fourth District in California.[11] It did not regard this action as an exception to the "no-politics" rule, but merely as support of its legislative program which Maguire had endorsed.

The union proved exceptionally fortunate in its first political endorsement. Maguire was a portly Irishman who had served in the California Assembly in 1875 and as Superior Court judge from 1882 to 1888.[12] He was now reëntering politics after four years of private law practice. Maguire pushed the seamen's program faithfully and energetically, and was vigorously supported by the sailors. So active was Furuseth's championship that he was accused of being a member of the Democratic party's water-front organization, the Neptune Club. This he stoutly denied, stating: "... as an executive officer of the Sailors' Union of the Pacific, I do not believe that it would be wise to affiliate myself with a political party."[13]

Interest in the seamen's bill was kept alive by frequent articles in the *Journal*[14] and by resolutions introduced at national labor conventions. Finally, in December, 1893, Furuseth reported that Congressman Maguire had divided the sailors' program into six bills which he would soon introduce in Congress.[15] A few months later Maguire asked the union to send a representative to Washington to explain the bills. Furuseth thought that W. J. B. Mackay should go, probably because this Scotsman was the closest facsimile the union possessed of a competent native American seaman—the type considered most likely to influence congressmen. Besides, Furuseth himself was being held in San Francisco as a witness in connection with the bombing of the Curtin boardinghouse. At the last moment Mackay could not go and Furuseth's presence in court was not needed, so half by accident Furu-

Lobbyist for Seamen

seth was launched upon an eventful career as lobbyist for the sailors.

Furuseth left San Francisco for Washington on March 6, 1894. He was joined in Chicago by T. J. Elderkin, secretary-treasurer of the National Seamen's Union, which had been established two years before. In Washington they met the president of the NSU, Charles Hagen of New Orleans, and John R. Bell of New York. The four union representatives testified for two and a half hours on the Maguire bills at a hearing before the House Committee on Merchant Marine and Fisheries.[16]

Furuseth was shocked at the ignorance of congressmen on maritime matters, but pleased with their apparent eagerness to learn.[17] When the other representatives returned home, Furuseth went to New York, where he secured written statements from the consuls of maritime nations to show that the condition of American seamen was inferior to that of foreign seamen.[18] He returned to Washington to present these statements to the subcommittee charged with considering the Maguire bills. In the meantime the shipowners had become alarmed and began to flood Congress with mail denouncing the bills as "arbitrary and unjust," "communistic and subversive of discipline," and charging that the bills would "place a premium on desertion."[19]

The key to success lay in convincing Representative Nelson Dingley, the recognized authority in Congress on maritime affairs. Furuseth secured Dingley's promise that he would not oppose H.R. 5603, a bill to repeal the 1890 law.[20] Hearings were held on this bill on June 15, and the committee unanimously reported it out favorably. Success in the House seemed almost certain, but at the last moment Albert J. Hopkins of Illinois objected to the bill's introduction under unanimous consent and General Henry H. Bingham of Pennsylvania prevented its consideration by a filibuster.[21] But Furuseth was not discouraged. The congressmen had been impressed with the seamen's case, and he was certain that the bill would pass in the next session.

When Furuseth returned to San Francisco in the late summer of 1894, he found that the SUP was rapidly disintegrating. Frequently a quorum could not be gathered, and meetings which had formerly lasted until long past midnight were now adjourned at nine o'clock or earlier. Funds were so low that it was suggested that the union dispense with the major expense of printing the *Coast Seamen's Journal.* In fighting this proposal Furuseth said:

The last thing we should think of touching is the *Journal,* make it stronger, brighter, better if possible, but you may do anything else but reduce it now when we need it more than ever. We need it to speak to the people of the United States to tell them our misery, our hunger, our hope. We need it to urge our claims on Congress. We need it to help defeat our opponents.

As a result of Furuseth's efforts, the handful of members voted 12 to 8 against economizing by dropping the *Journal*.[22]

That fall, while denouncing the current trend in the labor movement toward political action, the union again enthusiastically supported Maguire's campaign.[23] Speaking at the Labor Day celebration, Furuseth denied that he had entered politics:

I am not a politician and have never talked politics, purely as such, in public. I speak from the standpoint of a seaman and a citizen. There can be no suspicion of politics in the assertion that a nation cannot be secure in peace nor victorious in war if she is dependent upon strangers, mercenaries, to guard the nation's rights. I speak for that party, any party, any governmental system, which will restore to the nation a patriotic marine....[24]

Maguire was reëlected, and he asked the sailors to send a representative to the short session of Congress to give his bill the final push it needed. Neither the SUP nor the National Seamen's Union had the funds to support a representative, but fortunately the American Federation of Labor chose to send Furuseth and Adolph Strasser to Washington. On February 18, 1895, President Cleveland signed the first Maguire bill.

The new law abolished imprisonment for desertion in the coastwise trade, prohibited allotment of any kind in that trade, and exempted a seaman's clothing from attachment. "The enforcement of its provisions," warned the *Journal*, "rests with the seamen themselves through their unions."[25] The sailors determined to capitalize on their new freedom, and shortly after Furuseth's return to San Francisco in March, 1895, they demanded higher wages. After a few months of strenuous effort, which left less than $4,000 in the union treasury, they were forced to admit that the expected upturn in business had not materialized, and the struggle was postponed.[26]

During the fight the union had made use of the Maguire Act to force captains to pay back to the sailors advances which they had given to the crimps.[27] It was found, however, that the law was not entirely satisfactory. In the first place, if a sailor signed on a vessel without going through the shipping commissioner, an advance could be paid and no one would know. In a reversal of their former stand, the sailors now demanded that everyone be required to sign before the commissioner. Second, the shipowners hired any "farmer" or "hobo" on shore to take the place of men on strike. This could be prevented, the sailors thought, if owners were required to hire competent crews.

Lobbyist for Seamen

The most impressive demonstration of the inadequacy of the Maguire Act was the *Arago* decision.[28] In May, 1895, Robert Robertson, John Bradley, P. H. Olsen, and Morris Hanson signed articles before the shipping commissioner in San Francisco to sail on the barkentine *Arago* to Knappton, Washington, then to Valparaiso and other foreign ports, and return to the United States. When the sailors reached Oregon, they decided they did not want to make the foreign journey. Believing that they were protected under the Maguire Act, the men quit their vessel in an American port. The master had them arrested and brought back to the ship; then they were taken to San Francisco in chains. Furuseth petitioned for a writ of habeas corpus and hired H. W. Hutton to defend the men.

The case was recognized as extremely important because, if a seaman could be arrested when the articles included a non-American port, it would be a simple matter to insert such a port in all articles of agreement, and the Maguire Act would be worthless. Perhaps the most frightening aspect of the incident was that men had actually been arrested and brought back to their vessel. The seamen had long realized that, before the Maguire Act was passed, owners had the legal right to take such action, but in practice it had not happened within the memory of any of the coasting sailors. No master would bother to arrest a deserting seaman when it was easier to hire a substitute in his place. The actual arrest of a deserter shocked the union, and it was decided to make a test case of the affair.

The union based its defense on the Thirteenth Amendment to the Constitution, which forbids involuntary servitude. On December 26, 1896, the Supreme Court handed down the "Second Dred Scott Decision." The majority opinion held that the seaman's contract, based upon ancient maritime law, was different from other contracts, that the purpose of the Thirteenth Amendment was not to give the sailor freedom to violate his agreement, but to prevent peonage of the type prevalent in Mexico. Justice John Harlan, who dissented, laid stress upon the consequences of the decision. What difference did it make, he asked, whether a man stood with lash in hand compelling labor or whether this was done by the government with United States marshals? Would a domestic employee who refused to fulfill a contract to work for six months be required to live up to the terms of that contract? The sailors were stunned and dismayed by the decision. The *San Francisco Examiner* succinctly expressed their point of view: "According to the highest tribunal which can pass on the matter, the difference between a deep-water sailor and a slave is $15 per month."

Other legal cases under the Maguire Act did not fare so badly. In commenting on the act after it had been in operation for one year, the *Journal* wrote:

Taken altogether, it may be said that the Maguire Act has been a great success.... It has increased the seaman's self-respect by decreasing the power of the crimp. It has placed him on a plane of equality with other citizens by guaranteeing him the right to work or quit at will when in port. It has increased his self-reliance by guaranteeing that the wages he earns shall be paid in full into his own hands.[29]

WHITE ACT, 1898

Late in 1895 Furuseth returned to Washington to work for enactment of the remaining Maguire bills. From five in the morning till long past midnight he wrote letters, talked with congressmen, attended hearings, and spent lonely evenings in his bare hotel room preparing for the next day's work. His bitterest opponents conceded that he was the most intelligent sailor they had ever met. Congressmen treated him with the respect usually reserved for an elder statesman.

The Fifty-fourth Congress held extensive hearings on the Maguire bills and on various substitutes and compromises that had been introduced. The shipowners assembled their strongest forces to oppose the seamen's program and perhaps to repeal or amend the Maguire Act. Vernon C. Brown, president of the Maritime Exchange of New York, was their principal spokesman. At the request of Eastern shipowners, Representative Phillip D. Low of New York introduced a bill that was more "reasonable." Furuseth felt it was so full of loopholes that it was only a meaningless mouthing of pleasant phrases.

Two opponents particularly annoyed the seamen because of their obvious effect upon congressmen. One was Eugene T. Chamberlain, United States Commissioner of Navigation, who favored limiting allotment to one month's wages instead of abolishing it completely, and who testified that the complaints of the sailors were exaggerated, especially as to the inadequacy of the forecastle space. The second was the American Seamen's Friend Society, an organization that maintained missions and boardinghouses in thirty-one ports throughout the world. The *Journal* charged that the society was under the control of merchants, shipowners, and philanthropists who contributed to its support. "The American Seamen's Friend Society," said the *Journal*, "cannot glorify God and help American seamen by prayer alone.... The seaman's condition must be improved to the point of humanity before he can be made amenable to mental or spiritual efforts."[30]

To counteract this powerful opposition required a skillful tactician like Furuseth.[31] He kept his ultimate objective clearly in mind, found his opponents' weaknesses, and massed his attack where it would be the most effective. His stated objective was to revive the American merchant marine and man the ships with American citizens. By law, no foreign vessels could compete in the coastwise trade of the United States, but in the foreign trade American vessels had almost disappeared from the ocean. The story was told of a British captain who, seeing a vessel carrying the American flag in the South Pacific, feigned great surprise and exclaimed: "Why bless my heart, that must be a Yankee ship. I remember seeing that flag when I was a boy. The poor fellow must have drifted off the coast and got lost."[32] American sailors were as scarce as American vessels. For even in the coastwise trade, it was estimated at the time that only 18 per cent of the total crew including officers, who had to be citizens, were Americans. No congressman could argue against Furuseth's stated objective. That he also wanted to build a strong union was not stated, but was implicit in his every act.

Analyzing his opponents' weaknesses, Furuseth found that the American officer's world-wide reputation for "buckoism," cruelty to the men, was the most vulnerable spot. For several years the union had been publicizing examples of sadism,[33] and Furuseth had proposed printing a compendium of these outrages. The pamphlet, entitled *Red Record*,[34] became the seamen's most effective weapon. Every trade unionist in America had an opportunity to read with horror the matter-of-fact listing of crimes. Every congressman was supplied with a copy to ponder his individual responsibility for the continuation of such a situation. In the ten years before publication of *Red Record* in 1895, sixteen known deaths had occurred under circumstances justifying the charge of murder. Many instances of cruelty resulted in the loss of eyes, limbs, or teeth. In only seven of the cases listed were convictions obtained. In the rest, the officers were exonerated for lack of evidence, or their actions were deemed justifiable discipline. The highest penalty inflicted was a $1,000 fine and a one-year prison sentence. Penalties in the other cases ranged from $25 to $100.

A sample of the less gruesome cases described in *Red Record* follows:

HENRY B. HYDE, Captain Pendleton, arrived in San Francisco, April, 1893. First mate of the ship charged with breaking a seaman's wrist by a blow with a belaying pin, and otherwise ill-treating him. All hands tell a straightforward story in the courts, plainly proving his guilt. Case dismissed on ground of "justifiable discipline."

T. F. OAKES, Captain Reid, arrived in San Francisco, May, 1893. Captain Reid and First-Mate J. McKay charged with cruelty to seamen, the latter on twenty-eight distinct indictments. McKay's case dismissed on the second trial. In the case of Captain Reid six seamen gave direct evidence of his cruelty and bore on their persons the actual wounds inflicted. Spectators in the court expressed indignation and confidence of a conviction. Reid made no defense. Case dismissed. Jury returned the verdict that "a shipmaster has the right to beat a seaman who is unruly."

BEAR, United States revenue steamer, Captain Healy. Three seamen, Holben, DaWertz and Frandsen of the American bark *Estrella* charged that while discharging coal into the *Bear* in the harbor of Oonalaska, in June, 1889, Captain Healy, without provocation, ordered them placed in irons and confined in the forepeak of the *Bear*. Then they were triced up, with their hands behind them and their toes barely touching the deck. The punishment lasted for fifteen minutes, and the pain was most excruciating. They were then tied with their backs to the stanchions and their arms around them for forty-two hours. They were then put ashore and made to shift for themselves. The seamen accused both Captain Healy and Captain Avery of the *Estrella* of drunkenness and gross incapacity. Healy exonerated by the Navy Department.

It did not matter that the shipowners denied personal responsibility for the crimes of their officers, or claimed that the charges were exaggerated or that such conditions existed only in the deepwater trade. Upon them lay the onus of defending an intolerable situation. As a partial solution the union proposed that a vessel be made liable for any injury inflicted upon a seaman by an officer. Furuseth explained that the intention was not to punish anyone, but merely to make maltreatment of the men so expensive for a shipowner that he would not employ officers who used such methods. The precedent for making a vessel liable for the acts of its officers had already been set by Congress when it made the owners responsible for fines levied when the captain neglected to show proper lights in a harbor or made some other mistake.

Furthermore, experience had shown that in practice it was impossible to collect damages from a "bucko" mate.[35] Before the vessel reached port, the guilty officer would be put ashore to disappear so that the seamen could not place charges against him. When the ship was ready to leave, he would mysteriously reappear. Even if charges were made, it was necessary to prove that the brutal treatment had been motivated by malice or revenge. "The statute reads in such a way," explained Furuseth, "that no jury on God's earth will ever convict." Moreover, after preferring charges, the sailor would meet still other difficulties. While waiting for the trial, he would be held in jail as if he had been guilty of a crime, because he could not afford to stay in a boardinghouse, and if he were not present at the proper time the charges would be dropped. Or he might find on the day of the trial that his most important witnesses had been "liquored-up," and their appearance in court in so disreputable a condition would have been disastrous.[36] Liability of a vessel—making cruelty expensive to a shipowner—was at least a partial answer.

The brutal treatment of seamen was not Furuseth's major concern. Brutality was only a symptom of a much more serious malady, but it was a means of putting Congress in a sympathetic mood to listen to the rest of the story. Cruelty was practiced not out of sheer meanness, but to drive inexperienced men to do work they did not know and did not want to learn. Such men were obtained by shipowners through the crimping system. Abolish advance and allotment in the foreign trade as they had been abolished in the coastwise trade, and the crimp would disappear because he could not make a dishonest living. To make sure that the crimp would not use some subterfuge to get his pound of flesh, it was merely necessary for Congress to make the sailor a free man.

Again the shipowners were placed on the defensive. They argued that the crimp was a necessary evil of the shipping industry and that giving sailors the right to desert was unthinkable. "Why?" asked Furuseth.

When a vessel is delayed, it may mean 24 hours demurrage—possibly $100 or $150, but what will the owner of a glass factory lose by having its furnaces go cold; half a million dollars. What will a cotton planter lose by not being able to pick his cotton when it is ripe? Is there any good reason why, because I am a sailor, I should have shackles put upon my hands and made to feel that I, of all men, am the one upon whom the United States is putting the stamp of servitude?[37]

Furuseth patiently explained the relationship of these conditions to the building of an American merchant marine. In the early days all the sailors were American citizens. The captain and the crew came from the same town and discipline was easy. As competition increased and profits grew smaller, seamen began to be cheated. Native Americans refused to accept the lower standards. In seeking replacements, owners utilized the crimps, who found men without previous experience. These men had to be driven to their tasks. This brutality drove more American seamen out of the merchant marine, until now less than 10 per cent of the sailors were citizens.

Furuseth also found the shipowners vulnerable for failing to supply adequate forecastle space and sufficient provisions for the crew. When the owners mustered "expert" testimony to show that the sailors were exaggerating, that foreign vessels with which they competed had lower standards, and that they provided better food and quarters than were required by law, Furuseth had a cogent answer. He submitted testimony he had obtained from foreign consuls to show that the laws of their countries set higher standards than those required on American vessels. He submitted the scale of provisions of California penal institutions, which was superior to that required of American shipowners. And he delivered a *coup de grâce* by pointing to the actual results of inadequate diet and improper living conditions. The San Francisco Marine Hospital treated 391 cases of scurvy between 1872 and 1888. American vessels carried less than 20 per cent of the trade from the port of San Francisco, yet of the 391 cases, 235 were from American ships.

For seven months Furuseth remained in Washington, planning, pleading, and explaining. With the assistance of Sereno E. Payne, chairman of the House Committee on Merchant Marine and Fisheries, two bills were reported out which represented a compromise between the seamen's program and that of the "friends" of the seamen. In commending the bills for favorable consideration the committee said: "The seamen are inclined to be radical in their demands, while the owners, with the proverbial timidity which attaches itself to invested capital, are reluctant to consent to any changes that savor of untried experiments."[38] On the whole, Furuseth was satisfied, and expressed the hope and belief that the Senate would follow the House's example of approving the bills.

Upon his return to San Francisco in June, 1896, Furuseth found the condition of the union little improved. In fact, in January, 1896, shipowners had signed a formal agreement with the boarding masters to freeze the union out of the water front. The owners agreed to hire a specified proportion of their men through the houses, and the boarding masters promised to refuse rooms to any men who went out on strike.

Maguire ran for Congress in the fall. Again the seamen supported him while at the same time applauding Gompers' nonpartisan stand on politics within the AFL.[39] In addition to his duties as secretary, Furuseth worked for Maguire's reëlection and wrote letters seeking support for the seamen's bills. Impressed by the effect of organizations like the American Seamen's Friend Society upon congressmen, he set about winning wide popular support for the bills. Upon his return to the East in December, 1896, Furuseth spoke before the Social Reform Club of New York and other groups which he thought might be helpful to the seamen.

When Furuseth arrived in Washington he was dismayed to learn that the Senate Committee on Commerce had discarded the House bills

Lobbyist for Seamen

and had approved a substitute prepared by E. T. Chamberlain and introduced by Senator Frye of Maine. The substitute permitted allotment, provided for imprisonment for desertion at the discretion of the court, and forbade punishment without "justifiable cause."

Senator Frye was a strong antagonist. Furuseth marshaled his forces carefully for the battle.[40] He sent hundreds, perhaps thousands, of letters to men he knew in the labor movement. He asked them to have their unions write letters to congressmen; he suggested they contact local newspapers, influential political bosses, or personal friends of their congressmen. He urged mass meetings to protest both the Supreme Court's decision in the *Arago* case and the Frye bill. The SUP mailed marked copies of the *Journal* to every newspaper in Maine in an effort to influence the senator.[41] Furuseth prepared a memorial to Congress in which he said that the Senate had "inadvertly" approved a bill that would reëstablish flogging in the American merchant marine. He contrasted the practices of foreign countries with those of the United States. "Do they [foreign nations] organize societies to protect dogs, and cats and other animals and permit men who may not defend themselves, short of mutiny, to be beaten? They protect the animals and the seamen, too."[42] In a melodramatic message read at the SUP birthday celebration, Furuseth wrote:

Oh ye patriots! Was it for this that ye gave life and all during the War for Independence? What, now, has become of the inalienable right to liberty for which you fought and of which we have been so proud? Was it for this, you loyal soldiers, that your bones were left on every battle field from Bull Run to Appomattox? Oh Lincoln! was it for this that your hair grew grey before its time, that your face became sad, and got stamped upon it the air which denotes the burden bearer? Was it for this you died? Oh ye Christians, was it for this that our Teacher, our Saviour, gave his bloody sweat at Gethsemane, his blood on Calvary? No, a thousand times, No![43]

Senator Frye was so annoyed by the petitions, letters, and newspaper articles that he refused, as chairman of the Committee on Commerce, to call up any bill. Senators friendly to Furuseth advised him to stop the agitation in order to allow Frye the opportunity of introducing a bill that might possibly be amended on the Senate floor.[44] Furuseth hoped that this tactic might work, because he was convinced that a majority of the senators favored his bills, but the session ended without any action.

Furuseth remained in Washington for the opening of the new session of Congress. Senator Stephen S. White of California introduced S. 95, a bill embodying the seamen's major demands. After visiting several former abolitionists to interest them in the sailors' involuntary servitude, and after holding a series of mass meetings in the East, Furuseth returned in April, 1897, to San Francisco, where the effect of the gold strike in the Klondike was serving as a sharp stimulant to the ailing maritime industry. Men were working again and many of them were rejoining the union. Efforts to organize the deepwater sailors, however, proved premature.[45]

An incident occurred that summer over which the sailors chuckled for a good many years. It illustrated Furuseth's flair for making news and his ability to turn an embarrassing situation to the union's advantage. The grand marshal of the Fourth of July parade invited the sailors to participate. Although the union's membership had increased, most of the men would have been at sea on the Fourth and the union would have made a sorry showing. Furuseth therefore declined the invitation to take part in this march of free men:

We, therefore, sir, being mindful of our status—that of involuntary servitude—which was in no way modified by the declaration of individual freedom, feel that it would be an imposition on our part to take advantage of your kindness and inflict our presence—the presence of bondsmen—upon the freemen who will on the Fourth of July celebrate their freedom and renew their allegiance to those principles which have made nations and men great.[46]

In December Furuseth made his annual trip to the AFL convention and then went on to Washington, where he plunged into activities in support of the White bill. Several brief hearings were held on S. 95. What annoyed Furuseth most was the willingness of the "friends" of the seamen to compromise the bill. He blamed one watered-down version on some of the "sky pilots" or "Holy Joes" whom he had cajoled into concerning themselves over the sailors' plight.[47] The war with Spain delayed consideration of seamen's legislation for several months, but Furuseth remained in Washington to point out the lesson of the shortage of qualified American seamen to serve in the Navy. The White bill was finally reported out on June 23, and was passed by the Senate on July 2, 1898. As amended, it permitted allotment up to one month's pay in the foreign trade and allowed imprisonment of one month at the discretion of the court for desertion in a foreign port; it did not provide for enlarged forecastles or for two watches at sea.[48]

When Congress took its summer recess, Furuseth returned to San Francisco. Elections in the fall resulted in the defeat of most of the Democratic party candidates, including Maguire for governor and James H. Barry for Congress. These defeats must have discouraged many members of the union, for there was opposition to any further

Lobbyist for Seamen 43

legislative efforts. A long and heated debate took place at the meeting on November 21, just before Furuseth went back to Washington, on the desirability of spending $200 for legislative expenses.[49] The National Seamen's Union paid Furuseth's expenses to the AFL convention. The AFL paid his transportation to Washington and his salary and expenses for acting as its legislative representative. The item under debate at the SUP meeting, therefore, was the money for pamphlets, typing, postage, and other costs chargeable to the seamen's bill. The expense was approved by only a narrow margin.

The White bill, as it had passed the Senate, came up in the House of Representatives in December. Furuseth left Washington to attend the AFL convention in Kansas City, Missouri. Some congressmen halfheartedly introduced amendments to restore the bill to its original form. On December 13 the House quickly disposed of most of these amendments and passed the bill substantially as it had come from the Senate. On December 28, 1898, the amended White bill became law.[50] The AFL convention endorsed Gompers' estimate of the bill as a step in the right direction, but as falling short of "that full freedom to quit at will and move freely from place to place, which is the inalienable natural right of man, and without which freedom loses its meaning and becomes but an empty phrase...."[51]

Since their "Appeal to Congress" in 1892, the seamen had rectified most of their grievances through the Maguire Act and the White Act. The major accomplishments were the right to quit work in any American port, prohibition of allotment in the coastwise trade, slightly larger forecastle space, an improved scale of provisions, the right of a majority of the crew to call for a survey of seaworthiness, penalties for unreasonably delaying payment to seamen, a reduction in the penalties for various offenses committed by seamen, the requirement that masters hire full crews "if obtainable," and transportation back to the United States if a vessel was wrecked in a foreign port. The acts fell short of satisfying the sailors' demands in that the law still permitted imprisonment for desertion in a foreign port and allotment up to one month's wages in the foreign trade, the vessel was not liable for injuries inflicted upon the crew by the officers, and the captain could still insert in the articles a provision that wages due a seaman be paid at the master's option.

Furuseth returned to Washington in 1900 and 1901, but his primary concern then was with legislative matters in which the AFL was interested. Congress was unresponsive, and he summed up his efforts for the AFL as a failure.[52] He continued to push the seamen's program[53] and tried to defeat a bill forbidding anyone to board a vessel without the master's consent. Though the bill was aimed at the crimps, Furuseth realized that it could also be used to keep union agents off the ships. He was successful in amending the bill so that it became ineffective,[54] but he was unable to secure any further legislation beneficial to the seamen. However, the legal basis had been laid which allowed the union to take advantage of the economic upswing that took place at the close of the century.

IV. LABOR THEORIST

ALTHOUGH FURUSETH always considered himself first and foremost a member of the Sailors' Union of the Pacific, it was inevitable that a man of his stature would play an important role on a larger stage. He became a leader in the San Francisco Federated Trades Council; his abilities received prompt recognition from officers of the American Federation of Labor; and he succeeded in building a national organization of seamen. On this broader stage, Furuseth was forced to work out a philosophy of the labor movement. As local secretary of a sailors' union, he could limit his horizon to wages, hours, and working conditions. As a national figure of some prominence, he had to have ideals and goals.

SAN FRANCISCO LABOR MOVEMENT

Until the great strike in 1901, Furuseth never held an important elective position in the San Francisco labor movement. His frequent absences, at first with the fishing fleet and later in Washington, made the acceptance of such a post impossible. However, other members of the Sailors' Union—Frank Roney, W. A. Bushnell, Alfred Fuhrman, W. J. B. Mackay, and Walter Macarthur—served successively as president of the Federated Trades Council. This is eloquent testimony to the capabilities of these associates of Furuseth, and to the importance of the Sailors' Union in the affairs of the San Francisco labor movement. Furuseth was elected to represent the sailors in the Federated Trades Council in 1887,[1] and he attended the weekly meetings almost every Friday night when he was in San Francisco. His abilities were utilized on many committees of the labor council, especially on those dealing with the constitution and bylaws.[2]

Furuseth's skill as an inspirational speaker was frequently in demand.[3] In his early speeches he emphasized the necessity for organization in order to achieve the Christian goals upon which the labor movement was based. His uplifting and ennobling words made his listeners feel that they were part of a great crusade. They were not petty seekers for an extra slice of bread. They were searchers after truth, fighters in the struggle to fulfill the ideals of Christianity, guardians of the Declaration of Independence and the Constitution, an army dedicated to extending religious and political democracy to the industrial field.

Furuseth's high-pitched, sometimes rasping voice was capable of becoming deeply sonorous. In the heat of argument his flashing eyes combined with his sharp tongue and impassioned tones to wither the enemy. The strong Scandinavian accent in which every *j* sounded like a *y* never noticeably troubled his Irish, German, and Scandinavian audiences. And this accent, which he kept all his life, never seemed to bother Furuseth or to make him self-conscious. The audience, however, was conscious of Furuseth. His appearance was striking. Although he was not so gaunt as he became in later years, his tall figure, his long arms, his beaklike nose, his ordinary sailor's clothes, and his poise and ease on the platform brought him attention even before he began to speak. His reputation for complete honesty, for devotion to the workers whom he served, and for total disinterest in any personal gain won him a respectful hearing at all times.

Although Furuseth's sentences were often long and complex, his thoughts were easily followed. He held his audience by the logic of his argument, the novel twist or interpretation of an old idea, and the absolute sincerity with which he spoke. There were rare occasions when he used the tricks of the orator, but most of his speeches were delivered without bombast or acting. At a time when a reference to Chinese coolie labor or a personal attack on the wealthy would have brought forth a cheer from any working-class audience, Furuseth refrained from such cheap tricks. He would point out that Collis P. Huntington employed 75,000 men and held the destiny of 300,000 men, women, and children in his hands, but this was merely to stress the inequality that existed between the individual worker and the individual employer. The lesson to be learned was the necessity for organization:

If you be opposed to absolutism, join your trade union.... If you be a Christian and hope for the coming of the Kingdom for which you pray, then support organization. If you be a workman hoping for better times to come in the immediate future, then organize. Organize into trade unions because you who are in the same trades understand each other best, and mutual grievances give mutual sympathy. Let us organize together that we may bear each other's burdens, but above all, let us join together that we may study jointly, study that we may jointly know, and know that we may act jointly in the interest of peace and progress in the times dangerous and doubtful, which, according to all students of sociology, are coming, times in which it may be decided for ages to come whether wealth shall rule man or man be "a man fo' a' that."[4]

To the modern reader, many of Furuseth's speeches appear to contain long, involved introductions and a great many asides, but careful examination shows that these are not mere ramblings. Furuseth was trained in a period when listening to speakers was entertainment, and when the leisurely development of an idea was not cut short by limitations of time. Even to his contemporaries, however, Furuseth's speeches and reports seemed "lengthy." Although he could be brief and to the point, when he wanted to make a speech there was no way of cutting him short. In speaking extemporaneously at conventions, Furuseth might ramble occasionally, but in his prepared speeches the introductions and asides were all intimately connected with the topic. His Labor Day speech was always as carefully prepared as the parade, the floats, the music, and the entertainment that preceded it. Although the grammarian, the logician, or the historian might be able to find fault with Furuseth's speech, the worker who listened was untroubled by such criticism. Furuseth's talk was, aside from the beer and the dancing, the high point of Labor Day. It lifted the worker's spirits and ennobled him in his own eyes.[5]

At the meetings of the Federated Trades Council, Furuseth frequently participated in the debates that enlivened the sessions, for he enjoyed matching wits verbally. Many of the arguments were over personalities, jurisdiction, or trivial matters, but the hottest debates arose from the conflict between Socialists and "trade unionists."[6] The enmity between these two labor groups in vying for the loyalty of workingmen was often much greater than their enmity toward the bosses. Although the conflict took many forms, the fundamental difference lay in the attitude toward politics. Socialists (a broad term taking in many shades of opinion) believed that working people could best advance their own interests by concentrating upon the election of Socialists to office. Once elected, these men would change the laws to bring justice to the workers. Socialists did not oppose unions, strikes, or boycotts, but held that their value was limited to a temporary advantage won at great cost. For no sooner would the workers get a wage increase than it would be wiped out by an increase in prices.

On the other hand, "trade unionists" were not interested in "pie in the sky by and by." They wanted better wages and working conditions now. On this, labor could unite. On politics, they insisted, history showed that labor would divide and ruin itself. Just as Socialists did not discount the value of strikes and boycotts, so "trade unionists" did not deny the value of political activity. They supported political candidates friendly to labor and they worked for legislation in the interests of labor, but their primary reliance was on the strength of the trade union. Sometimes the lines of division were not too clear.

Furuseth was always with the "trade unionists," but, like Samuel Gompers, his philosophy of the labor movement went far beyond being merely "wage conscious." To him trade unionism was a way of life. Its objectives were just as humanitarian and its interests just as wide as the objectives and interests of the Socialist movement.[7]

NATIONAL LABOR MOVEMENT

Furuseth first met Gompers in 1891, when the president of the AFL came to San Francisco to prevent a schism in the labor movement. Alfred Fuhrman had withdrawn the West Coast brewery workers from their national organization. Because the San Francisco Federated Trades Council recognized Fuhrman's group as the official Brewery Workers' Union, the council was suspended from the AFL. Consequently, Fuhrman began to organize a Pacific Coast federation outside the AFL. His efforts met with a sympathetic response because most of the West Coast unions felt that they had been neglected by their sister unions in the East.[8] Gompers' speaking tour of the Pacific Coast successfully nipped the separatist movement in the bud. In Walter Macarthur, then president of the Federated Trades Council, and Andrew Furuseth, secretary of the Coast Seamen's Union, Gompers found stanch allies.[9]

The two men met again in December, 1891, at the American Federation of Labor convention in Birmingham, Alabama, where Furuseth represented the San Francisco Federated Trades Council. His entrance upon the scene of the national labor movement was a stormy one. For three days a special committee debated whether or not to seat the suspended San Francisco organization in the convention. In defending his right to be seated, Furuseth impressed the delegates with his "clear, eloquent, and forcible speech—a speech remarkable for its logic, and absence of superfluous phrase."[10] And behind the scenes he negotiated a compromise between the brewery workers in San Francisco and their national officers present at the convention.[11]

Furuseth was finally seated at the 1891 convention. He missed the 1892 convention but, with two exceptions, he represented the seamen's national organization at every annual convention of the American Federation of Labor from 1893 to 1936.[12] His abilities and his loyalty to Gompers received recognition by his appointment with almost monotonous regularity as either chairman or secretary of the Committee on the President's Report—one of the most important convention committees. It was the duty of this committee to go over the president's yearly report and to comment on the recommendations made. Although the committee seldom publicly disagreed with the president, the items it chose to stress set the tone of the organization for the ensuing year.

In addition to his duties on the committee, which ordinarily occupied

Labor Theorist

three or four days of full-time work, Furuseth introduced resolutions pertaining to seamen's legislation, international affairs,[13] injunctions,[14] and arbitration. In accordance with a general practice of the AFL, there was seldom any debate or controversy when a member organization introduced a resolution as long as it dealt strictly with the craft. Thus, when the seamen asked the AFL to endorse the Maguire bills or the White bill pending in Congress, there was no opposition. If they had asked the federation to condemn these bills, there would have been no opposition.

Furuseth prided himself on his parliamentary ability at the conventions. He was trained in the democratic school of the Sailors' Union, where he frequently acted as chairman during the periods when he was not the union secretary. There were men at the sailors' meetings who knew every parliamentary trick. The chairman had to be physically strong to awe the rowdies, and sharp-witted to outmaneuver the tacticians on the floor. Furuseth made use of this union experience at the AFL conventions. He frequently made procedural motions or tried to maneuver reports or resolutions with which he disagreed into the most unfavorable parliamentary position.

A labor convention is much more than an occasion to pass resolutions and elect officers. Many of the delegates who attended the AFL conventions came year after year; this made the gathering each December a sort of social occasion. In addition to the official social affairs, there were informal gatherings in hotel rooms, lobbies, and saloons. Sometimes these informal groups discussed momentous questions; they settled problems of jurisdiction, decided upon joint campaigns, and picked candidates for office. Undoubtedly, many delegates came to the convention with nothing more on their minds than having a good time. Furuseth was not in this group. He could enjoy the social aspect of the convention as well as any other delegate, but he felt that this should be subordinate to what he considered the main work of the gathering. Quite frequently he favored holding an extra night session, meeting on a Saturday or a Sunday, or cutting out an entertainment. Usually he was a minority of one on such proposals.

Looking back at these early conventions of the AFL, one is amazed at the brashness of the handful of delegates, representing a tiny segment of the working population, in speaking in the name of all labor. A few of the delegates actually represented organizations with more than 25,000 members; many of them, like Furuseth, often represented unions that existed mostly on paper. During the 1890's the seamen seldom met as a national organization. The strongest single unit was the Sailors'

Union of the Pacific, and after its defeat in the strike of 1893 there were many meetings when a quorum of fifty members could not be assembled. This did not seem to bother Furuseth. Speaking in the name of all American seamen, he was the equal of any delegate to the convention, and he was almost always one of the dozen most vocal.

The issue that disturbed the national federation was the same one that troubled the San Francisco Trades Council—the fight against the minority of Socialists. In debates Furuseth always sided with Gompers, opposing any move that would turn the AFL into a political movement, and he campaigned vigorously against the proposal made by some Socialists that labor disputes should be settled by compulsory arbitration.[15]

In the forge of political debate at these conventions, the Norwegian sailor hammered out a philosophy of the trade-union movement which was to remain with him for the rest of his life. He brought to these gatherings the sailor's desire to be free, coupled with the sailor's training in working together for the mutual welfare of all. He had already read widely, especially in the fields of history and philosophy. Above all, he brought a fierce protectiveness for his fellow sailors. His experiences with Haskell and other Socialists were not such as to make him sympathetic to their cause. By the time he became active in the national labor movement, he was convinced of the necessity of securing remedial legislation for seamen. It was obvious to him that this could not be accomplished by a utopian scheme of supporting a labor party. The seamen, by the nature of their occupation, were disenfranchised. The solution lay in influencing the already established political parties to support labor's cause. But the foundation of Furuseth's philosophy rested on the belief that anything that labor got must be secured by its own organized strength. Philosophically, but not practically, Furuseth believed that the role of government in the conflict between workers and employers was to allow complete freedom for both sides. He asked for no favors from the government, but he also asked that the government show no disfavor to the workers.

Narrow craft unionism, typical of the AFL of this period, was in line with a sailor's experience. Although he lived on board a vessel with cooks, stewards, and firemen, he regarded these men as somewhat beneath him—or at least in a separate category. They all were workers employed by the same owner under the same captain, but it was the universal experience that sailors organized their own unions independent of any of the other crafts on the vessel. This exclusiveness was even more pronounced between shore workers and seagoing personnel. Furu-

Labor Theorist

seth thought about his sailors in the same way that an employer thinks about his business. The first thought of the businessman is not, "Will this product be of value to my community and my country?" but more like Furuseth's criterion, "Will this action or this legislation be good for sailors?" This "business unionism" was more in keeping with the late nineteenth-century American philosophy than were the utopian ideals of the Socialists. The union was an instrument for getting something for the worker here and now. Above all, it elevated the individual worker so that through his organized strength he could speak to the employer as an equal instead of as a servant or a slave.

The philosophies of Samuel Gompers and of Andrew Furuseth before the turn of the century were so similar that it is difficult to point up differences. They influenced each other in their thinking and even in their phraseology. Their meetings after 1893 were quite frequent. They associated closely for two weeks at the annual convention and they saw each other in Washington, where both spent some time every year. Furuseth was legislative representative for the AFL from 1894 to 1901, when the seamen could afford to maintain him as their representative. In 1897 the AFL moved its headquarters from Indianapolis to Washington, and the association between Gompers and Furuseth became even closer than it had been before.[16]

As a legislative representative for the federation, Furuseth was concerned with more than seamen's legislation.[17] In 1898, for example, the AFL Executive Council was also interested in bills dealing with the eight-hour day, labor injunctions, immigration, and convict labor. Until the White Act was finally passed, Furuseth devoted most of his time to seamen's bills, but he also appeared frequently before committees and spoke to congressmen about other legislative matters. He was particularly concerned with abolishing the use of injunctions in labor disputes. This question so fascinated him that he made a special study of the legal history of the injunction. Few people, either in Congress or in the labor movement, knew as much about injunctions as did this self-taught sailor.

NATIONAL SEAMEN'S UNION

During the period from 1890 to 1901, when Furuseth spoke in the name of all the seamen of the United States, he tried to turn his empty boast into reality. Seamen had organized on a local basis even before the Coast Seamen's Union was formed in 1885. The Lake Seamen's Union had maintained an organization of sailors on the Great Lakes since 1878.[18] Unions had existed on the East and West coasts, but were of a transitory character. Because most of the Great Lakes and coasting sailors were Scandinavians, and because the nature of their occupation involved frequent chance contacts, it is reasonable to assume that the various seamen's groups were aware of each other's existence. There is some evidence of a limited communication among these unions before 1885,[19] but the molding of a national seamen's organization waited upon a more opportune time and more dynamic leadership.

When Alfred Fuhrman attended a convention of brewery workers in 1888 in Chicago, he spoke with representatives of the Lake Seamen's Union, who manifested a desire for greater unity among seamen.[20] In 1889 Samuel Gompers helped to organize the Atlantic Coast sailors, and they carried on correspondence with sailors on the Pacific Coast.[21] The Eastern sailors suggested a national organization of seamen, but the Coast Seamen's Union considered the proposal premature.[22] The first real impetus came from the tour of Atlantic, Gulf, and Great Lakes ports in 1890 by the CSU delegates returning from the international convention in Glasgow.[23] As a result of their reports, the Coast Seamen's Union decided, on November 24, 1890, to ask the sailors' unions throughout the country whether they were interested in forming a national organization. The idea was further explored by Andrew Furuseth on the occasion of Samuel Gompers' visit to San Francisco in 1891.[24]

Events in San Francisco that year served to emphasize the necessity for organizing nationally. Facing a conflict with shipowners, and the possibility of importation of nonunion men, the newly formed Sailors' Union of the Pacific first voted to spend $5,000 to send an organizer to the East Coast, but later rescinded the motion. Instead, the Emergency Committee, elected to conduct the fight against the owners, recommended the calling of a national seamen's convention. A month later, in December, 1891, at the AFL convention in Birmingham, Alabama, Furuseth discussed the matter with delegates—none of them seamen—from other parts of the country.[25] He returned to San Francisco via Chicago, where he stopped to confer with the Great Lakes sailors. Thereafter events moved rapidly. On April 22, 1892, delegates from the Great Lakes, the Gulf Coast, and the Pacific Coast met in Chicago and established the National Seamen's Union. They elected Charles Hagen of New Orleans president and T. J. Elderkin of Chicago secretary-treasurer, and set as their main goal the organization of the East Coast.

Furuseth was not a delegate to the convention. At this time he had resigned as secretary of the Sailors' Union and was working on the Columbia River. The SUP delegates, John Haist, Frank Waterhouse, and Thomas Finnerty, were not completely satisfied with the loose federation established in Chicago, but they deemed it better than no organization at all.

Although regular correspondence was maintained,[26] no real progress was made in organizing the seamen. The second convention in 1893 tried to enlarge the jurisdiction of the union to include firemen, but with little success. At this convention Furuseth, who was again absent because of the West Coast strike, was elected legislative representative. While he was speaking for the seamen in Washington, the National Seamen's Union was rapidly disintegrating.[27] Even Furuseth's own union, defeated and demoralized, became a shadow of its former self. No attempt was made to hold a convention in 1894. In July of that year, the president, Charles Hagen, mysteriously disappeared.

Although Furuseth held no office in the national organization, his victory in securing passage of the first law drafted by seamen made him the logical choice to revive the NSU. Before returning to San Francisco in 1895, he visited the Eastern branches to discuss the new law. By the end of the year it seemed feasible to call another convention.[28] Elaborate preparations were made by the sailors in New York as hosts of the nine delegates who attended.[29]

Aside from picking a new president, T. J. Robertson, and retaining Elderkin as secretary-treasurer, the convention accomplished very little. Furuseth remained in New York for several weeks trying to organize the Scandinavian seamen. Although he reported some success, his efforts did not result in permanent organization. None of the seamen's groups showed any strength during 1896 and no convention was called. When Robertson resigned in February, 1897, Furuseth was chosen by the executive board to serve as president until the next convention. That convention was not to meet until December, 1899. For three years with Elderkin, and another year with Walter Macarthur,[30] Furuseth kept together a semblance of a national organization of seamen.

Furuseth's duties as president were anything but pleasant, for he faced trouble on both the Atlantic and the Great Lakes. When he went east in 1897 for the AFL convention in Nashville, Tennessee, he met J. Havelock Wilson, who had come with other fraternal delegates from the British Trades Union Congress. Whatever differences they had had in Glasgow in 1890 were submerged in their common problem. The British seamen's union had been wiped out and Wilson was trying to rebuild it. He rightly judged that he could reach more British seamen in New York, where they would be drawn together by the common bond of being foreigners in a strange land, than he could in British ports where sailors were afraid to be seen at union meetings.

Furuseth took Wilson to union headquarters in Boston, where a formal agreement was reached between the Atlantic Coast Seamen's Union and the representatives of British sailors.[31] Wilson was to go to New York, whence most of the steamships sailed, for the purpose of organizing seamen. Those who regularly sailed on British vessels would become members of the British union, and the others would join the Atlantic Coast union. Wilson was a fiery speaker able to arouse an audience to a fever pitch of excitement, and he was successful, together with Andrew Furuseth, in recruiting a great many men—men who quickly dropped out when the emotional impact of Wilson's speech had subsided.[32] The transitory nature of the membership was only a minor irritation. Wilson himself became the major irritation. He was accused by agents in Boston and New York of acting as if the Atlantic Coast Seamen's Union was a branch of the British union. Furuseth resented this attitude, and though outwardly remaining friendly, he was probably happy to lend Wilson $50 to buy passage home.[33]

Without Wilson's aid, the agents on the Atlantic Coast who reported to Furuseth usually did not do very well. They depended on dues for their living, and quite often they did not take in enough money in a week to buy coal for the stove. The agent in New York, F. H. Bureyson, wrote that he would have to resign because his clothes were so shabby that he could not be seen in polite company. Furuseth finally persuaded him to accept a small personal loan and to remain on the job—only to have him disappear a year later with the union funds. Rather than publicize this, the fifth such incident in one year, Furuseth replaced the shortage out of his own pocket.[34]

In addition to his troubles on the Atlantic Coast, Furuseth was faced on the Great Lakes with violent opposition to his leadership. In part, the Great Lakes sailors claimed that they were paying an undue proportion of the expenses of the national organization without receiving any benefits. Their per capita dues were spent in organizing the East Coast while those of the Atlantic unions were always remitted. They finally ceased paying dues, thus leaving the Sailors' Union of the Pacific as the only organization which actually paid the per capita levy.

To placate the Great Lakes sailors, Furuseth offered the presidency of the national union to their secretary, William Penje. In reply he received an insulting letter, asking what right Furuseth had to offer the job. Furthermore, Penje wrote, he did not approve of the way in which the affairs of the NSU were being managed: "I could under no circumstance accept an office in an organization, which in my estimation is rotten.... I think the present one is dead, and if it is not, it ought to

Labor Theorist 55

be."³⁵ Only by playing up to Penje's "big head" and by capitulating to the demands of the Great Lakes sailors was Furuseth finally able to get them to agree to the calling of another convention in 1899, at which time Penje was elected president.

In the year preceding the convention, Furuseth proposed and conducted an amazing organizational campaign. The White Act had just become law in December, 1898. The seamen had campaigned for total abolition of allotment in order to destroy the power of the crimps. The law, as passed, still permitted allotment in the foreign trade but limited it to a maximum of one month's pay. Previously the crimp had received $10 per month; thus, on a three months' voyage, he was allotted $30. Under the new law, if the sailor's wages were $20 per month, the crimp could not receive more than $20. It was now in his interest to raise wages to $30 so that he could make as much as he had before.³⁶

Recognizing the mutual interest of the crimps and the union at this point, Furuseth tried to make use of a provision of the law which he had opposed in Congress, to organize the seamen by using the crimps. Only when one realizes how savagely the sailors hated the crimps, how bitterly Furuseth had campaigned against them in Washington, how eloquently he denounced them on every occasion as slave catchers and procurers—only then can one grasp the significance of his plan. It was simple. The crimps were to be organized in every city. The union would agree to ship all its men through the organized crimps. In return the crimps would agree not to hire anyone who did not belong to the union.³⁷ Had the plan worked, every seaman would have had to join the union. Eventually Furuseth might have been able to throw out the crimps and deal directly with the shipowners, but at the moment there seemed no way to build the union independently because the crimps controlled shipping in all Atlantic ports and in the Pacific foreign trade. Some crimps were willing to work with the union because they were afraid that, if they demanded higher pay for the seamen, the union might underbid them and take the shipping away from them.

The plan did not work at first on the Pacific Coast because the crimps preferred to deal with shipowners rather than with the union. Instead of raising wages, the West Coast crimps agreed to lower wages; the difference was returned to the crimp by the shipowner. Thus, on a four months' trip, the crimp supplied men at $15 instead of the former wage of $20, and the shipowner saved $20 in wages which he turned over to the crimp. In addition, the crimp received one month's allotment of $15, making a total of $35. Under the old system he would have made $40, but he preferred to coöperate with the shipowner, whom he trusted, rather than with the union. This alliance of shipowners and crimps was destroyed by a strike of Pacific Coast sailors in 1899, which raised wages and forced the boardinghouse keepers to work with the union.

The plan failed on the East Coast because of internal opposition in the union to any association with the crimps,[38] and because the crimps themselves failed to organize effectively. Only in Boston did the crimps combine. In other cities, despite the best efforts of Furuseth and those agents who agreed with his plan, there were enough crimps unwilling to coöperate with the union to make the entire plan ineffective.[39] If necessary, the shipowner could always go down to Philadelphia or Baltimore to pick up his crew when he could not obtain them at his price in Boston.

The justification for working with the crimps was that they would get their advance whether or not the union coöperated, because law and custom so provided. Under Furuseth's scheme, the sailors would have obtained higher wages and the union would have been effectively organized. The danger that the crimps might take over the union was not discussed.

When the national organization of seamen finally met in December, 1899, it represented about 3,000 members. The lack of organizational progress was not due to want of effort, but reflected the general decline of the labor movement during this period. Drastic changes were made at the convention. The name of the organization was changed to the International Seamen's Union of America. The country was divided into three districts: the Atlantic and Gulf coasts, the Great Lakes, and the Pacific Coast. In each district three unions were to be organized, corresponding to the three departments on a vessel: the deck crew, the engine crew, and the stewards and cooks. Each district union was given almost complete autonomy. It had the right to establish branches in any city in its district. The function of the national organization was to help with organizing activities and to continue the legislative work in Washington. Per capita dues were assessed, but as a concession to the Great Lakes sailors, they were allowed to keep their per capita tax for organizational purposes. William Penje was elected president and William H. Frazier of New York secretary-treasurer.[40]

No longer charged with the responsibility of the national union, Furuseth nevertheless made organizational tours of the Atlantic and Great Lakes ports in 1900 and 1901.[41] Upon his insistence, the SUP sent sizable sums of money to organize the Great Lakes union. With increasing prosperity, his appeals to seamen became more effective. Membership rose rapidly. In March, 1901, the firemen on the Pacific Coast became the first maritime organization, except for the sailors, to join the new national union.[42] Perhaps Furuseth would soon be able to speak in the name of all American seamen.

V. FIGHTER

LIKE ALL OTHER UNIONS at the turn of the century, the seamen's unions experienced a phenomenal growth in membership. Such expansion brought growing pains to the Sailors' Union of the Pacific and problems to its part-time secretary, Andrew Furuseth.[1] During the period from 1893 to 1898, when recovering from the drubbing administered by the Shipowners' Association, the union maintained about a thousand members and a treasury ranging from $5,000 to $10,000.[2] In 1901 it had an active dues-paying membership of 3,188 and a treasury in excess of $42,000.[3]

By taking advantage of the general economic upswing and the prosperity of Pacific Coast ports after the acquisition of the American empire in the Pacific, the union gradually drove wages up and improved conditions aboard ship. In 1898 this was accomplished merely by refusing to ship out on vessels that offered less than the union scale at a time when labor was in great demand. In 1899 the union conducted a full-scale strike against the Shipowners' Association which resulted in costly delays of sailing vessels on the Pacific Coast.[4]

It was a strange strike, for most of the members, as experienced seamen, were probably already getting the $40 per month demanded by the union. So apathetic was the membership that it was impossible to elect a strike committee or to get anyone to accept the responsibility for conducting the strike. The entire task fell upon the secretary, who communicated with the owners, provided room and board for striking seamen, supervised the patrols that kept scabs from boarding the vessels, and conducted the negotiations that ended the strike. The union was satisfied when the owners finally agreed to pay the scale, but Furuseth tried to obtain a more permanent advantage. He wanted a signed agreement. This the owners refused to grant. He also wanted them to close their shipping office. To this they agreed. It is not clear how seamen were to be hired, but from what is known of Furuseth's activities in the East earlier in the year, it is almost certain that he tried to work out some arrangement for hiring through boardinghouses approved by the union. Whether or not he was successful is not definitely known.

At the same time that the union was demanding higher wages on sailing vessels, it began a vigorous campaign to organize the men on steam schooners. Nick Jortall, former secretary of the Steamship Sailors' Union, was placed in charge of the drive. Of more than a thousand steam-schooner sailors who had joined the SUP in 1891, only a handful remained. The former members were the most bitter opponents of the SUP because they feared that should the union once again become powerful, they would be forced to pay up four or five years' back dues. To win these "old-timers" back to the union, it was decided to allow them to rejoin upon payment of one year's dues—$9. The older men began to return to the fold, and with them came the young steamship sailors whom they had previously discouraged from joining the union. In June, 1899, the steamship sailors won an important victory when the Pacific Coast Steamship Company raised wages of the deck crew $5 per month and allowed Nick Jortall's brother, Chris, to use the docks of the company to conduct union business.

The new members who flocked into the union upon the heels of each victory soon created an internal problem which challenged Furuseth's leadership. Actually, no one openly attacked Furuseth, but blows were aimed at his lieutenants, Ed Rosenberg and Walter Macarthur. Rosenberg served as temporary secretary of the union when Furuseth was absent in the East, and Macarthur was editor of the *Coast Seamen's Journal*. Both men had established reputations in the labor movement on the West Coast, and Macarthur was widely known throughout the United States as editor of one of the leading labor newspapers in the country.

Ostensibly, the issue was whether the *Journal* should continue to be printed by James H. Barry's publishing firm. Barry, an active member of the Typographical Union, was an important figure in San Francisco labor politics and a long-time friend of the Sailors' Union. Rosenberg and Macarthur favored continued publication of the *Journal* by Barry. A second group composed of Ed Anderson, Nick and Chris Jortall, and John Kean wanted to change to a new firm which had made a lower printing bid. After several weeks of heated debate, the union voted on February 19, 1900, to give the business to the new firm. Rosenberg and Macarthur immediately resigned in a huff. In explaining his action to Furuseth, who was absent in Washington, Rosenberg wrote:

> I did not want to play to the dungaree sailor element by pretending that I was one of them. Their filthy language, their beastly carousing, their dirt, I despise, and I shall always say so. It is evil and it should be fought against. I am no saint nor holier than thou person, only a "white shirt sailor" and it is the white shirt sailors who have made the union what it is today. There are some demogogues [he mentions Jortall] among the white shirt sailors who for lust of power or for personal gain play to the dungaree sailor by raising a howl at someone for being stuck up.[5]

It is quite evident that the real issue was not who should publish the paper, but who should control the union. The leadership of Furuseth and his lieutenants was being challenged by the new members—who now constituted a majority—led by a few of the old-timers.[6] Ed Anderson as treasurer was obviously irritated by Furuseth's pledge at the ISU convention to contribute $2,000 of SUP money to the organizing campaign on the Great Lakes. This had been done without consulting Anderson or the union.[7] Other objections to the Furuseth group included charges that they were wasteful of union funds, that some of them had proved incompetent, and that the *Journal* was being used to promote the personal political advantage of its editor in the San Francisco labor movement.

Furuseth's personal popularity was still high, and no direct attack on him would have been wise.[8] Since his presence in San Francisco would have been unwelcome to the group temporarily controlling the union, John Kean made a motion to ask Furuseth to remain in the East to organize the Atlantic Coast. One of the Jortall brothers suggested that perhaps Furuseth should stay there for the rest of the year. Upon the advice of his friends that any work he might accomplish in the East would be counterbalanced by complete disruption of the union on the Pacific Coast,[9] Furuseth returned to San Francisco as soon as his legislative duties for the AFL permitted at the end of June.

During the months of his absence, Furuseth had had to conduct the fight for his lieutenants by mail. His strategy in this first serious challenge to his leadership was to insinuate that his opponents were playing into the hands of the Shipowners' Association by awarding the printing to a plant that also did printing for the association. In a mildly worded rebuke to his chief, Nick Jortall said that he failed to follow Furuseth's logic. "The men here," he wrote, "have faith in the superior education and intelligence of a few, but that supposed superiority should not be abused and used as a whip."[10]

What Furuseth could not do by mail, he quickly accomplished upon his return to San Francisco in July, 1900. He picked a fight with the new editor of the *Journal*, John Vance Thompson. He insisted that the secretary and not the editor should have charge of certain records, and he demanded that the editor publish in full the legislative reports. He won on both issues, and at the first packed meeting in many months, on September 17, Thompson resigned.

The internal wrangle smoldered for the rest of the year, but it dissipated in the face of the common enemy in the City Front Strike of 1901. The last evidence of the feud was the defeat of Ed Rosenberg as a delegate to the ISU convention in November by the insurgent faction. But in January, 1901, Walter Macarthur was reinstalled as editor of the *Coast Seamen's Journal,* thus ending a year of turmoil over control of the union paper.

CITY FRONT STRIKE, 1901[11]

The first year of the new century also saw efforts to consolidate the phenomenal gains in membership made by all the water-front unions. Within the SUP, Furuseth concerned himself with the classical problem of all trade unions—to interest new members in the work of the organization. Educational meetings were held for their benefit, and Furuseth was authorized to hire an assistant to meet the increasing demands of the enlarged membership upon the secretary's time.

Outside the Sailors' Union, Furuseth recognized the necessity for greater coöperation among the water-front organizations. Largely owing to his efforts, a jurisdictional controversy with the longshoremen over the loading and unloading of vessels was settled by making the ship's rail the boundary line. In December Furuseth wrote to the other water-front unions proposing a maritime federation. Past attempts to unite the jealous maritime factions had all ended in failure, but the times were different now and the need was more urgent. Workers were joining unions, and unions were affiliating with their national, state, and local bodies.[12] On the water front, the fifteen to twenty different groups spelled danger. Any one of them could precipitate a fight with the owners which would put all of them out of work. Furuseth may have thrown his prestige behind the newly formed City Front Federation of all water-front unions in order to help the weaker ones, but it is more likely that he was concerned with preventing the younger and less experienced unions from calling premature strikes or making unreasonable demands upon shipowners.

As usual, Furuseth left for the East in December, but his stay was shorter than in previous years. There was too much brewing in San Francisco. The sailors were preparing demands to present to shipowners, and were considering whether to try to enforce a nine-hour day. The firemen on the Pacific Coast were responding to the call of the International Seamen's Union to come under its enlarged jurisdiction. A fight was developing in the new Central Labor Council which threatened, and finally resulted in, the withdrawal of the building trades unions. The efforts of the AFL organizer, Jefferson D. Pierce, were continuing to bring fresh recruits to the already swollen membership of the San Francisco labor movement. The California State Federation of

Fighter

Labor had been organized during Furuseth's absence. And in April, 1901, shortly after his return to San Francisco, a group of employers met to form a new organization, the Employers' Association, to meet the challenge of that industrial Frankenstein—the trade union.

Furuseth's first task was to try to secure a written agreement with shipowners. The sailors demanded union recognition, a $5 per month increase in pay, and a one-year contract. The Shipowners' Association would not sign an agreement unless the union promised to supply men only to members of the association, but the union refused to be used as a club to force all vessels into the association.

While his sailors battled the shipowners, Furuseth saw the Employers' Association effectively beat down every effort of the uptown unions to improve their conditions or extend their organization. When the metal polishers went on strike on April 1, many employers were willing to settle with the union, but they were informed that any firm that signed an agreement would have its supplies cut off. The Metal Polishers' Union was forced to capitulate. When the cooks and waiters struck on May 1 for a ten-hour day and a six-day week, the restaurant owners who signed with the union found their oyster and meat supplies cut off. A few days later, the carriage and wagon workers were notified that negotiations with their employers were terminated on the advice of M. F. Michael, attorney for the Employers' Association. This was the first public acknowledgment that a united group of employers was fighting the unions. The association's membership, however, remained a secret, with Michael as the only spokesman.

By the early part of May it seemed that the two conflicting forces would soon involve the entire city in open warfare. Organized labor spoke of calling 40,000 men out on strike. Mayor James D. Phelan invited labor and business leaders to a conference, and the Central Labor Council asked the Employers' Association to agree to arbitration. Michael, speaking for the association, said the employers had nothing to arbitrate. He likened the situation to that of a burglar who, surprised by his victim, proposes they get the mayor to decide who should have the property.

It was obvious by now that the Employers' Association intended to break one union at a time. Labor's wisest course might have been a strategic retreat, but this was impossible. Most of the strikes that had been called thus far involved newly formed unions inexperienced in the labor movement and anxious for immediate results. These groups might have been restrained, but one of the most powerful unions in the city, the Machinists' Union, was already committed to strike action.

The American Federation of Labor had decided to concentrate on one industry at a time to win the nine-hour day, and the iron trades had been picked as the first. Workers in these trades had given the employers six months' notice that the nine-hour day would go into effect on May 1. When that time came, there were too many small unions out on strike to allow the Central Labor Council to concentrate on the iron trades, and so the date was postponed for twenty days. On May 20, since no further delay could be made without acknowledging defeat, the Machinists' Union called its men out on strike. Again the Employers' Association stepped in to prevent any firm from coming to terms with the union.

In July the newly formed Butchers' Union felt the heavy hand of the Employers' Association. The union displayed union-shop cards in all retail establishments that had signed agreements with it. The nonunion shops began to lose patrons. They appealed to the Wholesale Butchers' Association, which in turn notified all retailers that those who displayed the union card would get no meat. Within a few days the workers capitulated.

On July 26, every beer-bottling plant in San Francisco paid off all its employees and posted a notice:

> From this day forward, we intend to operate our own business and operate it under the following conditions: 1) We will recognize no representative or walking delegate or official of any labor union. If our men have any grievance, we will adjust the same with them as individuals, but not as an organized body. 2) We will submit to no more dictations as to whom we shall employ and whom we shall not employ and how we shall run our business.[13]

Those who wished to return to work under the new conditions were welcomed back.

Watching these events, the sailors knew that their turn would come soon. In the latter part of May they had secured an agreement with the largest steamship company in the West, the Pacific Coast Steamship Company, but it was evident from what was happening uptown that soon no agreement would be worth the paper on which it was written. Furuseth went quietly to all those he knew with influence among the employers, urging them to take steps to prevent open warfare.

Any incident could have ignited the powder keg that set off the general struggle between capital and labor. Ironically, it was the innocent arrival of delegates to an Epworth League convention which precipitated the conflict. They had contracted with the Morton Special Delivery Company to handle their baggage. This company, which was nonunion, found that it could not deliver all the baggage, and it appealed to the Morton Drayage and Warehouse Company for help. The teamsters in the latter company were union men and, adhering to their contract with the Draymen's Association, they refused to work with a nonunion firm. The Draymen's Association, however, had joined the Employers' Association, and the union firm was told to lock out its employees until they agreed to work under orders from the employer—not the union.

The lines of battle were sharply drawn. Businessmen throughout San Francisco canvassed their employees on whether they were loyal to the employer or to the union. In every trade workers were forced into the position of making a choice between their union and their job.

In addition to those already on strike, 6,400 teamsters were now locked out. At the meetings of the Central Labor Council and the City Front Federation on July 26, there were insistent demands for a general strike of all labor, but the older, more experienced men were able to delay any action.

For the next few days the leaders of the San Francisco labor movement frantically sought to avoid an open conflict.[14] On the urging of the Municipal League's Conciliation Committee, the teamsters agreed to the employers' demand to meet with their own employees, but not with representatives of the union. A committee from the City Front Federation waited upon the mayor, the president of the Steamship Managers' Association, and the president of the Chamber of Commerce, urging them to use their good offices to settle the dispute. The federation proposed that all men be taken back to work, that a conciliation committee composed of representatives of employers and workers try to settle all differences, and that both sides agree not to participate in any sympathetic strikes or lockouts until the conciliation committee had reached an agreement. The mayor called two conferences to which the labor leaders responded, but representatives from the secret Employers' Association failed to appear. M. F. Michael did, however, send a letter to the mayor in which he repeated the stand of the association's members: they had no objection to men joining unions, but they would not agree to hire only union workers. The Draymen's Association would agree to take back the men when they recognized the right of the employer to run his own business.

Offered no line of retreat, the San Francisco labor movement drew up its battle lines. The City Front Federation, representing 15,000 water-front workers, met Monday night, July 29, and voted to support the 6,400 locked-out teamsters. (Since the total organized labor movement of San Francisco was estimated at 25,000, this very nearly amounted to a general strike of all labor.) The Sailors' Union, meeting in its own headquarters, greeted the news that Furuseth brought from the City Front Federation with cheers. At the San Francisco Athletic Club, where 2,000 teamsters were anxiously awaiting news of the federation's decision, the announcement brought forth a demonstration that no intercollegiate football match ever surpassed. "Men fell over each other in their excitement, and when a minute later the doors were opened, it was a torrent of shouting humanity which poured out into Sixth Street."[15]

The City Front Federation wisely selected Furuseth as strike manager. Politically, he represented the most powerful union on the water front. Employers respected him as a fair-minded and level-headed union leader. The workers knew him better and trusted him more than any other man on the water front. He had experience in influencing public opinion for a cause, and this fight was labor's *cause célèbre*.

The port of San Francisco was closed. At least half of the business in the city came to a halt.[16] Mayor Phelan tried to get some agreement, but found both sides intransigent. Furuseth characterized the terms offered by the Employers' Association as an insult to organized labor. He said the employers had no objection to unions as long as they existed for purely social or charitable purposes. They assumed, he said, that labor was either "wanting in brain or lacking in power."[17]

At the Sailors' Union meeting Monday night, August 5, Furuseth told the men to prepare for a long siege. The immediate need was to supply relief funds to the longshoremen, for they were the weakest link on the water front. The sailors voted $1,000 for this purpose, authorized the expense of putting men up at boardinghouses until the fight was over, and made plans to open a restaurant to feed the strikers. Furuseth reported on the meetings of the City Front Federation and the San Francisco Labor Council, which had met the previous day to map plans for an aggressive campaign to extend the fight to still more industries.

With 20,000 angry men out of work, San Francisco remained relatively calm for the first few days. There was no occasion for violence because the employers and the police made no attempt to challenge the supremacy of the labor movement. But after a week of stalemate, George W. Newhall, president of the Board of Trustees of the Chamber of Commerce and, incidentally, a member of the Police Commission, called upon the mayor to provide additional police protection or to ask the governor for help from the state militia. Mayor Phelan at first resisted. In a letter to the Chamber of Commerce, he wrote: "Instead of proclaiming that disorder exists, I must say that up to date the workingmen of San Francisco have acted with moderation and with prudence which becomes citizens of a free country whose privileges they understand and appreciate."[18] A few days later, however, he complied with the demands of the Employers' Association and authorized the hiring of additional policemen to ride on the wagons driven by scab teamsters. The mayor apologetically explained that he had had to choose between hiring policemen who would be under the discipline of the police department, and allowing the employers to hire private guards under no discipline.

Furuseth and other labor leaders were furious. They demanded the ouster of Police Commissioner Newhall on the ground that the police department's role should be that of a neutral agency enforcing order. It could not be neutral with the leader of the employers' group on the Police Commission. Furuseth pointed out that during the month of August, 1901, the number of arrests had declined almost one half in comparison with August of the previous year. There had been less violence with 20,000 workingmen on the streets than when 7,000 Navy men recently were on leave in San Francisco. Most of the "crimes" charged to labor would, in ordinary times, be considered water-front incidents—rolling drunks, brawls, and accidents.

Many of the special police hired for the strike were ex-convicts, prize fighters, and professional strikebreakers. Such men made the task of preserving order more, instead of less, difficult. Furuseth pleaded with his men not to be provoked. "Do not oppose these men," he begged in a hoarse whisper at the Labor Day exercises in Mechanics Pavilion. "Turn yourself into martyrs, suffer any indignity, but don't permit them to draw you into any violence."[19] He warned them that violence was the best way to defeat the purposes of the strike. "Look with suspicion upon and have nothing to do with anyone who suggests violent action of any kind."[20] As the strike dragged from days into weeks and weeks into months, however, the number of beatings and sluggings increased. Even though union leaders denied it, at least some of the hundred such cases reported in the *San Francisco Chronicle* were directly attributable to the strike situation.[21] Businessmen clamored for additional protection. A citizens' committee was formed to raise $180,000 to enable the city to hire more policemen.

Disturbed by the activities of the police department and by rumors that provocations to violence would increase, Furuseth laid his case before the mayor. By this time, Mayor Phelan was already too far committed to retreat, and Furuseth got no satisfaction from him. He left the conference with the impression that "the clubbing of peaceable, innocent men would continue until they would consent to resume work."[22] Though labor was dissatisfied with the mayor's attitude, businessmen were equally convinced that his actions were not vigorous enough. They tried on several occasions to involve Governor Henry T. Gage, but the governor replied that, from his own personal observations and from reports of city and county officials, he could see no justification for sending the state militia to San Francisco.

Besides countering the employers' efforts to use the police force of the government to crush the strike, union leaders had several other problems to meet. They had to uphold the morale of the strikers, maintain good public relations, and find a weak spot in the enemy's ranks. Furuseth saw these problems clearly and worked toward their solution.

The greatest danger was that the workers would be starved into submission. To prevent this, the unions opened a restaurant, put the men up in boardinghouses, gave strike benefits, and donated money to the weaker unions. Publicly, Furuseth scoffed at the idea that the men could be starved out. "The banks are more likely to bust," he said, "than we are likely to lose our cause by starvation."[23] But providing for 20,000 strikers was an expensive undertaking which even the best union treasuries could not support. At the end of September the Typographical Union launched a general campaign for funds. Money came from unions in San Francisco which were not on strike and from maritime unions all over the country, but the labor movement as a whole did not appear to support the strikers.

Preventing scabbing was important in sustaining morale. In addition to the usual picket lines, unions as far away as Nevada were asked to contact scabs being imported by the Employers' Association. Union men boarded trains en route to San Francisco to induce scabs to desert long before they arrived at their destination. Considerable success was reported, except with the large groups of Negro strikebreakers.

Another group of scabs with whom the unions had little success was composed of students from the University of California. The unions sent a letter to the president of the university, Benjamin Ide Wheeler, in which they asked: "Is it one of the marks of a liberal education that those who receive it gratuitously should do what even uneducated men consider vile and infamous? Labor is honourable, but not all labor. There are conditions which make it dishonourable, and your students have placed themselves in these conditions."[24] President Wheeler facetiously replied that denying students the right to work would be discriminating against the sons of workingmen who had to earn their way through college.[25]

Fighter

Proper communication with the strikers was important for good morale. Fortunately, William Randolph Hearst's *Examiner* vigorously championed the cause of the workingmen, though it stood alone among the daily metropolitan papers which heaped calumnies upon the labor unions. Morale was also maintained by frequent mass meetings and parades. The Metropolitan Temple was filled to overflowing on August 8. Two weeks later, 9,000 men marched silently four abreast down Market Street with only one banner at their head—the American flag. The Labor Day parade and the meeting afterward attracted 20,000 people. And again on September 21, the Metropolitan Temple was filled to capacity. At all these meetings Furuseth was a featured speaker. His theme was: Victory is assured; refrain from violence. He stressed that the purpose of the strike was to maintain the Christian principle that men have the duty of assuming the burdens of their fellow men. Another, more inflammatory speaker, who appeared during the later stages of the strike, was Father Peter C. Yorke. He was so effective that the newspapers attacked him with more venom than they directed at the strike leaders.

In a strike that lasted for ten weeks and involved many conflicting and jealous unions, a remarkable degree of unity was maintained. With the exception of the Building Trades Council, every union in San Francisco presented a solid front against the enemy. The Building Trades Council, however, was the strongest and best organized section of labor's army. P. H. McCarthy, its president, had withdrawn all his unions from the Central Labor Council and refused to recognize its authority. In an effort to extend the strike and to involve the building trades workers, it was decided to call out the teamsters who hauled gravel and sand. Had this tactic worked, the strike would have become general. McCarthy, however, threatened to start his own union of teamsters. The issue was never resolved because the strike ended before the two union groups had a chance to annihilate each other.

The creation of a favorable climate of public opinion had begun long before the actual outbreak of hostilities. The unions won the preliminary phase of this battle. They definitely established the impression that they were being forced to fight and that they had sought every honorable means to avoid a strike. Furthermore, their antagonists were a secret organization, "a mercantile Mafia," composed of wealthy, "money-mad" capitalists.

To counter labor's initial advantage, Michael sent a letter to Mayor Phelan outlining the position of the Employers' Association.[26] The letter was conciliatory and vague. Labor could easily have agreed to all four terms for settlement, but Furuseth asked for a clarification of point three. Confirming labor's suspicions, Michael replied through the mayor that point three would pledge labor not to engage in any sympathetic strike or boycott. Such a pledge, Furuseth pointed out, would even prevent labor from contributing to the support of striking workers.

Furuseth, however, did not close the door to further negotiation. In fact, he continued to emphasize the point that union leaders were willing to sit down at the conference table, but they had no one with whom to confer. "If three of their number," he pleaded, "would meet three of our side, it would be easy to reach an understanding." And he added pacifically, "They are not hard-hearted men, but they do not understand us. They do not know our hopes and aspirations. When they are willing to meet us, I think we can reach peace and not have any additional hard words to forget."[27]

When the strike was a month old, the Draymen's Association finally did consent to a meeting, but only on condition that the employees meet with their employers as individuals and not as representatives of any union. Furuseth ridiculed the employers' proposal, but he was careful not to antagonize public opinion by refusing the offer. Employees of the draying companies did appear at a conference, but the only significance of the meeting was that the Employers' Association had allowed the Draymen's Association to meet with the workers on any basis.

Outside organizations were encouraged to try their hand at settling the dispute. The conference with the Draymen's Association was due to the efforts of the Municipal League's Conciliation Committee and the Municipal Federation of Improvement Clubs. The San Francisco Board of Supervisors also tried to bring about a meeting of the contesting parties. Furuseth, S. H. Goff, and Rosenberg of the Labor Council responded promptly to the call of the supervisors. Michael procrastinated and finally agreed to bring members of the Employers' Association to meet with a committee of the supervisors provided the names of the men who attended were kept secret. When the meeting was held, the Employers' Association committee took under advisement the proposal to meet with representatives of labor. Then, after repeated proddings by the Board of Supervisors, they finally took refuge behind the technicality that the Employers' Association was not a direct party to the dispute between the individual employers and their workers. The supervisors considered the employers' attitude untenable.[28]

Labor also tried to use the meetings of the Board of Supervisors as a public forum. Resolutions were introduced to censure Police Commissioner Newhall, to require the newly deputized policemen to wear uniforms, and to condemn the Employers' Association. Although the supervisors side-stepped most of the issues, the debate served to publicize labor's cause.

Cognizant of the importance of winning public support among farm groups, the Labor Council issued a special "Appeal to Farmers" and a letter to the "Interior Press." They made much of a statement attributed to Frank Symmes, president of the Merchants' Association and chairman of the executive committee of the Employers' Association, in which he said, "If, by reason of a struggle we are making on principle and in defense of individual liberty of action, the grain crop can't be moved without surrender of our position, *let it rot.*"[29] Labor appealed to the community of interest it shared with the farmer: "Let us ask you to consider who are likely to be your friends, the capitalists or we. You belong to the great army of toilers, so do we."[30]

An incident remote from San Francisco and the situation there hurt the strikers. On September 6, President McKinley was shot by a crazed anarchist. The *San Francisco Examiner* had been carrying on a vigorous attack against the Republican president. It had also been the only spokesman for the strikers among the daily press. All the other newspapers immediately accused the Hearst newspaper of inciting acts of violence such as the assassination and the San Francisco strike.[31]

Undoubtedly the most important task facing the strike leaders was to destroy the solidarity of the employers. To do this, they attempted to use one group of employers against the others. They failed. When the City Front Federation went on strike, the primary purpose was to force the shipowners to use their influence within the Employers' Association to force a retreat. This failed. The grain brokers appealed to labor shortly after the start of the strike to make some provision for moving the harvest, protesting that their relations with labor had always been friendly. Furuseth replied that nothing could be done until the brokers went to the Employers' Association and used their influence to bring about a settlement of the whole dispute. This failed. The Retail Merchants' Association and the Retail Grocers' Association, whose members might feel the boycott power of labor, did vote to ask the Employers' Association to end the conflict. But the Merchants' Association, consisting of the larger firms, voted to back the policy of its board of directors in supporting the Employers' Association. It rejected an appeal that had been sent by the unions to the individual members of the association in an attempt to disrupt their unity. Even the most concerted efforts to boycott firms suspected of being leading members of the Employers' Association failed to break up the solid front that employers presented to labor.

The end of the strike came suddenly and unexpectedly. Governor Gage called representatives of the Draymen's Association to meet with him at 2:00 P.M. on October 2. A short while later, this group met with representatives of the union. By 4:00 P.M. they announced a settlement. One of the conditions was that the terms would not be made public, so that the strike would not be refought by pen or mouth. The *San Francisco Chronicle,* however, reported that the Draymen's Association had agreed to take back striking teamsters without discrimination "where they were needed." The union agreed to work with nonunion men and not to interfere with the business of the employer. All sympathetic strikes and boycotts were to be called off. The strike of the machinists and other iron trades workers for the nine-hour day would not be affected by this settlement.[32]

George Renner, business manager of the Draymen's Association, told reporters he could not reveal the exact terms, but he thought the strike had taught labor the lesson that it could not interfere with the business of the employer. He predicted, "We have seen the end of labor troubles for a good many years." Furuseth kept his remarks more in the spirit of the settlement. He simply announced to the throngs of sailors who greeted his arrival at union headquarters: "If the Governor says that the strike is off, the strike is off." When pressed by the men about the terms, he refused to say anything except, "The settlement is all right."[33]

Several questions present themselves. What were the terms of the settlement? No one knows, but subsequent events indicate that the terms published by the *Chronicle* were substantially correct. The right of labor to participate in boycotts and sympathetic strikes was not mentioned in the newspaper, so labor probably retained this face-saving clause. Second, why did Furuseth and the other labor leaders call off the strike? Some of the weaker unions may have reached the limit of their financial resources,[34] but this was certainly not true of the Sailors' Union. The financial report for December, 1901, showed more than $40,000 on hand—only a few thousand dollars less than was in the treasury at the beginning of the strike.[35] Furthermore, only a start had been made at collecting funds from unions outside San Francisco. Morale does not seem to have played a part. There is no evidence that any large number of strikers were returning to their jobs before the settlement.

The presence of Governor Gage at the negotiations suggests that he may have threatened to call out the militia in order to get labor to accept unsatisfactory terms. The time of year may have been a factor, because winter always brought to San Francisco a large number of unemployed who would take the place of strikers. But probably the best explanation is that after ten weeks of fighting, labor had come to the conclusion that it could not win. The Employers' Association was too strong. It had made its members fear the displeasure of the association more than any harm they might suffer from the unions. Good strike tactics require ending a strike quickly when the cause is lost. A better settlement might have been secured by prolonging the fight, but it probably would not have been worth the price.

Furuseth had nothing to be ashamed of. He had been beaten by superior forces, but his generalship had been masterful. His forces emerged intact. They would be ready to do battle again at a more opportune time. Such thoughts were hardly consolation for eating humble pie, but Furuseth had tasted the bitter dish before. He would taste it again.

Aftermath of the Strike

One of the significant results of the City Front strike was the development of the Union Labor party in San Francisco. The organization had been started before the strike was settled. The leaders of the Sailors' Union vigorously opposed siphoning off labor's efforts from the industrial to the political field, but as the 1901 mayoralty campaign progressed, pressure from the rank and file of the unions was so great that even the stanchest antagonist of political action capitulated. In October the *Coast Seamen's Journal* came out in full support of the Union Labor party candidates.

To counteract the apparent unity of labor on the political question, the daily newspapers printed a letter written by Furuseth during the strike in which he termed the Union Labor party "a sad mistake." In the meantime, like most conservative trade-union leaders, Furuseth had changed his mind. The strike had shown the necessity of taking the control of the city government out of the hands of the Employers' Association. "We find now that both the Republican and Democratic tickets are as distinctly class tickets as the present government, and, inasmuch as we are to have a class government, I most emphatically prefer a working class government."[36]

The victory of the labor party in the election encouraged further political activity. A move was initiated to draft Furuseth to run for Congress, but Gompers advised against such action.[37] He was in San Francisco to attend a meeting of the AFL Executive Council, which was trying to restore harmony to the divided labor movement in the city. At a sailors' meeting he praised their leader: "Furuseth has stood at the doors of the Capital, like a panther watching, like a lion attacking. No scheme has been hatched against you that he has not exposed, and by exposing it, defeated it."[38] Then he told the story of a fight between two men on the stage of an English theater. The audience gasped in horror as the stronger man lifted his opponent above his head and was about to dash him to his death among the spectators. Then Charles Lamb, the English wit, shouted, "Don't waste him, throw him at the fiddlers." The audience laughed; even the men on the stage relaxed, and a life was saved. "Don't waste Furuseth by sending him to Congress," warned Gompers. "Don't throw him at the fiddler even. Keep him where he is, where he can be of real service to you, and where he can preserve his good name and retain your esteem."[39]

Gompers probably would not have made such a speech if Furuseth had really wanted to go to Congress.[40] Other labor leaders just as valuable had run for office, had been enthusiastically supported by Gompers, and had made a good record for themselves when they were elected. Furuseth preferred to keep his roots in the labor movement, where he could live without the necessity of compromising his ideals.

Meanwhile the shipowners tried to push the advantage they had gained from the strike to eliminate the Sailors' Union from the water front. Steam-schooner sailors reported that they were being discriminated against. The sailing-vessel operators reorganized their association to include all vessels and reëstablished their own shipping office. The union charged that their hiring system amounted to black-listing of union men, but the association answered that an identity card was used only for the purpose of eliminating drunks.

After several months of sparring, during which the sailors demonstrated that their union was still very much alive, the owners signed the first written contract with the Sailors' Union in March, 1902.[41] Furuseth was absent in Washington during the negotiations, but it was his insistence upon the need for a written agreement that finally persuaded the sailors to accept a contract not entirely to their liking.[42] The union rejected the owners' proposal for a sliding scale of wages based on freight rates over which the sailors had no control, and instead obtained a flat rate of $40 for inside ports. Both sides agreed upon a nine-hour working day in port. Committees were established to handle grievances. Aspects of the agreement which caused considerable criticism were the provisions against participating in any sympathetic strike and the term of the agreement, only six months instead of a year, which

Fighter

would bring the contract up for renewal during the dullest shipping period. Paradoxically, Furuseth had to convince the sailors to renounce the sympathetic strike—a principle that he had recently so stoutly defended.

Such compromises were necessary in order to attain the primary objective of building the Sailors' Union, for the most important clause of the agreement provided for a new method of hiring which would increase the strength of the union. The owners would continue to hire through their own shipping office, but they promised to obtain their men either from the union or from boardinghouses approved by the union. This arrangement would eliminate the crimp from the coasting trade. With the power to give or withdraw approval, the union could be assured that the sailors got a fair deal in the boardinghouse and that they were shipped out at the union scale.

Friendly, even cordial, relationships existed between the sailors and the owners for four years after the City Front strike, because Furuseth held firm to two guiding principles. First, he insisted that the union make no unreasonable demands upon the owners. When freight rates declined, he used this as an excuse to postpone asking for higher wages; when prices declined, he pointed out that the maintenance of the same wages meant an actual increase in buying power. He opposed the establishment of a union hiring hall as an experiment that had twice ended in failure; but by eliminating the boardinghouses from the agreement in 1904, he insured that virtually all hiring was done through the union. Despite great pressure from the rank and file, Furuseth insisted on keeping the clause demanded by the shipowners prohibiting sympathetic strikes. When necessary, he even dropped a clause providing for preference in hiring for union cooks and stewards. The only important issue pushed by the union was the demand for mess rooms (instead of eating on deck) and improved forecastle space.

Second, Furuseth insisted upon compliance with the spirit and the letter of the contract. He had a highly developed sense of the obligations incumbent upon those who had won economic and legislative privileges. Writing to William Gohl, the union agent in Aberdeen, Washington, Furuseth expressed his disgust with those who held these privileges lightly:

New found freedom is a terrible burden. Improvements and privileges paid for by the sweat and blood of others feel easy and are held cheap by those who did nothing to acquire them. Men who cannot use freedom could not have acquired it and cannot keep it, and it is bitter to contemplate that it is thrown away, nay, sold at the price of a few drinks. Of course, if they cannot be persuaded by their comrades or taught by the past, then the crimps and the shipowners will teach us all, that we are responsible for each other, that the honest worker and the sober man must suffer for the shirker and the drunk.[43]

Increasing the sailor's skill and responsibility, supplying competent crews, and eliminating drunks and loafers became major items in Furuseth's program to make it profitable for the owners to deal with the union. So insistent was he upon the sanctity of the contract and so single-minded was his purpose in building the Sailors' Union that he fought against members of his own union, the Central Labor Council, and the State Federation of Labor when they tried to involve the sailors in sympathetic strikes to help other labor groups. Even when it meant walking through picket lines to work with scabs who were provided with police protection, Furuseth insisted upon rigid observance of the contract.

1906 STRIKE

Peace on the water front was shattered after the disastrous earthquake in 1906.[44] Discontent had started long before, but Furuseth had been able to hold off the insistent demands for wage increases by pointing out that freight rates were depressed. By the winter of 1905, however, the cost of living had risen to new highs and the sailors would no longer accept the old wage rates. Many of them left the sea to take jobs ashore, and the union members voted down a proposal to renew the agreement at the same rates. After prolonged negotiations for an increase failed, the union decided to take a referendum vote on whether to inaugurate a new wage scale providing for a $5 per month increase on May 1, 1906.

While the sailors were voting on the referendum, San Francisco was struck by the earthquake. Labor promised to coöperate in rebuilding the city by abolishing jurisdictional lines and not taking advantage of the catastrophe to ask for higher wages. But the unions had no control over wages in such extraordinary circumstances. Skilled labor was scarce and employers were willing to pay premium rates. Since employers made no attempt to control skyrocketing prices, wages and prices raced after each other in a dizzying spiral.

The shipowners, however, made no offer to increase wages. In 1905 they had joined the United Shipping and Transportation Association and had posted bonds of $60,000 to pledge that they would not raise wages without the consent of the association's executive board. The union claimed that this association was dominated by the Southern Pacific Railroad Company which was deliberately fostering a strike in the maritime industry in order to divert traffic to the railroads.

Fighter

Furuseth was absent in the East during most of the negotiations with the owners, but he returned about the middle of May. A few days later the union decided to renew its request for a $5 wage increase—a bold gesture because no other union wanted to seem to be gouging the public at a time when the city was struggling to get back on its feet. It was especially bold because almost all the supplies needed to rebuild the city would be coming in by ship. The owners rejected the sailors' demands, partly on the ground that as members of the United Shipping and Transportation Association they were not authorized to offer more than a $2.50 increase.

The sailors decided to institute their own wage scale beginning on June 1. No seaman would sail after this date unless he received the $5 increase. When the owners began a general lockout involving all maritime workers, the sailors were in a dilemma. Many of the other waterfront unions, especially the longshoremen, were too weak to put up a fight. To unite with them would mean that the sailors would have to support them financially during the strike and morally in the strike settlement. On the other hand, if the other unions did not strike, they would be in a position to scab on the sailors. The seamen chose the second alternative. The sailors, the cooks and stewards, and the firemen deliberately withdrew from the City Front Federation and advised the longshoremen to go back to work if they could.

Without the support of the seamen, the longshoremen had no choice but to return to work on the employers' condition that they would do any work required of them. Sometimes this meant loading scab-manned vessels, and occasionally they were even required to man the ships. Only the longshoremen in San Pedro and Aberdeen, many of whom were also members of the Sailors' Union, refused to accept the status of scabs. On the other hand, the sailors loaded and sailed vessels to Alaska where the longshoremen were on strike. This action was justified on the ground that to do otherwise would be to punish the owners who were willing to pay the union scale.[45]

Furuseth was elected strike manager for the three seagoing groups. The sailors demanded $50 per month for sailing to inside ports, the firemen demanded restoration of overtime pay for work done aboard ship when they were supposed to be off duty (a right they claimed to have lost due to an oversight in the last contract), and the cooks demanded an increase from $30 to $35 for the lowest-paid men. The strategy of the strike was to divide the shipowners and to make it unprofitable to sail with nonunion crews. From the beginning there were a large number of owners who willingly paid the increased scale, and the association hoped to involve them by precipitating a general waterfront tie-up. Furuseth guarded closely against any incident anywhere on the coast which might lead to such a tie-up. This may also partially explain why the seagoing unions withdrew from the City Front Federation.

Furuseth used every trick to make the strike costly to those owners who refused to pay the union scale. Labor was scarce in San Francisco. To secure crews, the owners had to go to Chicago, Mexico, Hawaii, and Australia. Of two hundred men who were recruited in Chicago, only six arrived in San Francisco; the others had deserted. Most of them had been members of the Lake Seamen's Union and had used the strike to secure a free ride to California at the expense of the shipowners. A group of "Kanakas" who came from Hawaii deserted when they reached San Francisco; a union member had been on board and had "educated" the Kanakas on the situation. The group from Mexico was held up in port for several weeks, at least, while the courts heard arguments as to whether the Alien Contract Labor Law had been violated. In the meantime, the vessels did not move and the shipowners paid the expenses.[46]

Use of the courts and government agencies to annoy the shipowners played a prominent part in this strike. When vessels could not be stopped by putting aboard a dummy crew which would desert at the last minute, Furuseth wrote letters to the Department of Labor, the inspector of immigration, and other government officials calling attention to various violations of the law.[47] Without exception, these charges were investigated and considered ill-founded, but they served to delay vessels in port while the investigations took place. Perhaps more important was the thought that must have occurred to Furuseth: if the laws were rewritten, the vessels might actually be prevented from sailing. A vessel manned by Chinese sailors who did not understand English could hardly be considered ready for an emergency at sea, even though the existing law did not define competency in terms of being able to understand the language of the officers. Young boys who were being lured aboard vessels under false pretenses were actually being shanghaied even though the law as written did not cover this situation. The subtle interpretations that government officials chose to give to maritime law go far to explain the stubbornness with which Furuseth later fought for his particular wording of seamen's legislation. His insistence was not due to crankiness or unyielding pride of authorship. Rather, his phraseology was carefully designed to prevent a repetition of interpretations of the law such as were made in the 1906 strike.

The owners also used the courts. They secured a number of injunctions enjoining the union and its officials from interfering with their ships. Furuseth was now directly involved in a matter upon which he had become one of the recognized authorities in the American Federation of Labor. His extensive study of the injunction had led him to the conclusion that it was an abuse of the equity powers of the courts which, if allowed to continue, would bring an end to individual liberty.[48] The union violated the injunctions. When the strike ended, the shipowners agreed not to prosecute, but the Hammond Lumber Company, which did not settle with the union, did attempt to secure a judgment against Furuseth and other union officers. Fremont Older, editor of the *San Francisco Bulletin,* asked Furuseth about the possibility of a jail sentence. Furuseth's answer has become a classic in American labor history. Speaking slowly in his Scandinavian accent, he replied: "They can't put me in a smaller room than I've always lived in, they can't give me plainer food than I've always eaten, they can't make me any lonelier than I've always been."[49]

Furuseth and the union members were less worried about going to jail than was H. W. Hutton, the union attorney, who had his professional reputation at stake. Ellison, who was acting as union secretary, wrote to the agent in Aberdeen that the officers would welcome a month of rest in jail to emerge at the end of that time as the idols of the labor movement.[50] Furuseth was denied his martyrdom. The Hammond Lumber Company won its case, but in the process of appeal through the courts, no judgment was ever executed. It is of interest to note that while Furuseth was advising AFL leaders to go to jail rather than pay expensive court costs to fight injunctions,[51] his own union was using every legal recourse to keep him out of jail.[52]

The court hearings brought out the ferocity of the 1906 struggle. Longshoremen loading nonunion vessels were beaten up. The union sent a launch to meet all incoming vessels for the purpose of convincing scabs by argument, if possible, and by force, if necessary, to desert nonunion ships. On one occasion, as the launch drew alongside the schooner *National City,* the captain fired at the men and killed Andrew Kelner. In Aberdeen, a gunman hired by the Shipowners' Association murdered A. Wahlstrom in a barroom fight.

As in previous strikes, the owners asked for additional police protection. The mayor was now Eugene E. Schmitz of the Union Labor party, who had already lost considerable labor support because of several unsavory deals which were soon to be revealed as outright corruption. Despite the importance of recapturing labor's support and despite the statements of police captains that the situation was under control and the water front was unusually quiet, the mayor assigned fifty special police to the strike. He turned down Furuseth's suggestion that he refuse additional police protection unless the owners would allow the union free access to their docks and ships to talk to the scabs. However, Mayor Schmitz did a great deal to change public opinion concerning the strike. At first most people regarded the union as a villain who was taking advantage of San Francisco's plight to win a wage increase. But the mayor, with the consent of the union, offered to arbitrate the issue. When the owners refused to arbitrate a wage increase of 16 cents per day, they were placed in the position of stubbornly refusing a reasonable demand.

Since shipping was so brisk, the union had difficulty in supplying sufficient crews to man union vessels. The members, therefore, did not suffer much personal hardship.[53] The union spent more than $25,000 to conduct the strike, but the delays and inconvenience undoubtedly cost the shipowners much more, even though they claimed to be doing more than their normal amount of business. In October, after five months of fighting, the firms still remaining in the association (with the exception of the Hammond Lumber Company) reached an agreement with the union. The terms were not made public, but the seamen received a substantial increase.

The union's victory marked the beginning of fifteen years of peaceful employee-employer relationships. Problems continued to arise, but they were all settled without recourse to work stoppages until the post–World War I antiunion drive.

LONGSHOREMEN VERSUS SEAMEN

The same thoroughness and ferocity with which Furuseth fought the shipowners came into play in fighting the encroachments of other unions upon the seamen's domain. With the rapid expansion of trade-union membership, craft lines were blurred and sharp conflicts over spheres of influence became common occurrences in the American labor movement. Samuel Gompers watched his unions attempting to carve up the labor market very much as the nations were trying to carve up the world. His power to stop the unions was about as great as his power to stop the nations, for each union recognized the authority of the American Federation of Labor only when it pleased to do so. "There is no short-cut to the elimination of jurisdiction disputes," said Furuseth in agreeing with Gompers. "It is the nature of men, individually and collectively, to hold and increase themselves in authority."[54]

Jurisdictional problems were no novelty to Furuseth. Almost from the moment that he joined the Coast Seamen's Union, he had been battling longshoremen and steamship sailors.⁵⁵ The latter had been absorbed into the Sailors' Union of the Pacific, but the longshoremen continued to present a problem.⁵⁶ Ordinarily, the sailor detests doing longshore work; once he has reached port, he is eager to taste the pleasures denied him by long days and nights of hard work and celibacy. But in the California lumber trade, as previously noted, the sailors had to do the loading in the isolated spots where the ship stopped to pick up cargo. What may have begun as an enforced duty soon turned into a prized privilege. For the Pacific Coast sailor found that his skill in loading and unloading lumber earned him a steady job, and he could demand higher wages because he was doing work comparable to that of higher-paid shore workers. Steady jobs and higher wages meant harder work, but from Furuseth's point of view this made the seaman a workingman instead of a temporary hired hand. It had a further importance to the union. When a ship was loaded by longshoremen, any crew could be picked up to sail the vessel, but if the ship was loaded by seamen—experienced seamen—the same men who loaded it would also sail it. Such experienced men were invariably union members.

There was more to Furuseth's battle with the longshoremen than his desire for higher wages, more steady work, and better union control. He felt a deep-seated distrust of all people on shore. The sailor was considered a fair target by every unscrupulous moneylender, boardinghouse keeper, or prostitute. It is no wonder that continued experiences with such representatives of shore life made the sailor resentful, but it takes a little more understanding to appreciate his distrust of men who made their living as longshoremen, painters, cooks, engineers, and the like. Without using the words, Furuseth believed in the wage-fund theory. That is, there was a given amount of money which the shipowner could pay out in wages. This had to be divided among longshoremen, sailors, riggers, teamsters, and many others. The men who sailed the ships represented a minority of the workers employed in the transportation industry. What would happen if the sailors united with the other transportation crafts? When the question of dividing the limited amount of money in the wage fund arose, the shore workers would outvote the minority and take the biggest share, leaving the poor sailor—as usual—with nothing.

It can hardly be doubted that the organization of the steward and engineer departments of the International Seamen's Union was at least partly a result of the fear that shore unions would gain a foothold on the ships.⁵⁷ In 1901 the cooks and stewards on the Atlantic Coast joined the ISU, but on the Great Lakes these workers joined the Hotel and Restaurant Employees' Union. Since shipping on the Great Lakes was seasonal, most of the cooks and stewards worked aboard ships only during the summer and took jobs in hotels and restaurants during the winter. They could see no reason for holding membership in two unions. But Furuseth raged. His primary argument was that everyone working aboard a vessel was subject to maritime law; shore unions knew nothing of maritime law, were doing nothing to improve it, and could do nothing to protect their members on board ship. When, despite Furuseth's arguments, the AFL convention decided in favor of the Hotel and Restaurant Employees' Union in the coastal trade,[58] the ISU disregarded the convention's decision, organized separate locals of marine cooks and stewards,[59] and eventually forced the hotel and restaurant employees to relinquish all claims to jurisdiction.

When the tugboat pilots on the Great Lakes joined the International Longshoremen's Association, Furuseth was not overjoyed that these men had finally recognized the necessity for union organization. When officers of the pilots' union later testified before Gompers that the ILA had materially benefited all the members and that they were anxious to remain in that union,[60] Furuseth was not convinced that he had made a mistake in estimating the ability of the ILA to handle maritime workers' problems. He did not insist that the pilots should be forced to join the ISU, but since they were covered by maritime law, he felt they had no right to belong to a shore union.

On the Pacific Coast, the sailors had arrived at an arrangement with the longshoremen which allowed both groups to work in armed harmony most of the time. It was understood that sailors had charge of the cargo as far as the ship's tackle could reach. Furuseth even lent a hand in organizing the longshoremen, but he never allowed the sailors to place their union in jeopardy in order to protect the dock workers. This was a difficult position to uphold since many of the sailors worked as longshoremen when they could not find jobs aboard ship. On several occasions the longshoremen asked the Sailors' Union to refuse to accept cargo from nonunion men. Furuseth always rejected these requests on the ground that maritime law made it mandatory for a sailor to obey orders. Under the law a sailor would lose half his earned pay if he walked off a ship, whereas a longshoreman would lose nothing. Moreover, the SUP contracts stipulated that sailors would accept cargo from any longshoremen, regardless of their union affiliation. On one occasion when a union crew refused to accept a load of lumber from men who were scabbing on striking longshoremen, Furuseth sent union sailors from San Francisco to take the place of the crew which had walked off the vessel.[61] Furuseth might have been thinking of the sanctity of the contract or expressing his reverence for the law, but he was principally concerned with preserving his union and protecting his men. If the sailors struck every time nonunion longshoremen handled cargo, they might succeed in organizing the dock workers, but they would break their own union. The Sailors' Union lived in peace with the longshoremen because it was more highly organized and therefore in a position to make the rules.

While peace reigned on the Pacific, trouble brewed on the Great Lakes. For many years the Great Lakes Seamen's Union had accepted as members only helmsmen and watchmen, even refusing to admit other men of the deck department. As the era of the sailing ship came to an end at the turn of the century, such exclusiveness could not be maintained, for every deck hand was a potential helmsman. The union therefore began to admit a larger proportion of the ship's personnel. The firemen, however, were regarded with contempt as an inferior breed. Since many of them were recruited from the longshoremen who loaded coal onto the vessels, it was not surprising that they should turn to the ILA for relief from the long hours of backbreaking work before the blazing furnaces.

Furuseth led the fight against this invasion of the maritime jurisdiction. The ISU convention in December, 1899, passed a strong resolution in favor of organizing the firemen,[62] which Furuseth took to the AFL convention a few days later. When the AFL offered to arbitrate the dispute, Furuseth flatly refused on the ground that there was nothing to arbitrate. The ILA was exceeding its jurisdiction in taking in maritime workers. In January William Penje, president of the ISU and secretary of the Great Lakes Seamen's Union, talked with Daniel O'Keefe, president of the ILA. O'Keefe told Penje that he had no objection to the firemen's joining the ISU or forming an independent union, provided this was the desire of the men.[63] When Penje talked to leaders of the firemen's union, he discovered what O'Keefe already knew—that the men would not leave the ILA. Penje then wrote to Furuseth flatly refusing to carry out the ISU convention mandate, because, he said, a fight with the strongly organized firemen would only end with their convincing the deck hands not to join the sailors' union.[64]

Penje retreated. Not so Furuseth. At the 1901 ISU convention he spearheaded an organizational drive to bring all seagoing groups under ISU jurisdiction, in accordance with the constitutional provision for three departments in each district. In retaliation, the ILA changed its name to the International Longshoremen's and Marine Transport Workers' Association. Furuseth referred to it as "that long name organization." Walter Macarthur called it "a heterogeneous hodge-podge of incongruous conglomerates... neither fish, flesh, nor good red herring."[65] Beginning in 1902, every AFL convention became the stage for a debate between seamen and longshoremen. Furuseth said that the adoption of the new name meant an invasion of maritime jurisdiction which the original AFL charter did not authorize. O'Keefe replied that the new name was simply in line with the practice of all longshoremen's unions in Europe. Since his union had joined the International Transport Workers' Federation, it had innocently adopted a similar name. Furuseth argued that the new name was not only a threat to seamen, but to all transportation unions—teamsters, carmen, and others. O'Keefe denied that his union was planning to invade the jurisdiction of any union, and he was convincing enough to get the support of the other transportation unions on most issues. O'Keefe taunted the seamen for their failure to persuade the firemen on the Great Lakes to join the ISU. He said the firemen remained with the longshoremen because the ILMTWA increased its membership from 300 in 1899 to 4,000 in 1904, and its members' wages from $30 to $65 per month. Then, with a jibe at Furuseth's legalistic approach to jurisdictional fights and maritime problems, he said: "Are these men going to attach themselves to an organization which can do nothing for itself or for them? Perhaps it is good practice for a man who has nothing better to do (our friend) to study law for twenty years, but we bring results that are practical."[66]

To many AFL delegates the controversy over a name was inane. Some of them, thinking in terms of their own jurisdictional problems, believed the real issue was control of membership. It is doubtful that most of them grasped the basic consideration that motivated Furuseth—the separation of maritime workers from shore workers. At the 1904 convention the delegates voted against the resolutions of both the longshoremen and the ISU.

In the meantime incidents multiplied. On the Pacific Coast the longshoremen informed the sailors that they would no longer allow them to work cargo on foreign vessels. They claimed that the sailors were working as longshoremen at lower wages and did not actually sail on the ships after they were loaded; instead, nonunion crews were allowed to take over to sail deepwater.[67] Furuseth made an open declaration of war[68] and told the longshoremen to withdraw from that "long name" organization. When they refused, the sailors organized new locals. Working hand in hand with employers, they refused to accept cargo from

Fighter

members of the ILMTWA. At Furuseth's personal request the companies put guards aboard the ships to protect the sailors from violence. Port police, local judges, and city officials coöperated with the owners and the sailors to break any longshore union that refused to follow the instructions of the Sailors' Union.[69]

Frantic appeals from Gompers and the AFL Executive Council, imploring Furuseth to end this spectacle of open civil war, were printed in the labor press of San Francisco. Furuseth said Gompers was straddling the issue when he asked the sailors to stop forcing ILA locals to withdraw from their international. The sailors, Furuseth argued legalistically, were not asking locals to withdraw from the ILA, but from the ILMTWA—an organization not recognized by the AFL. By the end of 1905, Furuseth had successfully forced every longshore union on the Pacific Coast to join the Pacific Coast Federation of Longshoremen. He could now bargain with the longshoremen in the East from a position of strength. If they wanted their locals back, they would have to make concessions to the sailors.

With the utmost diplomacy, Samuel Gompers finally persuaded both sides to meet in Erie, Pennsylvania, on April 18–20, 1906. It took even more diplomacy to keep the representatives together for three days. Walter Macarthur and Andrew Furuseth presented the case of the ISU; H. C. Barter and John A. Madsen spoke for the longshoremen. The conference ended in agreement on only one subject—a resolution expressing concern and horror at the news of the San Francisco earthquake.

The conference is important chiefly because a verbatim transcript of the entire proceedings was printed,[70] giving an excellent picture of Furuseth as an extemporaneous speaker, a debater, and a lawyer. The proceedings were conducted like a congressional inquiry, and Furuseth behaved like the professional that he was. The entire first day was spent in quibbles on two questions. First, what organization did Barter and Madsen represent? Furuseth maintained that unless they represented the ILA, the only organization recognized by the AFL, they had no business at this meeting. The other question was whether this was a court of arbitration or merely a "gab fest." Furuseth wanted Gompers to act as arbitrator in accord with the decision at the last AFL convention, but he had difficulty in defending the principle of arbitration which he and Gompers had been attacking for several years.[71] Macarthur solved the dilemma by drawing a distinction between arbitration, when applied to disputes between labor and capital, and "suasion," referring to internal labor affairs. The problems of the first day were settled by allowing the longshoremen to call themselves what they liked and by deciding not to decide anything about the matter of arbitration. The following two days were spent in hearing testimony of witnesses and in debate. In rehashing the old arguments, Furuseth revealed himself as a skilled trial lawyer.

After delaying for more than a year, Gompers handed down an arbitration award that has served with minor changes to this day.[72] The award was a tribute to Furuseth's stubborn will, his legal talents, and his devotion to the men whom he served, for it provided that the long name be dropped and that the Pacific Coast formula for settling the jurisdiction between the two groups be used nationally. The longshoremen did not accept the award as binding upon their organization, but continued pressure from the seamen on the West Coast and persuasion by Samuel Gompers, who made a special trip to their convention in 1908, finally convinced them. At the AFL convention of that year Furuseth met with the delegates representing the longshoremen, and Gompers' award was accepted by both sides. The remaining question of what to do with the seagoing members of the ILA was settled by allowing them to stay in it. Furuseth could make this concession because the firemen on the Great Lakes had already withdrawn from the ILA and were operating under an independent charter. Gompers was able to point to the settlement of the longshoremen-seamen controversy as one of the major achievements of the 1908 AFL convention.[73]

Since 1900, Furuseth's stature had grown in the labor movement. As the leader of two important strikes on the West Coast in 1901 and 1906, he was probably the best-known labor leader on the coast. Having defeated an important revolt within his own SUP, he was now so solidly entrenched that his leadership would not be seriously questioned for twenty years. His victory over the longshoremen presented him in a new light to AFL delegates—as a fighter as well as a skilled parliamentarian with an astute legal mind. During this period he was making friends, testing ideas, and developing as a lobbyist par excellence. All these experiences were soon to be combined in the attainment of what he considered the crowning achievement of his career—the La Follette Seamen's Act.

VI. LABOR LEADER

ON THE OCCASION of the twenty-fifth anniversary of the birth of the Sailors' Union of the Pacific on March 6, 1910, Andrew Furuseth had an opportunity to review his accomplishments. His article, characteristically entitled "The Struggle Yet To Come," was devoid of any personal triumphs, but it recorded what the seamen had been able to do as an organized group:

Advance and allotment to "original creditors" have been abolished in the coastside trade and reduced to one-third in the foreign trade. The power to imprison a man for violation of his contract to labor has been abolished in the domestic trade of the United States.... The right to administer corporal punishment has been abolished.... But above all, the seamen must look to the future. What we have gained is as nothing compared to what must be gained.[1]

THE MAN

After twenty-five years in the labor movement, Furuseth had become well known, not only on the Pacific Coast, but nationally and internationally. Although he had never been photographed, his features were familiar to seamen all over the world. His hair had become almost completely white, his chiseled features even more angular. His face was weathered but not worn, and his kind, flashing hazel eyes belied an otherwise gruff exterior. At fifty-six Furuseth was still a husky man, long-limbed and loose-jointed. As he grew older, he became thinner, creating the illusion that he was getting taller. Furuseth never paid much attention to his dress. It was generally believed that he would not wear a suit of clothes until it had been properly wrinkled, that he washed his suits instead of sending them to the cleaner, and that he ironed his clothes by putting them under his mattress—sailor style.[2]

There was much about Furuseth that was mere conjecture, because he had a phobia against personal publicity and he assumed a dignity and an aloofness with even his closest associates which precluded intimacy.[3] Only as a personal favor to Senator Robert La Follette, after the passage of the Seamen's Act in 1915, did Furuseth finally consent to having his picture taken. Until that time he had even refused to be part of the traditional convention photographs in which the seamen's representatives appear indistinguishable from any group of businessmen.[4] To Victor Olander, Furuseth explained his aversion to being photographed by saying that he wanted the sailors' fight for personal liberty to be associated in the public mind with all seamen, and not merely with Andrew Furuseth.

"Cold to men while on fire for man" is the way one writer summed up the common impression of Furuseth.[5] He had many associates and acquaintances, but few, if any, friends. Although in speaking informally to or about Furuseth, people customarily referred to him as "Andy," no one ever really became intimate with him. Any sailor could stop and chat with Andy. He knew almost every sailor on the West Coast and thousands all over the country. He knew them as sailors, as union members, but not as people. He allowed them to know him in the same way. Many men who knew Furuseth well cannot recall that he ever inquired about their health, their family, or their financial status even in a perfunctory manner. He was, however, considered a "soft touch." Any derelict sailor could get a "loan" from Furuseth.

His associates in the trade-union movement were primarily the "white-collar" sailors and the non-Socialist intellectuals.[6] Men like Walter Macarthur, Paul Scharrenberg, and Victor Olander came closest to being his confidants. All had experience before the mast; they were well read and literate; they were good speakers, active union members, and admirers of the "Old Man." But they were not servile followers. Furuseth would not have respected them had they been "yes men." The disagreements between Macarthur and Furuseth after the former resigned as editor of the *Coast Seamen's Journal* in 1913 to run unsuccessfully for Congress became so great that for the next twenty years they hardly spoke or wrote to each other.

At AFL conventions and in Washington, D.C., Furuseth could frequently be found in the company of John P. Frey or Samuel Gompers. In Frey he found a match for historical discussions and philosophical debate. Gompers he loyally supported as his chief, but he enjoyed baiting the president for compromising the principles in which they both believed. Most of the time, however, Furuseth was alone.

Furuseth was well acquainted with shipowners, especially on the West Coast. He could drop in on them and have a friendly chat— usually about shipping conditions and the progress of maritime legislation in Congress. The attacks of shipowners upon the union were not meant as personal attacks upon Furuseth, whom most of them regarded as a completely honest labor leader who used his influence to restrain the seamen from making unreasonable demands. Some owners like James Rolph, John D. Spreckles, and William Denman lent valuable aid to Furuseth's legislative program.

Among newspapermen and magazine writers, Furuseth was almost

Labor Leader

universally admired. He could always count on getting "inside" information from the Washington press corps when other sources failed. Furuseth was friendly with many "Lords of the Press" like William Randolph Hearst,[7] but he was most closely associated with Fremont Older of the *San Francisco Bulletin*.[8] Older, like most people who got to know Furuseth, admired him for his honesty, sincerity, and complete reliability.

In Washington there was scarcely a congressman who did not know and respect Andrew Furuseth. His knowledge of the maritime law of all countries of the world amazed congressmen—he did not fit their stereotype of either a lobbyist or a labor leader. His ability to stand up against the best maritime lawyers the shipowners could hire evoked their admiration. When other men might have been firmly cut off at a congressional hearing for being long-winded, Furuseth was politely allowed to continue his testimony and enter long documents into the record.

There were many members of the House of Representatives who were union members or who owed their election to labor's support. Men like James Maguire and Edward J. Livernash, who came from San Francisco, were especially anxious to please Furuseth. William B. Wilson of the United Mine Workers had been closely associated with him at AFL conventions, where they alternated for a time as secretary and chairman of the Committee on the President's Report. In Congress Wilson was of immense help to the seamen, and when he later became secretary of labor in Woodrow Wilson's cabinet, he remained true to their cause.

It was in the Senate, however, that Furuseth had his closest "friends." During the graft prosecutions of "Boss" Abraham Ruef in San Francisco, Furuseth was one of the few labor leaders to insist on a thorough house cleaning. He refused to support the Union Labor party and sided with Fremont Older and District Attorney Francis J. Heney. Through them he became acquainted with the leading Progressive Republicans. Gompers and the AFL leaders had already established cordial relations with the Democrats. Heney gave Furuseth a letter of introduction to Robert La Follette, who was so impressed by the Norwegian seaman that a lifelong friendship started.[9] There was probably no one outside the union to whom Furuseth was closer than Bob La Follette. The association was based on more than a mutual interest in improving the lot of seamen. If they did not always agree, they at least respected each other's opinions on national and international politics, on philosophy, literature, and life. One of the few families for whom Furuseth evinced a personal concern was the La Follette family. He had a standing invitation to have breakfast with the La Follettes every Sunday morning, and he came as close to leading a family life at those breakfasts as he ever did in his entire life.

At fifty-five, when he met La Follette, Furuseth's philosophy had fully matured. It would not change basically the rest of his life. One guiding principle in deciding whether any measure was right or wrong was to determine whether it would be good or bad for seamen—especially Pacific Coast sailors. A second guiding principle was a mixture of laissez-faire economics and a doctrine of self-help. Third, Furuseth had a fervent belief in individual liberty bordering on anarchy. In practice, when these principles conflicted with each other, as they often did, the welfare of the seamen usually triumphed over the others.

Some observers have remarked that Furuseth was "class unconscious."[10] It is true that he could see the faults of his own class and that he could understand and sympathize with the actions of employers, but he always took pride in being "a simple sailor." If he sided with an employer, it was because he thought it was in the best interest of all the seamen. He agreed with the Socialists in recognizing the class interests of sailors and shipowners, but he did not agree that these divergent interests need necessarily lead to the overthrow of the ruling class. A *modus operandi* could be reached.

No organized religion claimed Furuseth's allegiance. He cultivated ministers and priests who threw in their lot with the union, but those who disagreed with the organized seamen in any respect he condemned as "sky pilots."[11] In common with many labor leaders of the period, Furuseth did not actively oppose or support any religious group. His personal view undoubtedly was that the union expressed the ideals of Christianity more truly than any church.[12] Over and over again, Furuseth hammered away at the idea that "the labor movement . . . means the seeking for some form of industry in which the Christ idea shall hold full control. . . ."[13] The equality of all men before God had been won in the religious field by the triumph of Christianity. The equality of all men in the industrial field would be won by the trade unions:

What is it [unionism] doing today? It takes the individual who under modern conditions feels himself utterly helpless and crushed. It gives him new ideas, new hopes and new determination. It lessens pauperism by the introduction of mutual help done in a brotherly way, guaranteed as a right. . . . It tends to sobriety in life, to moderation in speech and to determined resistance to all attacks on liberty wheresoever found. It gives the weak the strength and endurance of the strong, to the rash it teaches caution, upon the careless it urges circumspection, it makes in general for a stronger manhood, a happier womanhood and a brighter childhood.[14]

The union also fulfilled another important role in Furuseth's philosophy. As a voluntary association of free men it was a means whereby the individual could help himself by helping others. He emphasized the necessity for each man to help himself by improving his skill as a worker and by increasing his knowledge, but above all by joining a union.

Liberty was Furuseth's slogan. He fought to make the seaman a free man, and he fought for freedom and democracy within the labor movement. Speaking at the 1912 convention of the AFL, he admonished the delegates who were about to force the steam fitters to submit to the jurisdiction of the plumbers' union:

... there never was a body of men in love with their own power that did not always think their power was for the good of the poor fellow who had to obey. The trouble with most of you—excuse me for saying so—is that it is a long time since you have had the shackles. It is so long ago you have forgotten how they feel. It is something like the woman who, having rings in her nose and rings in her ears and on her ankles, thinks they are ornaments—forgetting that they were chains once on a time....

You are making an awful mistake in your policy in trying to compel what you should obtain by voluntary action....[15]

With Jefferson, whom he quoted, Furuseth believed that "that government is best which governs least." Commenting on the insurance and pension aspects of German maritime law, the *Coast Seamen's Journal* remarked, "The animating idea of American statesmanship is that it is better to suffer under individualism than to succeed under paternalism."[16] To reconcile this with his role as a lobbyist did not seem incongruous to Furuseth, for he argued that the seamen merely wanted the government to allow the free play of economic forces. Give seamen their freedom, allow them to leave their jobs like any other worker, and they would be free to strike against crimps, low wages, brutal masters, and intolerable living conditions. There were aspects of the legislative program which did not fit into his basic philosophy: regulation by law of the hours of work in port, size of forecastles, food scale, manning of the vessel, and many others. Contradictions? Perhaps. But there is no contradiction if every thought and every action are gauged against the measuring rod of what would benefit the sailor.

After 1910 Furuseth began spending more and more of his time in the East. Some years he would come back to the Pacific Coast for only a few months. He remained, however, in constant communication with the Sailors' Union of the Pacific, received the minutes of every meeting, and continued to hold the title of secretary. This was not simply an honorary title even though the secretary pro tem did most of the actual work.

Upon his return from the East, Furuseth usually made a visit to all branches, beginning in Seattle and going down to San Pedro. At these meetings he reported on the progress of his legislative efforts and discussed local problems with the union leaders in each port. In San Francisco all the component units of the International Seamen's Union usually held a large meeting to hear his report. Unless he was invited, Furuseth did not assert his prerogative as president of the ISU (he had been reëlected in 1908) to visit the meetings of the firemen, the cooks and stewards, or other units of the international, but he did regularly attend the meetings of the Sailors' Union.

After visiting the branches Furuseth often went on what he liked to call "fishing expeditions." These were his visits to shipowners, port captains, shipping commissioners, and shipping masters. They were friendly visits in which Furuseth, while ostensibly relating his experiences in Washington, fished for information about the intentions of the shipowners. Union leaders placed considerable faith in Furuseth's uncanny ability to diagnose, through his friendly chats, how the shipowners would react to demands for a pay raise or for better working conditions.

Furuseth drove himself as hard in San Francisco as he did in Washington, continuing to put in a twelve- to sixteen-hour day. By seven in the morning he left his room at 59 Beaver Street, which he kept the year round even when he spent only two or three months a year in the city. On his way to the union office he stopped for a solitary breakfast, invariably consisting of a "snail" and coffee. At the office, after reading his mail, Furuseth spent most of the day typing his own letters hunt-and-peck style. With a cigar or a pipe hanging from his mouth, he carried on an extensive correspondence with congressmen, government officials, union officers in other countries, and SUP agents in every port on the Pacific.

Sometimes the union leaders who had carried the load during the many months of Furuseth's absence were resentful of his criticism and of his evident desire to take over the smallest details of union administration. But quite often they were relieved to throw off the mantle of responsibility. Ellison, secretary pro tem, once wrote: "I have got pretty near all the dose I can stand of abuse and complaint, and shall be happy when Furuseth comes here to relieve me."[17]

Labor Leader

Furuseth never entered into the idle talk that was common in any union office, but he could be lured away from his typewriter to participate in a good argument. He would listen attentively to the debate and when he thought he had grasped the situation, he would join in enthusiastically. Politics and religion were forbidden topics, but even when these taboos were obeyed, there were still union policies, legal problems, and other matters which often resulted in heated controversies. Furuseth genuinely enjoyed these verbal battles.

Most of the union officials kept regular office hours. At noon they all went down to lunch together, but not Furuseth. He would go alone for his coffee and snails—he seemed to live on this diet—whenever the spirit moved him. In the evening, if he wanted a better meal, he would go to the Fly Trap or the Hofbrau, again usually alone; but occasionally before a meeting some of the men would join him. Eating was not one of Furuseth's pleasures. He enjoyed a good meal and had a particular fondness for oysters, but he was satisfied with almost anything that was set before him.

Outside the union, Furuseth allowed himself little divertisement. Occasionally he would spend an evening at the home of Paul Scharrenberg, Walter Macarthur, or Selim Silver, but if he did not have a union meeting, he ordinarily spent his evenings reading. He read avidly, especially in the fields of history and maritime affairs, for he regarded the study of history as essential to the progress of mankind. Furuseth also enjoyed classical music, the opera, and plays, and he occasionally indulged in these pleasures. In San Francisco he usually attended the opera or the theater by himself, but in Washington and Chicago he sometimes went with Victor Olander.

Furuseth had few "vices," though he did smoke and drink. He felt that drinking was entirely a personal matter except when anyone entered a union meeting or showed up for work under the influence of alcohol. Such behavior reflected unfavorably on all seamen. Gambling he also regarded as a personal matter. A union rule forbade gambling in the union hall, but in 1910 the rule had been relaxed to such an extent that the headquarters resembled a miniature Monte Carlo. Several years later, when an argument over gambling resulted in a serious stabbing, the rule was strictly enforced by Furuseth's orders.[18]

If women may be listed as one of the sailors' vices, Furuseth was guiltless. As far as anyone knew, he had never had any relationship with women. The sailors speculated, though not in Furuseth's presence, that he was a woman hater, but his public utterances and the testimony of one of his secretaries make this unlikely. He believed that a woman's place was in the home keeping the family together, and that the modern industrial system, by forcing women and children into the factories, was seriously impairing the human race.[19] Furuseth often pointed out that the goal of a sailor was not a wife in every port, but enough money to support a wife in one port and a union in every port. Observing his beardless face, some sailors whispered that their leader was "queer." One of the few times that anyone heard Furuseth raise his voice in anger was when he accidentally overheard such a discussion.

Although others might speculate that Furuseth had deliberately rejected a family life so that he could devote himself to the seamen's cause unhampered by family ties, Furuseth never found it necessary to explain his obvious disinterest in the opposite sex. In practice, he was married to the union. It received more devotion, more loving care than any woman could expect.

WEST COAST ACTIVITIES

Union activity in San Francisco meant political activity. The Union Labor party had inextricably involved every union leader. Furuseth gave the movement his belated blessing after the failure of the 1901 strike, but he was disturbed by the effects of labor's participation in politics. "For nearly three years the labor movement has been drifting slowly but surely upon the rocks of personal ambitions."[20]

Watching the unsavory alliances that Boss Ruef of the Union Labor party was making with businessmen and saloonkeepers, the sailors were forced first into silence and then into open opposition. When the Board of Supervisors quietly granted a franchise to Patrick Calhoun's notorious United Railroad Company to build an overhead trolley shortly after the San Francisco earthquake, even the Labor Council gasped a protest against the obvious collusion between a monopolist and the members of the board. The *Coast Seamen's Journal* angrily exclaimed, "The Ruef party, of San Francisco, has been weighed and found wanting."[21] On May 5, 1907, the street carmen went on strike against the United Railroad Company. Furuseth and Fremont Older believed that the strike had been deliberately precipitated by Calhoun, secretly in league with Union Labor party officials and the president of the Carmen's Union, in order to divert the pending graft investigation—an investigation that subsequently proved that Calhoun had paid $200,000 to Boss Ruef and the San Francisco Board of Supervisors for the overhead trolley franchise. Furuseth failed to prevent the carmen from falling into Calhoun's trap, but he did keep the strike from involving all the unions in the city.[22]

Labor Leader

Mayor Schmitz appointed Furuseth to a committee of fifty labor and business leaders to halt the spread of a strike which was the bloodiest in the history of the San Francisco labor movement. Furuseth coöperated with the committee to the extent of cautioning against violence, but he soon became convinced that Mayor Schmitz was not sincerely interested in bringing about a settlement. He proposed that the United Railroad Company be required to put street cars in operation on all lines in accordance with the terms of their franchise. Thus the company would have been forced to reach a settlement with the union or lose its franchise. The suggestion was not heeded, and Furuseth resigned from the Committee of Fifty. His efforts to bring about a solution, however, did not cease. He was afraid that if the strike did spread, it would involve the Sailors' Union, which, because of depressed shipping conditions, would have been at a distinct disadvantage in fighting the shipowners.[23] Because he was willing to compromise the street carmen's strike on almost any conditions, Furuseth was severely criticized by many labor leaders.[24]

He made himself still more unpopular by almost singlehandedly opposing any involvement of the labor movement with the Union Labor party. P. H. McCarthy of the building trades unions had made an about-face in his former opposition to the labor party and was now trying to take control of Boss Ruef's machine.[25] From his intimate association with Fremont Older, Furuseth knew of the disclosures of corruption which were soon to be made. He wanted a clean break so that labor could disassociate itself from these scandals, but an overwhelming majority overruled him.[26]

Despite the unpopularity of his position, Furuseth for years maintained his opposition to the labor party. In 1909 he supported Francis J. Heney against Charles M. Fickert for district attorney because Heney favored continuation of the graft prosecution.[27] When Fickert won, the *Journal* deplored the victory of the Union Labor party as a victory for dishonesty, graft, and corruption.[28] In 1911 Furuseth supported James Rolph against P. H. McCarthy for mayor.[29] For this he was branded a "scab" and a "traitor to labor." He was denied the platform at meetings called to discuss nonpolitical subjects, and he was threatened with violence.[30] John J. McNamara, one of the brothers who was being held in jail in Los Angeles for the bombing of the *Times,* was induced to write to Macarthur and Furuseth asking them to support the Union Labor party candidate or to remain neutral, since defeat of the labor party would hurt the defense.[31] At the time the McNamaras had not confessed their guilt. The letter from the labor martyrs was intended to put Furuseth in a most unfavorable light if he continued his opposition to McCarthy. Although Macarthur and Furuseth denied that the election in San Francisco had any connection with the attempt of the Los Angeles Merchants' and Manufacturers' Association to convict the McNamaras, their popularity did not increase—especially when McCarthy lost the election. Furuseth's courageous stand on an unpopular position lost him the support of many labor people, but it won the respect and admiration of a group of Progressive Republicans who were to aid materially the seamen's program in Congress.

This was not the sum of Furuseth's political activities during these years. When he was not involved in city elections, Furuseth spent a considerable amount of time campaigning for Livernash for Congress in 1904, Maguire for governor in 1908, against Taft for president in 1908, and for Macarthur for Congress in 1910.[32] He argued that while it was wrong for unions to support political candidates, it was permissible for union officials, acting as citizens, to participate in politics. Publicly Furuseth supported Gompers' maxim that in politics labor should reward its friends and punish its enemies; but in private he wrote to the secretary of the AFL, Frank Morrison, that labor could not support any Republican candidate because even those who held union cards came under the caucus rule of "Uncle" Joe Cannon once they were elected to Congress.[33] For a man who believed that labor's strength should be concentrated in the economic field,[34] Furuseth was about as deep in politics as any man could be.

The economic front on the Pacific Coast was relatively quiet for the sailors from 1907 until after World War I. With the exception of the Hammond Lumber Company ships, the sailors had almost complete organization of all coastal vessels. Wage reductions were effectively resisted during times of depressed trade,[35] and wage increases were gained during better times. The Hammond fleet, however, was a source of constant annoyance to the union. Without mentioning names, Furuseth told the membership in 1907: "Whenever there are vessels sailing with non-union men and they get along without any delay or trouble, they are a constant invitation to other vessels to do the same thing."[36] He asked the members to treat as a scab any union member who dishonored the union contract, but held that on nonunion ships it was the duty of members to get aboard and stir up dissatisfaction.[37] When the union failed to win over these crews, Furuseth started a correspondence with A. B. Hammond in which he tried to convince the lumber merchant that it would be to his advantage to have an agreement with the union. In reply, Hammond charged the union with being irresponsible and arbitrary. He ridiculed Furuseth's sudden concern for the Hammond crews, and charged that privately Furuseth had offered to substitute experienced union members for the present crews. Hammond and his captains were well satisfied to operate without union interference.[38]

Efforts to eliminate the nonunion competition of the American-Hawaiian Line in the Hawaii trade were similarly unsuccessful.[39] Competition from deepwater seamen also plagued the union, but there was little point in attempting to organize these seamen until the crimps' control in the foreign trade could be broken by legislative action.[40]

For several years Furuseth spent part of his time on the West Coast lobbying in state legislatures to repeal antiquated laws which made it a crime to induce seamen to desert their ships. The laws had always been violated by crimps, but Furuseth felt that they might be applied against the union. In 1913, after six years of union lobbying,[41] Governor Hiram Johnson finally signed the bill that repealed the last such state law in the country.

Injunction Issue

At AFL conventions Furuseth continued to bring to the attention of the delegates the seamen's legislative program, their duel with the longshoremen, and their major economic battles. He was, however, much more than the seamen's representative to the AFL. He was already considered one of labor's elder statesmen. Although he customarily supported Gompers, he could not be relied upon to give unswerving devotion to the chief. His individualist philosophy of self-help made Socialists anathema to him. He aligned himself with no group. He fought for what he believed to be right and attacked what he believed to be wrong with never any thought of how his actions might affect his political position within the labor movement or whether anyone would support him. On some occasions he failed to secure the support of his fellow delegates from the ISU. Even his stanchest admirers, Scharrenberg and Olander, sometimes voted against him. Although delegates listened respectfully to his opinions, he lacked the political power to effect the program that he championed, because he always acted as an individual instead of as a member of a group.

On the question of injunctions, which plagued the AFL, the delegates were especially dependent upon Furuseth's advice. All labor was agreed that the use of injunctions in labor disputes had to be eliminated, but few men had made a sufficiently thorough study of the historical and legal aspects of the problem to suggest a plausible solution.

Furuseth's keen interest in the injunction stemmed from the Debs case in 1894.[a] His early writings indicate more than a casual knowledge of the subject. As the AFL legislative representative at the turn of the century, he had attempted to secure remedial legislation. Afterwards he frequently testified before congressional committees and spoke before many labor gatherings to drive home his point that "labor is not property."[43]

Going back to Roman law, Furuseth discovered that injunctions had been used by the tribunes to protect the people from arbitrary acts. In England, the king once held all the legislative, executive, and judicial power in his own hands. At a time when there were not many laws, the king would issue a decree to cover an immediate situation. As more and more laws became accepted, the power of the king to issue decrees was decreased, then transferred to a court of Star Chamber, and finally severely limited by the Bill of Rights. The right of the courts to rectify situations not covered by law is known as equity. The injunction is one form of equity, but, said Furuseth, it was never meant to be applied to labor: "The modern use of the writ of injunction, especially in labor disputes, is revolutionary and destructive of popular government."[44] As equity was understood in England at the time of the adoption of the United States Constitution, the courts could use it only to protect property or property rights when there was no remedy at law. Now, argued Furuseth, the injunction is used in labor disputes on the assumption that business is property and that interference with business is interfering with property rights. If it is true that business is property and can be protected by the courts, then a business should be able to secure an injunction against competitors who might tend to diminish its income. But business is no more property than is labor; business and labor are both personal matters.

> The fundamental principle of American law is that there shall be no property rights in man. A man's labor power is part of him; it fluctuates with his health; decreases when he grows old, and ceases at his death. It cannot be divorced from man, and therefore, under our system cannot be property....[45]

If the judiciary is allowed to include business and labor within the meaning of property, then the judges sitting in equity could become the irresponsible masters of all those who earn their living through business or labor. The courts, by extending their equity power, substitute personal government for government by law. The despotism of the judiciary is as much to be avoided as the despotism of the executive. Not only labor, but all those who believe in individual liberty, must oppose the use of injunctions in labor disputes.

Labor Leader

Injunctions—proclamations—used contrary to and destructive of constitutional guarantees of individual freedom are usurpation, whether they take place in a monarchy by the king, or in a republic by a judge. The power is the same, the result is the same, and a people who will endure, become serfs, will deteriorate and die.

If we are the true sons of our fathers who bought our freedom with their blood, we must and will protect it even if it land us in prison for contempt of court....

It is ours to choose between passive resistance to usurpation and permitting our women to be destroyed and our children to be stunted.[46]

Furuseth advocated a two-pronged attack—resistance and legislative reform. Defiance of the injunction might result in being sent to jail, but he pointed out that there was no disgrace in going to jail—the disgrace came from the reason one was sent there.[47] At the 1908 convention Furuseth proposed "that when the judge issues injunctions in labor disputes it is the duty of organized labor to go to jail." The delegates overruled him by voting overwhelmingly to substitute, "we insist it is our duty to defend ourselves."[48] The following year, however, the delegates agreed with Furuseth in principle that the use of injunctions in labor disputes was an illegal usurpation by the courts and that they should not be obeyed. On the other hand, Furuseth agreed that the Bucks Stove case, which took away labor's right to boycott, was of such importance that it should be tested in the courts.[49]

The decision of the Supreme Court in the Danbury Hatters' case, that contempt of the injunction could be either criminal (with a fine or imprisonment as punishment) or remedial (with triple damages as the remedy), made the AFL decide to spend union funds in fighting cases in the courts rather than paying them out as damages.[50] With this philosophy Furuseth disagreed. As a minority of one at the 1912 convention, he proposed that the workers be advised to take legal steps to put their property beyond the reach of the law.

While most labor leaders contented themselves with denouncing the judges, Furuseth aimed his blows at the legislative branch where he felt the responsibility lay. The "Bill of Grievances" which he and Gompers wrote in order to dramatize the antilabor bias of Theodore Roosevelt and the Republican Congress in 1906[51] asked Congress to take legislative action to limit the powers of the courts. Many bills were introduced purportedly to accomplish this purpose. Furuseth insisted that any bill that labor supported must specifically declare that labor was not property. The Clayton Antitrust Act, passed during the early years of the Wilson administration, met this qualification, but Furuseth did not join with those who hailed it as labor's Magna Charta. He said that the act, though affording relief, did not go far enough.[52] Besides being an individualist, Furuseth also had a reputation for being a pessimist. He did not dampen labor's enthusiasm for the Clayton Act.

INTERNATIONAL LABOR LEADER

In 1908 the AFL rewarded Furuseth for his faithful service by electing him to represent the American labor movement at the British Trade Union Congress to be held in Nottingham, England, September 7–12, 1908. This honor was bestowed on one or two Americans each year to perpetuate the annual exchange of delegates.

Furuseth took a patronizing attitude toward the British delegates to the convention, who, he thought, showed "imperfect understanding" of labor problems by voting to ask for a government inquiry into pending trades disputes. He was pleased, however, that the congress was less "socialistic" than formerly and was beginning to concern itself with industrial problems. This conclusion was undoubtedly Furuseth's wish rather than an accomplished fact.[53]

Taking advantage of the AFL's offer to pay Furuseth's expenses to Europe, the International Seamen's Union asked him to attend the convention of the International Transport Workers which met in Vienna on August 24 and 25.[54] Furuseth arrived in Europe in the middle of July. In the month before the convention he visited Sweden, Norway (where he had his first reunion with relatives in at least thirty years), Germany, Holland, Belgium, England, France, Switzerland, Italy, and finally Austria.[55]

In every country Furuseth tried to talk to seamen, to trade-union leaders, to businessmen and government officials. He was particularly concerned in his investigations with the problem that was his primary interest—freedom for the seamen. Wherever he went, he determined to what extent the seaman was treated as a free man, how his status compared with that of other workers in the same country, and how the freedom of workers in European countries compared with that of American workers. He investigated both the laws and the actual practice in each country. Other matters that concerned him were the standard of living, especially for seamen; the history of the trade-union movement, again related to seamen; and the philosophy of the trade-union leaders, especially leaders of the seamen.

Nowhere in Europe did Furuseth find a sympathetic hearing for his plea that seamen should be treated as free men. "They do not seem to feel the chains." "It does not seem as if the men are really conscious of their serfdom." "The Dutch workmen...seem beautifully unconscious...." "To the [French] seaman himself it comes almost like a blow when you tell him that he also should be under the aegis of the French motto—'Liberté, Egalité, Fraternité.'" At the International Transport Workers' convention, Furuseth's proposals for abolishing imprisonment for desertion, for establishing a manning scale and a standard of efficiency, were ridiculed by Paul Miller, the German seamen's delegate, as "anarchistic." He said that Furuseth was a *wolkenschreiber* (cloud-pusher) and his proposals were so preposterous that no one would dare take them into the German Reichstag. The American proposals were not even discussed on the floor of the convention.

By the end of his tour Furuseth had concluded that everywhere in Europe the workers were under the influence of Socialists, who were looking, not for freedom, but for relief through government regulation:

> One thing seems certain. European statesmen are gradually—by law, by regulations, by judicial decisions and industrial and personal inducements—casting a net about the workers ... which they will some day pull tight around the squirming mass of workers who now talk and think of political power to control the state, while the state is quietly taking away their power in industry.
>
> The British and French workers partly see this tendency and will resist it, with possible success. My impression is that workers in other nations fail to see the drift, because they are looking elsewhere.[56]

During 1909 Furuseth kept up an extensive correspondence with seamen's representatives in Europe. The ISU issued an appeal "To the World's Seamen" calling for an international conference of seamen to meet before the International Transport Workers' convention in Copenhagen in August, 1910. Furuseth denied to his European correspondents that his proposal was an attempt to split the seamen from the longshoremen and railroad workers at the international convention, but this was undoubtedly his real purpose. The seamen, he felt, could be convinced to adopt the American legislative program for freeing the seamen of the world, but in a convention dominated by shore workers the American program would receive slight understanding or support.[57]

Returning to England in July, 1910, Furuseth plunged into an exhausting speaking tour to help the British seamen's union prepare for a strike against the International Shipping Federation. It was the decision of the British union to extend the strike to the United States and Europe which brought about a meeting of the seamen who were attending the sessions of the International Transport Workers' convention in Copenhagen. At the sailors' meetings (which were conducted under the jurisdiction of the parent organization), plans for an international strike to begin early in 1911 were made.

At the general sessions, Furuseth introduced a legislative program to be presented to the legislatures of the respective countries. His program called for abolition of imprisonment for desertion, abrogation of treaties that provided for the arrest of deserters from foreign ships, and establishment of manning scales and standards of individual efficiency. The Socialists, who dominated the convention, did not attack the program itself, which Furuseth had explained as carefully as if he were talking before a legislative committee, but they were quick to pounce on the phraseology, claiming it smacked of "begging" and "servility." They were not pleased with Furuseth's outspoken opposition to them in principle and to their proposals for publicly owned boardinghouses, workmen's compensation, and other social welfare schemes. They resented the way in which Furuseth had meddled, in alliance with J. Havelock Wilson, to back up the faction of the non-Socialist seamen's union in Norway.[58] Although they did not like Furuseth or his ideas, the Socialists could not very well go on record as opposing freedom for the seamen. They allowed the resolutions to pass unanimously but with the provision that each delegation would rewrite the legislative proposals to meet the needs of its own country.[59]

Furuseth hailed the results of the Copenhagen convention as a great victory for the American position. In the sense that he was able to use the pronouncements of the conference to further his legislative program in Congress, this was true, but in Europe his efforts remained merely a scrap of paper which the Socialists whom he had antagonized did not bother to carry out.

The actual weakness of the International Transport Workers was shown in the "international" strike that had been planned for 1911. Despite brave utterances to the contrary, it is obvious that the strike was largely confined to the British Isles. The British union won a sweeping victory, but not because of any support from the ITW.[60]

Furuseth could not attend the ITW convention called for 1913 because he was tied up with legislation in Washington. Then the war came, and though contact between the seamen's unions of America and foreign unions continued, there were no further conferences until after the war.

INTERNATIONAL SEAMEN'S UNION, 1900–1915[61]

Back in America, there was enough to do without being concerned with the seamen of all the world. When Furuseth turned over the presidency of the ISU to William Penje of Chicago in 1899, he did not give up his interest in the organization. As legislative representative he kept in constant touch with every port, and it was natural that this communication should include organizational matters. Whenever he traveled on legislative business or to attend conventions, his trips were utilized to build the seamen's union. While the nominal leadership rested with the president and the secretary-treasurer, William Frazier of New York, the *de facto* leadership was in the hands of Andrew Furuseth.

From 1900 to 1903 the ISU practically tripled its membership, growing to almost 20,000.[62] This was largely due to the growth of the maritime unions on the Pacific Coast, to the extension of ISU jurisdiction to firemen and cooks and stewards, and to organization of the steamshipmen on the Great Lakes. On the Atlantic Coast, where organization was needed most urgently, the union was beset by organizational and factional problems which were never really solved during Furuseth's lifetime. Furuseth tried to organize the Negro deck hands who constituted the majority of the crews on the Atlantic coastal sailing vessels, but failed because of internal opposition and the reluctance of the men to join. His attempts to organize the Gulf seamen were similarly unsuccessful.

The Atlantic marine firemen succeeded in forming an organization, but in 1904, against the advice of Furuseth and Frazier, they plunged into a disastrous strike which broke the union. As a result of the strike, Dan Sullivan, secretary of the Atlantic Coast Marine Firemen's Union, and William Frazier became bitter enemies. It was, perhaps, in the hope of reconciling the differences existing on the East Coast that Furuseth accepted the post of secretary-treasurer at the 1904 ISU convention. However, his duties in Washington and on the Pacific Coast, where the SUP was involved in a conflict with the longshoremen, prevented him from functioning. Frazier reassumed his office and held it until 1913.

In 1908 Penje wrote that he could not attend the convention because of a pending dispute with the shipowners on the Great Lakes, and that he could no longer be a candidate for president. Furuseth tried to convince Victor Olander of Chicago to accept the position, but Olander declined on the ground that the recognized leader of the seamen ought to be the president.[63] Furuseth was then elected to that office, which he held until his death.

Another result of the firemen's strike was that organizational work on the Atlantic Coast had to be started again from the beginning. The ISU engaged a full-time organizer, Fred Benson, with authority to hire assistants and spend large sums of money. In 1907, for example, the union spent upward of $10,000—more than a third of the total income for the year—to pay for organizational expenses on the Atlantic Coast.

Again the difficulty was that the Negro, Italian, and Spanish-speaking seamen would not join. Benson employed five Negro organizers for twenty weeks without any success. The Spanish-speaking marine firemen refused to join the ISU on the Atlantic so long as it was dominated by Dan Sullivan, who had a reputation for discriminating against all foreigners. Only in Mobile, New Orleans, and Philadelphia did the union have any success whatsoever.

Furthermore, the members of this insignificant organization on the Atlantic began feuding among themselves. Benson had organized marine workers on the boats which operated in New York harbor. Sullivan said that this was an invasion of the jurisdiction of marine firemen. Furuseth had to make a special trip to New York in January, 1908, to try to bring peace. While he was in New York all sides agreed to "bury the hatchet," but shortly afterward the fight broke out with renewed fury and spread over the entire Atlantic seaboard.

Sullivan demanded that the ISU executive board issue an appeal for financial aid for the marine firemen in the Gulf district who wanted to go out on strike against a $5 wage cut. Upon the advice of George C. Bodine, an attorney and former sailor who had been elected to the executive board, the board decided that the time was not propitious for a strike and advised the men to accept the wage cut. Sullivan then moved the headquarters of the Marine Firemen's Union to New Orleans and declared that hereafter the marine firemen of the Atlantic would remain outside the ISU because the International and Benson had followed a policy of trying to wreck his union. In retaliation, the ISU set up the Marine Firemen, Oilers, and Watertenders Union on the Atlantic and Gulf coasts under the direct supervision of the executive board. Bodine was put in charge of organization work in the Gulf ports. And thus began another factional fight.

In 1909 and 1910 the ISU was successful in organizing large numbers of firemen. This was due largely to the efforts of organizer Fred Benson, a speaking tour by J. Havelock Wilson and Thomas Chambers of the British seamen's union, and especially the help of a group of Spanish-speaking firemen under the leadership of James Vidal, José Berengher, Juan Martinez, and Secundino Bruge. Furuseth gave the Latin leaders his highest compliment by praising their moderation and their grasp of trade-union affairs. With Sullivan out of the ISU (running his own saloon and crimping establishment), the Latins, who comprised 85 per cent of all the firemen, flocked into the union in response to the appeals made by the Spanish language weekly published by the union.

Bodine aligned himself with another organizer, Charles H. Sheraton.

Labor Leader

Both of them cultivated the Spanish-speaking firemen. At the convention in 1910 Bodine, in alliance with the Latin group, made his first serious bid for power by trying to wrest control of the Atlantic firemen from the executive board. William Frazier, the union secretary, was accused of hindering the work of organizing the Latin firemen because he had put William Rogers in charge of the drive. Rogers had appointed agents in Boston and Philadelphia who were boarding masters, prejudiced against the Spanish-speaking men and generally incapable of organizing them. Ed Anderson was chairman of the convention committee that investigated the charges. He and a majority of the committee severely criticized Frazier for his management of the organizing campaign, but Furuseth, seizing upon a technicality, won postponement of a decision for a year until the charges had been investigated more fully. Frazier was barely reëlected secretary over George Bodine; a few years later, he was to betray Furuseth's loyalty with the worst kind of treachery.

The 1911 convention was a battle royal in which Furuseth was challenged on every principle and tactic. As a member of the committee investigating the charges against Frazier, Furuseth brought in a report whitewashing the agents in Boston and Philadelphia. Rodriguez, the agent in Boston, it was admitted, did charge seamen for drinks and for lodging, but he had resigned for the good of the union. Oscar Carlson, the agent in Philadelphia, had referred to Latins derogatively as "Dagos," but "Carlson is not an educated man; he is a seaman, with the prejudices and feelings of a seaman. He believed himself hounded, and he struck back foolishly, but in the opinion of the committee, not viciously."[64] The committee's recommendation not to remove Carlson on the ground that his removal would create discord among the non-Latin elements was upheld by the convention.

Bodine, Sheraton, and almost all the Atlantic Coast delegates even challenged Furuseth's legislative program. The Wilson-Spight bill, which contained all the features later to be included in La Follette's Seamen's Act, was attacked on the grounds that it provided imprisonment as a punishment for disobedience to orders, that its language provisions would operate to the detriment of the Spanish-speaking members, and that it exempted large numbers of maritime workers from its benefits.[65] Bodine favored a bill introduced by Representative William S. Greene.[66] When the Greene bill was defeated by the convention, Bodine's supporters refused to testify with the other convention delegates before a congressional committee that was holding hearings on the Wilson-Spight bill. Later, some of the dissidents even testified against the ISU bill.[67]

The minority criticized Furuseth for interfering in the affairs of the Norwegian seamen's union. They attempted unsuccessfully to get support from the convention for the *Waterfront Journal,* a newspaper edited by Sheraton.[68] They disagreed with the ISU delegates to the AFL convention who had voted against the establishment of a Transportation Department within the AFL. The delegates held that the legal status of seamen made their problems so different that they could not be in the same department with longshoremen. The Atlantic representatives felt that the fight with the longshoremen had gotten out of hand and that the seamen had to coöperate with shore workers. They were defeated. Bodine's faction approached the same matter from another angle by proposing to invite Tom Mann of the British dock workers to come to America. The victory of the British seamen's union in the 1911 strike had been due to the remarkable solidarity among all maritime crafts. The proposal was defeated on the ground that the ISU could not afford to pay the transportation expenses.

Elections, which were ordinarily a routine matter of casting a unanimous ballot for the incumbents, were this time hotly contested. Even Furuseth was challenged by Bodine. With almost solid support from the Pacific Coast and the Great Lakes, however, Furuseth and Frazier carried their entire slate into office.

At a time when Furuseth needed unity among the organized seamen, at least, the Atlantic Coast became a shambles of rival organizations. In a brief three-day strike in 1911, which was an outgrowth of the British "international" strike, the Atlantic Coast unions had actually won recognition from a few of the major steamship companies.[69] Attempting to follow up on this victory in 1912, the unions were shattered. The defeat was especially bad because of factional problems. The seamen's unions in New York had joined the Waterfront Federation of New York and Vicinity, an organization dominated by the longshoremen. It was this organization under a new name, the National Transportation Workers Federation of America, which called the 1912 strike without the approval of the ISU. But the federation was riddled with dissension from the beginning. The cooks and stewards refused to join the strike; non-Latin firemen offered to scab on Spanish-speaking firemen, who had withdrawn from the ISU in disgust over its conservative policies; and the Atlantic Coast Seamen's Union quit the strike at the end of July. The firemen, the only important organized group left facing the employers, had to capitulate.[70]

Several important developments affecting the ISU resulted from this strike. James Vidal decided to join the Industrial Workers of the World, and almost every Spanish-speaking fireman went with him. The IWW was now firmly entrenched on the water front. It gained complete control of the port of New Orleans, where it conducted an unsuccessful strike in 1913. It even invaded Furuseth's stronghold on the Pacific Coast and made substantial inroads, especially in San Pedro and Seattle. Furuseth castigated the "wobblies" as the tools of the shipowners. He charged that they had no respect for or understanding of the skill necessary for a seaman—they regarded the sailor as a "traveling longshoreman."[71]

In 1913 the ISU chartered a new organization to cover the firemen on the Atlantic Coast under the direction of the discredited Oscar Carlson. This was obviously a maneuver, not to capture the majority of firemen who were Spanish-speaking and already lost to the IWW, but to win the loyalty of the minority group of Anglo-Saxon firemen. Attempting to bring some sort of order out of the confusion surrounding the East Coast maritime unions, George Bodine urged the sailors and the firemen to join in a single organization. Since this was contrary to the policy of the ISU, Bodine's union was "read out" of the international in 1913. He tried to secure recognition as an independent AFL union and then as a local of the International Longshoremen's Association, but Furuseth blocked these efforts.[72] A new organization, the Eastern and Gulf Sailors' Association, was set up by the ISU as the spokesman for Atlantic Coast sailors.[73]

In the midst of this internal turmoil, William Frazier—the man who had loyally served as secretary of the ISU since 1899 and whom Furuseth had so faithfully shielded from attack—suddenly disappeared on March 7, 1912, with more than $3,000 of the union's funds. Furuseth summed up the situation on the Atlantic in December, 1912, in a private report to the officers of the SUP. If someone were elected in whom the men had any confidence, he said, something might yet be salvaged, but it looked as if things would continue as they were "until there is nothing left, even of the wreckage."[74]

The charge made by the dissident elements now outside the union, that the ISU was an international in name only, contained a great deal of truth. The seamen on the East Coast had been destroyed by internal squabbles. The seamen on the Great Lakes had been crushed by the United States Steel Corporation. Faced with the growing strength of the Lake Seamen's Union,[75] the Pittsburgh Steamship Company, a subsidiary of U.S. Steel and the largest carrier on the Great Lakes, persuaded the Lake Carriers' Association to refuse to renew the annual agreement with the union which had been in effect from 1903 to 1908.

At the opening of the shipping season in 1909 the association adopted an open-shop policy and a "Welfare Plan" providing free reading rooms and death and shipwreck benefits.[76] It opened hiring rooms in all Great Lakes ports. In order to join the Welfare Plan, a seaman had to renounce his union membership and accept a continuous discharge book, which was surrendered to the master at the beginning of a voyage and was returned at the end of the trip with the master's rating. If a sailor deserted or "talked union," his book would be turned in to the association.

Furuseth tried to avoid a long strike on the Great Lakes. He asked Olander to secure, through Gompers, an introduction to Judge Elbert H. Gary, chairman of U.S. Steel, in the hope that a peaceful settlement could be achieved without prolonged conflict.[77] When this failed, Furuseth exhorted the union members to make the necessary sacrifices to save themselves from industrial peonage.[78] He objected to reports in the newspapers which seemed to appeal to the labor movement as a whole for funds to win the Great Lakes strike when it was less than a year old.

> An organization of some twenty thousand members, eighty per cent of them single, and between the ages of twenty and forty, more than half of them not involved in any struggle that amounts to anything, telling the world—"We are spent; you must give us of your strength, of your money." Not for me. If the seamen cannot win this fight, then we have got to learn to endure. To live by the grace of others is not to live at all.[79]

By his public silence, however, Furuseth tacitly condoned the appeals to the labor movement, which became increasingly frequent as the strike became less and less effective over its three-year period.[80] In the first year alone, it was estimated that the ISU spent $127,000 on the strike.[81] Finally, on March 18, 1912, the Lake Seamen's Union admitted defeat and went back to work without a contract, but with a promise by the Lake Carriers' Association that it would not discriminate against union members. A few officers were left to keep up the pretense of a union.

Even in Furuseth's home domain, there were rumblings of discontent. Aside from the wobblies, an organized group tried to capture the delegation to the ISU convention in 1911 by appealing to the membership to vote for men who were rank-and-file seamen instead of union officeholders. Ellison, who for many years had been secretary pro tem of the SUP, deserted to the Bodine faction. He later became an important official of the rejuvenated City Front Federation. Furuseth darkly hinted that Ellison was a government agent—a highly improbable charge, but typical of the viciousness with which he could attack any

Labor Leader 107

opponent within the labor movement. The organization on the Pacific, however, was too solid to be disrupted.

The 1913 convention of the ISU in Seattle reflected the organizational status of the seamen, for whom Furuseth was speaking in Congress on the eve of their greatest legislative triumph. There were twenty-four delegates to that convention. No one was present from the Atlantic. One delegate represented the Great Lakes. All the others were from the Pacific Coast. Even in 1915, when the ISU was beginning to make some gains, the secretary reported that of its total income of slightly more than $11,000, the Pacific Coast unions contributed more than $9,000.[82] This was the army that Furuseth led into the halls of Congress.

VII. THE SEAMEN'S ACT

TRAVELING TO INTERNATIONAL CONVENTIONS, fighting longshoremen, dabbling in San Francisco politics, lobbying in Washington, organizing a union, and participating in its internal factional disputes occupied most of Furuseth's time. But it was part of his genius that he never lost sight of the common sailor to whose welfare he had dedicated himself. That sailor might not always have agreed, had he been asked, that what Furuseth did was in his best interests, but no one could know Furuseth without being convinced of his genuine concern for the seaman whose plight he understood even better than "Poor Jack" himself.

PLIGHT OF POOR JACK

To the leaders of the seamen's union the Maguire Act and the White Act had not been panaceas which solved all the sailors' problems, but tools by which the seamen, through organization, could solve their own problems. To some extent, this had been done. But some of the fundamental difficulties remained. The sailor was still among the lowest-paid unskilled workers; he faced long periods of unemployment even in the best of times; he lived in unsanitary, crowded conditions and sailed on unsafe ships which were so seriously undermanned that masters drove him unmercifully to perform the necessary ship's duties. In the foreign trade he suffered even worse conditions because of competition from foreign seamen, especially Asiatics, and he was still subject to the exactions of the crimp.

In response to an inquiry from a lady who wanted to know what kind of literature she should take to seamen, Furuseth summed up the sailor whom he knew. The men, he wrote, were usually well educated, they could read in their native language, and most of them read English. They had all received an early education in religion and were ashore often enough to have the opportunity to consult with their spiritual advisers. "Of course they do wrong, who does not. The life which they are compelled to live brings this about. They are compelled to desecrate the Sabbath by doing work which might well be left to Monday and the wages they receive make home ties out of the question." However, he added hopefully, seamen were trying to better their conditions. Some of them were leaving the sea. Perhaps, he suggested (probably seriously), the best books the lady could bring would be on how to find remunerative employment ashore.[1] Edward Livernash of San Francisco echoed these sentiments when he told the House of Representatives: "Sea life, as compared with land life, is unworthy of Americans...."[2] Furuseth wrote that the sea was gradually becoming "the domain of those who fought life's battles and accepted defeat, of the sewage of the Caucasian race and of such of the races of Asia as felt that their condition could be improved by becoming seamen."[3]

The change from sail to steam should have made life at sea safer and easier. Vessels, now independent of the vagaries of the wind, could make regular runs with much larger pay loads.[4] The certainty of ocean travel attracted passengers for an ever-growing tourist trade which brought about a revolutionary increase in the size of the stewards' department. Steam-operated winches and other laborsaving devices were capable of saving hundreds of man-hours of backbreaking toil. But instead of receiving the benefits of the industrial revolution of the sea, the skilled sailor found that he could be and was replaced by cheap unskilled labor. The size of the deck crew remained the same although the cargo became heavier and the ships became larger, so that the sailor complained he had more to do on a steamship than on a sailing vessel.

Steam and modern means of long-distance communication robbed the sailor not only of his skill, but of the romance and glamor of sailing. In the early 1800's boys ran away from home to go to sea. In the 1900's they were being offered the alternatives of going to jail or going to sea. The shipowner treated the seaman as an unskilled laborer who needed only enough intelligence to paint, scrub, and do hard manual labor. Wages were regarded by the owner and the sailor more as a reward than as compensation for labor performed. An able-bodied seaman could make from $20 to $45 per month depending on the port from which he sailed, his destination, the type of vessel, and the prevailing economic conditions. At no time were his wages sufficient to support a family. Usually there was not enough to support himself after he finished paying the crimp, the boarding master, the tailor, and all the parasites who preyed upon him as soon as he went ashore. Whatever money he had left, he spent "like a drunken sailor," because it was like a reward that he had never expected. Besides, the sooner he spent his money and went into debt to the boarding master, the sooner another ship would be found for him by the crimp.

All too often the sailor found that even his miserly wages could not be collected. Upon reaching a port in South America or China, he would be given leave without any money to face the blandishments on shore. Crimps and runners would meet the sailor, offer to lend him money, and find a place for him in a boardinghouse, provided he deserted his ship. The captain who owed the seaman several months' back wages was not sorry to have the man desert and forfeit his pay. In fact, he might even make the work so heavy, the petty tyrannies so great, that he practically invited the seaman to desert.[5]

Cases of actual cruelty aboard American ships were not so common as they had been in the nineteenth century, but the *Coast Seamen's Journal* could still report instances when captains put men on biscuits and water for punishment—in one case for thirty-five days—or instances when men were put in irons with their hands above their heads for fourteen hours.[6] Discipline aboard ship was of utmost importance, and Furuseth stoutly defended the right of the captain to punish men who were guilty of disobeying any lawful command at sea.[7] But discipline ought to be based upon law, and not upon the arbitrary whim of the captain or his mates.

Sailors did not often complain of cruelty. Their "gripes" usually concerned their living quarters and their food. The law required that each crew member be provided with seventy-two cubic feet of space aboard ship—an area six-by-two-by-six. "Too large for a coffin," said Furuseth, "and too small for a grave."[8] The foc'sle for the deck and engine crews and the "glory hole" for the stewards were invariably placed by the ship's designer where not even the cargo could be stored. There was little or no provision for ventilation. In these crowded, dirty, vermin-infested holes with the stench of leaky oil and human sweat, the men were expected to spend their time off duty. When the weather did not permit eating on deck, the men went to the galley with their own tin plates and returned to eat in the forecastle. Not even the union suggested that they were entitled to a separate mess room. No wonder that a high percentage of lung ailments existed among men who were leading the healthy outdoor life!

Old sailors swore that on the barrels of pork put on board for the crew were printed the words, "Not fit for human consumption." They described their food as "old horse, old hog, and hardtack, shadow soup and humbug with three quarts of water per day for cooking, washing and drinking." Undoubtedly the complaints were exaggerated, but their number and picturesqueness indicate that the sailor, at least, did not think he was being properly fed. On one occasion when some men complained that they were not being given the full scale of provisions required by law, the captain replied by providing the legal minimum of food—uncooked, because the law did not say that the food had to be cooked.

Seamen's Act

When a sailor spoke about a "leaky tub," he was not speaking figuratively. He actually believed that many of the vessels upon which he sailed were floating coffins, but he could not leave the vessel without forfeiting his wages. In addition, a common complaint of the old sailor was that most crew members were too inexperienced to do the work aboard ship and so the burden was shifted onto the old hands. Most captains frankly admitted that a majority of the men they hired were incapable of doing a seaman's work. Even these conditions, bad as they were, were threatened by foreign competition. Already the "American" merchant marine, exclusive of the officers, was manned by less than 10 per cent native Americans. Now these crews faced displacement by Orientals, who were more docile, willing to work for less money, and able to subsist on smaller rations.

Furuseth kept his hand, his heart, and his mind close to the sailors who voiced these complaints. He knew that the captain who practiced cruelty was the exception rather than the rule. He was well aware that most vessels supplied more than the legal food rations and provided better quarters than were required by law. But he also knew that the seaman occupied the bottom rung of the social and economic ladder. It was his aim to make the seaman the equal of any other skilled worker, and he thought that part of the answer lay with Congress.

Legislative Program after the White Act

Following their success in securing passage of the White Act in 1898, the seamen did not press an aggressive legislative campaign.[9] Furuseth continued to go to Washington, but he spent a large part of his time lobbying for or against measures in which the AFL was interested. Among others, he worked for the AFL anti-injunction bills, an eight-hour day for government employees, and legislation prohibiting the interstate transportation of the products of prison labor; he opposed such measures as contract labor laws in Hawaii. For the sailors, Furuseth guarded the gains made in the Maguire and White acts against attempts to reëstablish imprisonment for desertion, and allotment and advance in the coastwise trade.

Two minor proposals made by the seamen at the turn of the century were the abolition of tow barges and log rafts and prohibition of the Kalashi-Watch. Barges and rafts were used by shipowners to cut costs, but they were a menace to commerce because they had to be cut loose in severe weather. The Kalashi-Watch was a method of dividing the work so that a skeleton crew maintained a watch at night and every member of the crew was on duty during the day. The union pointed to the loss of the *Walla-Walla* off Cape Mendocino as a tragic example of what could happen to vessels operating under this economy watch. No matter how justified, these were both make-work measures. Nothing was accomplished in Congress on either proposal until both were incorporated into the comprehensive measure to be known as the "seamen's bill."

During the first decade of the twentieth century, the Sailors' Union, in common with the rest of the labor movement in the West, emphasized legislation to exclude Orientals. On the Pacific Coast, the American-owned Pacific Mail Steamship Company employed Chinese almost exclusively, and other companies used them in the stewards' department. The Chinese could be hired for one fourth the wages of American seamen. Furuseth worked to renew the Chinese Exclusion Act and to extend it to all Orientals in the hope that either the Department of Justice or the courts would rule that American ships were American soil, thus excluding Orientals from employment. However, though for all other purposes a United States ship was considered American territory, the courts held that the Exclusion Act did not apply to the hiring of Chinese on American vessels.[10]

The SUP then turned to the Commerce Department, asking it to rule that vessels with Chinese crews who could not understand English were improperly manned and would be denied permission to clear the port. The sailors cited the decision of a federal court that the Pacific Mail Steamship Company was not entitled to the benefits of the limited liability laws because it had sent its vessel, the *Rio de Janeiro*, to sea improperly manned. The court held that the "competent crew" required by law meant one that could understand the language of the officers, and that the loss of life and property when the *Rio de Janeiro* sank just outside San Francisco was due to the negligence of the company in hiring an incompetent crew. The Department of Commerce refused to take any action on the sailors' request. Nor was it any more sympathetic to their demand that the department prosecute the steamship companies for violation of the Alien Contract Labor Law.

Whenever bills were proposed to subsidize the merchant marine, Furuseth, who opposed subsidies in principle, tried to tack on an amendment that would deny them to vessels employing Orientals. Congress was no more sympathetic than the executive branch of the government.

From every outward expression, Furuseth joined wholeheartedly in labor's narrow, prejudiced view of all Orientals. When Chinese no longer manned the vessels, Furuseth was equally bitter toward Filipinos.

Seamen's Act

He never publicly attacked the Negro race (though no Negroes are members of the SUP), and he took pride in "being as much devoid of nationality [as distinguished from race] feeling as any man."[11] It is difficult to reconcile the high personal regard in which leaders of the Japanese and Indian seamen's unions held Furuseth with his public utterances.[12] One of his chief arguments for passage of seamen's legislation was always that, unless white men were brought back to the sea, the yellow race would win mastery of the sea and, with it, mastery of the world. Few labor men, even on the West Coast, outdid Furuseth in the chauvinism he voiced on this question.[13]

While the West Coast union gave preference to anti-Chinese legislation, seamen on the Atlantic and the Great Lakes concentrated their efforts on various manning bills. In 1900 they introduced a bill that would make it mandatory to carry a specified number of seamen depending upon the size of the vessel. The manning scale was based on a report made by a British commission that had studied sailing vessels. The same crews were necessary on steamers, argued the *Coast Seamen's Journal*, because the steam power might fail.[14] After the wreck of the *Rio de Janeiro* and the burning of the *Slocum* on June 15, 1904, when 935 passengers were drowned or burned to death, the argument shifted to the need for experienced seamen. Subsequent bills stressed the importance of efficiency. They provided that at least 75 per cent of the deck crew, exclusive of officers, be able-bodied seamen (A.B.'s) with a minimum of three years' experience at sea. The union also opposed subsidy bills that failed to provide minimum standards of efficiency, and legislation that would give to the local boards of the Steamship Inspection Service the power to decide the number and efficiency of the crew for each individual vessel. In 1909 the essential features of these various bills were put into the seamen's bill, and agitation for a separate manning bill ceased.

DEVELOPMENT OF THE SEAMEN'S BILL[15]

Furuseth's legislative horizons went far beyond a manning bill, far beyond a prohibition of the use of barges and rafts. Although he wrote letters and articles, made speeches, cornered congressmen, and testified before congressional committees in support of these ameliorative measures, he believed none of them would basically help the seaman until he had become a free man. The White Act had given a measure of freedom to the sailor in the coastwise trade, but until that freedom was extended to all American sailors—in fact, to all the sailors of the world—the seaman would continue to come to Congress as a mendicant.

In a paean to freedom, which he called "God's greatest gift to man," Furuseth explained why it was fundamental and of paramount importance:

> Only the free can organize into a trade union. Bondmen may organize, but only with the view of gaining freedom. That is, they may organize against the state. They may organize a revolution, and they may go into the field to gain freedom by force of arms; they may go to the people to plead for it. They cannot organize a trade union because they are not in possession of the trade union weapon, namely the power to throw the employers' business out of order by refusing to labor. Having obtained this power, the men can then organize effectively on trade union lines. They can, being free men, go to the employer and ask for a redress of grievances and if refused, they may cease to labor....
> He [the employer] meets representatives from the men and industrial democracy has begun....
> When the disciples of the Nazarene were worried about food, clothing and shelter and came to Him for advice, He told them to cease to worry about those things and to seek first the Kingdom of Heaven, and all other things would follow. If we apply ordinary analysis to this answer, we shall find that its meaning is simple.
> There being universal Fatherhood, a universal Brotherhood follows of itself as a logical necessity. All being equal before the Father, this then must be the Kingdom. No masters, no peons, no bondmen—all freemen. Seek ye first freedom and all else shall be added, that is, all else must follow....[16]

As long as the seaman was bound to the vessel as the serf was bound to the soil, he would occupy an inferior status. Furuseth's study of history led him to the conclusion that seamen during feudal times had been among the freest of workingmen.[17] The master of the vessel had shared the hardships and dangers of the sea with every member of the crew. With the rise of capitalism, the owner stayed on shore. He insured or overinsured his vessel and cargo so that his self-interest no longer necessitated hiring the best crews. Men were now kept at sea, not by being the best treated and the highest paid, but by laws that made it a crime against the state to leave a vessel.

The first part of Furuseth's philosophy was that the seaman must be free. The second part was that the shipowner must be regulated, his freedom curtailed. Furuseth would not have approved of thus placing the two parts of his philosophy in juxtaposition. This, however, is exactly what he believed. Modern insurance, limited liability laws, and the increasing safety of navigation had made it possible for the shipowner to send to sea leaky vessels with incompetent crews without fear of losing money. It was therefore necessary for the state to step in and set minimum standards for the protection of the crew and the passengers.

Seamen's Act

The evolution from Furuseth's philosophy to the Seamen's Act was a gradual process of combining many separate bills and demands into one composite bill. The first bill to contain many of the essential features of the future Seamen's Act was introduced by Edward J. Livernash of San Francisco on March 11, 1904. It established a system of watch at sea and a nine-hour day in port, with the provision that no unnecessary work be done on Sundays and holidays. It increased the penalty for failing to "pay off" promptly at the end of a voyage, provided that a majority of the ship's crew might ask for a survey of the vessel's seaworthiness, and abolished imprisonment for desertion in a foreign port.

In the next session of Congress, Representative Thomas Spight of Missouri introduced a similar bill, which in addition called for increased forecastle space, the abolition of corporal punishment, payment of half wages in port, and more butter and water in the seamen's food scale. The same bill was introduced again in 1908. Congress, dominated by standpat Republicans, gave scant attention to the seamen's proposals, and none of them reached the floor for debate. Only as a substitute for subsidy proposals or as extraneous discussion on naval appropriation bills did the seamen even have the opportunity to present their views.

An important alteration in the seamen's bill came about as a result of Furuseth's attendance at the sessions of the International Transport Workers' Federation in Vienna, where he found the European seamen unsympathetic to his "humble supplication ... that the nations issue a decree of emancipation" for the sailor.[18] If the European seaman would not strive for his own freedom, America would strike a blow for the freedom of all the seamen in the world. Hence Furuseth included a proposal which he had made several years before merely as a humanitarian gesture,[19] but which now became the cornerstone of the seamen's bill: that the United States abrogate all treaties providing for the arrest, detention, and return of seamen deserting in an American port. Any seaman coming to America would be a free man.

If foreign seamen could desert in American ports, foreign shipowners would be forced to hire crews in those ports at American wage scales, or they would have to pay the same rates to their European crews to keep them from deserting when they got to America. But this was not all. In order to put foreign and American shipowners on an equal footing, all the provisions regarding safety, manning, allotment, and advance in other proposed legislation were included in the seamen's bill and made applicable to foreign ships in American harbors. For example, the provision that 75 per cent of the crew of each department should be able to understand the language of the officers was made applicable to a British vessel. If the British vessel carried Chinese or Lascar crews who could not understand the officers' orders, it would be denied clearance from an American harbor. The British would thus be forced to hire crews meeting American standards if they wished to trade with the United States.[20]

Many of the new ideas were incorporated into the bill introduced by Representative Spight on May 21, 1909. With a single bill embodying most of the seamen's proposals, Furuseth threw his full energies into arousing public sentiment to force Congress to take some action. The highlight of the campaign took place during the ISU convention in December, 1909, when eighteen hundred seamen in New York paraded through the streets and ended the evening in a mass meeting at Cooper Union. J. Havelock Wilson, who was in New York organizing British seamen, and Samuel Gompers, who arrived dramatically in the middle of the meeting after a bout with the Supreme Court in the Bucks Stove case, were, along with Furuseth and Victor Olander, the principal speakers of the evening. The son of William Lloyd Garrison sent a message for the men who were not freed by the Emancipation Proclamation. The theme of freedom set the dominant tone of the meeting and the campaign that followed.

Increased agitation and the acquisition of a "strong earnest friend,"[21] Senator Robert La Follette, led to the first full-scale hearings on the seamen's bill in February, 1910. William Frazier, Olander, Furuseth, and other leaders of the ISU who testified before the House Committee on Merchant Marine and Fisheries were certain that they had created a favorable impression. But the final days of the session passed without any action because Representative William S. Greene of Massachusetts, chairman of the committee, and Representative William E. Humphrey of Washington prevented the committee from meeting.[22] Furuseth was bitter. To a fellow labor lobbyist, he wrote, "I can appreciate what an awful job you ... have trying to accomplish something worth while; getting glad hands and fair promises by the cartload, and very little else."[23] But he vowed that the agitation would continue "even though the consummation be deferred for a thousand tomorrows."[24]

The election returns in 1910 gave Furuseth new reason to hope for the success of the seamen's bill. Many congressmen favorable to the bill had been reëlected, the Progressive Republicans and the Democrats had scored gains, and William B. Wilson, of the United Mine Workers and a close associate of Furuseth's at every AFL convention, was elected to the House of Representatives. When the new Congress met, Wilson

Seamen's Act

introduced the seamen's bill in the House as H.R. 11372 and La Follette introduced the same bill in the Senate, S. 468. In hopeful anticipation of the hearings on the bill, the ISU changed its 1912 convention site from San Francisco to Baltimore in order to have all the delegates available to testify before the House Committee on Merchant Marine and Fisheries.

All the delegates were available, but all of them did not testify in favor of the bill. George Bodine and the delegates from the Atlantic Coast expressed their preference for a bill introduced by Representative Greene. Although the Wilson bill had some commendable features, they said, certain of its provisions were so objectionable that they would rather see the entire bill defeated. Bodine argued that the clause requiring 75 per cent of each department of the vessel to understand the language of the officers was impractical because there was no way to test accurately whether the men understood the orders. He was undoubtedly concerned with the large number of Spanish-speaking firemen who could not have passed a rigid language test. He objected to the efficiency ratings of "able seaman" and "ordinary seaman" which would be given by government inspectors. Such "branding" of seamen by the government, he said, was contrary to the philosophy of the ISU. Furthermore, the idea that a man needed three years' experience at sea in order to do the work of a sailor on a modern steam vessel was ridiculous. He had personally been at sea for ten years and had never seen a sailor lower a lifeboat except for a drill. Bodine's testimony was all the more damaging because it showed division among the seamen themselves.

Shipowner Opposition

Much more serious opposition came from the shipowners,[25] who in the past had been little concerned with seamen's legislation. They had approached the problem from an entirely different tack. Most owners stoutly believed that American seamen were already the best paid and the best fed in the world, and they argued that these high standards forced them to operate at a disadvantage vis-à-vis foreign shipowners. The solution, to the owner, was obvious: subsidize the American merchant marine in the same way that Congress passed tariff laws to protect the high wages paid in American manufacturing concerns.

Although he denied that he opposed subsidies in principle, Furuseth led the ISU in fighting every subsidy measure proposed in Congress. As early as 1888 the *Coast Seamen's Journal* had pointed out the fundamental fallacy in the shipowners' request for subsidies.[26] Wages constituted less than 12 per cent of the total operating cost of a vessel,[27] and, moreover, the shipowner in the foreign trade could hire his crews, with the exception of the officers, any place in the world. The shipowner in the coastwise trade was already protected by law from competition by foreign vessels. With logic and truth, the seamen argued that the owners wished to keep labor on the "free list" while they received the benefits of protection for their business. It was on this basis that Furuseth opposed the Hanna-Payne Shipping Subsidy Bill in 1899 and the recommendations of the Merchant Marine Commission in 1905. The Naval Reserve feature of the subsidy bill growing out of the commission's recommendations further angered the seamen. It was proposed that sailors be given the opportunity of volunteering to serve in the Naval Reserves, for which they would be paid $25 per year by the government.[28] Furuseth argued that if this devious method of forcing seamen into the Navy were adopted, it would merely result in the shipowner's cutting the sailor's wages by $25. Furuseth introduced a resolution at the ISU convention in 1906 protesting

... against being used as a key to open the treasury and as a pack mule to carry away the plunder. We are too ill-paid and poor to live like other men, but we have yet, in spite of our status under the law and the pity with which we are considered, sufficient self-respect to appreciate the true value of the gift which this bill contemplates forcing upon us.[29]

Furuseth even argued that subsidies would not help the merchant marine, but the railroads. Because the railroads picked up the freight, they could practically dictate which ships would get the business, and therefore they could control the ocean freight rates. Furthermore, they had their own fleets in which they could lower the rates by an amount corresponding to the subsidy. This would allow them to increase railroad rates without raising the total freight costs to the shipper.[30]

The ISU deviated from its unalterable opposition to subsidies only on those rare occasions when it thought the existing mail subsidies could be used to exclude "Mongolians" from the crew. It was also hinted that there might be some justification for subsidizing sailing vessels because they were excellent training grounds for sailors.

Most members of Congress were unconvinced by the shipowners' pleas for help against foreign competition. They were aware of the shocking decline of the American merchant marine, but they were not agreed upon a solution to the problem. Furuseth's proposal to equalize wages and standards through the seamen's bill appeared to have merit to some congressmen. It would cost the government nothing. If Furu-

Seamen's Act

seth was correct, it would act to raise wages and standards on foreign vessels to the American standards so that competition would be on an equal basis.

At the 1912 and subsequent hearings on the seamen's bill, when it seemed possible that it might be favorably reported to Congress, the shipowners united in their efforts to defeat it. The only exceptions were James Rolph, whom Furuseth had supported in the San Francisco mayoralty campaign,[31] and Rudolph Spreckles.[32] The owners had no particular objection to that portion of the bill which allowed seamen to desert, because they had seldom tried to reclaim deserters. They did object to being forced to give the seaman half of his earned pay in any port on the ground that he would squander it on drink. To this, Furuseth replied that not only was the seaman entitled by right to his pay, but shore leave without money put him at the mercy of the crimp and the boarding master.

The most important objections of the shipowners concerned the provision for language qualifications and the specification that 75 per cent of the deck crew be able seamen with three years of sea experience. If such provisions were included, they contended, there would not be enough seamen to man the ships. This would put the American merchant marine into the hands of a few "irresponsible strike leaders."[33] Furthermore, such rigid qualifications were unnecessary on a modern steamship; any sailor could be taught everything he needed to know in a few months.

Furuseth's pride in his "profession" was sorely wounded by the suggestion that the sailor was an unskilled laborer. Indignantly he explained the myriad duties expected of a seaman and the knowledge and experience necessary to perform these duties. Most of all, he emphasized that while many men could do a seaman's work under ordinary circumstances, in emergencies, when life and property were at stake, it was absolutely essential to have trained, experienced personnel. Anyone could polish the brass on a fire engine, but only the trained fireman was capable of quick and accurate response when a fire occurred.

SAFETY AND THE SEAMEN'S BILL

In the midst of this controversy, when the House committee was deliberating over which, if any, bill should be reported out to Congress, there occurred one of the worst disasters in maritime history: the sinking of the *Titanic* on April 14, 1912. When this luxury liner had been launched early in 1911, the *Coast Seamen's Journal* had prophetically remarked: "No matter how strongly ships may be built, no matter how scientifically they may be equipped with means of communication and life-saving, in the last analysis safety depends on boats and seamen to man them."[34] A few days before the disaster, Furuseth had written to the House committee pointing out that limited liability laws, by protecting the shipowner against loss, had tended to lower the requirements for safety equipment and to decrease the number and efficiency of the personnel.[35] Safety was the new theme now used to drive home the need for the seamen's bill. Statements from *Titanic* survivors and from congressional committees which investigated the disaster were cited to emphasize the necessity for having enough lifeboats and enough qualified men to man them.[36]

The majority of the Committee on Merchant Marine and Fisheries, led by Rufus Hardy, William B. Wilson, and J. W. Alexander, reported favorably on the seamen's bill on May 2, 1912. In line with the lessons of the *Titanic,* the bill retained the requirement that 75 per cent of the deck crew be able seamen and, in addition, required that there be sufficient lifeboats for all passengers with two able seamen for each boat. The minority turned in a blistering report a few days later: "This bill is the most extreme and revolutionary in all probability that has ever been favorably reported to this House." They objected strenuously to all features of the bill which tried to dictate to foreign nations what language their crews should speak, what qualifications they should have, and what safety devices their ships must carry. They objected to the provision allowing foreign sailors to desert in the United States because it would "encourage the scum of all the foreign sailors," those who had no respect for their agreements, to desert in this country. Most important, "this bill . . . would not change conditions in the coastwise trade. Ninety-three per cent of our foreign trade is carried on in foreign ships manned by foreign sailors. Of the few ships that carry the 7 per cent of our foreign trade, not 10 per cent of their crews are American citizens."[37] The only reason for recommending such a bill, the minority charged, was to win votes in the coming elections in November, 1912.

If it was true that the seamen's bill was a matter of "playing politics," then both Republicans and Democrats were guilty, for the principle of the bill was endorsed at the two national conventions. The Democrats, who controlled Congress and who were soon to win the presidency, declared:

> We urge upon Congress the speedy enactment of laws for the greater security of life and property at sea, and we favor the repeal of all laws and the abrogation of so much of our treaties with other nations as provide for the arrest and

Seamen's Act

imprisonment of seamen charged with desertion or with the violation of their contract of service. Such laws are un-American and violate the spirit, if not the letter, of the Constitution of the United States.[38]

With both parties now pledged to the bill, its passage seemed assured, but Congress moved slowly. It was not until August 3 that the House approved the bill with slight amendments. In the Senate it was referred to the Committee on Commerce, and Furuseth expected quick approval from a committee that he thought was sympathetic. However, objections from the shipowners, especially the Lake Carriers' Association, delayed action until the short session in January, 1913. Thirteen days of hearings added nothing new to the arguments that had previously been made.

It was now confidently expected that the bill would be reported out favorably. "Of course," Furuseth wrote, "understand that there is nothing certain in the world, or in Washington. There is no use trying to sell the hide before we have shot the bear, but things really look good."[39] But nothing happened. Senator Theodore H. Burton, chairman of the subcommittee considering the bill, called Furuseth several times to meet with representatives of the shipowners so that some compromise could be arranged. When Furuseth saw that Burton was attempting to water down the bill, he obstinately announced that he would rather see the bill defeated than approved in the form in which Burton wished to present it to the Senate.[40] La Follette and friends of the seamen in the Committee on Commerce decided to risk the chance of amending the bill on the floor. The bill reached the Senate on March 2, and most of the serious features to which Furuseth objected were removed.[41] On March 4, the last day of the Congress, the bill was sent to President Taft.

Years of work were about to be climaxed with success. The bill was not all that the seamen had asked, but it could be construed as a clear victory. Imagine the elation at AFL headquarters where Furuseth had his office. Imagine the feelings of this lonely man as he went to his bare room in the National Hotel. As he sat on his iron cot, he must have mentally composed the telegram that he would send to the Sailors' Union of the Pacific on the occasion of their birthday on March 6. Then imagine the letdown when he learned the following day that President Taft had vetoed the seamen's bill on the ground that it might create "friction with the commerce of foreign nations."[42] He hurried back to San Francisco to cushion the shock to the seamen which he knew would be worse than his own disappointment. As consolation, he assured them that President-elect Wilson was expected to favor the bill in its original form. Perhaps Taft's veto had been a blessing in disguise.

A New Campaign

In April, after less than a month in San Francisco, Furuseth returned to Washington to help guide his bill through Congress.[43] He had obviously decided to miss the ISU convention which was scheduled to meet in May in San Francisco; he knew that it would, in fact, be little more than a meeting of the West Coast unions. There was practically nothing left of the union on the Atlantic, and the Great Lakes unions were too weak and poor after a three-year conflict with the Lake Carriers' Association to be able to send more than one delegate.

While waiting for Congress to act on the seamen's bill, Furuseth occupied his spare time during April, July, and September, 1913, visiting the Atlantic unions in an effort to salvage something from the strife-dismembered organization. Not even within his own union did he find a ray of hope or encouragement to help him face the trials in Washington. The weakness of the SUP and the growing strength of the IWW made him fear that the wobblies would take some drastic strike action which would alienate Congress and ruin the chance of passing the seamen's bill at a time when victory seemed so close."

But victory was much further away than Furuseth expected. La Follette introduced his bill (S. 4) in the Senate on April 7, and Alexander introduced a similar bill (H.R. 4616) in the House of Representatives on May 3. Senator Knute Nelson introduced the watered-down version (now S. 136) which President Taft had vetoed. Despite very favorable opinions on the La Follette bill from William B. Wilson, now secretary of labor, and William C. Redfield, secretary of commerce, the subcommittee recommended the Nelson bill to the full committee.[45]

Interminable delays followed. Important members of committees absented themselves from Congress, priority was given to tariff and currency legislation, and the Wilson administration failed to give the bill immediate support because Secretary Redfield wished to await the outcome of the International Conference on Safety of Life at Sea which would meet in London in November, 1913. By the middle of June, Furuseth wrote dejectedly:

> With all my soul I wish this was over, or at any rate that they would tell me if there is no intention of acting this session.
> I am almost afraid of the thoughts that come to me at times. Prospects of action, then delay; then more good prospects, and then more delay....[46]

All Furuseth's friends assured him that Congress would soon take some action. La Follette conferred with him regularly on strategy. Senator James P. Clarke, chairman of the Senate Committee on Commerce and a close friend of La Follette, repeatedly told Furuseth that his committee was sympathetic and would take prompt action. Judge Alexander, chairman of the House Committee on Merchant Marine and Fisheries, who had long been a friend of the seamen's bill, added his assurances. In the administration, Furuseth had a loyal supporter in William B. Wilson. Even the president, in personal interviews with Furuseth on April 21 and again in August, expressed his interest and support. But nothing happened.

It seems obvious that President Wilson and his legislative leaders were following the advice of Secretary of Commerce Redfield to postpone action until after the London conference. Furuseth feared that conference, which he knew would be composed primarily of shipowners. The strategy that he worked out with La Follette was to secure passage of the seamen's bill before the conference, so that it would serve as the basis for instructions to the American delegation. In the race to secure early enactment, Furuseth was aided by the congressional reaction to the sinking of the *State of California* on August 20, 1913, with the loss of thirty-one lives. Pointedly, Furuseth called attention to the lack of qualified seamen aboard the ship as the reason for the failure to launch sufficient lifeboats in a calm sea to save all the passengers.[47] The disaster undoubtedly influenced the Commerce Committee to report the Nelson bill to the Senate on October 2, but with a recommendation that action be delayed until after the London conference.

Singlehandedly, La Follette defeated the move to postpone debate and maneuvered the seamen's bill onto the floor of the Senate. On October 16 he offered his own bill as a substitute for the Nelson bill. Another marine disaster, the burning of the *Volturno* with a loss of more than two hundred passengers on October 11, had given the pro-seamen forces a psychological advantage and the public support of the influential National Consumers' League.[48] Furuseth and his friends had shouted so loud and so long about safety at sea that they were generally conceded to be the experts on the subject. Therefore, when La Follette's bill came up for discussion in the Senate on October 21, it was possible for its advocates to beat down weakening amendments offered by Theodore Burton of Ohio and Augustus Bacon of Georgia. In fact, several amendments were added which strengthened the safety measures of the bill. Aside from La Follette, who had made this bill a very personal matter, other senators who spoke in favor of the measure were Duncan U. Fletcher of Florida, George Sutherland of Utah, George W. Norris of Nebraska, Albert B. Cummins of Iowa, John Sharp Williams of Mississippi, and Harry Lane of Oregon.

Furuseth watched the three-day debate with tense excitement from the Senate gallery. He heard La Follette's tribute to him:

> Mr. President, of course I am a landlubber, and have to take my tutelage from those men who have been at sea. I never shall be able to express my very great obligation to Andrew Furuseth, who for the last four years has called upon me almost every Sunday morning to talk with me about this legislation. Andrew Furuseth is a sailor. He is a Norwegian Americanized, one of the most intelligent men it has been my good fortune to meet. For nineteen years he has been sitting up there in that corner of the gallery waiting to be made free. Whatever I happen to know about this subject, I have acquired from talking with him.[49]

On October 23, when the bill was adopted with only one dissenting vote, Furuseth rushed from his corner in the gallery into the corridors, crying out, "This finishes the work Lincoln began." Tears were running down his cheeks. He put his hands to his throat, saying: "I am choking, I am so happy."[50]

LONDON CONFERENCE ON SAFETY OF LIFE AT SEA

In the meantime, on October 3, 1913, Furuseth learned that he had been appointed by President Wilson to be one of the American commissioners to the London Conference on Safety of Life at Sea.[51] This was an unexpected and unwelcome honor. Furuseth remembered a similar international conference in 1908 whose recommendations he had criticized at the time because they showed more interest in safety appliances than in the men who handled those appliances.[52] He suspected that the recommendations of this conference would be used to weaken and postpone the seamen's bill.[53] The conference would be dominated by shipowners, especially British shipowners, who would oppose the high manning provisions of the American bill and the granting of freedom to the seamen. In a dilemma, he wired John H. Tennison, secretary pro tem of the SUP: "Fear to accept or decline. Acceptance may mean loss of right to fight and a weakening of our position. Refusing may mean losing the good will of the President."[54]

It was not until a few days before the final sailing date on October 30 that Furuseth decided definitely to accept the president's appointment. All the friends of the seamen's bill advised him to accept, arguing that the president knew Furuseth's position and expected him to present his views. Secretary Redfield assured him that all the commissioners could go with "mind free and tongue loose."[55] Alexander, who had also been appointed a delegate, said that even though he had been unable to secure the House's approval of the seamen's bill in the few days before sailing time, he would personally consider himself instructed by the bill passed by the Senate.[56] Furuseth's friends further pointed out that to decline would be interpreted as unwillingness to face the international experts on safety, and that acceptance would give him an opportunity to present a minority report if the conference did not adopt his view.

All Furuseth's fears were justified. The conference opened November 12 and was hardly under way when Furuseth began writing confidential letters to his friends indicating that he was ready to resign. The American delegation adopted a rule that no proposal would be made by any delegate unless it was approved by the majority of the delegation. Feeling that he had been assured of the right to express his personal opinions, Furuseth refused to be bound by the decision. "I simply refuse to obey and let them all rave."[57] His most serious objection was that the meeting was really a "conference on safety to owners on shore."[58] The proposals made for an international treaty were far below the standards set by the seamen's bill passed by the Senate. Passenger vessels were to be required to carry lifeboats for 75 per cent of the passengers instead of "boats for all," and to provide four certified "boat handlers" instead of two able seamen for each lifeboat.

Furuseth refused to adopt the reasoning of the majority of the delegation that the standards established by the conference were an important advance because they exceeded the existing standards in many countries. He refused to believe that these were minimum standards and that each country could adopt higher ones if it wished; he argued that the minimum would also be the maximum. Hiding behind the international treaty, a foreign vessel entering an American port would not be subject to the standards set by the United States in the seamen's bill. The crew, for example, would not be required to understand the language of the officers, because the international treaty allowed the use of interpreters.

When, in opposition to Alexander and Furuseth, Eugene T. Chamberlain, commissioner of navigation, and George Uhler, head of the Steamboat Inspection Service, led the American delegation in approving the conference proposals, Furuseth wired President Wilson asking him to reverse this stand. When he received no reply, he decided to resign from the commission on December 24.[59] He spent Christmas Day contemplating what effect his resignation and the recommendations of the conference would have upon the seamen's bill. The effect was not good. William B. Wilson politely told Furuseth that the resignation was unfortunate. Redfield was displeased. Even Alexander, who had supported Furuseth in London, was noticeably chilled by what he considered the intractable attitude of an obstinate old seaman.[60]

Congress Procrastinates

This was no time to lose friends. Ever since the La Follette bill had come to the Senate floor, the shipowners had been conducting a campaign of lobbying and publicity against the bill.[61] Their attack was directed both against the credibility of the proponents of the bill and against the bill itself. Sitting in the Senate gallery for nineteen years, they said, hardly qualified Furuseth to speak as a seaman. The experts in London did not find it necessary to adopt the standards he advocated. George W. White, president of the Association of Passenger Steamboat Lines, wrote: "If it [the seamen's bill] should become law, it would mean the most serious marine disaster in our history." Representatives of the Great Lakes Carriers' Association vehemently shouted that the nonsensical provision requiring lifeboats for all passengers would so limit passenger space on the Great Lakes vessels that none of them could operate at a profit during the four summer months on which their entire business depended. Moreover, the requirement that the vessel must carry two A.B.'s for every lifeboat would double the size of the crew.[62]

So strong were the protests and the demands for further hearings that the House Committee on Merchant Marine and Fisheries consented to take additional testimony. Hearings were held at various times from December, 1913, to March, 1914. Although special emphasis was given to the problem of inland waterways, all the old arguments on the bill were repeated. Furuseth summed up the hearings in a report to his membership:

> The hearings on our bill closed yesterday, (Friday the 13th and full moon). If anybody is superstitious and thinks it is unlucky it ought to be to those who caused the hearings to be held. We did not ask for any hearings, that is sure.
>
> The hearings were a perfect carnival of criticism on the sailors and witnesses testified that they were "mere creatures; they needed no skill or experience; anybody could do a sailor's work; they might need a month's experience or so, but they would not need more than three or four months even at the wheel." In short, it was the unanimous opinion of those representing the steamship companies that they did not need any sailors. Then came along the representatives of the sailing vessels and said they did not need any sailors. . . .
>
> If the people of the United States could have listened to the testimony, there would either be a fundamental sweeping change from existing conditions, or feeling that, they would never travel by sea unless they were compelled to. The testimony is such as necessarily brings to the minds of any person a conviction that everything at present is done with a view of cheapness and that the whole effort is toward the safety of investments for those on shore instead of safety of life to those at sea, regardless of whether they be passengers or seamen, male or female, children or adults. . . .[63]

While the hearings were in progress, Furuseth assigned to Olander, who had been sent to Washington to help him, and to Edward H. Nockles, a labor leader from Chicago, the task of winning support for the seamen's bill in the House. A special series of seven letters, laying heavy stress on the safety provisions, was mimeographed and distributed to each member. Since many of the letters were delivered personally, Furuseth had an opportunity to talk to many congressmen. He concluded that most of them were woefully ignorant of maritime matters.

For himself, Furuseth took the responsibility of defeating in the Senate the London Convention on Safety of Life at Sea. Woodrow Wilson had recommended to Congress on December 2, while Furuseth was in London, that action on seamen's legislation be postponed until the results of the London conference were known. Many of Wilson's followers in Congress interpreted this to mean that the Senate should approve the international convention before the seamen's bill was approved. Furuseth reasoned that if this were done, the bill would be modified to meet the lower standards of the convention, which was to be effective for seven years. If the Senate approved it, he argued, all legislation for the benefit of the American merchant marine would be impossible until the international agreement expired.

The president submitted the convention to the Senate on March 20, and hearings were held in April. Although the Senate did not act on the convention until December, 1914, it played an important part in the strategy of passing the seamen's bill. Since the shipowners expressed their willingness to abide by the decisions of the London conference, approval of the convention would undoubtedly satisfy the public that Congress had acted to insure safety at sea. Furuseth knew that if the president should make a strong statement in favor of ratification, the Senate would respect his wishes. It was for these reasons that Furuseth reluctantly proposed that the London convention be approved after it had been amended to provide that the United States reserved for itself the right to impose higher standards for all ships in American ports. With this amendment, the treaty was ratified by the Senate on December 16.[64]

Meanwhile, after holding the seamen's bill for more than seven months, the House Committee on Merchant Marine and Fisheries reported out a substitute bill on June 19, 1914. This bill, largely the work of the chairman, Alexander, lowered most of the safety provisions to conform to the international convention, exempted Great Lakes vessels from most of them, failed to require a three-watch system for firemen, and weakened the equalization aspects of the Senate bill—to all of which Furuseth strenuously objected.

Furuseth was in a quandary. To allow the bill to be considered on the floor of the House might result in an entirely unsatisfactory measure which could not be changed in a conference committee. To hold it in committee for further amendments might delay action until it was too late. La Follette, from his sick bed, and William B. Wilson advised trying to get a better bill from the committee. By pointing to the recent sinking of the *Empress of Ireland* on the St. Lawrence River with a tragic loss of 1,026 lives, Furuseth was successful in getting more stringent safety regulations applied to the "inland marine." Alexander also consented to several other changes, but he was adamant in refusing to include provisions that would require foreign shipowners to pay seamen half their wages in American ports and would deny legal recognition to any allotment paid by a foreign shipowner.

The bill was still far from satisfactory, but time was running out, and the friends of the seamen agreed to take their chances in a conference committee. The bill was reported on August 27 and passed by unanimous consent.[65] The following day the Senate disagreed with the House bill and asked for a conference, but Senator Clarke requested reconsideration of the motion so that the Committee on Commerce could restudy its bill in the light of the war that had just broken out in Europe. New hearings were held, and their scope was extended to allow the Great Lakes shipowners to testify that they were also opposed to the House version of the bill.

All that fall, Furuseth alternated between hope and despondency. La Follette had been ill all summer, Olander had returned to Chicago for a political campaign, William B. Wilson was out of Washington a large part of the time, and Furuseth felt the tremendous responsibility which he carried alone. In one of his low periods, on October 17, he wrote: "The bill has not passed and it is plain that it will not be at this session, and the Lord God only knows when, or if at all."[66] When the session came to a close without any action by the Senate committee, his disappointment was the more bitter because he had allowed himself to believe that he would succeed. The Democratic party's congressional campaign handbook for 1914 had spoken of the seamen's bill as an accomplished fact;[67] but when President Wilson failed to fulfill the promise of his party, Furuseth preferred to place the blame on the president's advisers, Eugene Chamberlain and George Uhler.[68]

During November and part of December, Furuseth visited Baltimore, Philadelphia, New York, and Boston, speaking before groups of seamen wherever he could find them. Reporting to the new secretary-treasurer of the ISU, Thomas A. Hanson, he commented on his meeting in Bos-

Seamen's Act

ton: "The spirit or temper which exhibits itself there was extremely disheartening to say the least."[69] At his meeting with the union in New York, seventeen members attended. Open meetings held at the sailors' missions were more successful, especially when there were no competing attractions of free fights or other entertainments; sometimes his audiences numbered more than a hundred men. Furuseth concluded that the seamen were waiting for the La Follette bill to become law before they seriously tried to organize.[70]

Instead of being discouraged, Furuseth returned to Washington in December with renewed vigor. La Follette was feeling much better, and he could now lend his support to pushing through the bill. One of the first results was to block the move made by the administration to get the Senate to adopt the Convention on Safety of Life at Sea without the qualifying amendment which Furuseth thought necessary. Then, shortly after the Christmas recess, on January 4, 1915, the Senate Committee on Commerce reported its disagreement with the House version of the seamen's bill and asked for a conference.

For two months, while the conference committee deliberated, rumors flew thick and fast. It was said that the committee had agreed on the Alexander version of the bill, that the president had indicated he would not sign the La Follette version, and that the committee would delay action until the president could pocket veto the bill. Furuseth feared the worst but he expressed growing optimism. This was based on his confidence in the members of the conference committee, on the public support for the bill, on the influence of the seamen's friends in the Senate, and on the need of the administration to win the support of the Progressive Republicans on the ship-purchase bill then in the Senate.

VICTORY

As the Sixty-third Congress drew to a close, the conference committee finally agreed on February 23 to report the seamen's bill substantially as it had been introduced by Senator La Follette. The House of Representatives approved the bill on the 25th, and the Senate began debate on it the next evening. Senator Fletcher briefly explained the bill. Senators Henry Cabot Lodge and Elihu Root opposed it on the ground that its provisions for unilaterally abrogating commercial treaties might lead to serious international complications. The following day, February 27, Senator Burton, an old opponent, spoke against the bill. Senator James K. Vardaman spoke for ten minutes, and then the bill was agreed to without debate. Furuseth recognized that one of the main reasons the bill passed was "that the opponents were taken unawares and were out of the Senate Chamber." Senator Hoke Smith of Georgia stormed into the Senate and "raised a row." He moved for a reconsideration, but La Follette was able to rally 39 votes against 33 to table the motion to reconsider.[71] All that was left now was the highly dubious task of getting the president's signature.

As the bill went to the president, it consisted of twenty sections.[72] Fifteen of these were revisions of previous statutes and five were new provisions. One of the new sections provided that the seamen should not be required to do any unnecessary work on Sundays or holidays while the vessel was in a safe harbor. At all other times in port, nine hours would constitute a day's work.

The bill defined an able seaman as one who was nineteen years old with at least three years' deck experience at sea or on the Great Lakes. An able seaman on the Great Lakes had to have only eighteen months of experience. A graduate of a school ship could become an able seaman after one year's experience. Sixty-five per cent of the deck crew (that is, sailors) had to be A.B.'s, and 75 per cent of each department of the vessel had to understand the language of the officers.

Another section dealt with lifeboats and safety appliances. Ocean-going vessels were required to carry lifeboats and pontoon life rafts sufficient for every passenger aboard. Vessels on the Great Lakes which traveled more than three miles offshore were subject to the same provisions, except that from May 15 to September 15 they might operate with lifeboats and rafts for only half of the passengers. Each vessel was required to have one A.B. for every lifeboat it carried.

To avoid the loophole through which shipowners had evaded paying seamen for injuries received at work, the law provided that the courts were not to consider officers to be fellow servants with the seamen under their authority. The last new section required that all accidents resulting from the towing of rafts or barges be reported to the secretary of commerce.

Of the fifteen amendments to preëxisting maritime law, the most important were the provisions to abolish imprisonment for desertion, to allow seamen to receive half pay in every port of loading or unloading (and expressly forbidding the "master's option" that had been used to make seamen sign away this right), to increase forecastle space, to improve the scale of provisions, and to prohibit the payment of advance or allotment. These provisions now applied to the foreign as well as the coastwise trade.

The bill made most of its provisions applicable to all vessels in American ports, and it provided that after suitable notice had been given to foreign governments, any treaty in conflict with the bill would be abrogated. It was this feature of the bill that gave President Wilson serious concern. The United States had commercial treaties with twenty-two nations which provided for the arrest, detention, and return of seamen who deserted. More important (because foreign shipowners seldom tried to reclaim deserters) were the provisions that foreign owners had to give their seamen half pay on demand in American ports, that any advance or allotment already paid by the master would not be recognized as legal payment in the United States, and that 75 per cent of the crew had to understand the language of the officers. Foreign shipowners had already vigorously protested to the State Department.[73]

In answer to a plea from Furuseth asking President Wilson to sign the bill which had just been delivered to him, the president expressed his doubts in a letter dated March 2:

What is troubling me at this moment is that it demands of the government what seems a truly impossible thing, namely the denunciation of some twenty-two commercial treaties.... To throw the commercial relations of the country into disorder and doubt just at this juncture might lead to the most serious consequences, and upon that ground I am debating very seriously whether it is possible for me to sign this bill or not.[74]

When Furuseth learned that the president had sent the bill to the secretary of state, William J. Bryan, he recognized the symptoms of defeat. In January, however, Furuseth had twice talked at length with Bryan, and he felt he had made a favorable impression. Although he knew that the president had been doubtful all along about the application of the bill to foreign vessels, he could hope for the best. He did not know that on the same day the bill had passed the Senate, Bryan had recommended to the president that it should be politely pocket vetoed.[75] On Tuesday, March 2, Senator John Kern and seven other senators went to see President Wilson to urge him to sign the bill, while Furuseth, La Follette, and Senator Robert L. Owen called upon Secretary Bryan. Although Bryan seemed genuinely affected by Furuseth's appeal, he again recommended to the president that the bill not be signed.[76]

That evening Furuseth went with Senator La Follette to visit the president. La Follette talked with Wilson for fifteen minutes, and then Furuseth was called into the room. He probably knew that he had only a few minutes to present his case. In those few minutes, twenty years of work might be done or undone. If the president refused to sign now, the seamen's bill was killed for the duration of the war and perhaps forever. Years later, Furuseth could not remember what he told the president, and he did not leave any contemporary account of his conversation, but surely he was flushed with excitement and eloquence, and surely he stressed the aspect of freedom which he knew would appeal to the president. After fifteen minutes, he was dismissed. La Follette remained with the president for another hour before he joined Furuseth. The president had not yet made up his mind.[77]

March 3, no news. Furuseth waited as the hours passed by. Thursday morning, March 4, no news. Only a few hours remained before Congress would adjourn. An hour before adjournment, Furuseth learned that the president had signed the bill. That afternoon the news was released to the press. Wilson explained his decision in a letter to Newton D. Baker, who was the attorney for the Great Lakes Carriers' Association for many years and who later became secretary of war: "I debated the matter of signing the bill very earnestly indeed, weighing the arguments on both sides with a good deal of anxiety, and finally determined to sign it because it seemed the only chance to get something like justice to a class of workmen who have been too much neglected by our laws."[78]

La Follette was overjoyed for his own personal achievement, for his friend, Furuseth, and for what they had done for the seamen of the world. To the Sailors' Union of the Pacific he wired on March 6:

> As you meet to celebrate the thirtieth anniversary of your organization I rejoice that in the Providence of God I am permitted at last to hail you as free men under the Constitution of our country. The Fourth of March, 1915, is your emancipation day. The act approved by President Wilson makes America sacred soil and the Thirteenth Amendment finally becomes a covenant of refuge for the seamen of the world. In the years to come, as you commemorate this great event, you should dedicate a part of the service to the memory of Andrew Furuseth. Except for his intelligent, courageous and unswerving devotion to your cause for twenty-one years you would be bondsmen instead of free men today.[79]

Furuseth's immediate reaction to the news can only be imagined. But the following day he sent his greetings to the Sailors' Union expressing his elation and his sober sense of responsibility for making the Seamen's Act effective: "I celebrate with you ... the freedom gained and the larger hope for the future. When the act just passed becomes operative we shall be free and have the power to protect our freedom. Freedom ever demands loyalty and prudence."[80]

VIII. USING THE SEAMEN'S ACT

THE INK had barely dried on President Wilson's signature on the Seamen's Act when outraged shipowners, newspapers, and magazines began to malign it as they had never done while Congress was considering it. Long before the act went into effect on November 4, 1915, dire predictions were made that it would lead to serious international complications, that it would drive the American merchant marine off the seas, that its safety features were not enforceable, and that there were not enough seamen qualified to meet the high standards it set. These led a host of other charges.

SHIPOWNER OPPOSITION

Leaders in the fight to secure repeal of the act were Robert Dollar, a shipowner who operated most of his vessels under the British flag until wartime conditions forced him to seek protection under American neutrality, and R. P. Schwerin, manager of the Pacific Mail Steamship Company. Both operated companies in the Pacific trade with Chinese crews and white officers. Both claimed that the language clause of the Seamen's Act would deprive them of their Chinese crews and thus make it impossible for them to compete against Japanese vessels. They circulated the story that upon receiving news of the act's passage, Japanese shipowners had celebrated the fact that the United States had legislated itself out of the transpacific trade. William B. Wilson recalled, however, that two years earlier Schwerin had testified before a congressional committee that the Pacific Mail Steamship Company was going out of business because the Panama Canal Railroad Act of 1912 discriminated against shipping companies owned by railroads. Furuseth took genuine delight in quoting Schwerin's remarks to the committee on February 1, 1913: "I want to say that I am done with the American flag forever. I would not raise my hand to raise a dollar for the American flag...." This was the man who set himself up as the champion of an American merchant marine—manned by Chinese crews. Schwerin now told newspapermen that his company was going out of business because of the Seamen's Act. The truth was that the company was being reorganized to divest itself nominally of Southern Pacific Railroad ownership so that it could take advantage of favorable toll rates through the Panama Canal.[2]

Aligned solidly with Schwerin and Dollar were the shipowners on the Atlantic and the Great Lakes, the chambers of commerce in every major port, and the United States Chamber of Commerce. They said they had no objection to freedom for seamen since shipowners had long abandoned their right to force the return of a sailor to his vessel. They had no objection to abolishing allotment and advance because these practices had largely disappeared when the modern steamer with its short voyages supplanted the old-time sailing vessel. The extra quart of water and the extra ounce of butter required by the law would work no hardship because American vessels habitually provided much more than the legal minimum. The unacceptable features of the new law were the "arbitrary" manner in which foreign treaties were abrogated, the language clause, and the provision for half pay for seamen in port.[3]

To answer the charges, Furuseth wrote articles, communicated with friendly journalists, and spoke before any group that would listen.[4] Despite several attempts by the seamen and by neutral and even scholarly groups to arrange for a debate between the shipowners and Furuseth, no shipowner would accept the challenge.[5] Pleading with his audiences to give the Seamen's Act a fair trial, Furuseth told them that Congress had followed the advice of the shipowners for one hundred and fifty years. As a result, the United States had practically no American merchant marine and no American sailors. The new law would, for the first time, place American shipowners on an equal footing with foreign owners. Furuseth charged that American owners were tools of the International Shipping Federation, dominated by British shipowners, who opposed any proposals for building an American merchant marine. Congress, he emphasized, as if it were the clinching point, had listened to the shipowners' arguments, had considered them very carefully, and had rejected them.[6]

Government Misinterpretation

It was true that Congress and President Wilson showed no disposition to reconsider their approval of the Seamen's Act. The subject had been debated too long to have it reopened.[7] It was not through Congress that the shipowners were afforded relief, but through the administration of the law by the Department of Commerce.

Within a few months after passage of the act, Secretary Redfield interpreted the language clause so broadly that it was meaningless. In his view, it was possible for the Chinese crew of the *China* to pass the language test by answering in pidgin English the questions asked by the officers in pidgin English, complete with gestures. Crew members were expected to understand routine orders connected with their jobs, but the fundamental purpose of this section of the act—to eliminate Chinese seamen—was defeated by not requiring 75 per cent of the crew to have real competency in the language of the officers.[8]

On the other hand, the Department of Commerce interpreted the physical examination required for an A.B. certificate so strictly that many men who had been sailing for twenty or thirty years were disqualified. Union members who were color blind, had missing fingers, or were otherwise physically deformed, began abusing Furuseth as vigorously as the shipowners—and probably in less temperate language. Furuseth did succeed in securing modification of the physical examination so that "old-timers" who had demonstrated their ability to do a seaman's job were perfunctorily passed,[9] but he had little sympathy for the Johnny-come-lately's who complained because they could not meet the A.B. requirements. "There are, on the Atlantic," he wrote to Percy Pryor, secretary of the Atlantic Seamen's Union, "men who feel themselves incapable of coming up to the standard of the Able Seaman and, they feeling their weakness, are out against the whole thing, but these are not seamen, they are wasters. . . ."[10]

Whenever the Department of Commerce was asked to interpret the Seamen's Act, the decision was almost always in favor of the shipowners. When it was asked whether the provision for improving the forecastle applied to vessels built after 1897, as Furuseth claimed, or to those built after passage of the act, the department held that it applied only to vessels built after 1915.[11] When it was asked to rule on the meaning of "watch-and-watch" at sea, the department decided that this provision meant that all members of the crew should be on duty an equal number of hours, but it did not require an equal number of men on each watch. Thus the shipowner could have four men on duty during the night and twelve men on duty during the day instead of halving his crew—eight men on and eight men off. Since eight men were not sufficient to man a vessel during the day, the owner would have been forced to hire additional sailors except for the department's ruling.[12]

Secretary Redfield also ruled that foreign vessels whose safety regulations were equal to American standards would not be required to undergo inspection by American officers. Since the laws of most nations satisfied Redfield's rather loose interpretation of equal safety standards, their vessels were thus exempted in practice from the requirement of meeting American standards in every respect. Vessels of foreign nations were also exempted from other equalization features of the law.[13]

Despite the fact that the Department of Commerce had eight months' time to put the "able seaman" section of the act into operation, it failed to provide forms for the men to apply for their certificates until a few days before the effective date. This resulted in a scarcity of men with the proper certificates so that vessels had to be allowed to sail without complying with the law. Furuseth intimated that the failure to certify able seamen until the last moment was a deliberate attempt on the part of the department to create the impression that the law was impractical because there were not enough qualified seamen available to meet its requirements. He wrote bitterly: "The eight months granted by the statute for the preparation to enforce the Act were expended in an effort to find ways and means to avoid the law...."[14]

Relationships between the organized seamen and the Department of Commerce reached a low point after the sinking of the *Eastland* in July, 1915. This vessel, loaded with summer excursionists, was moored to a wharf in the Chicago River when it suddenly overturned, drowning approximately a thousand men, women, and children. Furuseth and Olander charged that the responsibility for the disaster should be placed upon the department's Marine Inspection Service, which had granted clearance to an unseaworthy vessel. Inspectors who were too conscientious about safety provisions, said the union leaders, did not hold their jobs long. Redfield and George Uhler were indignant at the implication that they were morally responsible for the *Eastland* disaster.[15]

Despite every pressure that Furuseth could bring upon congressmen and members of the administration, the Department of Commerce continued its string of adverse decisions.[16] So serious did Furuseth consider its attacks on the law that for two years he left Washington only under the most urgent necessity. He became the lonely guardian of the act as he had been its lonely advocate. He worked as hard to get favorable decisions from the administration as he had worked to obtain favorable consideration from Congress. Secretary Redfield denied that his department was construing the law for the benefit of shipowners, but reports from every port indicated that his generous interpretation was being supplemented by decisions of the local inspectors and customs collectors charged with its enforcement, who were allowing wholesale violations to continue.[17] Furuseth reported disgustedly, "There does not appear to be anything that can be done with the Department itself and this is recognized by practically everybody."[18]

No relief could be requested from Congress, for to raise the question of interpretation of the law might lead to its complete emasculation. President Wilson was too busy with other matters to interfere with the rulings of the department except in most unusual cases. Consequently,

Furuseth began a series of costly court cases to test the rulings on such questions as forecastles, advance, watch-and-watch, and the language provisions. Gilbert Roe, an associate of Robert La Follette, and Silas B. Axtell, a young maritime lawyer in New York, handled most of the cases that went to the Supreme Court. Furuseth was not a silent client. His letters to the attorneys indicate that he considered himself at least an equal in suggesting the cases to be tried, the precedents to be cited, and the line of argument to be used. Every case was followed by Furuseth as if the fate of the entire Seamen's Act depended upon the decision, but even when court rulings were favorable to the seamen, which was not often, the unions were in no position to take advantage of their triumphs.[19]

Before the courts handed down any decisions and before pressure from Gompers, William B. Wilson, and other friends of the seamen forced the Department of Commerce to modify some of its orders, America entered the war. The Seamen's Act was virtually suspended for the duration of the conflict.

It is difficult to assess the true value of the Seamen's Act either to the American merchant marine or to the seamen prior to America's entry into the war. Even Furuseth admitted at first that it was wartime conditions, and not the act, which forced wages up on European and American ships.[20] But at the ISU convention in December, 1917, he said that it was a serious mistake to regard the war as the cause of increased wages for seamen. Without taking into consideration the shipping depression at the start of the European war, he reasoned: "The first increase in wages came four months after the Seamen's Act had come into operation, but more than eighteen months after the war in Europe commenced."[21] In actual fact, the law was so loosely interpreted and so badly enforced that it could not be considered a major cause of the higher wages or of the increase in American merchant marine tonnage.

Organizing a Union

From the union's viewpoint the Seamen's Act was of value to the extent that it aided in the organization of seamen. Furuseth had tried to use the act in December, 1914, four months before its enactment, when he toured the principal Atlantic ports. He had found the sailors apathetic. He had found the shipowners uninterested in his offer to help them secure qualified seamen to meet the standards to be required by the act. He had concluded that organization would have to wait until Congress passed the law.

But Furuseth's first task was to handle several long-postponed problems on the Pacific Coast. For a year he had unsuccessfully been trying by correspondence to halt the trend of the Sailors' Union of the Pacific toward a working agreement with the longshoremen.[22] A second problem was unemployment, which had hit the maritime industry on the Pacific so badly in 1914 that the union, with Furuseth's disapproval, had spent union funds to feed its members. The unemployed, led by a group loyal to the Bodine faction and by some IWW men, could attend meetings while the employed were at sea. They were thus able to override the seemingly hardhearted attitude that the only permanent solution was for some of the men to seek other employment.[23] The opening of the Panama Canal presented a third problem because the Pacific Coast would no longer be isolated from the competition of lower-paid seamen on the Atlantic.[24]

The unemployment problem dissolved before Furuseth arrived in San Francisco in April, 1915, because of an upturn in maritime trade. The problems of the longshoremen and the Panama Canal were solved by becoming inextricably intertwined.

By mail, Furuseth had been unable to prevent the sailors from joining the Waterfront Workers' Federation in San Francisco. In fact, it was only by pleading that the entire fate of the seamen's bill depended upon continued peaceful relations in the industry that he succeeded in preventing the sailors from joining other maritime workers in demands that would undoubtedly have led to a strike just as the bill was receiving its final consideration by Congress.[25] In San Francisco, Furuseth was more successful in detaching the sailors from the longshoremen. He reminded his men of past experiences with the longshoremen, especially their final treachery when they had publicly announced their opposition to the seamen's bill on the ground that it allowed ships to go to sea with sailors so fatigued from handling cargo that they were incapable of handling the vessel.[26] He warned the sailors that if they failed to listen to the lessons of history and fell into the trap of refusing to handle cargo from nonunion longshoremen, they would lose their jobs and the longshoremen would take over all the cargo work.

These arguments might not have prevailed had Furuseth not been able to demonstrate their truth by the problems that arose from interocean travel through the Panama Canal. West Coast ships carried experienced crews who were paid high wages because they customarily helped in the loading and unloading of vessels. When they arrived on the Atlantic, the longshoremen refused to allow the sailors to help in the unloading. The sailors were indignant because the owners started reducing the size and the wages of the crew to meet Atlantic competi-

Using the Seamen's Act

tion. "It seems that we must fight our way over every inch of ground," wrote Furuseth, "if it be not against the owners, then it is against the workers who were, in their opinion, benefited by our helplessness and degradation."[27] In retaliation, he went to the owners and convinced them that slightly larger crews would be able to handle all the cargo if the longshoremen refused, and this could be done with a saving to the owners.[28] To Percy Pryor, secretary of the union in Boston, Furuseth wrote that if the longshoremen refused to handle cargo, then the sailors ought to take the jobs at regular longshore wages.[29] Furthermore, he pointed out that Atlantic seamen's wages would always be lower than those on the Pacific until seamen insisted upon their right to handle cargo within the ship's rail. In addition to these arguments and the demonstrated conflict in interests, Furuseth charged that German agents were trying to cripple American shipping by offering longshoremen $10 per week if they walked out. By these methods he kept the SUP from becoming involved in what might have developed into a general West Coast tie-up.[30]

In 1916 the conflict flared up again when the longshoremen went out on strike. The sailors were sympathetic despite the veiled criticism of the strike leaders in the *Coast Seamen's Journal*. To restrain the sailors from becoming involved, Furuseth was called back to the Pacific Coast in September, 1916. Although he met an extremely hostile reception from the longshoremen, especially in Seattle where he was booed on the streets, he succeeded once more in preventing the seamen from sacrificing themselves for the benefit of shore workers.[31]

While Furuseth was in San Francisco, another matter that attracted his attention was the case of Tom Mooney, arrested for allegedly exploding a bomb that killed several persons during a Preparedness Day parade. Despite overwhelming evidence that Mooney had been "framed" by false testimony secured by District Attorney Fickert, most labor leaders in San Francisco refused to take up the case. All too vividly they remembered the McNamara case, and besides they disliked Tom Mooney because he was a radical who had tried to organize the San Francisco carmen without the sanction of the Central Labor Council. Those labor leaders whose sense of justice was outraged were afraid to make any move because the president of the Central Labor Council, A. W. Brouillet, was known to be working with Fickert. No action could be taken for Mooney until Brouillet was deposed, and everyone feared to take the initiative against a man who many believed was an agent of the Employers' Association. Moreover, war hysteria made it unsafe to stand on the side of the unpopular bomb-throwing radicals.

In this crisis some of the men who wanted justice done called upon Furuseth for help. He was back in Washington involved in negotiations with hundreds of government officials on seamen's affairs. He knew Mooney, and he knew that Mooney had worked with wobblies and had a reputation for threatening violence. All the things that Mooney stood for, Furuseth abhorred. Yet the men in San Francisco had chosen wisely, for Furuseth was convinced that Mooney had not received a fair trial, and he made a special trip to San Francisco to lead the fight against Brouillet. He stayed only long enough to speak before the Central Labor Council, where he rallied the doubtful, awakened the lethargic, and encouraged the timid. When Furuseth finished speaking, there was no doubt as to the outcome. Brouillet was ousted.[32]

Furuseth made several other brief visits to the Pacific Coast before the outbreak of the war, but most of his time was spent in the East.[33] When he was in San Francisco in 1915 shortly after passage of the Seamen's Act, the Pacific seamen decided that the only way to protect and raise their standards was to organize the seamen on the Atlantic Coast. Accordingly, they sent Furuseth and Patrick Flynn, secretary of the Marine Firemen's Union, back east with a $5,000 campaign fund to make use of the act to get the seamen into the union.[34]

Conditions in the East were far from favorable for organization. Shipping on the Great Lakes was very depressed, and seamen who ordinarily left the coast to take the better-paid summer jobs on the Lakes remained in the Atlantic ports. Moreover, the East was now flooded with scores of refugee seamen seeking work in the coastwise trade. Shipping on the Atlantic was in the doldrums. No wonder that Furuseth and Flynn were disappointed in the size of their meetings and the response of the men. One meeting in Hoboken, New Jersey, attracted more than 800 men, but the other twenty-eight meetings in Great Lakes and Atlantic ports yielded a total attendance of less than 1,800.[35] Most disappointing were the firemen. Furuseth wrote:

> The sailors are coming in fairly lively, and if it continues and increases, we shall have them in fairly good condition by the 4th of November. [This is not in accord with other much more pessimistic reports.]
>
> The firemen are in much worse condition,—nationality prejudice is running mad among them. The Irish and Liverpool Irish in Boston, after their manner born, think themselves superior to everybody else. They would like an organization of their kind, supported by contributions from somebody else. They think themselves vastly superior to the Dutchman, but will tolerate him as a contribution payer, but when it comes to the Spaniard, they don't like him to be even that; and as for themselves, they have little or no capacity for living...."[36]

But at least the seamen gave Flynn and Furuseth a sympathetic, if not an enthusiastic, hearing. The shipowners, on the other hand, gave them a cool reception. Furuseth asked them to allow union representatives aboard their vessels to explain the Seamen's Act to the men. It was tacitly understood that the purpose of such visits would be to sign up union members. If the owners refused to permit the sailor to have a visitor in his own home (the ship), then the union could harass them with the regulatory features of the act. If the owners agreed, the act could be inaugurated on November 4 in an atmosphere of friendly relations between shipowners and their crews.

To the union's request, the owners replied that friendly relations already existed between themselves and their men. Furthermore, one of them wrote:

> It is our understanding that this law was passed at the request of and with the full knowledge of all the seamen in the United States, and that they were all fully familiar with all the conditions which they desired to accomplish by the Act, and that being the case, I am somewhat at a loss to understand where your educational assistance now is necessary.[37]

After several such chilling replies, Furuseth concluded: "The idea that we could do anything with the shipowners was a fool's dream; they will do nothing except what they are compelled to do."[38] He became firmly convinced that the shipowners were deliberately creating conditions that would drive experienced men from the sea, so that when the Seamen's Act went into effect, they could show that there were not enough able seamen to run the vessels as required by law.

In January, 1916, the entire shipping picture changed. Because foreign shipowners had raised wages as a result of the war and were hiring large numbers of American seamen, a sudden shortage of qualified men developed. The men on individual vessels asked for and received increases of $5 per month. In March, union and nonunion seamen held meetings all along the Atlantic Coast to demand $45 per month and 25 per cent extra for vessels going into the war zone. On April 14, sailors, firemen, cooks and stewards, and even seamen on foreign vessels answered the union's call to strike in order to enforce its demands. It was really no contest. Seamen were scarce, profits were high, and all the shipowners agreed to pay the new scale.[39] Furuseth's role in the strike had been to encourage "skirmishes" during the first few months in order to build up morale, to discourage full-scale "war" until the union was in a position to win a quick and decisive victory, and to avert any strikes on the Great Lakes and the Pacific until the Atlantic wage issue was settled.[40]

The result was phenomenal. Not only did wages go up in all other districts,⁴¹ but the seamen began flocking into the union as they had never done before. The total membership of the International Seamen's Union jumped from 16,000, which it had maintained for five years before the passage of the Seamen's Act, to more than 30,000 by the end of 1916. The sailors on the Atlantic tripled their membership, and the Great Lakes union doubled in size. The number of union firemen also increased. Growth on the Pacific Coast was less phenomenal because the industry was already highly organized.⁴² As important as the increased wages and membership was the improved morale, which was so high that Furuseth feared the members were under the impression that they could attain anything they desired.

A strong union was Furuseth's most coveted achievement. He believed the Seamen's Act was not the goal but the tool by which the sailors could build a union. Congress could merely create the conditions that would make freedom and equality with other workers possible. Only by their own efforts through the union would the men be truly free. Although less than half of those employed in the seafaring trade had taken advantage of their freedom under the Seamen's Act to join the ISU, the goal of complete organization was in sight. Nothing was impossible. Then came America's declaration of war.

IX. WORLD WAR I

When Congress declared war on April 6, 1917, Furuseth was in San Francisco. He immediately wound up his affairs and returned to Washington. On the long train ride he had time to reflect on his attitude toward the war and his plans for the future. Just a few weeks before, on March 12, he had met with representatives of seventy-eight AFL and five independent unions to clarify the position labor should take toward America's impending entry into the war. He and Olander had not objected to the statement unanimously adopted by the labor conference in support of the American government,[1] but Furuseth had approached Gompers afterward to prophesy: "That sounds the death-knell of the A.F.L., and your forty years work for labor you have destroyed today."[2] Now he was going back to Washington to prevent his own prediction from materializing.

Furuseth and War

In common with the rest of the organized labor movement, Furuseth had always opposed American imperialism and American involvement in war.[3] When many Americans demanded the annexation of Hawaii, he had dissented. Rather than opposing it on principle as imperialism, as did Walter Macarthur and other labor leaders, Furuseth felt that the most effective argument was that Hawaii would be a source of cheap slave labor which would be used to lower the standards of American workingmen.[4] But whatever his argument, his opposition had been vigorous.

Furuseth had taken the lead within the labor movement in warning against becoming so emotionally entangled in the affairs of Cuba that the United States would be drawn into a war with Spain. When war did come, he had exploited the nation's need for skilled men in the Navy by pointing out that remedial legislation was necessary to bring Americans back to the sea. Privately, however, he had written to the union agents advising them to let the scabs join the Navy, but to keep the union men in the merchant marine.[5]

Furuseth had also opposed the building of a canal in Panama or Nicaragua. It is likely that this opposition was based on his fear that the canal would put the West Coast sailors in competition with the lower-paid Atlantic sailors, but publicly he opposed it on the ground that it would plunge the United States into a war of conquest to control the entire Caribbean area.

On many of these issues, Furuseth had started out in agreement with the majority opinion in the labor movement, but when most of the other leaders retreated and then became enthusiastic supporters of policies that they had once opposed, Furuseth refused to change. It made no difference to him that overwhelming public opinion and even his associates supported Hawaiian annexation, war with Spain, and the building of an interocean canal. He was prepared to stand alone.

Now, too, he must stand alone. Again he had started off with the majority in the pious hope that "with the growth of trade unionism in all countries and among all races, the workers will be less and less inclined to kill each other in the interests of their masters."[6] When the war in Europe broke out, he took a unique position which distinguished him from the Socialists, the pacifists, and Gompers. Although he agreed that America should not become involved, he said that American workers should know that the war in Europe was too fundamental to be blamed upon any particular government. Individuals and nations were striving for the fruits of their toil and for national independence. He protested the pacifist "cry for peace where peace is not nor can be, because of the present wrongs imposed and suffered," and he derided those who called for an international police force, because, he said, "no matter how [it is] organized or controlled in our present stage of development, [it] can mean only suppression, stagnation and despair."[7] He even opposed participation in an organization designed to promote a world court on the grounds that "peace is always the main desire of those who are satisfied, that is to say; those who are not disturbed by any new and to the World strange ideas.... The judges would be issuing injunctions against pestiferous agitators who will persist in disturbing the peace with their cries about wrongs...."[8]

When the *Lusitania* was sunk by German submarines, Furuseth might have been one of the first to denounce the cowardly attack on an unarmed merchant vessel. Instead, he chose to denounce the owners because they had sent the ship out improperly manned with inefficient seamen, loaded with war materials, and in defiance of German warnings. He was mainly concerned with pointing out that if the owners had met the standards of the Seamen's Act, many lives could have been saved.[9]

As a close associate of La Follette, Furuseth championed many of his friend's proposals. He urged labor people to support La Follette's resolution calling upon the president to assemble all neutral nations for the purpose of halting the European war.[10] He gave the senator encouragement when he decided to filibuster against Wilson's proposal to arm American merchant vessels.[11] His attitude toward preparedness was echoed by the *Coast Seamen's Journal:* "Organization and more organization is the only kind of 'preparedness' over which the workers have a right to become enthused."[12] The organized sailors in San Francisco endorsed his stand by refusing to participate in the Preparedness Day parade since labor was opposed to military preparedness and did not need to be artificially stimulated for true preparedness.[13]

Conditional Support of the War Effort

But war had come. It would have been suicidal for labor to have opposed the war, and Furuseth undoubtedly recognized this.[14] His disagreement with Gompers was based on two points. Furuseth bore the Germans no personal ill will. In response to proposals by the unions in Allied nations that seamen pledge themselves not to sail with German seamen in retaliation for the submarine campaign, Furuseth refused to condemn the sailor who was merely acting under orders. "Hatred once developed," he wrote to J. Havelock Wilson of the British seamen's union, "does not cease with the war and it will then be used by the shipowners to pit seamen against seamen in the economic struggle."[15] Furuseth had no sympathy with Gompers' Alliance for Labor and Democracy, a group he viewed as a collection of "parlor pinks" and "57 varieties" of Socialists and liberals (though they were actually conservative trade unionists) who wanted the war fought to the bitter end.

His primary difference with Gompers, however, concerned the disposition of labor to promise everything in support of the war without receiving anything in return.[16] The *Coast Seamen's Journal* asked editorially:

> Has he [Gompers] been steadfast to the course mapped out by his constituents, the workers, or has he yielded to the fawning of the plutocratic press that has so suddenly changed its curses to praises?...
>
> To conquer the world for the workers is indeed a glorious and worthy aim. To follow Mr. Gompers when he leads in that direction is a great privilege. To criticize and oppose him when he heads in the other way should be a sacred duty.[17]

For himself and his seamen, Furuseth preferred independence to support the administration, provided something could be gained from such support. This policy was never enunciated, but his actions spoke louder than any resolution. He refused to accept any office in the government which might place him in the position of managing any part of the transportation industry. On every occasion he bargained for as much as he could possibly get for the seamen. Fortunately for Furuseth and the sailors, President Wilson and Secretary William B. Wilson upheld the organized seamen on every controversial issue to such an extent that the question of withdrawing support from the administration never arose.

Furuseth aided the government's war efforts while protecting the interests of the seamen. Upon arriving in Washington he went to the United States Shipping Board, the agency charged with the responsibility of building the merchant marine, and suggested that it might be able to solve its immediate problem of finding ships' carpenters by appealing to the Brotherhood of Carpenters. He also pointed out that when the merchant fleet was built, it would be necessary to find men to man the vessels. This could be accomplished, he thought, if the government called a conference of shipowners and unions for the purpose of attracting the thousands of men who had left the sea before the passage of the La Follette Act. The Shipping Board initiated such a meeting on May 8, 1917. After a series of joint conferences, an agreement was reached on August 8 which provided for increased wages and allowed the unions access to the docks and the vessels. The unions agreed not to enforce the closed shop on those vessels they controlled, in order to allow the government to put young men on board to receive practical experience in seamanship.[18]

Upon Furuseth's insistence, the agreement was embodied in a formal "Call to the Sea," which appealed to the patriotism of former seamen. The "Call" bears many of the characteristics of Furuseth's writing:

TO ALL SEAFARING MEN ASHORE OR AFLOAT

The nation that proclaimed your freedom now needs your services. America is at war. Our troops are being transported over the sea. Munitions and supplies are being shipped in ever increasing quantities to our armies in Europe. The bases are the ports of America. The battlefields are in Europe. The sea intervenes. Over it the men of the sea must sail the supply ships. A great emergency fleet is now being built.... Your help is needed to prove that no enemy on the seas can stop the ships of the nation whose seamen bear the responsibility of liberty.

America has the right, a far greater right than any other nation, to call upon the seamen of all the world for service. By responding to this call now you can demonstrate your practical appreciation of freedom won.[19]

This "Call to the Sea" was to be signed by all parties—shipowners, unions, and government—who had signed the August 8th agreement. Although the agreement was originally limited to the Atlantic Coast, the Pacific Coast shipowners quickly endorsed the terms of the pact.

On the other hand, the Great Lakes Carriers' Association balked, refusing to allow the union access to its ships and docks. Furuseth maintained that the "Call" could not be issued until all parties concerned proved their sincerity by signing the agreement. He thus tried to place the Lake Carriers' Association in the position of impeding national defense by stubbornly rejecting any dealings with the union. In September the ISU on the Great Lakes issued an ultimatum to the association to sign the "Call to the Sea." To prevent a strike, the United States Shipping Board frantically negotiated with the unions and the shipowners. The union agreed not to strike while the government talked to the Great Lakes shipowners, who finally agreed to abolish the Welfare Plan used on the Great Lakes since 1909; but they persisted in their refusal to recognize the union.[20] The "Call to the Sea" still could not be issued.

The situation was allowed to rest until July, 1918, when the union again demanded the signature of the Great Lakes Carriers' Association and a raise from $85 to $100 per month. The ISU condemned the association for its "duplicity, treachery, and outright refusal to cooperate with the government...."[21] A strike deadline was set for July 29. Again the association expressed willingness to abide by all the terms of the agreement as to wages, hours, and other conditions, but absolutely refused to recognize the union in any way. This did not satisfy Furuseth or the other union leaders. Rather than risk a tie-up on the Great Lakes, at the last moment the Shipping Board ordered the shipowners to sign the agreement. Furuseth had succeeded in parlaying a patriotic appeal into a weapon that completely broke the strangle hold of the hated Welfare Plan. By signing, the owners had not only recognized the union, but had also recognized its right to talk to the men on the companies' docks and ships.[22]

Wages and working conditions were also improved on the Atlantic and the Pacific. The labor policies of the Shipping Board and the high freight rates discouraged the owners from offering any resistance to labor's demands. In May, 1918, the Atlantic shipowners agreed to pay higher wages, thereby wiping out the differential between Atlantic and Pacific ports, and in addition they paid a 50 per cent bonus on vessels going into the war zone.[23] Although Furuseth recognized that his bargaining position had been improved by the war, he told the seamen that they could maintain their wages after the war provided they became union men in fact as well as in name. "The power that gave can take also and much more swiftly. It is up to us to do our full duty (as seamen and as union men) now, and then we shall be safe."[24]

In return for the government's support, the union consented to suspension of the able seamen's requirements in the La Follette Act and agreed to coöperate in a recruitment and training program for merchant marine personnel. Old-timers regarded the new recruits as draft dodgers who saw in the merchant marine a way to escape military duty.[25] They complained that the newcomers were worthless aboard a vessel. Union officials realized that in coöperating in this training program they were creating a huge reservoir of men to threaten the future standards of the union. However, they loyally carried out their pledge. In fact, Furuseth insisted that shipowners should disregard their preference for A.B.'s as crewmen and employ trainees. He asked the union members to show the new men how to be good seamen, and he added prestige to volunteers for the merchant marine by persuading President Wilson to issue a special proclamation emphasizing the importance of this service to America.

The Sea Service Bureau, a subdivision of the Shipping Board, was responsible for recruiting and training merchant marine personnel. Furuseth coöperated with the bureau, but he vigorously opposed all suggestions to bring this program under the control of the Navy. Mounting public criticism of high wages paid to sailors, charges of drunkenness and inefficiency, and the complaint of shipowners that there was a shortage of men led the Shipping Board to propose that vessels be manned with Navy personnel.[26] By appealing to President Wilson, by demonstrating that skilled seamen were available if conditions were suitable, by showing that vessels already taken over by the Navy required two or three times the number of men necessary to run them under private control, and by securing the coöperation of the union men whom he advised to "try to give our 'friends' as little ammunition as possible," Furuseth was able to block the move to transfer the merchant marine to Navy control except for the troop transports.[27] There is little doubt that under Navy administration the union would have perished. Furthermore, Furuseth was probably correct in predicting that men would not volunteer so readily for the dangerous and arduous duties of a seaman during wartime if they had to accept military discipline and military pay.

To secure an adequate supply of seamen, Furuseth suggested that former seamen be declared draft-exempt if they registered for sea service. A general order was issued exempting men working in industries vital to the national defense, but its application to seamen was left up to local draft boards. Toward the end of the war Furuseth was successful in securing the release of experienced sailors from the Army.[28] He also recommended to the government that an estimated 5,000 German seamen be allowed to work in the coastwise trade since "a sailor's loyalty is to his ship, not the flag."[29] A strange argument in wartime! In addition, Furuseth pointed out that the recruitment problem would be solved when wages and living conditions at sea were made equal to those of shore workers.

One of Furuseth's most important contributions to the war effort was to keep the demands and actions of organized seamen within reasonable bounds. This was no easy task with prices rising much faster than wages. Furuseth appealed to their patriotism and to their gratitude for the Seamen's Act. Unless the men kept the vessels moving, he threatened, the Navy would take control. Furuseth asked the union officers to repay President Wilson for his fight against the "union wreckers" by "seeing that the vessels are not delayed. . . . Of course this will not be easy, but it can and must be done."[20]

Furuseth's loyalty was handsomely repaid when the Shipping Board agreed in August, 1918, that all its vessels under lease to private owners on the Atlantic would grant preference to union men in filling 60 per cent of the able seaman jobs.[31] But when Furuseth tried to get a 100 per cent preference clause for the unions on the Pacific a few months later, the Shipping Board balked. Commissioner Charles R. Page, in charge of personnel, wanted to issue instructions providing merely that there be no discrimination against union men. Furuseth argued that the Pacific Coast unions had controlled 98 per cent of the tonnage before the war; they had consented to allow graduates of the Sea Service Training Schools aboard the ships, but they had never agreed to give up the closed shop. He notified Page that if instructions were issued without providing for the closed shop on the Pacific, he was through.[32] To Tennison he wrote, "If we cannot get decent treatment while the war is yet on, we know what we are going to get when it is over and we might as well die raising hell as crawling on our knees with our forehead to the ground. . . ."[33] President Wilson intervened to prevent the issuance of any instructions,[34] but the changed attitude of the Shipping Board, dominated by shipowners, signaled an approaching about-face in government policy toward the unions.[35]

When the war ended, the ISU had increased its membership by 50 per cent over the prewar years. The Atlantic unions had doubled in size,[36] and all the unions were stronger numerically and financially. New, vigorous leadership had arisen on the Atlantic Coast, which was now the largest district in the international. The unions on the Pacific controlled virtually all shipping, and on the Great Lakes they were making rapid strides now that the Welfare Plan was no longer in effect.

Paris Peace Conference

With union affairs progressing satisfactorily, Furuseth turned his attention to the forthcoming Peace Conference, suspecting that an international plot was afoot to destroy the Seamen's Act. His fears were aroused by a statement by Edward M. Hurley, chairman of the Shipping Board, that he was going to the Peace Conference to secure equalization of standards in the merchant marines of the world. To Furuseth, equalization with European nations meant lowering American standards to foreign standards.[37] "The question of the Peace Conference makes me shiver," he wrote. "There is where the seamen may be stripped of all hope or where the seamen may become free in all countries."[38]

His suspicions were intensified by friends in Washington and by union officials in New York.[39] As soon as he learned that President Wilson was planning to go to Europe, he warned him that the International Shipping Federation would attempt to use the Peace Conference to destroy the Seamen's Act and thus prevent the United States from building a merchant marine.[40] Furuseth decided that he would have to attend the conference to protect the freedom that he had gained from Congress.

> Seven centuries in the abyss of slavery; three years of God's free air, then back to the abyss.... If such is to be our fate, I want to make one last real fight for freedom no matter what the consequences may be....[41]

> I dread this trip. It is worse than anything I have so far tried.[42]

Furuseth arrived in England in December. He made inquiries of shipowners and of union and government officials concerning the action to be taken on the Seamen's Act at the Peace Conference. When everyone denied any knowledge of plans to discuss the act or even to consider any matters dealing with seamen, Furuseth became all the more suspicious. He extracted a promise from J. Havelock Wilson that the British seamen's union would support the American law, but Wilson refused to help extend the principles of the act to Europe. Furuseth had feared, even before he left the United States, that Wilson had been seduced by the "fawning press" and the honors bestowed upon him during the war,[43] but he had no more success with the executive board of the British union. He tried to tour the Scandinavian countries to secure support for his position, but his travels were restricted by passport regulations, and he made only limited headway in the countries he visited. Even when representatives of many of the European seamen's unions met to form the International Seafarers' Federation,[44] Furuseth could not dissuade them from taking the same position as J. H. Wilson. In fact, it was at the seamen's conference in Paris on March 11–14, 1919, and not at the Peace Conference, that a proposal was adopted to ask for a meeting with the shipowners to establish a standard wage for all seamen.[45]

The Peace Conference[46] did not discuss seamen in particular, but established the International Commission on Labor Legislation, of which Samuel Gompers was elected chairman. Furuseth was not an official delegate, so he sat through most of the sessions in a corner of the room. He wrote notes to the commissioners and consulted with them on strategy. Gompers left the conference with the impression that all Furuseth's objections to the proposed charter for an International Labor Organization under the League of Nations had been met by the adoption of amendments which Furuseth himself had suggested. He discovered later, however, that after the conference Furuseth had written a letter to President Wilson denouncing the League of Nations and the International Labor Organization as a plot to kill the American merchant marine—the only material gain that the United States had made from the war.

The debate on labor's attitude toward the League of Nations took place at the AFL convention in June, 1919. The largest numerical opposition to the proposed Treaty of Peace and to the League came from a group of Irish nationalists who were only concerned with making sure that nothing in the treaty could be used to hinder the independence of Ireland. When a qualifying amendment was added to allay their fears, this resistance melted away. The most serious opposition came from Furuseth because he argued on principle.

That the delegates considered this topic important is attested by the amount of time allotted for debate. That the officials of the AFL thought the issue important is shown by the number of prominent labor leaders who took the floor. President Wilson was concerned. He sent several of his close advisers to consult with labor and to try to influence the convention.

Andrew Furuseth opened the debate on the resolution of the Committee on International Affairs:

> It is a disagreeable job that I am now endeavoring to perform. I have struggled with myself for two months. . . .
>
> Mr. Chairman, I lost in the fight. I cannot, no matter what the consequences may be, keep my peace now. It is the only place in which I can enter my protest, and whether that protest be heard or not, or whatever the result may be to me, there is something in me that ceaselessly, night and day, commands me to

speak.... It may be it will be stated that I am opposing here something that President Wilson wanted, and that my gratitude to him should be of such a nature as to keep my mouth shut... but my nature is such that I cannot follow blindly, no matter who it may be, and I cannot accept without protest the diluted labor propositions that, under pressure, the President of the United States felt himself compelled, no doubt, to accept....

He then proceeded to argue that Section 23 of the Covenant of the League of Nations established a superlegislature that granted to the League the power to determine humane and just labor conditions in all the member nations. The superlegislature had the power to make recommendations or draft conventions. Recommendations would be made to Congress and would be acted upon in the same manner as all labor legislation, but draft conventions were treaties that would be discussed by the Senate in secret, like any other treaty. There would not be any way for labor to know what the Senate was considering behind its closed doors. Approval of the peace treaty would establish the authority of this superlegislature forever, because there was no provision for amending a peace treaty. Once adopted, it would become part of the supreme law of the United States. True, upon Furuseth's protest, a clause had been added to provide that no action taken by the League should be construed to "diminish the protection afforded by... existing legislation." But Furuseth asked, "Who is to determine whether what they propose is to diminish or to increase it? The League itself in the last extremity...."

As an example of the way in which the League would act to destroy all that the American labor movement stood for, Furuseth pointed to the labor charter adopted in Paris. Instead of approving labor's right to "free association," it granted labor the right of joining "lawful combinations." But who would determine what was lawful? The League of Nations. The Peace Conference refused to include a section patterned after the Thirteenth Amendment to the Constitution on the ground that there was no slavery in Europe. But when the matter was raised of applying the principle of this amendment to allow seamen to leave their vessels in safe harbors, the conference promptly voted it down. The American delegates secured the adoption of a phrase from the Clayton Act which stated that labor should not be regarded as a commodity or an article of commerce; but the drafting committee changed this to read that labor should not be regarded as "merely" a commodity or article of commerce, thus "changing an absolute negative to an equally absolute positive...." The conference changed the American principle of "equal pay for equal time" for women to the less satisfactory principle of "equal pay for equal value." After citing a number of other examples, Furuseth concluded that "there isn't a solitary thing here that leaves any of the American ideals in this document...."

One of the main dangers to American labor was the way in which the International Labor Organization was to be constituted.

> Who is to sit in this wonderful body? One man representing labor.... Then there is one representing the employers... and two representing the United States government. That is three to one as I read it. It might not be now, because Woodrow Wilson has the appointing power, but what will it be under his successor do you think?
>
> Now, then there are four men for each nation.... But, mind you, the British Empire has twenty-four because it is represented over and over again.... What chance have you got? Have men all of a sudden become saints? Are men no longer controlled by their interests? I have found no evidence of it anywhere, and I can't accept that philosophy.

He concluded by pointing out how the superlegislature, dominated by British capitalist interests, would act to destroy American sea power by emasculating the Seamen's Act. "And so from whatever side I look at it, from the labor question and from the seamen's question, I can't vote for this thing...."

Furuseth then sat down to listen to a withering attack on his position by every top official of the AFL. Matthew Woll led off by pointing out that every agreement is a restriction upon sovereignty. Every union that joined the AFL gave up part of its sovereignty. No superlegislative body was being created because no act of that body would be valid until ratified by all the contracting parties. Although the United States might gain little at first from efforts to improve standards, those efforts would be helpful in raising standards throughout the world.

William Green of the United Mine Workers, while expressing his "profound regard" for Furuseth, averred that Furuseth did not fully understand the labor clauses. He readily admitted that the document was not perfect, but neither was any agreement between employers and workers. To reject the Covenant of the League of Nations because it was not perfect would mean a return to the theory of the survival of the fittest, with war as the only method of settling international disputes. Another miner, J. H. Walker, said that he had been stumping the country for the League of Nations. Everywhere he had spoken, he had found opposition to the labor provisions of the covenant—from employers especially—but he had never expected to find opposition in a labor convention.

The principal speaker, however, was Samuel Gompers. His speech was partly a personal attack on Furuseth and partly an argument for approving the League's covenant. Of Furuseth he said: "Some people are so constituted that if you were to give them Paradise, they would find some fault with it." He charged Furuseth with an unpardonable breach of organizational etiquette when he wrote a letter to President Wilson without consulting the labor delegates. Despite repeated inquiries, Furuseth had failed to reveal the contents of his letter. In Paris, he said, Furuseth had congratulated him for securing adoption of amendments that had been suggested by Furuseth, but now he opposed the same documents. Gompers ridiculed Furuseth's warning that labor's rights would be destroyed in secret sessions of the Senate, for it would act upon conventions openly arrived at by the International Labor Organization and known to everyone. He demanded that Furuseth produce the names of English labor leaders who, as Furuseth had charged, were "shocked" at the League's covenant. All the British labor organizations had endorsed the covenant. He ended by quoting a telegram he had just received from President Wilson in which the president stated that the labor provisions of the covenant, although slightly weakened, "will constitute a most serviceable Magna Charta."

ISU delegates to the AFL convention reported that Furuseth had received a tremendous ovation when he finished speaking. This may have been so, but it never materialized in votes. Of more than 30,000 votes cast, only 420 opposed the committee report endorsing the League. Two of the five ISU delegates went along with the majority. Many of those who voted with Furuseth did so because they feared Irish independence might suffer or for other reasons of their own.

The entire affair illustrates many facets of Furuseth's character: his suspicion of international conferences dominated by governments and businessmen; his jealous regard for the welfare of the seamen; his complete disregard of personal political ambitions; a certain amount of presumptuousness in believing that seamen and labor leaders in Europe and America were all wrong, and only he was right; and a bulldog tenacity in holding on to ideas and policies long discarded by the rest of the labor movement.

X. CHANGING FORTUNES

IN 1919 there were more serious problems confronting the sailors of America than opposition to an ephemeral League of Nations. Just before Furuseth had come to the Atlantic City convention of the AFL, he had met with shipowners, other union officials, and the United States Shipping Board on June 4–6. Freed from wartime restrictions, the seamen, like other workers, were eager to consolidate their gains and to win improvements in working conditions while the postwar prosperity lasted. The purpose of the conference called by the Shipping Board was ostensibly to find a method for handling labor disputes in the maritime industry. The conference had grown out of a demand by the Atlantic union in the spring of 1919 for what it called "a modification of the working rules." These changes included an eight-hour day in port, a three-watch system for the deck crew, and, most important, preferential hiring for union members.[1]

1919 STRIKE SUCCEEDS

During the war the Shipping Board, as the largest single employer of maritime labor and the agency that practically paid the bills for all the shipping companies, had actually determined wage policy.[2] The government was anxious to shed this responsibility, and at the conference in June the board proposed the establishment of a commission of shipowners and seamen to adjust disputes. The owners agreed, but the union refused until the owners would grant union preference. Without such a clause they could break the union, which would then lack equal bargaining power in the joint commission. The June conference and other meetings on the same subject broke up without agreement. The owners objected to what they called a closed shop for the foreigners in the seamen's union, but when the union offered to amend its demand so that preference would be given to American citizens first, and then to union members, the hypocrisy of the shipowners was exposed by their rejection of this proposal.

On July 10 the firemen on the Atlantic went out on strike. Within a few days 40,000 men had left their ships. In addition to their former demands, they asked for an increase from $75 to $90 per month for firemen and sailors. Circumstances favored the strikers. Employment opportunities on shore were good, the companies were still making enormous profits, and the Shipping Board maintained a "hands-off" policy. Three weeks later, the strike was settled on the basis of a $10 increase. The union did not win a preference clause, but this did not make much difference because the strike had served to organize almost all the seamen on the Atlantic. They won an eight-hour day in port and the three-watch system for some but not all of the deck hands. As Furuseth predicted, the Pacific Coast shipowners granted similar concessions a few months later without a strike.[3]

Furuseth's role in the 1919 strike is extremely interesting. He played a leading part in all the prestrike negotiations with the government and the owners. It was undoubtedly Furuseth who suggested the preference clause for Americans as a solution to the shipowners' objection to the closed shop for the union. He tried desperately to avoid a strike, but he failed. Once it began, he apparently played little part in it beyond issuing public statements in its support and attempting to keep the Shipping Board neutral. In the middle of the strike, before a settlement was in sight, Furuseth decided to go to the Mayo Clinic for observation.[4] Whatever ailed Furuseth was not a sudden emergency. His decision to go at this time indicates that he had no control over the Atlantic unions conducting the strike, and that they, perhaps, had little desire to have him interfere in their affairs. The essential difference between them appears to have been over the demand for preference for Americans. Furuseth thought this clause most important. The Atlantic union leaders obviously would find it difficult to justify to at least 50 per cent of their members, who were not citizens, a clause that gave preference to citizens before union members. It was much easier to demand and justify a pay raise. Furuseth was out of sympathy with an increase because he believed that this would reëstablish the differential in wages between British and American seamen which had been wiped out during the war.[5]

The time had passed when Furuseth was the union. He had helped to bring the infant Atlantic organization to maturity. Now it was strong numerically and financially.[6] It no longer felt it needed Furuseth's help in Congress or the financial aid he once wheedled for it from the Pacific Coast. The Eastern sailors cried for independence, and they got it. Their first effort in 1919 under extremely favorable circumstances was successful.

Government and Shipowners Defeat Union, 1921

The next attempt in 1921 shattered the organization so that it never revived.[7] On January 25, 1921, the American Steamship Owners Association and Admiral William S. Benson of the Shipping Board re-

Changing Fortunes

quested the unions on the Atlantic to accept a reduction in wages. The unions offered to meet with the owners on condition that the existing contract not be modified to the "length of driving the American from the sea." A series of meetings was held in April. The owners pointed to a world-wide shipping depression. Freight rates from New York to Liverpool, for example, had fallen from a high point of $3.21 per hundred pounds in 1918 to 41 cents in 1921.[8] Thousands of seamen in Atlantic ports were standing in soup lines.[9] The owners, supported by Admiral Benson, proposed a 15 per cent wage reduction and a modification in working rules.

Union officials, under Furuseth's guidance, attempted to delay the wage reduction or to trade it off against other concessions by placing the problem of maintaining an American merchant marine before the question of wages and hours. Furuseth charged that the conditions offered by the shipowners were part of an international conspiracy to drive Americans from the sea.[10] The union repeated its request that citizens be given first preference in hiring, and union members second. It asked for enforcement of the La Follette Seamen's Act and abolition of the Sea Service Bureau, which was continuing to recruit seamen when there already was a surplus.

The shipowners refused to grant any kind of preference clause,[11] and they disclaimed all responsibility for enforcing the Seamen's Act or for maintaining the Sea Service Bureau. The union then rejected their request for a reduction in wages. It correctly concluded that the 15 per cent cut was on base pay and that the actual reduction would be closer to 35 per cent, since all overtime would be eliminated by going back to the two-watch system in which men worked eighty-four hours per week instead of fifty-four hours, as on the three-watch system. An additional important change in the working rules, to which the union objected, was the provision that withdrew the right of union officials to visit the docks and vessels.

Since the owners and the union could not come to an agreement, Admiral Benson announced that beginning May 1, 1921, the wages and working conditions offered by the owners, which he considered reasonable, would go into effect on all government vessels. This meant that the new conditions would become effective on all vessels because the government owned or leased 70 per cent of the merchant marine. Before the deadline, Furuseth offered to submit the entire matter of the maintenance of an American merchant marine to the president. It may have galled him to propose arbitration, a procedure he had long and vigorously opposed, but there was no alternative. Nothing more could be gained by negotiation and the union was in no position to fight, with thousands of men idle and ready to scab. A decision by the president, even if it were unfavorable, would provide the union with an excuse for not striking. Admiral Benson and the shipowners refused to allow the union this "out."[12]

On May 1 any seaman who refused to work under the new rules was locked out. Any owner who leased government vessels was forced to accept the Shipping Board's decree for fear that the vessels would be taken back by the government. The seamen fought valiantly but vainly. They defied injunctions on the East Coast. On the West Coast, where the owners had presented similar demands to the seamen, the men answered the union's call to strike even though half the union members were already unemployed. Because of the many scabs available, the ISU had to depend upon the Marine Engineers Beneficial Association, a group of key licensed officers who were also on strike, to keep the vessels from sailing. But the MEBA on the Atlantic Coast was a new organization inexperienced in striking. When it capitulated, the strike was lost. On government vessels the original offer made to the union was put into effect, but private owners did not feel bound by any agreement, and wages were slashed still further.[13]

Furuseth had foreseen the disaster that followed the 1921 strike, but even among his closest associates he had acquired a reputation as a "calamity howler," and they had given his warnings slight heed. In 1920 he had urged the ISU to establish schools in seamanship to replace the training schools set up by the Sea Service Bureau and to raise the standards of skill among seamen so that they would become indispensable to the owners. Although the ISU authorized an expenditure of $15,000 for such union schools, the response from the membership was so apathetic that the program never developed.

Furuseth had also cautioned against overconfidence. The swollen membership of all the unions represented book members with a high turnover. They were not educated in the principles of unionism, and they could not be relied upon in a crisis. The arrogance of some of the new men had manifested itself in a growing disrespect for the authority of the ships' officers—conduct unbecoming a true seaman.[14] In December, 1920, Furuseth had predicted a "panic of limitless proportions" and had advised union officers to teach their members that it was easier to raise wages on the floor of a union meeting than in a conference with the owners.[15]

His pessimistic warnings went unheeded. But it is doubtful that his advice could have saved the union from the owners' determination to free themselves from the shackles imposed upon them by the war. They deliberately provoked a strike in order to break the union; a reduction in pay could have been negotiated, but the humiliating conditions attached to the reduction forced the union to make a stand. Captain Walter Peterson, spokesman for the Pacific Coast shipowners, told an investigator many years later, "I was hired during 1921 to break Andy Furuseth's union, and I broke it."[16]

DECLINE OF THE ISU

Furuseth saw the membership of the ISU crumble from 115,000 in 1920 to a low of 16,000 in 1923—the same number of members the union had had before passage of the Seamen's Act.[17] The members melted away, vanished, disappeared. Only the hard core remained. To these men Furuseth preached, "We have lost a battle, but we will win the campaign." In secret instructions to the officers, he advised them to make use of the "Oracle." The "Oracle" was the technique of harassing shipowners with last-minute delays and inconveniences, now made simple by the Seamen's Act. For example, a seaman who failed to receive half of his pay in port could libel his vessel and hold it up until the owner paid him in full. Sailors working on vessels that did not operate on the two-watch system and firemen on vessels that did not use the three-watch system could, under the Seamen's Act, leave the ship at a critical moment and demand full pay. Since there was no penalty for desertion beyond the forfeiture of half pay, the seamen could quit at a time most inconvenient for the shipowner. The key to the effectiveness of the "Oracle" was the willingness of the members to sacrifice their jobs or part of their pay, or both, for the benefit of the union. Time and again Furuseth called upon the seamen to make the necessary sacrifices. He explained that the Seamen's Act was not their golden goose, but the gun with which to shoot the goose. The membership failed to pull the trigger.[18]

Even the officers of the union were less than lukewarm to Furuseth's pleas. The acting secretary of the SUP wrote: "As to working the oracle, that might have been alright years ago, today the men won't do it, they seem to have lost heart, it is a sad state of affairs and the only thing to do is go along the best we know how, until times improve."[19]

For a veteran like Furuseth, who recalled the sacrifices willingly made by others in the past, it was often difficult to conceal contempt for those unwilling to give up a day's pay to strike a blow for their own freedom. He pleaded with the men, but instead of giving him a sympathetic hearing, many shouted back at him that their lot was due to his misguided devotion to an outmoded craft unionism.

FIGHT AGAINST THE IWW

It did little good for Furuseth to argue that craft unionism had nothing to do with the union's defeat, that the seamen's unions in France, Holland, Sweden, and Norway, which were organized on an industrial basis, had also suffered defeats in the postwar period. Instead of blaming craft unionism, he said, the sailors should blame themselves. Battles were won by the spirit, the devotion, and the strategy of the membership, not by forms of organization.[20] Nevertheless, many union members were strongly attracted by the philosophy of the Industrial Workers of the World, that all maritime workers should unite for a common goal. In the holocaust of defeat, the wobbly philosophy of the total emancipation of the workingman from exploitation spread so rapidly that it threatened to engulf the ISU.

Since 1913, when the Spanish-speaking firemen had left the ISU to join the IWW, the remaining wobblies within the union had lain dormant or had formed small, ineffective units of the Marine Transport Workers' Industrial Union.[21] After the war, taking advantage of internal differences in the ISU and the large influx of new members, they aligned themselves with sympathetic factions to achieve important changes. On the Atlantic they were successful in moving the union headquarters from Boston, where for more than twenty years a handful of men had run the organization, to New York, where the overwhelming majority of the membership resided. They also put considerable effort into organizing Negro and Oriental seamen. On the Pacific Coast they were even more effective. Against Furuseth's advice they established a rotary hiring system in the union hall. This system (now in effect in all maritime unions) was opposed by Furuseth because every attempt at rotary hiring in the past had ended in failure, with members blaming the union because they could not take jobs offered to them. On the other hand, Furuseth argued, captains charged with the responsibility of vessels and passengers could not pick men they could trust. He predicted that the government would step in to destroy the rotary hiring system and the union.[22] The greatest victory for the wobblies came in January, 1921, when they elected J. Vance Thompson as editor of the *Coast Seamen's Journal*. Although Thompson was probably not a wobbly, he was sympathetic to many of their ideas, and he gave them an opportunity to express these ideas in the union's official newspaper.

The strength of the IWW in the Atlantic Seamen's Union became apparent immediately after the 1921 strike, when its adherents were successful in overruling the officers' decision to discontinue the strike

Changing Fortunes

relief program which had been costing the union $6,000 per week. The officers claimed that all the real seamen had found jobs after the strike, but the unemployables, led by IWW agitators, came to the meeting and, after a near riot, took over the organization. On the technicality that the union had never legally notified the state of Massachusetts, under which it was incorporated, of its change of address to New York, the officers moved the funds and records back to Boston, where they could operate unhampered by the wobbly-ridden membership.[23]

The situation on the West Coast was even more serious. Seattle and San Pedro were almost completely under the control of the IWW, and in San Francisco the wobblies outnumbered the old-line union members at every meeting. In July, 1921, the steam-schooner operators came to the union with a proposal to settle the strike. Aside from a reduction in pay and other objectionable features, the operators insisted in a famous "clause 8" that the sailors agree to work cargo with any longshoremen whether union or nonunion. The SUP had agreed to similar clauses many times before, but the temper was different now. The sailors refused to scab on the longshoremen, and at their meeting on July 11 the agreement was rejected.[24]

Andrew Furuseth hurried back to San Francisco. He was convinced that the strike was lost and that it was better to accept any agreement rather than annihilation. Never in sympathy with the idea that the sailors should sacrifice themselves for the longshoremen, he believed that the rejection of the agreement was engineered by the IWW in order to waste the SUP's funds on a useless struggle so that the wobblies could take over the remains of the union. San Francisco was combed for every available sailor to attend a meeting at the Civic Auditorium, at which Furuseth spoke. Invoking the spirit of all the past martyrs of the union, impugning the honesty and sincerity of his opponents, and calling for a demonstration of personal loyalty to himself, Furuseth was able to arouse the members to such a pitch that Thompson and others who had led in the rejection of the agreement trembled for their lives. While police guarded the entrance, the riotous meeting inside the auditorium completely reversed its previous, almost unanimous stand.[25]

Furuseth then went to the operators with the union's acceptance of the agreement, but they refused to sign because the union was controlled by the IWW. Furuseth promised that within sixty days Thompson and all the leading wobblies would be expelled. The promise was fulfilled. The *Coast Seamen's Journal* was taken over by the ISU and transferred to Washington, D.C., where it would be completely out of the hands of the West Coast extremists. The owners, however, now refused to renew any agreement. When Furuseth offered to point out the wobblies who were sailing if the owners would give the union agents permission to visit the ships and docks, the owners replied that they knew the wobblies as well as the union agents did. Since the wobblies continued to sail, Furuseth concluded that the owners were in league with them. He used this and evidence disclosed by Basil M. Manly, former chairman of the National War Labor Board, to charge that the wobblies were employed by the owners for the purpose of destroying a real union. As long as employers continued "treating the sea as the cesspool of human society," he said, they would attract only "thieves, smugglers, and users of narcotics, dirty and crummy in person, dirty and revolutionary in speech...."[26] He intimated that the owners would like to see the sailors join with the wobblies so that the union would become subject to the criminal syndicalism laws. No charge was too base to be hurled against the union wreckers.[27]

The IWW returned Furuseth's attacks in kind. He was called "an armchair sailor," "an informer," "the personification of narrow American bigotry," "reactionary and a tool of the shipowners," "a grafter," and every other foul name in the IWW lexicon.[28] The spectacle of two rival labor organizations competing for the loyalty of the maritime workers continued for two years. The only fortunate result of this conflict was that the ISU and the ILA agreed on a temporary peace to enable both of them to resist the inroads made by industrial union advocates.

In the end, the combined forces of the AFL, the government, and the shipowners defeated the IWW. Without any real control of shipping anywhere in the United States, the Marine Transport Workers' Industrial Union answered the call of the General Defense Committee of the IWW to participate in a nationwide general strike scheduled for May 1, 1923, to force the government to free all political prisoners—those arrested under criminal syndicalism laws. In addition to this principal objective, other extreme demands were presented to the shipowners.[29]

The strike actually occurred on April 26. The ISU, of course, had no scruples about manning the ships that the wobblies deserted. Some ISU members went out on strike with the IWW, but most of them remained on their jobs while ISU officials negotiated with the United States Shipping Board in Washington. Furuseth was in San Francisco during the critical negotiations in April and May, but his long campaign against the wobblies finally "paid off." The Shipping Board agreed to grant a 10 per cent raise and other minor concessions. This effectively undercut the IWW strike. The men returned to work disillusioned with the IWW leadership, but they went back without joining the ISU.⁹⁰

Furuseth had coöperated with the government in a war in which he did not believe, for the purpose of helping the seamen build a powerful union. He had succeeded in building that union and in achieving the highest wage scale and the best working conditions for seamen in American history. He thought that the danger to these standards was in the Paris Peace Conference, but the enemy was at home. It destroyed his dream.

XI. DEFENDER OF THE SEAMEN'S ACT

ANDREW FURUSETH lived for more than twenty years after the passage of the Seamen's Act. He spent the major part of each of those years in Washington lobbying to enforce and to strengthen the act.[1] In all that time he failed to secure the passage of a single important piece of legislation. At first Congress was in no mood to consider either strengthening or weakening the Seamen's Act. Then came the war with its abnormal demand for seamen. The union sacrificed its legislative gains in return for more important contractual gains with the shipowners. Immediately after the war the union was so strong that it could win from the owners what it could not win from Congress. But the union's defeat in the 1921 strike marked the end of any concessions either from the shipowners or from Congress until the New Deal days.

IN THE COURTS

Failing to receive adequate administrative enforcement of the Seamen's Act after its passage in 1915, Furuseth turned to the courts rather than to Congress for relief because reconsideration by the legislative branch might lead to worse instead of better laws. Few unions spent as much money in litigation as the ISU.[2] As president, Furuseth decided which cases should be contested, which lawyers should handle them, and what line of reasoning should be used. Maritime attorneys, who had received unofficial blessings (and business) from the union, kept Furuseth informed on every important case that arose in any American port.

Most of the cases that the union fought through to the Supreme Court concerned interpretations of the Seamen's Act. They involved the authority of Congress to nullify seamen's contracts made in a foreign port; the question of whether the half-pay provisions applied to foreign seamen; the issue of whether the watch provisions meant that each member of the crew should serve an equal number of hours or whether the entire crew should be divided into equal watches; whether advances made in foreign countries could be deducted from wages earned when the seaman was paid off in the United States; the right of seamen to desert in a foreign port; the meaning of the term "half pay"; and many other questions.[3]

Although the courts upheld the constitutionality of the act, the decisions were generally adverse to the seamen's interests. A notable exception was the interpretation of the division of watches in *O'Hara* v.

Defender of Seamen's Act 165

Luckenbach, in which Justice Sutherland, who had been instrumental in securing passage of the act when he was a senator, wrote the opinion in favor of the union. Even after the decision, however, the vessels continued to run on Kalashi-Watch because the men actually preferred sleeping through the night rather than changing watches every four hours.

Usually Furuseth disapproved of taking any case that did not involve maritime law,[4] but there were some exceptions. He endorsed Paul Scharrenberg's vain attempt to prosecute the Dollar Steamship Company for hiring crews in violation of the Alien Contract Labor Law and the Chinese Exclusion Act.[5] He pinned great hopes on the attempt to outlaw the shipping offices maintained by the Shipowners' Association of the Pacific Coast on the ground that they were an illegal restraint of trade under the antitrust laws. After years of court battles on this case, a decision favorable to the union was obtained, but by that time the owners had revised the procedures of their shipping offices to come technically within the law. Unofficially, they continued to force all seamen to be hired through their offices.[6]

Many of the court cases were undertaken to secure clarification of the act or to reverse administrative interpretations of it. There is little doubt, however, that after 1923 the purpose of many of the lawsuits was to harass the shipowners with legal action at a time when the union had no economic power. Litigation could be minimized, Furuseth told the Shipping Board, if preference in hiring were given to union members.[7]

IN CONGRESS

Whenever the courts rendered adverse decisions, Furuseth attempted to plug the legal holes in the Seamen's Act by introducing remedial legislation. An opportunity to rectify the early "mistakes" of the courts and the administration appeared during consideration of the Merchant Marine Act of 1920. Confronted with the problem of what to do with the enormous merchant fleet built during the war, Congress turned it over to private owners at a fraction of the original cost and supported it by many indirect subsidies. To obtain the seamen's support or at least their silent consent to the subsidy provisions, several sections were added to the Merchant Marine Act to strengthen and clarify the Seamen's Act. This was done without Furuseth's approval or endorsement because he regarded the entire bill as wrong in principle. The act clarified the intent of Congress to make the abolition of advance and allotment applicable to foreign vessels. (The Supreme Court later held in *Jackson* v. *S. S. Archimedes*[8] that when these payments were made in a foreign port, they were legal and not covered under the act.) Perhaps the most important section enabled the seamen to sue for personal injury either under the common law or under provisions similar to existing railway labor legislation.[9]

Despite the unfavorable court decisions, the Seamen's Act could have been effective if the administration had interpreted and enforced it as the union leaders thought it should be. Repeated protests to the Department of Commerce, the Shipping Board, and other government agencies brought only slight improvement, largely because they were dominated by shipowners. Furuseth's main complaints concerned the failure to enforce the provision that 75 per cent of the crew must understand the language of the officers, failure to require vessels to carry the legal minimum of A.B.'s, nonenforcement of the watch-and-watch provisions, the granting of A.B. and lifeboat certificates to unqualified personnel, and decisions to lower the manning scales. As an example of how badly the law had been enforced, the *Seamen's Journal* in March, 1930, called attention to the fact that since January 1, 1925, not a single muster had been made of any vessel to determine whether the crew qualified under the A.B. requirements of the Seamen's Act.[10]

Failure to enforce the act, Furuseth believed, had resulted in a serious deterioration in the American merchant marine. In fact, the situation had become so bad that he advised his union brothers at the 1926 AFL convention: "If you can travel on the railroad, don't go on a ship. The kind of men that the shipowners have dug up from somewhere are of such an inefficient class that they could not do what is necessary for a seaman to do in the hours of danger."[11] The sinking of the British vessel, the *Vestris*, on November 12, 1928, with the loss of 110 lives gave Furuseth an occasion to denounce the "gentlemen's agreement" between the government and the shipowners to overlook the provisions of the Seamen's Act. The tragedy could have been avoided, he claimed, if the vessel had been adequately manned.[12]

Many of the defects in administration might be remedied, Furuseth thought, if the bureaus handling personnel problems, such as the Bureau of Steamboat Inspection and the Sea Service Bureau, were transferred from the Department of Commerce and the Shipping Board to the Department of Labor. The Department of Commerce and the Shipping Board were concerned primarily with profits and not with the welfare of the workers or the passengers. Bills to effect this transfer did not receive serious consideration from Congress. The Sea Service Bureau continued to recruit merchant marine personnel at a time when many experienced seamen were out of work. It was charged with black-listing

Defender of Seamen's Act

union men and even hiring aliens in preference to American citizens who were union members. The continued existence of the bureau after the war was a constant reminder to the union that the government would never allow it to gain a monopoly of merchant marine personnel. On several occasions Furuseth induced congressmen to introduce amendments to appropriation bills which would have denied further funds to the bureau, but this tactic was not successful.[13]

Other bills introduced through Furuseth's efforts also failed to pass; the little that the seamen asked was usually dragged through Congress for years and then dropped. Attempts were made, for example, to establish a load line in the coastal trade. Although an international treaty providing for load lines in the foreign trade was adopted, similar safety laws for the coastwise trade were defeated.

One type of legislation for which Furuseth lobbied, without success, was designed to secure from the government what the union could not accomplish through its own efforts. Reversing a long tradition of opposition to a continuous discharge book, the union proposed what it had formerly called an "industrial passport," provided it did not have a column for the master's comments and did not have to be surrendered to him when the voyage began. The book would be simply a record of the ships on which the seaman had served, the capacity in which he had served, and the length of service. Since some kind of identification was necessary, a government discharge book of this kind would be preferable to the shipowners' grade book, which could be used to intimidate the sailors and to black-list those who had the temerity to complain of conditions aboard ship. Moreover, a government-issued book would help the union by making the owners' discharge books illegal and by providing a means to eliminate radicals—first the IWW and later the Communists—from the merchant marine.[14]

In 1929 Fiorello La Guardia introduced a bill requiring that the stewards on vessels flying the United States flag be American citizens. The union could not enforce such a demand upon the owners, and Congress refused to do it. In 1923 and again in 1934, Furuseth tried to persuade Congress to end the shipowners' practice of hiring crews in foreign ports for round-trip voyages. The bill would have required every seaman on an American vessel to sign off when he reached an American port. Thus the men who would not take advantage of the Seamen's Act to desert at half pay would have to sign off at full pay. Nothing came of the proposal. In 1930, after the ISU had failed to abolish the owners' shipping offices by either union or court action, Senator Robert La Follette, Jr., introduced legislation to make hiring through government shipping offices compulsory. "No private shipping office," said Furuseth, "whether kept by the owners, unions, or individuals, has ever been able to keep itself honest and clean. Nothing but the direct selection by the man who has to have the work done has ever tended to the development of the right kind of men."[15]

The single piece of legislation that occupied a major part of Furuseth's time was an amendment to the Immigration Act of 1924. Furuseth had foreseen that the act would endanger the seamen's right to desert, but he had supported it because, with the rest of the labor movement, he believed that the restriction of immigration was paramount.[16] Under the new law, alien seamen were allowed to leave their ships and stay in the United States for sixty days. Stringent immigration quotas put a premium on smuggling aliens into the country, and one loophole through which they could enter was by signing on as a crew member and deserting in America. To stop this illegal entry, it was proposed that seamen coming ashore be required to put up heavy bonds. This, of course, would have made it impossible for any foreign seaman to desert his ship under the provisions of the Seamen's Act.

Furuseth objected to this solution. Instead he introduced in every Congress a bill that would require the steamship companies to leave port with a crew equal in size to that with which they had arrived.[17] He argued that shipowners or their officers were receiving from $200 to $1,000 for signing on extra crew members with the object of allowing them to desert in America. To prevent this, he proposed that officials of the Labor Department be allowed to examine the crews of incoming vessels, and that anyone found to be a mala fide seaman be deported at the expense of the vessel. To the shipowners' objection that it was impossible to determine who was a bona fide seaman and who was not, Furuseth answered that any experienced official could tell the difference. Furthermore, he proposed that no one ineligible to enter the United States as an immigrant (an Oriental) be allowed to enter an American port except under the flag of his own country. This, he said, would stop the illicit smuggling of men and narcotics by the Chinese crews coming into America.[18]

Perhaps nothing illustrates better the significance attached to Furuseth's proposals than the featuring of the defeat of the deportation bills in the lead editorial in the July, 1934, *Seamen's Journal*—the very month in which a West Coast maritime strike was bringing about a revolution in water-front labor relations. Part of the value of the bills was in their propaganda effect. The ISU came to Congress and the public with a plan for closing the loophole through which, it was esti-

Defender of Seamen's Act 169

mated, as many as 40,000 persons per year illegally entered the United States. The shipowners, on the other hand, had no solution except to abolish the seamen's right to desert, a policy now completely out of tune with the times. Illegal entrants came on ships, and it was natural for the public to feel that the responsibility for violating the law lay with the shipowners.

The deportation bills were also important because they preserved the equalization principle of the Seamen's Act. But even more significant was their potential effect on the merchant marine. The regulations with regard to alien crews, Furuseth believed, would be so burdensome to the shipowners that they would result in the use of citizens, and thus might stem the seemingly endless tide of aliens willing to take jobs on American vessels under any conditions. Furuseth told Congress that American seamen were demoralized by the sight of American vessels manned by foreign crews. The enactment of the King bill to deport aliens who had entered the United States under the guise of seamen was necessary for the morale of the American merchant marine, to keep American sailors from "drinking in communistic ideas until they have neither time nor patience for their own country's ideas."

The King bill, like all its similar predecessors, failed to pass even though it received considerable support from many who were sympathetic to the seamen and from others who were antagonistic to foreigners. Although there is little doubt that Furuseth was sincere in his arguments, he made use of antiforeign, pro-American feelings to advance the cause of American seamen—his men.[19] In every bill providing for subsidies to shipowners, he insisted that a subsidized vessel be required to carry a certain percentage of Americans in its crew. He carried on a continual battle with the United States Shipping Board and finally succeeded in obtaining preference for Americans on vessels operated with funds contributed by American citizens.

Furuseth had opposed the employment of Orientals on any ships except those of their own country long before the Seamen's Act was passed, and he continued his agitation as long as he remained in Washington. The new menace to American marine wage standards after World War I was the Filipino. Furuseth believed that the Filipino was especially dangerous not only because he would work for the same low wages as the Chinese, but because, as a resident of an American territory, he was considered a citizen for the purposes of the subsidy laws. Furuseth said that the Filipino was not legally a citizen and, furthermore, was a poor seaman. "I have sailed with Filipinos," Furuseth told a congressional committee in 1930. "I know from personal knowledge and experience that they are very difficult to live with on board ship. The reputation of the Manila man, as we seamen call the Filipino, is that of being treacherous, swift with the use of the knife, and always in the back."[20]

BEFORE PUBLIC OPINION

While Furuseth guarded the Seamen's Act against misinterpretation and lack of enforcement, shipowners expressed their own ideas about what ailed the merchant marine. Even though many provisions of the act were modified by administrative or court edict to conform with the owners' desires, there still remained numerous restrictions burdensome and irksome to them. Most irritating was Section 13, requiring that at least 55 per cent of the deck crew be able seamen. As soon as the war ended and the union moved to enforce this provision, which had been suspended during hostilities, the shipowners introduced a bill to reduce the A.B. requirement to 20 per cent and to lower the standards for an A.B. certificate for native-born Americans. Furuseth was ultimately successful in blocking the bill's passage in the Senate after it had received the approval of the lower house.[21]

Great Lakes shipowners tried to secure exemption from some of the safety provisions and from the A.B. and watch-and-watch requirements, but Furuseth thwarted them by reminding Congress of the *Eastland,* the *Empress of Ireland,* and other inland marine disasters. Representative Arthur M. Free of California repeatedly introduced legislation on behalf of the Pacific Coast shipowners. They were particularly annoyed by the provision for watch-and-watch at sea and by the frequent requests for half pay when seamen reached port. Their proposed bills would have permitted vessels to run on Kalashi-Watch and have given the master the option of deciding when and how much to pay his men. Furuseth's vigorous objection to these bills kept them from being seriously considered by Congress.

These piecemeal attacks on the Seamen's Act reflected the shipowners' desire for a complete revision of the maritime code. The government, the owners, and the United States Chamber of Commerce at various times in the 1920's made suggestions for such a reorganization. Furuseth often served on the commissions considering a new codification of the navigation laws. He always submitted a minority report. The majority, consisting of shipowners and their representatives, proposed among other changes that punishment for desertion in foreign ports be restored, that the half-pay provisions be amended to allow the captain to use his judgment, that punishment for delaying a vessel by failure to

Defender of Seamen's Act

report to work on time be increased, that the three-year experience requirement for obtaining an A.B. certificate be substantially reduced, that the opportunity for any water-front "sorehead" to delay a vessel by asking for a muster of the crew to determine whether it was in compliance with language and A.B. requirements be eliminated, that seamen be required to carry a continuous discharge book, that the watch requirements be substantially modified, that crew members be denied the right to call for a survey of seaworthiness, that owners be exempted from personal-injury suits arising from quarrels between crew members, and that shipowners and the government be relieved of the responsibility of bringing back seamen stranded in foreign countries.[22]

Some of these recommended changes were undoubtedly reasonable, but Furuseth made them appear monstrous proposals to reëstablish serfdom in the merchant marine. He told the Chamber of Commerce that its campaign against the half-pay provision, on the ground that seamen dissipated and bought narcotics, might "be effective with some simple-minded landsmen who know nothing about the seamen's life except what they read in the papers, and equally little about the seamen's earnings, but it will not work with members of Congress...."[23] Furuseth was willing to admit that seamen got drunk as often as any other workers, but real seamen did not rush off to dissipate their half pay in drink and dope. Such practices were carried on by the Chinese, by students, and by riffraff who were hired because they worked for practically nothing. The remedy for drunkenness and desertion, like most of the other evils complained of, lay in the hands of the shipowners. They had merely to pay decent wages to attract the real seamen back to the sea.[24] Analyzing one set of proposals, Furuseth wrote to the United States Shipping Board:

> The suggested amendments are based upon the assumption that neither skill nor experience is needed in the management and navigation of ships, and therefore ships may safely be sent to sea without seamen and manned by crews of casual laborers picked up on the streets. Having reduced the status of seamanship to that of unskilled labor, the proposed amendments would reduce the unskilled laborer himself below the status of ordinary humanity.[25]

Coupled with the demand for relief from the exactions of the Seamen's Act was the shipowners' continual cry for government subsidies.[26] Always the argument was that the high wages paid to American seamen prevented the American merchant marine from competing with foreign ships. This was a false assumption, Furuseth said. In the first place, wages were approximately the same, and where they were not, they would be equal if the Seamen's Act were allowed to operate. Second, wages constituted less than 2 per cent of the total operating cost of a vessel. Other experts placed the percentage of wage costs as high as 12 per cent, but it was generally admitted that substantial savings could be made by greater efficiency in the use of fuel and in loading and unloading, and that income could be increased by a more systematic solicitation of business.[27]

Even when Victor Olander, ISU secretary-treasurer, and Paul Scharrenberg, editor of the *Journal*, favored some limited form of subsidy, Furuseth was able to convince the 1926 ISU convention to go on record against all subsidies. It was agreed, however, that vessels should be "adequately compensated" for carrying mail.[28] To meet foreign competition, the convention held, the government should enforce the Seamen's Act and extend its principles. Shipowners should be allowed to buy their vessels any place in the world where the price was cheapest, and to repair their vessels in foreign ports without paying duties on such repairs. American railroads should be required to terminate agreements that gave foreign shipowners preference in handling cargo.

The result of government subsidies, Furuseth told the National Conference on the Merchant Marine in 1933, was to place a premium on inefficiency. At one time the owner's self-interest dictated that he hire the best men because they were the most efficient. Then the shipowners had convinced Congress that they needed subsidies to build an American merchant marine. Instead, they had used the funds to hire inefficient help—Chinese and other foreigners who were more amenable to control. Real seamen left the sea rather than submit to the humiliating conditions imposed by the owners. As a result the reputation of the American merchant marine had declined to such an extent that American shippers and passengers preferred to use foreign vessels.[29]

President Roosevelt's proposal to grant outright subsidies to shipowners, even though it contained a proviso that every crew member must be a citizen or eligible to become one, drew from Furuseth the comment, "I have never seen anything so rotten in all my years in Washington."[30] Told that the officers and men on the Atlantic Coast favored the subsidy proposal, he confided to George Larsen, acting secretary of the SUP, that they obviously did not know what they wanted.[31]

But Congress was forever in a generous mood to shipowners. The owners asked and Congress gave. Furuseth must have inspired, or at least agreed with, the editorial comment of the *Nation* on this give-away program under the Republicans in 1922. "Our wiseacres in Washington with as much grasp of the situation as a boy sailing peanut shells in a

Defender of Seamen's Act

bathtub, propose a subsidy that would keep American dollars at sea but leave American sailors ashore."[32] When shipowners countered this objection with the suggestion that seamen also be subsidized at $20 per month provided they joined the Naval Reserve, Furuseth told President Coolidge that sailors did not want to become "tipsters."[33] Moreover, any subsidies to seamen would be deducted from their wages. Putting men in the Naval Reserve was not an honest method of encouraging Americans to go to sea, but a subterfuge for creating a strike-breaking agency.[34]

If shipowners were sincere in their desire to build an American merchant marine, they would abandon their policy of ruling by "force and fear," cease hiring Orientals to replace Americans, and offer decent wages and better living conditions. For the solution to the problem was not in having more and more ships flying the American flag, but in having more and more seamen. Furuseth's continued repetition of this point, his insistence on liberty and actual sea experience as the basic ingredients for developing sea power, and his heavy emphasis on the importance of sea power are well illustrated in the following excerpts from his pamphlet, *Sea Power and Its Development*:

> Sea-power is in the seaman. Vessels are seamen's tools and tools finally belong to those who know how to use them.
> Sea-power has at all times meant World power. Those who controlled the sea always went where they wanted to go; stayed where they wanted to stay; took what they wanted and brought it home. Control over the sea has at all times brought independence and wealth. Sea-power was always in the seamen. The vessels (the tools used) have been altered and improved upon as experience and knowledge increased. But the sea has remained unchanged through all the ages. So also the seamen. The qualities of mind and body that were needed in the seamen of the earliest times are yet needed and there can be no real seamen where those qualities are not. The sea has been a prison wall to the weak and timid, a highway to the strong and a field of honor to the daring and venturesome men....
> To develop a large number of trained seamen, to foster and develop a tendency to the sea in the population, has ever been the care of statesmanship. Nations have fought over fishing grounds, not because of the fish to be caught, but the seamen to be trained in the use of those grounds.
> The sea-power of the Nordic Race was developed in freedom. The seamen of this race knew nothing of bondage as applied to themselves. The common hazard made them loyal to each other and ready to obey orders from their leaders. *They were patient of discipline, impatient of bondage....*
> Man is not by nature a seaman. The sea, the vessels, the life is so distinct from man's natural mode of life that it has always taken years of training to make a seaman. His thoughts and feelings need the training as absolutely as does his body. Nearly all real seamen began the life in early youth. It was always

one step at a time from boy to master. The sea has not changed. Human nature has not altered very materially. The training is as much needed as it ever was. Seamen are not made on shore. They are not taught in a correspondence school and very seldom in a training vessel as they are known and managed. As no man became a swimmer except by going into the water so no man, whatever his ancestry, becomes a seaman except at sea....[35]

EVALUATION

For more than twenty years Furuseth had fought for the enactment of the seamen's bill, and for another twenty years he had devoted himself to defending it from emasculation. A lifetime devoted to a single piece of legislation. Was it worth while?

The answer is not simple. Evaluation of the Seamen's Act is difficult because it was never interpreted by the courts as its originators had planned and never enforced by the administration as its advocates thought it should be, and because it became enmeshed with other conflicting legislation. Changing economic conditions, political considerations, and world events make it almost impossible to isolate the Seamen's Act as a factor in the evolution of the American merchant marine.[36] Although Furuseth was among the most vociferous in damning every administration for failing to enforce the act, he was, at the same time, adamant in insisting that it was fundamentally successful.[37] The criterion for a true evaluation should be the extent to which the act fulfilled its original promise.

The Seamen's Act would never have been proposed had it not been the intention of its originators to use it to build a strong union. It might be claimed that the act was responsible for the phenomenal rise of the ISU during the war and the immediate postwar period, but it would probably be more accurate to give the credit to the wartime scarcity of seamen, the favorable attitude of the administration, and the enormous total expansion of the merchant marine. When the Shipping Board began to look with less favor upon unions, when the merchant marine declined, and when economic conditions deteriorated, the ISU diminished to its prewar strength. During the twenties the union was too weak and its members were too apathetic to take advantage of the act for organizational purposes. The union might have deteriorated even further without the act, but this is questionable. The revival of the union in the New Deal era had little to do with the Seamen's Act.

Another important objective claimed for the act was to build the American merchant marine by forcing its competitors to meet American standards. Mountains of statistics could be cited either to prove or to disprove the contention that it accomplished this aim, but in light of the conflicting data presented by Furuseth and by the shipowners, one is forced to conclude that the evidence is not decisive. Wage differentials for the unlicensed crews on British and American vessels were about 30 per cent before the Seamen's Act was passed. During the war wages were almost equal. In the postwar period the difference of approximately 30 per cent was revived. But factors such as rates of exchange, number of holidays, pensions, unemployment compensation, and other considerations outside the wage scale—the types of vessels, the ports visited, and the routes taken—tend to confuse the true picture.[38] The increasing number of desertions in United States ports did not necessarily prove that foreign seamen were trying to equalize their wages; probably many of them were seeking to evade the immigration laws.[39]

Because of early administrative interpretations, the Seamen's Act never seriously tended to force foreign vessels to meet American safety requirements. Even on American vessels the language requirements, which were supposed to eliminate allegedly incompetent Chinese crews, failed to operate because the Orientals were taught enough English to pass the simple language test. And the provision for A.B.'s either was not enforced or was evaded by obtaining certificates, especially during strikes, from government officials who "coöperated" with the shipowners. In justice it should be said that the safety provisions of the act did raise American standards over those of most other nations.

The Seamen's Act was supposed to bring Americans back to the sea. Statistically it could be proved, especially during World War I, that the merchant marine was manned by a greater percentage of Americans, but was this owing to the act or to the declining supply of foreign seamen?[40] Wages rose and fell in response to economic conditions and the strength of the union, not as a result of the Seamen's Act.[41] Conditions aboard ship and the treatment of the men were improved materially, at least in part because of the changed legal status of the seamen. The act could be and was used to prod shipowners and masters into more humane treatment of their crews. Perhaps the most important accomplishments are incapable of measurement. These were a changed public attitude toward seamen, a realization on the part of the public and the seaman of the dignity and importance of his work, and an increasing self-respect which came with liberty.

More important than the act itself was the fight for the act. It gave the union a program. It held up an ideal of liberty more worthy of sacrifice than wages and hours. To the public and to Congress, this fight presented the union in a most favorable light. The campaign for legislative reforms brought about many of those reforms by the pressure of public opinion long before Congress took action.

Was the effort worth while? If one believes that the fight for human dignity, for freedom, and for self-preservation is worth while, then Furuseth made an important contribution to civilization.

XII. LONELY WARRIOR

FROM 1920 TO 1935 Furuseth assumed a prominent role in the affairs of the international seamen's unions even though he was out of step and out of sympathy with the philosophy of the overwhelming majority of European seamen. Seven times after World War I he visited Europe for the purpose of pushing his viewpoint, almost always without success. His objectives were to extend the principles of the Seamen's Act to European nations, to guard against measures that might nullify the act in America, and to safeguard the interests of the seamen as opposed to the longshoremen.

FREEDOM FOR THE SEAMEN OF THE WORLD

After his failure to realize any of his principles at the Paris Peace Conference, Furuseth looked toward the newly formed International Seafarers' Federation as the best agency through which he could push his program. In contrast to the International Transport Workers' Federation, it was not dominated by Socialists or by landsmen such as longshoremen and railroad workers. Besides the powerful British and American seamen's unions, the ISF consisted of representatives of seamen from France, Belgium, Holland, Norway, Italy, Sweden, and several other countries. The ISF proved to be a fragile agency.

In 1920 Furuseth, with Paul Scharrenberg and Oscar Carlson, attended a series of meetings in Europe. First, there was the International Conference of Seafarers in Genoa, Italy, on June 11–14. At this meeting the seamen discussed the proposals they would favor at the International Labor Organization Conference scheduled to consider maritime problems a few days later. The main purpose of the ILO conference was to draft an international convention for an eight-hour day and a forty-eight-hour week for seamen. Since there was little need to convince seamen of the necessity for such a convention, the preliminary meeting of the sailors' representatives spent considerable time debating Furuseth's proposal to extend the principles of the Seamen's Act to all Europe. Although the delegates from most nations expressed lukewarm approval of "Furuseth's law," the British union, with almost half the votes, defeated his motion. The British sailors argued that they had no objection to the law in America if American seamen wanted it, but they did not believe it proper for a seaman to be able to break his contract while denying his employer the right to "sack" a seaman protected under the same contract. They cited instances of Americans who deserted in British ports and then became so desperate for jobs that they offered to work in return for passage back to America, thus competing unfavorably with British seamen. They said that Furuseth exhibited typical American modesty in giving credit to the Seamen's Act for all wage increases in Europe during the war. Higher wages had been won by the men themselves through organization, not through the act. The British union had completely revolutionized the seamen's status through the international strike of 1911 long before the act was in effect.[1]

Since the United States was not a member of the League of Nations, American seamen were not allowed to participate in ILO meetings. A motion to seat an American as a delegate was defeated. The Americans then wrote to the ILO chairman that they had no desire to take part in a conference whose purpose was "not to liberate the seamen, to make them free men, but only to ameliorate the conditions of the yet remaining serfs."[2] Ironically, the conference (made up of one representative for labor, one for the shipowners, and two each from the governments of participating nations) adopted the principle that desertion was a civil and not a criminal offense, even though at their own meeting the seamen had voted it down.[3]

Although the ILO conference came as close to recommending Furuseth's principles as was possible in such an international gathering, he was extremely critical of its accomplishments. Proposals to provide shipwrecked sailors with unemployment indemnity and to establish employment agencies for seamen, he thought, were fraught with perils of black-listing. The convention setting a minimum age of fourteen for seamen would endanger the existing standard of age sixteen in most countries. Because of the opposition of British shipowners, the conference failed to agree on the major question—the limitation of hours of work.

Because J. Havelock Wilson thought that limitation of hours could be accomplished by direct negotiation with the shipowners, he called a meeting of the International Seafarers' Federation for August 5 in Brussels. Furuseth spent the intervening time in the Scandinavian countries propagandizing for freedom for the seamen.[4] In July the Danish seamen went on strike. Wilson was out of sympathy with the purpose of the strike and was opposed to the political leadership of the Danish seamen's union. He failed, as president of the ISF, to render any effective aid to the strikers who were members of his federation. Furuseth sided with Wilson. When he received $1,000 from the ISU for the strike, he turned the money over to the ISF secretary instead of to the strikers. The Scandinavian unions were thus alienated from the ISF, which they believed represented the narrow national interests of the British union, and were receptive to the invitation of the International Transport Workers to join a seamen's section. Other unions also deserted the ISF, and within a few years all that remained was a paper organization consisting of the stanchly loyal Furuseth and the British unions.

Although the main purpose of the August meeting of the ISF was to plan a campaign for the eight-hour day, Furuseth was allowed to present his program for freeing the seamen. Probably realizing that there was not much point in opposing the stubborn American, and hoping that he would support the British proposal for an international strike unless the eight-hour day was conceded, the British delegates allowed Furuseth's motions to pass without opposition. On the other hand, Furuseth and Scharrenberg abstained from voting on endorsement of the international strike on the rather flimsy excuse that they had not received instructions on this matter from their union.

In 1921 the ILO called another conference specifically for the purpose of discussing the eight-hour day. Since there would be no opportunity to introduce resolutions on freedom for sailors, the ISU did not send representatives. Officially the union explained that American seamen would not be present because United States shipowners would not be represented.[5]

Furuseth attended the secretariat meeting of the International Seafarers' Federation in Paris in July, 1922, where he joined forces with J. H. Wilson to prevent the complete disintegration of their organization before the onslaught of the International Transport Workers' Federation and the Red Trade Union International. He told the gathering that if the ISF decided to merge with the ITWF, the American seamen would withdraw. He was as much opposed to uniting with shore workers on an international level as on the local level in San Francisco. "How landsmen who know nothing about seamen's lives and seamen's traditions and do not care to know," he declared, "can possibly 'safeguard' the economic interests of the seamen will always remain a mystery to me."[6]

Returning to America after two months in Europe, Furuseth reported that the Continent was on the verge of plunging into another war. It was his firm conviction that Europe was divided between the "haves" and the "have-nots." The League of Nations, he thought, was established to protect the "haves," and the World Court was created to sanctify the League with the legal cloak of respectability which was once supplied by the Church or the monarchy. "In continuing to support the League ... we [the AFL] are ... submitting our hand to the shackles, our feet to the gyves and our bended back to the scourge."[7]

Furuseth's special venom was reserved for the International Labor Organization. In 1924 the ILO submitted to its member nations a draft convention for an International Seamen's Code, based on the results of the Genoa conference in 1920 and several subsequent meetings. Furuseth felt that the code violated the instructions of the Genoa conference, which had agreed to grant freedom to the seamen. Despite assurances from Albert M. Thomas, the director of the ILO, that the American Seamen's Act would not be endangered, Furuseth replied: "If the Labor Section of the League of Nations cannot find anything which it can do for the seamen, except bondage as you propose, then it were certainly better that the Labor Section had never been created." He accused the framers of the code of being ignorant of maritime conditions and advised the ILO to spend its time abolishing slavery where it was "rampant within the League's jurisdiction in place of trying to abolish freedom where it has been gained."[8]

To defeat the draft conventions, Furuseth went to Europe in the summer of 1925 and again in 1926. The original drafts were turned down at an ILO conference in 1925, but not because of the objections that Furuseth had made.[9] The revised drafts presented to the Ninth Session of the International Labor Conference in Geneva in 1926 did not meet Furuseth's approval either. The workers' group at the conference, composed almost exclusively of members of the ITWF, was not anxious to hear Furuseth repeat his "hardy annual" appeal to free the seamen, but it finally consented to admit him to a closed meeting for half an hour to present his case. He spent part of his time denouncing the provision for a continuous discharge book for seamen as an "industrial passport." (The ISU was at this time asking Congress to provide a continuous discharge book for seamen.) He attacked the provision for the repatriation of seamen, because, he said, the expense of repatriation was transferred from the shipowner to the seaman. But he aimed his main fire at those provisions that in his view made abandonment of post in a safe harbor a criminal offense. The fundamental error of the entire code, in his opinion, was that it failed to recognize that maritime law applied only to the ocean and the open roadstead, and that the master and servant law applied in the harbor.[10] Actually, of course, Furuseth would have been opposed to any international treaty, for he feared that the United States would have to adopt the lower standards set by such a treaty, instead of recognizing the principle of equalization provided for in the Seamen's Act.

Lonely Warrior

Furuseth was hard put to explain why the shipowners opposed the draft conventions and all the workers' delegates favored them. One explanation he fancied was that the shipowners secretly desired the conventions to pass, but they opposed them in order to get the seamen to vote for them.[11]

Furuseth's lobbying activities in Europe in 1925 helped to defeat the first drafts partly because his presence showed that the seamen were not united in their demands. He failed to achieve any substantial changes in the draft conventions of 1926 because he was isolated from the main stream of the European labor movement and from most of the seamen's unions.[12]

In 1929 Furuseth returned to Europe for the purpose of opposing an ILO draft convention which, he claimed, would exclude seamen from loading and unloading cargo. By the time Furuseth arrived, however, the original draft covering this particular section had been withdrawn. He stayed in Europe for six months, visiting different ports to determine the methods by which aliens were being smuggled into the United States under the guise of seamen. In Norway he visited his family for the last time, and he spent several weeks in England helping the British seamen's union in a struggle with a rival organization established by the British Transport Workers.[13]

While Furuseth was in Europe, the extremely important International Conference for Safety of Life at Sea was held in London. The Department of Commerce had asked William Green, president of the AFL, to name a labor representative to be a member of the American delegation. Familiar with Furuseth's attitude toward international treaties and his record at the 1913 Conference on Safety of Life at Sea, Green asked Victor Olander to serve, but Olander was unable to go. Furuseth was not asked, and it would not have been politic to invite any other member of the ISU. Furuseth's failure to comment on this slight indicates that he was hurt.

He had plenty to say about the treaty as it was finally drafted. From 1929 to at least 1936, he stubbornly opposed its adoption on the same ground on which he had opposed the 1913 treaty: it would nullify and eventually result in repeal of the Seamen's Act because it would permit foreign vessels to compete with Americans on the lower standards it allowed.[14] To a gathering composed primarily of shipowners, Furuseth exclaimed:

> Men, if you pass this treaty, what do you do? You surrender the right of the men in Congress to pass laws governing not only American ships but foreign ships coming within its jurisdiction.... You would surrender that, surrender

all the right to determine what kind of equipment, what kind of crew, what kind of conditions there shall be on board of the vessels on which your women and children are to travel. My God, men, where is your humanitarian sentiment and your national sentiment carrying you? . . .

What is it you want, gentlemen? Do you want a merchant marine? Do you want sea power or do you want money? If you want sea power and a merchant marine and will go after it honestly and truthfully, you will get the money too. If you go the other way, you will lose the money and all the rest.[15]

There must have been considerable criticism of Furuseth's international junkets both because many members failed to understand or agree with the purpose of these trips and because of the heavy drain on an almost empty union treasury. One two-month trip by Furuseth and two other officers cost the union $6,000 exclusive of their salaries.[16] The care with which Furuseth prepared the financial reports of his travels indicates that he was not unaware of the criticism, but he continued to make the trips because he was so completely convinced that representation in Europe was essential to the welfare of American seamen. He was also convinced that he had succeeded, against the combined opposition of European governments, shipowners, and seamen, in preventing the complete destruction of the Seamen's Act.

Upon his own suggestion to Secretary of Labor Frances Perkins, Furuseth was appointed as one of the American delegates to the Preparatory Technical Tripartite Meeting of the Principal Maritime Countries, held in Geneva under the auspices of the ILO from November 5 to December 6, 1935. Furuseth had been quite ill earlier in the year, and he seemed to be more interested in a vacation in Europe at government expense than in the purpose of the conference, which was to prepare an agenda for the 1936 ILO meeting. In Geneva, however, the eighty-year-old Norwegian spoke frequently, and often at great length, for the equalization principles of the Seamen's Act. But he made no important contribution to the meeting aside from adding interest by expressing a viewpoint shared by no other delegate.[17]

Because Furuseth was seriously ill during much of 1936, Paul Scharrenberg was chosen as the labor representative to the ILO conference that considered the agenda prepared the previous year. The draft convention to which Scharrenberg agreed must have shocked Furuseth, but there was no comment from the "Old Man." His day in international maritime politics had ended.[18]

An Unyielding Conservative

Just as Furuseth's policies became anachronistic on the international scene, so his conservative views served to isolate him from the main stream of labor's thinking in the United States and even in his own union. Because of his many years of devoted service, labor leaders gave his increasingly eccentric opinions a respectful, if not a sympathetic, hearing. Almost always in the minority at AFL conventions, with many of the old-timers no longer in attendance, Furuseth became a lonely figure who haunted the lobby rather than the convention floor. There he might at times be seen in animated discussion with younger, admiring delegates. He might be chiding the convention for deserting what he considered the principles of the trade-union movement, he might be explaining why shore workers never understand the seaman, or he might be discoursing on Assyrian land laws, the Code of Hammurabi, Shakespeare, or the Bible. Most of the "discussion" was a monologue.[19]

On the floor of the convention, Furuseth was never troubled by the thought that he might be offending influential interests, or past, present, or future allies. He spoke his mind even when he knew that his cause was hopeless and that his fellow delegates from the ISU would not support him. His speeches were usually lengthy and inclined to ramble. On one occasion Daniel Tobin of the Teamsters' Union interrupted Furuseth's prolonged discourse on the injunction, the Declaration of Independence, and world history to ask whether the speaker was for or against the proposition before the convention—a resolution against unemployment insurance.

Furuseth was inclined to oppose reforms and reformers. "Do-gooders" offended him by lumping together their accomplishments for criminals, prostitutes, and seamen. He attacked the Workers' Education Bureau, an arm of the AFL supported by intellectuals and left-of-center trade unions, because he claimed its publications advocated principles contrary to those of the labor movement.[20] He refused to allow the American Civil Liberties Union to use his name because that organization defended the civil liberties of wobblies.[21] He bitterly denounced the liberal and socialistic League for Industrial Democracy for advocating government ownership of the merchant marine, which, he said, was also the position of the Chamber of Commerce.[22]

When most of the labor movement had abandoned its traditional opposition to regulating labor relations by law, Furuseth argued against minimum wage laws even for women. Reliance on government, he warned, would destroy the labor movement. He characterized Paul Scharrenberg's proposal to amend the Constitution to give Congress the power to establish a six-hour day as "half-baked." If the principle were established that government could regulate the hours of labor, workingmen would soon find themselves being forced to work twelve instead of six hours per day.[23]

In the discussions on shortening the hours of work as a remedy for meeting the unemployment problem of the thirties, Furuseth not only opposed government regulation but also expressed serious doubts as to whether the trend toward shorter hours should be considered progress. Technological improvements and shorter hours would destroy civilization by destroying the skills that men had developed over the centuries. He suggested a revision of the patent laws to eliminate the destructive effects of automatic machinery.[24]

A cardinal point in Furuseth's philosophy was his respect for workmanship. He abhorred any idea, any society, that threatened to destroy the skilled free craftsman. He told the students at the University of California on Labor Day, 1927:

> Work is worship—to labor is to pray, because that is to exercise the highest, the divine faculties implanted in us as the sons of God. It matters not if the labor be the writing of a thesis or the digging of a ditch, it is the use of the same divine faculty to labor—to create—and upon its proper and free use depends the life of individuals, nations and races....[25]

Expressing the same idea somewhat earlier to a labor audience, Furuseth said: "Labor . . . is the continuation of creation. If it is exercised in freedom and in joy then there is ample reason why we should celebrate...."[26] To one so firmly convinced of the holiness, the dignity, and the joy of labor, the reduction of hours of work was not necessarily a blessing.

Old-age pensions and unemployment insurance also came under fire from the rugged individualist. Unemployment insurance, he thought, would require a system of industrial passports which would give the employer almost unlimited black-listing power, would strengthen the employer by granting him authority to decide whether or not the worker was entitled to insurance, and would rob "the working man of his independence and courage."[27] Speaking on old-age pensions at the 1926 AFL convention, Furuseth likened the labor movement to an army—a fighting army—which must be fed raw meat occasionally to keep it in fighting trim. An army does not win battles by looking after the wounded, but by fighting.

> Sometimes it is better to let the wounded die, sometimes it is better to let the old die than to sacrifice the fire of fighting and the ability to win battles on the part of those who are fighting.
>
> This appeal for old-age pensions, this appeal for sickness insurance, this appeal for unemployment insurance—what is it? When it comes to the point of real issue it is nothing more nor less than sentiment, that stands in the way of real fighting.[28]

Victor Olander (who spoke in favor of old-age pensions) had to explain to the shocked delegates that beneath his friend's rough exterior, which sometimes made him "a little irritating to the casual observer," was a heart, a mind, and a soul devoted to labor's welfare.

Furuseth was an outspoken exponent of all proposals to extend political democracy. He favored extension of the direct primary. He even defended the right to filibuster in the Senate on the ground that it allowed an opportunity for the people to make their will felt while the legislative mill stood still. He justified his opposition to flexible tariffs by arguing that they would remove from the people's representatives the basis of political democracy—control of the purse strings. In the debate on the tariff issue, he accused its advocates, such as Matthew Woll, of working with manufacturers' associations. Stung by the virtual accusation of treason to the labor movement, one of the delegates replied that Furuseth "has a theoretical knowledge of a great many questions and not considerable knowledge of some that he discusses at length."[29]

Furuseth was also conservative in his views on organizational matters. Just as he opposed "amalgamation" in his own union, he resisted the demands of industrial unionists in the AFL, especially proposals to combine with longshoremen. Whereas other crafts had combined in the Metal Trades and Building Trades departments, Furuseth killed the move to form a Marine Transportation Department.[30] On the problem of organizing Negroes, he opposed both the radicals who favored complete equality and the reactionaries who favored discriminatory practices. He believed that his own union had found the answer in organizing separate locals for Negroes.[31]

A further example of Furuseth's conservatism was his stand on workmen's compensation. Long after other workers had fought for and won workmen's compensation laws in almost every state, the ISU blocked any move to pass a federal law that would put seamen under similar legislation.[32]

In response to the insistent demand of the West Coast unions, however, Furuseth secured the introduction of several bills providing compensation for seamen.[31] But because he opposed insurance in principle, his support of these measures was only lukewarm. He believed that if shipowners could insure themselves against injuries, they would fail to take the necessary precautions to prevent them, such as hiring competent personnel and improving the gear and equipment. His apathetic support turned to outright opposition when he discovered that the seamen might lose the right to bring suit for damages. An American seaman who was injured or sick was entitled to maintenance and cure, wages in full for the duration of the voyage, and the right to sue for damages in either federal or state courts under employer liability laws. Furuseth refused to support any compensation bill unless it specifically retained the old rights.

No amount of argument or evidence changed his opinion. George Larsen, Paul Scharrenberg, and practically every West Coast union leader came to the 1923 ISU convention ready to concede that employer liability and workmen's compensation were incompatible in principle. The first recognized employer responsibility and the second recognized public responsibility for injuries. No other group of workmen was protected under both principles. They were prepared to give up the right to sue for damages. Too often seamen got nothing for their injuries because they were outwitted by clever lawyers, or their own attorneys took from one fourth to one half of their award. "Compensation is certain. An action in court is always a gamble," editorialized the *Seamen's Journal*.[84]

Furuseth convinced the convention to reject this argument, but only after assurances that several senators had promised him that a bill containing both remedies—compensation and liability—would be passed. The fact that shipowners favored a compensation bill and the Department of Labor issued statistical reports proving the advantages of compensation over liability laws made the sailors suspicious. The arguments for compensation made by friends of labor were discounted on the ground that they did not understand the special status of the seaman. To this day leaders of the seamen's unions oppose workmen's compensation—a heritage of Furuseth's mistrust of government and his conservative reliance on past remedies.

Perhaps nothing better illustrates Furuseth's inability to change with the times and his stubborn insistence on his own solution to problems than his stand on the injunction issue. Aside from the Seamen's Act, Furuseth was undoubtedly best known for his views on this issue—views that were already well known in the labor movement at the beginning of the century. His remedy for the labor injunction was for Congress to make a clear distinction between "the real labor power, which is not property but life, and the result of labor power in operation, which is property, capable of being owned by somebody."[85] He did not agree with those who attacked the courts for usurping power, for he felt that the courts had correctly interpreted the Sherman Antitrust Act. The attack should be made on Congress, which had the power to limit the equity power of the courts to jurisdiction over property, but not over labor.

Lonely Warrior

Labor's Magna Charta, the Clayton Act, had proved, in the hands of the courts, to be an entirely unsatisfactory remedy. To meet the renewed threat of "government by injunction," the AFL asked representatives of every international union to meet in Washington on February 23–24, 1921. Andrew Furuseth and Percy Pryor were present for the ISU. The conference adopted a ringing declaration which said in part:

> The only possible and practical remedy in the face of a power so usurped and so completely unjustified lies in a flat refusal on the part of labor to recognize or abide by the terms of injunctions which seek to prohibit the doing of acts which the workers have a lawful and guaranteed right to do.... Labor realizes fully the consequences of such a course but in the defense of American freedom and of American institutions it is compelled to adopt this course, be the consequences what they may.[36]

Spewing defiance at the court on paper was one thing. Carrying that defiance into action when labor was on the defensive was another. Furuseth castigated AFL leaders for failing to defy injunctions. "Don't tell me you have the guts to go to jail," he told them, "because you haven't. The best of you have refused."[37] Instead, labor leaders began searching for legislative relief. Samuel Gompers showed Furuseth drafts of several bills which had been prepared by attorneys. Disgusted with their approach to the problem, Furuseth wrote his own bill. He showed it to Gompers and several congressmen, and then (apparently without official approval from the AFL) had the bill introduced by Senator Shipstead.[38]

Labor's approach to the problem in the past had been to attempt to limit the use of the injunction in labor disputes. The Clayton Act had forbidden its use where union activities were lawful and peaceful. In Furuseth's view this was tilting at windmills. His bill proposed to limit the jurisdiction of the court by striking at the root of the problem. Injunctions are issued to protect property when there is no remedy at law. Under Furuseth's bill, federal courts of equity could consider as property only what was "tangible and transferable." For example, the court could protect a building from fire hazards because the building was tangible and transferable, but it could not protect a business from a strike because the business was not tangible. The bill attacked the doctrine that "expectancies," that is, expected profits and good will, were property rights.[39]

The 1927 AFL convention gave the Shipstead bill a qualified endorsement. Four months later the bill received the unanimous disapproval of the legal profession. On February 7, 1928, a meeting of representatives of all AFL unions in Washington failed to endorse any specific bill, but Furuseth's agitation for the Shipstead bill brought about a historic and extensive congressional inquiry into the problem of injunctions. Out of these hearings came a new bill supported by congressmen and attorneys friendly to labor. But Furuseth stubbornly refused to retreat or compromise on his bill. The spectacle of a self-educated sailor bandying legal history and terminology with the best attorneys in the country at these hearings was a sight that few spectators or participants forgot. The lawyers thought that Furuseth was all wrong, but they respected his knowledge of the subject, the skill with which he presented his arguments, and his complete sincerity.

Labor leaders were less charitable in their appraisal of Furuseth's obstinate support of the Shipstead bill. A special AFL committee consisting of Matthew Woll, Victor Olander, and John P. Frey, after working with friendly senators and consulting many attorneys, decided that Furuseth's remedy was impractical. It had no chance of passing and, even if enacted, would not solve the problem. They accepted instead a substitute for the Shipstead bill which eventually was passed as the Norris-LaGuardia Act.

On the closing day of the 1929 AFL convention, with two thirds of the delegates already gone, Furuseth engaged Woll and Olander in debate on their abandonment of the Shipstead bill. What he had to say of Woll was not kind. He did not mean it to be. He told the convention that when he listened to Woll's arguments, he could not tell whether he was listening to a "pettifogging lawyer" or to "the president of the Civic Federation."[10] He defended his own bill and attacked the substitute. The latter, he said, was an attempt to secure special privileges for labor which would never stand up in court, and furthermore, instead of limiting injunctions, it gave to the equity courts a mandate to issue injunctions. Replying to the claim that no reputable lawyer favored the Shipstead bill, Furuseth reminded the convention that one of the chief authors of the substitute bill was a professor of equity law (Felix Frankfurter). Would you, he asked, go to the Pope to get the arguments against immaculate conception?[41]

Olander, who had originally favored the Shipstead bill, came out publicly with Woll to attack his friend's bill and his reasoning. Olander idolized Furuseth, but he felt that his responsibility to secure united support for the substitute was more important than his personal feelings. The Shipstead bill also granted jurisdiction to equity courts, he said; Furuseth was quibbling over words. Olander recalled that Furuseth had been forced to admit at the Senate hearings that patents and franchises were property. If a patent was property because the piece of paper on which the patent was granted was tangible, then so was a labor contract. To forbid injunctions where personal rights were concerned would prevent the courts from abating nuisances, restraining public officials from illegal acts, enforcing orders of the Interstate Commerce and Federal Trade commissions, and taking many other actions beneficial to labor. As a clincher, Olander cited a hypothetical case in which a vessel loaded with perishable cargo was struck. Under Furuseth's bill the court could issue an injunction to prevent pickets from interfering with the removal of tangible property.

Not only did Furuseth persist at every convention in recording his solitary opposition to the official AFL position, but even after the Norris-LaGuardia Act had been passed and proved entirely satisfactory to labor, he told the convention: "We have got a bill that regulates the issuing of injunctions and bases it purely on equity power. Our anti-injunction bill, as it is piously called, is an authorization and instruction to the courts to issue injunctions."[42]

An exception to Furuseth's conservatism was his consistent support of Senator La Follette. In 1916 Furuseth deserted his post in Washington twice to go to Wisconsin to campaign for his friend in the primary and in the general elections. To the seamen, he justified the time spent in campaigning by explaining that La Follette's enemies were crucifying him for his support of the Seamen's Act. He quickly realized after a few speaking engagements, however, that the "people of Wisconsin know practically nothing about the Seamen's Act and they care less. . . ."[43] This did not stop him from returning to Wisconsin in the fall of 1916 and again in 1922 to help in La Follette's senatorial campaign. Even more out of character was Furuseth's attempt to boom La Follette as a presidential candidate on a labor ticket in 1920 and again in 1924.[44] When the AFL officially endorsed La Follette for president in 1924, the ISU swung its propaganda and organizational machinery into full-scale support of his campaign.

Unfortunately, the seamen were able to bring to the battle only light artillery and very little ammunition. It was a tattered and battered army that Furuseth tried to rally to repay the senator for the boon of freedom which he had conferred upon all seamen. The union, after a strenuous campaign among the seamen, raised slightly more than $4,200 for La Follette—an average of about 25 cents for each of the claimed members of the union.[45] Undoubtedly a considerable part of the total amount contributed was raised by Furuseth personally from sources outside the ISU. While Furuseth deserted his nonpartisan approach to politics to support enthusiastically the Progressive-Labor party candidate, the ordinary seamen, like the citizens of Wisconsin, appear to have been unconcerned with La Follette's role as the seamen's champion.

BITTER END

The response of the seamen to the La Follette campaign does not reflect unfavorably on the merits of his candidacy, for it was typical of the apathy with which they responded to any campaign. They were not only beaten, but they knew it. The IWW inspired a spark of resistance in 1923 and briefly in 1926.[46] The seamen on the Great Lakes called a strike in the fall of 1922, but strike action was not renewed in the spring partly because union officials feared that the IWW would use the occasion to scab. The Atlantic unions contemplated striking in 1926, but on the advice of Furuseth the action was postponed and finally dropped.

After the 1921 strike, the shipowners' complete control of the water front went unchallenged until the 1934 upheaval. Wages, hours, and working conditions were determined by the employers without any reference to collective bargaining. Seamen's wages returned to the prewar level, although by 1931 the cost of living had risen 60 per cent above that level.[47] Seamen seldom received pay for overtime work, though they all worked overtime. Half of the holidays once observed were canceled. Lower wages and longer hours could be endured, but the reign of terror, the favoritism, the company employment agencies, the long wait between jobs, the poor food and uncomfortable forecastles aboard ship were unbearable.[48] One indication of what shipowner control of the water front was accomplishing was that, by their own admission, the owners' shipping offices on the West Coast in one year hired more than 45,000 different seamen to fill an estimated 10,000 jobs—a turnover of more than 400 per cent.[49]

During this period unionism on the water front hit an all-time low in numbers, finances, and morale. The annual income of the ISU dropped from more than $100,000 in 1920 to less than $25,000 in 1925.[50] To meet the increasing financial deficit in 1929, the ISU accepted a $1,500 donation from the National Union of Seamen of Great Britain.[51] The ISU "convention" in 1927 consisted of nine delegates, and even the pretense of holding a convention in 1928 was abandoned. Internal feuding, bickering, and outright revolt continued to plague the union, especially on the Atlantic Coast. A low point was reached in 1925 when K. N. Nolan, who had succeeded Thomas A. Hanson as secretary-treasurer upon his death in 1922, suddenly disappeared with almost $4,000 in union funds. To restore some prestige and trust to the office, Furuseth persuaded Victor Olander to accept the job as a personal favor to him.

Olander, already a prominent figure in the national labor movement and secretary of the Illinois Federation of Labor, agreed to devote the few hours he could spare from his other activities to the ISU.[52]

Furuseth spoke bravely about the great things that could be accomplished by a few individuals imbued with the proper spirit, but he failed to find either the leadership or the following. The ISU sent Patrick O'Brien and G. H. Brown on an organizational tour in 1922, but they found the men so unresponsive that after a few meetings they reported that further efforts would be a waste of time and money. Furuseth, himself, made several organizing attempts, with no greater success.[53]

Failing to interest the men, the union turned more and more to the shipowners and the United States Shipping Board in hopes of reaching some agreement on union recognition, union preference, and access to the docks and ships for union agents. Although it galled him to beg for favors,[54] Furuseth was especially active in this effort. On rare occasions, he was even successful. When he failed, he would inform the public that the shipowners' policies had resulted in such deterioration of the merchant marine that he would advise anyone who wanted to get rid of a wife to send her on an ocean voyage, since it was easier to get rid of her that way than to send her to Nevada.[55] Summarizing employer-employee relationships and the weakness of the union at the ISU convention in 1930, Furuseth said: "As it now stands, there can be neither individual or collective bargaining."[56] He frankly admitted: "As a matter of substantial truth, the shipowner determines the wages and conditions."[57]

From January, 1930, until the fateful convention of 1936, the ISU held no national gatherings. Whatever semblance of an organization remained operated through its officers. Local meetings, when held, were so poorly attended that paid union officials constituted the majority of those present. Under such circumstances, with no restraint by an active membership, it is small wonder that some of the officials became corrupt, made excessive use of expense accounts, accepted bribes from steamship companies, and, in some instances, even took money from men whom they favored with jobs.[58]

In a small way, Furuseth tried to stem the internal corruption. As early as 1920, when he noted the $250 expense account granted to each of three SUP delegates to the ISU convention, he protested: "No wonder some of our members call that kind of trips junket trips."[59] When Paul Scharrenberg invited him to accept a free cruise through the Panama Canal to the New Orleans ISU convention on a United Fruit Company vessel, he turned down the offer.[60] The United Fruit Company was not giving free cruises to union officials for nothing. Furuseth often quoted the old maxim, "There is nothing for nothing and very little for a ha'penny in this world." He once wrote: "In all my life I have been looking for the person who really wanted to give something to the seaman for nothing, and I have not found that creature in the jungle anywhere."[61] To Scharrenberg, however, Furuseth explained that he felt it his duty to remain in San Francisco to campaign against Representative Julius Kahn, who had voted wrong on seamen's legislation.

Furuseth unquestionably tried in many other ways to maintain a clean, honest union, but he cannot be entirely exonerated. He failed to use the full power of the international office to wipe out every trace or even suspicion of corruption. In 1922, to meet the threat of the IWW, the international union was granted wide authority by the convention. This authority was used in 1936 to revoke the charter of the SUP when it was suspected of being Communist-dominated, but it was not used earlier against dishonest officials.

No one, not even Furuseth's worst enemies, ever accused him of personal dishonesty. He had no need to be dishonest. His physical wants were simple. His admirers made a legend of his tiny bare room in the Ebbitt Hotel in Washington. They pointed to the times that Furuseth turned down substantial wage increases. His disregard for money is evidenced by the gift to his sister of his life's savings of $3,000 to pay off the mortgage on her farm. Although part of the legend of his self-denial is true, he held to the principle that union officials should be paid as much as but no more than a worker in the trade.

Furuseth lived frugally, not because he was penniless, but because he placed little value on the things that money could buy. He spent part of almost every afternoon and evening reading; Norwegian folk tales, Shakespeare, the Bible, and history were his favorites. He enjoyed conversation, debate, and argument, and could sit for hours in the restaurant across from his hotel discussing problems with his old cronies. Most of all, he enjoyed his work. Every day in Washington he would arrive at the office at nine o'clock, dictate some letters, and then go off to attend congressional hearings or to corner congressmen. He was a busy man, respected by everyone. He believed that he was performing a valuable service. He did not need money."[62]

Although Furuseth did not want monetary reward for his work, in the trying days of the union's decline he would have welcomed an expression of confidence and appreciation. When the union was strong, Furuseth never expected or desired personal adulation. In 1918 Silas B. Axtell, after extravagantly praising Furuseth, proposed the collection of a fund for the purpose of erecting a statue in his honor. Furuseth scotched the move by writing that, although Axtell's motives were undoubtedly sincere, his proposal was an unconscious insult "to all the men who have understood our struggle." What the movement needed, Furuseth explained, was "men, not monuments."[63]

By 1929 his attitude had changed. He consented to sit for Jo Davidson, already a world-renowned sculptor. During the sittings the question arose of what would be done with the bust. Furuseth suggested that it should properly be in the headquarters of the Sailors' Union of the Pacific. Davidson agreed, but he demanded that the seamen express their desire for the bust by contributing to a fund. He did not care how much money was raised, but he insisted that none of it come out of the union treasury.[64]

Furuseth was proud of the bust. He wrote: "Those who have seen it think it is myself in a mood in which I have said something and am expecting an answer."[65] He hoped that the sailors on the Pacific would inaugurate a fund to purchase the bust, but after several broad hints failed to produce results, he laid the issue squarely before the officers. "It would serve as a real information as to what my real standing is amongst the men now. Do they really want me, or do they want to get rid of me? Have they some idea that my usefulness is over?"[66]

No collection was ever made, and the bust, which had been left by Davidson with Lincoln Steffens, was finally turned over to the Department of Labor. To Furuseth the officers of the SUP explained that Davidson's request was unreasonable, because it would be impossible to reach all the members of the union to ask for their contributions.[67] Furuseth accepted the explanation, but the knowledge that his single request for personal glory had been turned down must have hurt deeply. It was true, as the officers explained, that the times were not propitious for such a collection. Many men were out of work. The Communists and the wobblies were beginning a campaign of character assassination. On the other hand, a large collection in adverse times would have been a tribute, not only to Furuseth, but to the union for which he stood.

Ever since passage of the Seamen's Act, Furuseth's responsibilities as secretary of the Sailors' Union of the Pacific had been declining. His duties in Washington, his role within the national AFL, and the toll of years precluded any active participation in the daily affairs of his West Coast sailors. He gradually lost touch with the rank-and-file seamen whom he had known so intimately. The leaders of the union, while according him the utmost respect, often found it expedient to conduct union business without interference from Furuseth's obstinate dogmatism on many matters.

When, in the mid-thirties, the crisis came in which Furuseth might have exerted his influence to build a powerful, united seamen's union, he was too far removed from the membership, too old, and too ill to make a significant contribution. In 1930 he was involved in an auto accident and sustained a knee injury that seriously impaired his ability to walk. For some time he had been bothered with a stomach ulcer; finally, in 1933, he consented to go to St. Luke's Hospital in San Francisco for treatment. He attended the AFL convention in October of that year, but did not once take the floor—an unprecedented occurrence. He went back to the hospital for brief periods in 1934 and 1935, each time recovering more slowly.[68]

These were years of revolution in maritime labor relations. Furuseth played a part, but his effectiveness was curtailed not only by his ill health, but also by his unwillingness to evaluate and take advantage of the revolution. For example, to every other labor leader the National Industrial Recovery Act represented an unprecedented opportunity to organize, but to Furuseth the NIRA "gave to big business substantially the same powers exercised by the old master guilds. It endeavored to protect the worker in his right to organize, but constrictions pleaded for and accepted have left us face to face with company unions."[69] The task of creating a National Recovery Administration code for the maritime industry was assumed for the union by Victor Olander and Ivan Hunter. While they tried to secure a satisfactory code, Furuseth concerned himself with bills for the deportation of alien seamen.[70]

More serious than his failure to comprehend the importance of the NIRA was his failure to understand the changing temper of the men. The move toward what Furuseth called "amalgamation," which had been going on for more than twenty years, was reaching a climax. Many members regarded the separation of crafts in the maritime industry as highly artificial. Nor could a membership that had no experience in dealing with longshore unions understand Furuseth's insistence on remaining independent and aloof from a sister union at a time when the trend was for coal miners to support steel workers and for garment workers to help organize textile mills. Above all, Furuseth isolated himself from the men by his fanatic opposition to the union hiring hall.

The maritime NRA code ran into innumerable snags. The breakdown of collective bargaining during the twenties now resulted in a failure to provide any agency through which the workers could settle their compounding grievances. Malcontents, ambitious upstarts, opportunists, idealists, and political representatives of every hue were all eager to show the seamen the way out of their difficulties. The most active, the best financed, and the most disciplined of these groups was the Communist party. Control of the maritime unions was considered so important by the Communists that they employed four full-time functionaries on the water front of San Francisco alone.[71] After several unsuccessful attempts to organize seamen, in 1928 with the Marine Workers' Progressive League, in 1929 with the International Seamen's Clubs, in 1930 with the Marine Workers' League, the Communists finally struck fire with the Marine Workers' Industrial Union organized in 1932.[72] Furuseth often charged that the shipowners financed the Communists so that the government would have an excuse to step in to break the unions.[73] He never produced any proof, but there was no doubt that the Communists' success was in part due to the propaganda of the Chamber of Commerce, which labeled every protest against the intolerable conditions existing on the water front as a "Communist plot."

While ISU officials negotiated in Washington, seamen and longshoremen grew increasingly restless. The explosion occurred first on the Pacific Coast.[74] The longshoremen, who had been under the complete control of the "Blue Book" company union since the defeat of the ILA in 1919, unexpectedly won a strike in October, 1933. Like most new unions, the reorganized ILA was dominated by militant leaders who wanted to press their initial gains. They succeeded in calling a strike for March 27, 1934, but it was postponed upon the request of President Roosevelt. Efforts of a special Fact-Finding Committee appointed by the president to compromise the differences between longshoremen and stevedore companies proved futile, and a coast-wide strike was called for May 9. On May 15, the SUP voted to join the strike to enforce demands it had made upon the shipowners in August, 1933.

Joint action with longshoremen was something that Furuseth had consistently opposed for more than thirty years. Furthermore, he undoubtedly shared the concern of Olander and others about the effect of the strike upon the maritime code hearings in Washington. On June 27, Furuseth flew to San Francisco to participate in the hearings conducted by the National Longshoremen's Board appointed by President Roosevelt to mediate in the strike, which had assumed national importance.

If Furuseth had any following or reputation among the maritime workers, the Communists determined to undermine it just as they had effectively undermined Joseph P. Ryan, president of the ILA. They told the workers that "Andy Barnacle" was coming to San Francisco. "Weeping Willow Andy Feroshus" was responsible for "selling out" the 1921 strike, and the workers were warned to beware of another "sellout." Such intemperate language against the venerable union leader would once have brought the sailors to his defense, but now, repeated often enough to men who scarcely knew the "Old Man of the Sea" and who knew little of the union's history, the smear campaign was successful in blunting his effectiveness.[75]

Furuseth wanted the sailors to return to work provided the shipowners agreed to recognize the ISU as their bargaining agent. All other matters, he thought, could be arbitrated. This would mean that the seamen would go back to work without regard to what the longshoremen did, and it would leave for arbitration the most controversial issue of the entire strike—the demand for a union hiring hall. The SUP meeting at headquarters in San Francisco (which the Communists claimed was called on two hours' notice) endorsed the proposal for union recognition and arbitration by a vote of 173 to 76. But when Furuseth went to San Pedro on July 3 to get endorsement from that branch, he was not only overwhelmingly defeated, but was booed and hooted. Another meeting called in San Francisco on July 5, this time well packed, reversed the previous approval of Furuseth's proposal by a vote of 459 to 95. The temper of the men was against any settlement independent of the longshoremen. Besides, they were not ready to settle for the ethereal gain of recognition of the union.[76]

On July 5, 1934, the San Francisco Industrial Association tried to open the port. In the ensuing riot two workers were shot by the police. The governor sent the National Guard to the water front, precipitating a demand for a general strike in San Francisco. Many of the union leaders cautiously tried to avoid becoming involved, but the sentiment of the membership had been so aroused that it became impossible to prevent calling a general strike for July 16. Furuseth, who had been working with the union leaders opposed to the strike call, suddenly collapsed and had to be taken to the hospital.

He left the hospital for a few days to participate in the SUP meeting on July 29 which considered the shipowners' offer to arbitrate all differences with all maritime unions. The longshoremen had already voted to accept the offer and to go back to work on July 29. Furuseth was given three minutes to argue that the SUP ought to refuse to return to work for any company that failed to grant recognition to the ISU. He was voted down.[77] Two days later he presided at a huge bonfire in a vacant lot near the union office, where the seamen gathered to cremate the "Blue Books" which they had been obliged to carry since 1921. On paper, the seamen had won less than Furuseth had asked upon his arrival in San Francisco, but the struggle against the shipowners had served to unite the maritime workers, fill them with a sense of power,

Lonely Warrior

and inspire them with new militancy. The water front was never the same again.

Furuseth did not return to Washington until January, 1935. During the five months he had spent on the West Coast, most of the time in the hospital, the ISU had passed through a series of crises involving the militant elements on the Atlantic Coast. More and more, dissident groups were challenging the old-time leaders.

To take advantage of the discontent within the ISU, the Communists gave up their Marine Workers' Industrial Union and ordered all their members to "bore from within." Contrary to instructions from the ISU executive board, the SUP voted to allow former members of the MWIU into the union. But this was not its only sin. The SUP joined with the longshoremen and other water-front unions in the Maritime Federation of the Pacific Coast. It expelled Paul Scharrenberg from the union and refused to reinstate him when the international executive board directed it to do so. It also failed to live up to the agreement with the shipowners.[78]

There was no doubt in Furuseth's mind that his union had been captured by the Communists. During all of 1935 he kept up a constant stream of telegrams and letters urging his sailors to come to their senses, warning against the unconstitutional actions of the union, pleading with the men to take his advice. He refused to believe that the insurgent elements (whom he lumped together under the term "Communists") had an actual majority of the union. They might be able to get a majority to the meetings because many members were beholden to the ILA and Harry Bridges for jobs as longshoremen. The real seamen were at sea. On this basis he justified his refusal to abide by the decision of one SUP meeting instructing him to cease his support for a bill that would have given the master of a vessel the right to choose his own men, at a time when the SUP was advocating that men should be hired only by turn through the union hall. "Andrew Furuseth takes no orders from Communists," he wired to the union.[79] He sincerely believed that if all the "real" seamen could be gathered together, they could outvote the Communists just as they had been able to defeat the wobblies in 1921. Reports from the newspapers that opposed him and from his friends and allies indicate that he had completely misjudged the situation.[80]

Furuseth returned to San Francisco in September, 1935, hoping that he could oust the insurgents. The Central Labor Council accorded the eighty-three-year-old veteran a place of honor in the Labor Day parade, but the seamen turned a deaf ear to his pleas. He was forced to admit privately that the men he had known were a small minority in the union.[81] The rest of them, he charged, were under the domination of the longshoremen, who were winning the allegiance of the sailors by giving them part-time work.

He urged George Larsen, Selim Silver, and other old-time leaders to take the same drastic action to rid themselves of the Communists which union leaders on the Atlantic Coast had used. In Atlantic ports, new members had been denied the right to vote for one year, meetings had been adjourned whenever the union leaders thought that they might be outvoted, strong-arm methods had been used to oust disrupters from meetings, the police and the courts had been utilized to keep the militants out of control, and known Communists were prevented from securing jobs aboard vessels.[82] But if Furuseth thought such tactics could work on the West Coast, he completely misunderstood the temper of the men.

Furuseth considered anyone who opposed the official leadership of the ISU as a Communist. He failed to distinguish between those who had legitimate grievances and those who were using the grievances for their own political purposes. To all these men he said, "You have treated the seamen as a door mat upon which to clean your shoes and a cuspidor for the cleaning of your mouth."[83]

Exhausted and physically ill, Furuseth made a strong personal appeal:

> My nerves are out of shape and that is undoubtedly the reason for my sickness and that condition arises from the failure of the membership throughout the country so far to take such advice as I am compelled to give and because they evidently believe either that I am not telling the truth or, if I am telling the truth, that they know better than I do.... [U]nless I can get the sympathy and cooperation that is necessary ... I can see no hope for us.[84]

The leaders of the insurgents on the Pacific Coast did not attack Furuseth. Many of them, like Harry Lundeberg, were ardent admirers of the "Old Man." They leveled their attack against Paul Scharrenberg, Victor Olander, Ivan Hunter, David Grange, Henry P. Griffin, and other more vulnerable targets. They believed that Furuseth was being misled and misinformed by corrupt union officials in the East who were advising him.[85] This was not true. His analysis of the West Coast situation was entirely his own. It was consistent with his lifelong respect for the labor agreement, his hatred of all forms of collectivism, and his distrust of longshoremen and other shore workers.

That fall Furuseth attended the AFL convention, then journeyed to the ILO conference in Geneva, and returned to Washington in January, 1936, for the first ISU convention in six years. The organization had made tremendous strides in every port since the 1934 strike, but its ranks were so hopelessly rent by various factions that this convention was called to force the dissident elements into line. ISU officials on the Atlantic and Great Lakes had managed to retain control of the union apparatus even though they had lost control of the membership. On the West Coast they controlled neither. In order to strengthen the hand of the executive board, it was necessary to amend the constitution, but a two-thirds vote for a revised constitution could never be obtained so long as the West Coast unions opposed the amendments. The solution was obvious. Expel the SUP, which had given sufficient cause by repeated violation of the international executive board orders. Without the votes of the SUP delegates, the convention would be able to amend the constitution.

Presiding over the stormy convention for eleven days proved too strenuous for Furuseth. He was ordered by his doctor to remain in his hotel room. When, a few days later, the moment came to vote on the revocation of the SUP charter, Furuseth sent a message to the delegates: "It is with deep sorrow but under absolute conviction of necessity that I urge you all to vote unanimously for expulsion, and that I urge upon all the loyal members with whom I have lived and toiled for some fifty years ... to immediately affiliate with the union to be chartered."[86]

Those who knew the "Old Man" realized that his sorrow was not a literary expression. It was a wound so deep that he never recovered. His whole life had been dedicated to these men. He had argued their cause before shipowners, legislators, courts, and the public. He had battled longshoremen for their benefit. He had given unstintingly of his time and energy in their behalf. All the loving devotion and the fierce protectiveness of a mother had been lavished upon his union. What he was now doing was equivalent to throwing his only child out of the house. Sadly he wrote to George Larsen, "It seems that for forty years I have wasted my life and yet if I had to go through it again I would act in the same way."[87]

Furuseth was spared the knowledge of the total disintegration of the ISU, which he had helped to found. The convention put Paul Scharrenberg in charge of legislative activities in Washington, which left Furuseth with only the title of president. Two months after the close of the convention, Furuseth went to the hospital. Scharrenberg visited him frequently, and they undoubtedly talked of the unsuccessful efforts to establish a rival union on the West Coast. Perhaps Scharrenberg spared the old man the tragic news of events on the Atlantic and Gulf coasts, where a thoroughly discredited leadership was frantically trying to hold onto the membership by making deals with the shipowners.

By September Furuseth was more dead than alive. He was not allowed to see anyone. But he hung on until January 22, 1938. The following day, on Sunday, the body of Andrew Furuseth was placed at *lit de parade* in the auditorium of the Department of Labor Building, the first labor leader to be thus honored. At the funeral services on Monday, congressmen, members of the Supreme Court, and labor leaders paid their respects. The body was cremated and the ashes were turned over to the master of the *S. S. Schoharie*. On March 21 in latitude 47° 12′ north, the master assembled the crew for a brief ceremony. "Fellow shipmates," he said, "we are assembled here to execute the wish of Andrew Furuseth, venerable man, an unselfish worker for the betterment of seamen, who through legal means has done more to secure improved conditions under which you work than any other man." The ashes were then thrown into the sea.[88]

NOTES

ABBREVIATIONS

AFL	American Federation of Labor
CSJ	*Coast Seamen's Journal* (1887–1922), *Seamen's Journal* (1922–1937)
CSU	Coast Seamen's Union
ILA	International Longshoremen's Association
ILO	International Labor Organization
ILMTWU	International Longshoremen and Marine Transport Workers' Union
ISF	International Seafarers' Federation
ISU	International Seamen's Union
ITWF	International Transport Workers' Federation
IWA	International Workingmen's Association
IWW	Industrial Workers of the World
MTWIU	Marine Transport Workers' Industrial Union
MWIU	Maritime Workers' Industrial Union
NMU	National Maritime Union
NSU	National Seamen's Union
SUP	Sailors' Union of the Pacific

Notes to Chapter I

SAILOR

(Pages 1–10)

[1] Pronounced like Pure-you-beth, Fur-u-seth. Note in Walter Macarthur, Correspondence and Papers, 1890–1945, Carton 1, Bancroft Library, Berkeley, Calif.; Coast Seamen's Union, Treasurer's Ledger, 1885/1887, Bancroft Library, Berkeley, Calif., p. 59.

[2] Carl Lynch cited by Robert M. La Follette, *Congressional Record*, 79th Cong., 2d sess., 92:10 (March 14, 1946), 1360–1361.

[3] Walter Galenson, *Labor in Norway* (Cambridge: 1947), pp. 8–10.

[4] Most of the information on Furuseth's family and early life comes from a pamphlet by Bernt A. Sosveen, *Andrew Furuseth*, translated by Birgit Hallen and reprinted in Silas B. Axtell, comp., *A Symposium on Andrew Furuseth* (New Bedford, Mass.: 1948), pp. 51–60. Furuseth rarely referred to his life in Norway or to his sailing days except in a very general way. Some of his closest friends cannot recall any time when he reminisced about them. Although Sosveen's account of Furuseth's later life is none too accurate, he seems to have gone to considerable pains to check church and official records in Norway on the early years.

[5] Verified on CSU Application for Membership Card of Andrew Furuseth, in possession of Selim Silver, Oakland, California.

[6] Letter from Andrew Furuseth (descendant relative) to Norwegian Consulate General, New York, April 16, 1947, cited in Axtell, *op. cit.*, p. 48.

[7] Furuseth to Victor Olander, secretary-treasurer of International Seamen's Union of America, Feb. 26, 1931, cited in Knut Gjerset, *Norwegian Sailors in American Waters* (Northfield, Minn.: 1933), p. 172. In this letter Furuseth said there were six boys and two girls in his family. He unaccountably omitted a brother and a sister.

[8] Lynch, cited by La Follette, *op. cit.*, says that Furuseth left the Schjotz farm because he was beaten for stopping work long enough to take a drink of water. It is more likely that his term of service was over and, seeking the advancement that his later career indicates, he left simply because there was no opportunity to be anything except a farm hand.

[9] *Ibid.*

[10] Sosveen, in Axtell, *op. cit.*, p. 54, says that Furuseth purchased three fishing vessels, but after a dramatic shipwreck on one of them, he decided to give up the sea. No corroborating information can be found for the shipwreck story, and it was at least six years after this that Furuseth left the sea. It is a safe guess, however, that any Scandinavian who had sailed for seven years would have spent part of that time fishing on the Newfoundland banks, the Columbia River, or both.

[11] W. Clark Russel, "The Life of the Merchant Sailor," *Scribner's Magazine*, XIV (July, 1893), 1–19.

[12] *Two Years Before the Mast* (New York: 1841), p. 125.

[13] Charles W. Brown, *My Ditty Bag* (Boston: 1925), pp. 20–27. J. Gray Jewell, *Among Our Sailors* (New York: 1874), is an account of brutality to seamen written by the American consul in Singapore. The classic work on the subject of cruelty to seamen is International Seamen's Union, *Red Record* (San Francisco: 1895). Almost any issue of the *Coast Seamen's Journal* from 1887 to 1890 contains news on instances of cruelty. The items became less frequent, but continued as long as the *Journal* existed. Some of the better articles on the subject appear in the issues of February 8, 1893, pp. 4–5, and January 26, 1898, pp. 1–3, 5–6.

[14] Describing the plight of the seaman who comes ashore, Willis J. Abbot, *American Merchant Ships and Sailors* (New York: 1902), p. 370, says, "The seaman landing with money in his pocket in any large town is like a hapless fish in some of our

much angled streams. It is not enough to avoid the tempting bait displayed on every side. So thick are the hooks and snares that merely to swim along, intent on his own business, is likely to result sooner or later in his being impaled on some cruel barb." Information about the port of Philadelphia was gathered by an attorney for the Legal Aid Society: Frances Anne Keay, "The Sailor in Port: Philadelphia," *Charities and the Commons*, XVII (Jan., 1908), 712–716.

[15] The *Coast Seamen's Journal* has many articles on crimps; some of the best appear on March 1, 1893, pp. 1–2, and on March 8, 1893, pp. 1–2. Walter Macarthur, "A True Story," in Correspondence and Papers, describes the author's personal experiences with crimps in San Francisco. The Reverend James Fell, a representative of the Seamen's Institute, tells how the British used crimps in *British Merchant Seamen in San Francisco, 1892–1898* (London: 1899), pp. 69–99.

[16] James Carr, owner of a hotel on the City Front, testified at hearings before the California Labor Commissioner on July 6, 1892, that even married men would stay at boardinghouses as the only means of getting a job. *Coast Seamen's Journal* (hereinafter cited as *CSJ*), Nov. 9, 1892, pp. 8–9.

[17] How this system worked for British merchant seamen is described in Fell, *op. cit.*, pp. 131–134.

[18] *Ibid.*, pp. 100–123.

[19] California Bureau of Labor Statistics, *Investigation into Condition of Men Working on the Waterfront and on Board Pacific Coast Vessels, San Francisco, June 29–July 10, 1887* (Sacramento: 1887), p. 7. These are the conclusions of the commissioner of the bureau, John J. Tobin. The investigation describes experiences of seamen and includes testimony from boardinghouse keepers. See also Jewell, *op. cit.*, pp. 15–16.

[20] Testimony of Andrew Furuseth, California Bureau of Labor Statistics, *op. cit.*, pp. 21–27.

[21] Frank Roney says that Furuseth was a member of the Great Lakes Seamen's Union, but this seems highly improbable since Furuseth was a deepwater sailor when the Lake Seamen's Union was organized in 1878. He never mentioned having sailed on the Great Lakes. *Frank Roney, Irish Rebel and California Labor Leader. An Autobiography*, ed. Ira B. Cross (Berkeley: 1931), p. 452.

[22] Coast Seamen's Union, Minutes (hereinafter cited as CSU, Minutes), Jan. 27, 1890. The secretary reported that 1,300 sailors participated in the Alaska fishing season and averaged $40 per month.

[23] Furuseth to *CSJ*, July 21, 1889, cited in *CSJ*, Aug. 21, 1889, p. 1.

[24] U.S. Department of Commerce, *Advisory Conference on the Subject of Making Passenger Vessels More Secure from Destruction by Fire, May 3, 1916* (Washington: 1916), p. 53.

[25] Furuseth to *CSJ*, July 21, 1889, cited in *CSJ*, Aug. 21, 1889, p. 1.

Notes to Chapter II

UNION MAN

(Pages 11–27)

[1] Andrew Furuseth, Application for Membership Card, in possession of Selim Silver, Oakland, California.

[2] An outside port was one in which the vessel had no facilities for docking and had to load and unload while anchored offshore. Unless otherwise specified, the wages quoted were the monthly wages of able seamen, regarded as the basic wage upon which the wage system was structured. A seaman was customarily paid when he "signed off."

Notes

[5] See Ira B. Cross, *A History of the Labor Movement in California* (Berkeley: 1935), pp. 156–165, for a discussion of this organization, its philosophy, and its leaders in California. Source material on the organization can be found in the Bancroft Library, Berkeley, Calif., in Book of Ritual for the Invisible Republic, 1882, 2 vols., and in Minute Book of the International Workingmen's Association, San Francisco, Central Committee, 1884–6.

[4] Contemporary accounts of the formation of the union and its early struggles can be found in the files of the *San Francisco Chronicle*. The union held an annual birthday celebration at which it was the custom to have participants in the Folsom Street Wharf meeting recount their experiences. Their speeches can be found in any issue of the *CSJ* after the March 6 celebration. The best scholarly treatment of these early events is in Paul S. Taylor, "Chapters from the Early History of the Seamen of the Pacific Coast" (unpublished manuscript, 1920), Bancroft Library, pp. 46–50. Cross, *op. cit.*, pp. 166–186, sets these events in the scene of the general labor movement of the time. Lucile Eaves, *A History of California Labor Legislation* (Berkeley: 1910), pp. 40–82, contains a brief history of the California labor movement to 1908. Frank Roney, *Frank Roney, Irish Rebel and California Labor Leader. An Autobiography*, ed. Ira B. Cross (Berkeley: 1931), pp. 406–407, 471–472, gives the reminiscences of one who participated in the organization of the union. In a review of the book, Ekel (probably a pseudonym for Paul Scharrenberg) writes that Roney's recollection of the early history of the SUP is practically worthless. The criticism does not seem fair. *CSJ*, Nov., 1931, pp. 337–339. See also Peter B. Gill, "The Sailors' Union of the Pacific from 1885–1929" (unpublished manuscript, 1942), Bancroft Library, pp. 1–101. Many other secondary sources are available, but these are the best.

For the history of sailors' organization on the Pacific Coast before the formation of the Coast Seamen's Union, see Ira B. Cross, "First Coast Seamen's Union," *CSJ*, July 8, 1908; Roney, *op. cit.*, pp. 328–345; Taylor, *op. cit.*, pp. 1–45; Paul S. Taylor, *The Sailors' Union of the Pacific* (New York: 1923), pp. 35–45; "Extracts from the Minutes of the Seamen's Protective Association," in Ira B. Cross, California Labor Notes, Box 5, Bancroft Library. There is a collection of newspaper clippings dealing with this organization in Burnette G. Haskell, Notes and Reminiscence, 1879–1893, Vol. IV, Bancroft Library.

[5] *San Francisco Chronicle*, March 5, 6, 8, 10, 12, 18, June 8, 1885.

[6] Felix Riesenberg, Jr., *Golden Gate, the Story of San Francisco Harbor* (New York: 1940), p. 222.

[7] Major events of the strike of 1886 are from *CSJ*, March 6, 1895, p. 1; Taylor, *The Sailors' Union of the Pacific*, pp. 51–52; Cross, *A History of the Labor Movement in California*, pp. 179–183.

[8] *San Francisco Chronicle*, June 24, 27, 1886.

[9] *CSJ*, March 6, 1895, p. 1.

[10] This composite picture is based upon a study of CSU, Minutes, and SUP, Files (Sailors' Union of the Pacific, San Francisco). The SUP Files are a fairly complete record of all communications, financial records, leaflets, reports of committees, etc., from the organization of the CSU (which became the SUP in 1891) in 1885 to 1938. Everything is filed by date and subject in unnumbered boxes which occupy three shelves, thirty feet long. They are not open to public inspection.

[11] CSU, Minutes, Sept. 10, 1888. The secretary's salary was then $13 per week. Furuseth proposed an increase to $15 on November 25, 1889, and on January 20, 1890, but the motion failed to get the necessary two-thirds majority. *Ibid.*, Feb. 24, 1890.

[12] Taylor, *The Sailors' Union of the Pacific*, p. 54. This will be fully discussed in chapter iii.

[13] Walter Macarthur, "Coast Seamen's Journal" (unpublished manuscript, 1932), in Correspondence and Papers, 1890–1945, Bancroft Library, Berkeley, Calif., p. 3. In order to give the struggling paper needed support, Furuseth recommended including the *CSJ* financial records in regular union funds. CSU, Minutes, Oct. 28, Nov. 2, 1889.

[14] California Bureau of Labor Statistics, *Investigation into Condition of Men Working on the Waterfront and on Board Pacific Coast Vessels, San Francisco, June 29–July 10, 1887* (Sacramento: 1887), p. 3; *CSJ*, Nov. 16, 1887, pp. 3–4.

[15] CSU, Minutes, Oct. 8, 15, 1888; Feb. 4, March 18, 1889; *CSJ*, March 20, 1889, p. 1.

[16] Secretary's Report, CSU, Minutes, Jan. 5, 1889.

[17] This conclusion is based on a study of the names that appear in the minutes of the meetings and of the votes on referendums. According to the constitution, a referendum had to be voted upon at three consecutive meetings. At the first meeting, everyone present voted. At the second meeting, those who had already voted did not vote. About half of those present usually voted on the referendum. The same thing happened at the third meeting. Control of the group working on shore has been an important element in the politics of the Sailors' Union.

[18] No adequate biography has been written of this interesting personality. Cross, *A History of the Labor Movement in California*, pp. 156–165, has the best treatment. Roney, *op. cit.*, pp. 388–486, has many references to Haskell. There is considerable source material in the Bancroft Library, such as Cross, California Labor Notes; Minute Book of the International Workingmen's Association, San Francisco, Central Committee, 1884–6; Book of Ritual for the Invisible Republic, 1882; Kaweah Cooperative Colony Records, 1885–1891; and Haskell, Notes and Reminiscence, 1879–1893.

[19] Roney, *op. cit.*, pp. 388–390.

[20] *Ibid.*, pp. 471–472.

[21] Walter Macarthur to Mrs. Dombroff, Aug. 9, 1940, in Macarthur, Correspondence and Papers, Box 1. He says that he hardly knew Haskell, who was a "has-been" when Macarthur came to San Francisco in 1889.

[22] SUP, Minutes, Nov. 18, 1907.

[23] Roney, *op. cit.*, pp. 483–486.

[24] CSU, Minutes, Jan. 7, 14, April 15, June 3, 24, 1889; Jan. 27, 1890.

[25] Taylor, *The Sailors' Union of the Pacific*, pp. 57–63, has the best history of this organization. Will Lawson, *Pacific Steamers* (Glasgow: 1927), has excellent photographs of many steamers used on the West Coast.

[26] *CSJ*, Nov. 9, 1887, p. 3.

[27] CSU, Minutes, Dec. 23, 30, 1889; Jan. 20, 27, Feb. 3, Dec. 1, 1890; Feb. 2, 9, March 10, 1891.

[28] *CSJ* carried a story from England or Australia or both in almost every issue during this period. See, for example, *CSJ*, March 20, 1889, p. 1; July 22, 1891, p. 4; March 2, 1892.

[29] *CSJ*, Sept. 19, 1888, p. 1; Dec. 26, 1888, p. 1; June 11, 1890; CSU, Minutes, Dec. 10, 17, 1888; Dec. 16, 1889; May 12, 19, Aug. 11, 1890.

[30] No biography of this important British labor leader has been written, but the autobiography of one of his lieutenants contains a great deal of complimentary material on Wilson. Edward Tupper, *Seamen's Torch* (London: 1938).

[31] *CSJ*, Nov. 19, 1890, p. 1; [Furuseth,] "Report of Delegates," CSU, Minutes, Nov. 10, 1890. Publicly, the delegates were enthusiastic about the conference. See *CSJ*, Nov. 19, 1890, p. 2; Nov. 26, 1890, p. 1. Walter Macarthur, not having been present in San Francisco to hear the report of the delegates, and relying for his information on his ability to read between the lines of the *CSJ* and the British union's newspaper, *The Seamen*, wrote a blistering attack on Wilson and the convention. This article is, surprisingly, published in *CSJ*, Jan. 7, 1891, p. 1.

Notes

[32] *CSJ*, Nov. 19, 1890, p. 1; [Furuseth,] "Report of Delegates," CSU, Minutes, Nov. 10, 1890.

[33] CSU, Minutes, March 10, 1890, indicate that use was made of the subterfuge of gambling instead of direct payment for the chance.

[34] CSU, Minutes, Feb. 2, 9, 1891.

[35] April 8, 1891, p. 2. See also CSU, Minutes, March 30, April 1, 2, 6, 13, 1891. At a meeting on November 20, 1893, the union voted to ask the state to release Henry Ark from prison.

[36] CSU, Minutes, April 6, 30, 1891.

[37] SUP, Minutes, March 28, 1892.

[38] *Ibid.*, May 30, 1892.

[39] *Ibid.*, June 13, 1892 (Furuseth audited the books), July 5, 1892 (Furuseth was officially elected secretary with 445 votes to 81).

[40] Secretary's Report, CSU, Minutes, Jan. 3, 1891.

[41] CSU, Minutes, Feb. 9, March 9, 10, 16, 23, 1891; *CSJ*, March 18, 1891, p. 2; March 25, 1891, p. 1.

[42] CSU, Minutes, May 4, 11, 18, 25, 1891; SUP, Minutes, Sept. 8, 1891; Oct. 13, 1892.

[43] SUP, Minutes, Nov. 28, 29, 1891; *CSJ*, Dec. 2, 1891, p. 4; Dec. 16, 1891, p. 4; Dec. 23, 1891, p. 4.

[44] *CSJ*, Feb. 3, 1892, p. 4.

[45] SUP, Minutes, Nov. 9, 1891; *CSJ*, Feb. 17, 1892, pp. 4–5; June 29, 1892, p. 5.

[46] Furuseth to agents, n.d., in SUP, Minutes, Oct. 13, 1892.

[47] SUP, Minutes, Jan. 3, 1893; *CSJ*, May 10, 1893, p. 8; May 17, 1893, p. 8. Detailed financial records for the Shipowners' Association are available in John Kentfield and Company, Business Records, 1853–1923, Box 117, Folder 6, Bancroft Library, Berkeley, Calif., but the accounts give no hint of antiunion activities, which must have been handled through a separate fund.

[48] *San Francisco Examiner*, Feb. 11, 1894.

[49] SUP, Minutes, Jan. 23, 1893.

[50] *CSJ*, Jan. 25, 1893, p. 8; Feb. 15, 1893, p. 8; March 15, 1893, p. 8; April 5, 1893, p. 9; April 12, 1893, p. 9.

[51] *Ibid.*, March 8, 1893, pp. 4–5.

[52] SUP, Minutes, March 20, 1893.

[53] *Ibid.*, May 8, 17, July 24, 1893.

[54] *CSJ*, Sept. 13, 1893, p. 8; SUP, Minutes, Sept. 5, 8, 1893.

[55] The best general account of the Curtin bombing is in Gill, *op. cit.*, pp. 127–135. All San Francisco newspapers carried stories and editorials on the incident. An excellent collection of newspaper clippings on the bombing, the arrests, and the subsequent trials was kept by Burnette G. Haskell, who was one of the attorneys retained for the defense. Haskell, *op. cit.*, VI, 1–93.

[56] SUP, Minutes, Sept. 25, 1893.

[57] *CSJ*, Sept. 27, 1893, p. 8; Oct. 4, 1893, p. 8.

[58] SUP, Minutes, Oct. 2, 16, 1893.

[59] Furuseth to members, in SUP, Minutes, Oct. 3, 1893.

Notes to Chapter III

LOBBYIST FOR SEAMEN

(Pages 28–44)

[1] For a complete review of U.S. legislation affecting the personnel of the American merchant marine, see *CSJ*, Dec. 10, 1890, Special Supplement; Silas B. Axtell, *Merchant Seamen's Law* (New York: 1955); Walter Macarthur, *The Seamen's Contract*,

1790–1918 (San Francisco: 1919). Principal sources for Furuseth's legislative activities are *CSJ* and SUP, Minutes.

² Interesting anecdotes on shanghaiing are described in James H. Williams, "Shanghaied," *Independent*, LV (Dec. 31, 1903), 3102–3107.

³ Walter Macarthur to Mrs. Dombroff, Aug. 9, 1940, in Macarthur, Correspondence and Papers, 1890–1945, Bancroft Library, Berkeley, Calif., says the law was passed at the behest of shipowners who wished to rid themselves of the crimps.

⁴ *CSJ*, Nov. 23, 1887, p. 2; Jan. 25, 1888, p. 1; California Bureau of Labor Statistics, *Investigation into Condition of Men Working on the Waterfront and on Board Pacific Coast Vessels, San Francisco, June 29–July 10, 1887* (Sacramento: 1887), p. 8.

⁵ *CSJ*, Dec. 24, 1890, p. 2; Feb. 21, 1894, p. 7; CSU, Minutes, March 23, 1891.

⁶ See H. Rept. 911 on H.R. 5603, House Committee on Merchant Marine and Fisheries, 53d Cong., 2d sess. (1894).

⁷ Nov. 16, 1887, p. 3; Feb. 8, 1888, p. 1; Feb. 22, 1888, p. 1; Jan. 27, 1892, pp. 4–5. Samuel Plimsoll, *Our Seamen* (London: 1873), tells dramatically and clearly the story of British efforts at reform.

⁸ SUP, Minutes, Feb. 15, 1892; *CSJ*, March 2, 9, 16, 1892.

⁹ SUP, Minutes, Feb. 15, 29, March 21, 1892.

¹⁰ *CSJ*, March 23, 1892, p. 4.

¹¹ SUP, Minutes; *CSJ*, Oct. 19, 1892, p. 5; Oct. 26, 1892, p. 4; Nov. 2, 1892, p. 5.

¹² A story on Maguire's life appears in *CSJ*, Nov. 16, 1892, p. 9.

¹³ *CSJ*, Nov. 23, 1892, p. 5.

¹⁴ Some of the best were: on forecastles, Dec. 28, 1892, p. 8; March 29, 1893, pp. 1–2; on advance, Jan. 25, 1893, pp. 4–5; Feb. 1, 1893, pp. 4–5; on brutality, Feb. 8, 1893, pp. 4–5; on food, Feb. 15, 1893, p. 5; Feb. 22, 1893, pp. 1–2; March 1, 1893, pp. 1–2; March 8, 1893, pp. 1–2; March 22, 1893, pp. 1–2; on hours of labor, April 5, 1893, pp. 1–2; on manning, April 19, 1893, pp. 1–2.

¹⁵ SUP, Minutes, Dec. 26, 1893. The bills are printed and explained in *CSJ*: H.R. 5603, Feb. 28, 1894, pp. 2–3; H.R. 5605, March 7, 1894, pp. 2–3; H.R. 5606, March 14, 1894, pp. 1–2; H.R. 5602, April 11, 1894, pp. 1–2; H.R. 7295, June 27, 1895, pp. 1-2. Most of the bills were introduced in the House of Representatives on January 27, 1894.

¹⁶ Report of Secretary-Treasurer T. J. Elderkin, in *CSJ*, April 4, 1894, p. 7.

¹⁷ Furuseth, "Legislative Report," *CSJ*, Aug. 1, 1894, p. 7.

¹⁸ SUP, Minutes, April 9, 1894.

¹⁹ *CSJ*, May 30, 1894, p. 6; June 6, 1894, pp. 6–7; June 20, 1894, p. 6; Furuseth, "Report," *CSJ*, Aug. 1, 1894, p. 7.

²⁰ SUP, Minutes, June 18, 1894.

²¹ H. Rept. 911 on H.R. 5603; *Congressional Record*, 53d Cong., 2d sess., 26:8 (July 27, 1894), 7943–7945.

²² SUP, Minutes, Aug. 6, 1894.

²³ *CSJ*, Sept. 26, 1894, p. 6; Oct. 24, 1894, pp. 6–7; Oct. 31, 1894, pp. 6–7.

²⁴ *Ibid.*, Sept. 5, 1894, p. 6.

²⁵ *Ibid.*, Feb. 13, 1895, p. 7.

²⁶ In addition to *CSJ* and SUP, Minutes, for March–May, 1895, see *San Francisco Call*, March 20–24, April 3, 5, 10, 18, 19, 20, 23, 25, May 3, 1895.

²⁷ *CSJ*, May 1, 1895, p. 7.

²⁸ *Robertson v. Baldwin*, 165 U.S. 275 (1896); SUP, Minutes, July 15, 1895; March 2, 9, 1896; Jan. 17, 1898. *CSJ* carried articles on the case from July, 1895, through January, 1898.

²⁹ Feb. 26, 1896, pp. 6–7.

³⁰ June 17, 1896, p. 6. For the story of a similar society with which the SUP maintained friendly relations, see Missions to Seamen, *From the Bristol Channel to the Seven Seas* (London: 1935).

Notes

[31] A complete report of Furuseth's activities in 1896 is in his "Legislative Report," *CSJ*, Aug. 5, 1896, pp. 1-2. The arguments for and against the White bill, S. 95, during 1896 are best presented in *Hearings on Bills Relating to Rights and Duties of Seamen*, House Committee on Merchant Marine and Fisheries, 54th Cong., 1st sess. (1896).

[32] Elbridge S. Brooks, *The Story of the American Sailor* (Boston: 1888), pp. 296-297.

[33] *CSJ*, Feb. 22, 1888, p. 1 (contains interesting comments on Commodore Elbridge T. Gerry and Henry Bergh's new organization, The New York Society for the Prevention of Cruelty to Sailors); Jan. 15, 1890, p. 1; Aug. 15, 1894, p. 6; CSU, Minutes, Dec. 16, 23, 1889; Jan. 13, 1890.

[34] ISU, *Red Record* (San Francisco: 1895). For press comments on *Red Record*, see *CSJ*, Jan. 22, 1896, pp. 1-2, 7.

[35] Brooks, *op. cit.*, p. 299.

[36] Typical cases appear in *CSJ*, Aug. 3, 1892, p. 4; *New York Times*, May 14, 1896; James H. Williams, "Betrayed," *Independent*, LXV (Aug. 20, 1908), 407-413; (Aug. 27, 1908), 470-475. A former American consul relates many cases in J. Gray Jewell, *Among Our Sailors* (New York: 1874). The superintendent of the Sailors Haven in Charlestown, Mass., a former sailor, writes of his experiences in Stanton H. King, *Dog Watches at Sea* (Boston: 1901). The president of the British and Foreign Sailors' Society describes cruelty to British seamen in Thomas Brassy, "Tyrants of the Sea," *Contemporary Review*, XLIX (March, 1886), 403-412.

[37] *CSJ*, Aug. 12, 1896, p. 1.

[38] *Laws Relating to American Seamen*, H. Rept. 1868 on H.R. 6399, House Committee on Merchant Marine and Fisheries, 54th Cong., 1st sess. (1896), p. 1. See also *To Amend the Laws Relating to Navigation*, H. Rept. 1660 on H.R. 2663.

[39] SUP, Minutes, Aug. 31, 1896; *CSJ*, Aug. 19, 1896, pp. 6-7; Oct. 7, 1896, p. 6; Oct. 28, 1896, pp. 6-7.

[40] SUP, Minutes, Jan. 25, 29, Feb. 1, 8, 1897; *CSJ*, Jan. 26, 1897, p. 6; Feb. 3, 1897, pp. 1-3; Feb. 10, 1897, pp. 1-2; SUP, Files, Jan.-March, 1897. See especially letters from Horace Atkinson (N.Y.) and A. McDonnell (Boston). Furuseth, "Legislative Report," *CSJ*, May 5, 1897, pp. 1-2, is a brief summary of activities in Washington in 1897.

[41] Ed Rosenberg to Furuseth, Jan., 1897, in SUP, Files.

[42] *CSJ*, Feb. 10, 1897, p. 6; see also issue of Jan. 20, 1897, p. 6.

[43] *Ibid.*, March 17, 1897, p. 1.

[44] SUP, Minutes, Feb. 15, 22, 1897.

[45] *Ibid.*, July 12, 19, Aug. 23, Sept. 13, 1897; *San Francisco Call*, Sept. 12, 1897; *CSJ*, July 28, 1897, p. 7; Aug. 11, 1897, p. 7; Sept. 15, 1897, p. 6; Sept. 29, 1897, p. 6.

[46] *CSJ*, June 30, 1897, p. 1.

[47] *Ibid.*, Feb. 9, 1898, p. 6; May 18, 1898, p. 6; SUP, Minutes, May 16, 1898; Furuseth to Charles B. Stover, Social Reform Club, N.Y., May 6, 1898, in SUP, Files; see letters from John O'Sullivan (Boston) to Furuseth, 1898, in SUP, Files.

[48] *Congressional Record*, 55th Cong., 2d sess., 31:7 (July 2, 1898), 6629-6632; Furuseth, "Legislative Report," *CSJ*, July 27, 1898, p. 7. Changes that Furuseth wanted in the bill as passed by the Senate are detailed in a letter from Furuseth to S. E. Payne, July 6, 1898, in SUP, Files.

[49] SUP, Minutes, Nov. 21, 1898. That the legislative program was not too popular among seamen on the East Coast is evident from a letter from Robert Ashe (Boston) to Furuseth, March 10, 1899, and another from A. M. McDonnell, secretary of the Atlantic Coast Seamen's Union, to Furuseth [1898], in SUP, Files. McDonnell completely failed to grasp the significance of the legislation. He wrote: "... am I right in judging that there is some point in our bill which is unobserved by our antagonists which will be of immense benefit to the union—a something which is not observable without deep study."

⁵⁰ *CSJ*, Nov. 23, 1898, p. 6; Dec. 14, 1898, p. 7; Dec. 21, 1898, p. 6; Jan. 18, 1899, pp. 1–5, 11 (complete text and analysis of the White Act); *San Francisco Call*, Dec. 13, 1898; *Laws Relating to American Seamen*, H. Rept. 1657 on S. 95, House Committee on Merchant Marine and Fisheries, 55th Cong., 2d sess. (1898). One of the clearest explanations of the change in the status of sailors as a result of the act is in Walter Macarthur, "The American Seaman under the Law," *Forum*, XXVI (Feb., 1899), 718–731.

⁵¹ AFL, *Proceedings, 1899*, p. 13.

⁵² Furuseth and Thomas F. Tracy, "Legislative Report," *CSJ*, April 17, 1901, pp. 1–2, 7; April 24, 1901, pp. 1–2.

⁵³ SUP, Files contain briefs for many court cases testing the Maguire and White acts and correspondence on seamen's legislative affairs. See James H. Williams, "The Sailor and the Law," *Independent*, LII (Nov. 15, 1900), 2733–2737, discussing H.R. 4963 and the *Ethelred* case, in which British shipowners were fined for evading the White Act.

⁵⁴ SUP, Minutes, Feb. 5, April 16, 1900; *CSJ*, Feb. 14, 1900, p. 7; April 25, 1900, p. 6.

Notes to Chapter IV

LABOR THEORIST

(Pages 45–56)

¹ Walter Macarthur to Mrs. Ottilie Dombroff, n.d., in Walter Macarthur, Correspondence and Papers, 1890–1945, Carton V, Bancroft Library, Berkeley, Calif. According to Frank Roney, Furuseth was a delegate to the Federated Trades Council while Roney was president, but "took no part in its proceedings, giving no evidence whatever of the capacity for leadership which he was subsequently to show." But Roney's memory did not serve him well, for he resigned from the Federated Trades Council at the end of 1886, before Furuseth became a delegate. *Frank Roney, Irish Rebel and California Labor Leader. An Autobiography*, ed. Ira B. Cross (Berkeley: 1931), pp. 452, 524–526.

² CSU, Minutes, Nov. 26, 1888; Feb. 11, 1889; *CSJ*, Oct. 2, 1889, p. 1. The *CSJ* reported the meetings of the Federated Trades Council, and Furuseth's name is mentioned frequently.

³ Complete texts of his early Labor Day speeches may be found in *CSJ*, Sept. 7, 1892, p. 4; Sept. 9, 1896, p. 2 (also in *San Francisco Call*, Sept. 8, 1896); Sept. 8, 1897, p. 2. The description of Furuseth as a speaker is based on interviews with Selim Silver, Jack McDonald, and William McDevitt.

⁴ *CSJ*, Sept. 9, 1896, p. 2.

⁵ Ira B. Cross wrote an interesting description of early labor parades in San Francisco in *Labor Clarion* (San Francisco), Sept. 2, 1910.

⁶ *CSJ*, June 10, 1891, p. 9; Nov. 23, 1892, p. 4; Nov. 30, 1892, p. 4; March 25, 1896, p. 6; March 30, 1898, p. 7; April 6, 1898, p. 6; SUP, Minutes, March 23, 1896.

⁷ Louis B. Reed, *The Labor Philosophy of Samuel Gompers* (New York: 1930).

⁸ Ira B. Cross, *A History of the Labor Movement in California* (Berkeley: 1935), pp. 205–206.

⁹ Samuel Gompers, *Seventy Years of Life and Labor* (New York: 1925), I, 336–338.

¹⁰ AFL, *Proceedings, 1891*, pp. 22–23.

¹¹ *Ibid.*, pp. 29–30.

¹² The following account of Furuseth's convention activities and his philosophy is drawn from AFL, *Proceedings*, 1891–1901.

¹³ See chap. vi.

¹⁴ See chap. ix.

[15] Andrew Furuseth and Adolph Strasser, in the name of the AFL, opposed the Erdman bill in 1894 and 1895 because they claimed that it provided for compulsory arbitration. The railway brotherhoods, which were on the verge of joining the AFL during this period, favored the Erdman bill. They were so alienated by Furuseth's and Strasser's attitude that they never joined the federation. Gompers, *op. cit.*, II, 134; Lewis L. Lorwin, *The American Federation of Labor* (Washington: 1933), p. 57 n.

[16] Gompers, *op. cit.*, I, 229. Letters between the two men found in SUP, Files, were infrequent and usually confined to business matters. In one of the few personal letters, dated October 20, 1897, Gompers explained to Furuseth in three pages that there was no need to explain that he was always willing to step down as president of the AFL if a good trade unionist could be agreed upon to take his place.

[17] The work of AFL legislative representatives can be seen in the report of the president to the AFL conventions in the section titled "Legislation." Some of the complete reports appear in *CSJ*, Feb. 16, 1898, pp. 1–2; Aug. 24, 1898, pp. 1–2; Aug. 22, 1900, pp. 8–10; Aug. 29, 1900, pp. 8–11; April 17, 1901, pp. 1–2, 7; April 24, 1901, pp. 1–2.

[18] Henry E. Hoagland, *Wage Bargaining on the Vessels of the Great Lakes* (Urbana, Ill.: 1917), pp. 28–32, gives a brief history of the maritime unions on the Great Lakes before 1903.

[19] Roney, *op. cit.*, p. 452.

[20] *CSJ*, Aug. 8, 1888, p. 1.

[21] *Ibid.*, Nov. 27, 1889, p. 1; CSU, Minutes, Dec. 2, 1889. At the request of Samuel Gompers, the Coast Seamen's Union sent him $500 to be used for organizing seamen on the Atlantic Coast. CSU, Minutes, Feb. 10, 17, 1890.

[22] CSU, Minutes, March 17, 1890.

[23] *Ibid.*, Nov. 10, 17, 1890; *CSJ*, Nov. 26, 1890, p. 1. The membership on the Great Lakes was estimated at 3,000 men, loosely organized in district assemblies of the Knights of Labor. On the Atlantic there were six groups operating independently of each other. With the exception of the Boston group, with 2,000 members, all of them were small. The Gulf ports were well organized.

[24] The following account of the formation and early history of the National Seamen's Union is based on CSU, Minutes, 1890–1891; SUP, Minutes, 1891–1900; SUP, Files; *CSJ*, 1892–1901; and NSU convention proceedings published in *CSJ*. Arthur E. Albrecht, *International Seamen's Union*, U.S. Bureau of Labor Statistics, Bull. no. 342 (Washington: 1923), is perhaps the best published secondary work on the early history of the ISU.

[25] AFL, *Proceedings, 1891*, p. 44. George Watson Reid (N.Y.) had represented the International Association of Sailors and Firemen at the 1899 convention. John F. O'Sullivan (Boston) had represented the Sailors and Firemen's International Union in 1890.

[26] Excerpts from letters were printed in almost every issue of *CSJ* and were recorded in SUP, Minutes.

[27] For a candid view of union tactics on the Atlantic Coast during this period, read James H. Williams, "The Autobiography of a Labor Leader," *Independent*, LIV (Nov. 6, 1902), 2634–2638.

[28] Letter from T. J. Elderkin, Oct. 31, 1895, in *CSJ*, Nov. 6, 1895, p. 7.

[29] "The arrangements were quite simple by modern comparison, but they were quite elaborate for the simple-minded lot in the Atlantic Coast Seamen's Union. The walls of the union headquarters were decorated with two coats of paint, the floors were carefully scrubbed and treated to two coats of special anti-fouling composition. The old-fashioned slush lamps were discarded and up-to-date electric lights installed. The old spruce benches were discarded and neatly varnished, hardwood chairs were installed in their place. The boys invested $12.00 in a dozen bright

nickle-plated cuspidors to protect their new floors from defilement. A rug was contributed which was spread at the front door. It read, 'Clean your mortal soles.' Not one cent of the expenses was charged to the union. It was all contributed by the members." *West Coast Sailors,* July 2, 1937.

[30] T. J. Elderkin resigned in January, 1899, partly because of a conflict with the secretary of the Great Lakes Seamen's Union, William Penje. *CSJ,* Jan. 11, 1899, p. 7.

[31] A. M. McDonnell to Furuseth, April 7, 1898, in SUP, Files; *CSJ,* Jan. 12, 1898, pp. 5, 7.

[32] McDonnell to Furuseth, April 7, 1898; J. H. Williams to Furuseth, Feb. 2, 1898, in SUP, Files; *CSJ,* Jan. 5, 1898, pp. 5, 7; Jan. 12, 1898, p. 6; Feb. 2, 1898, p. 7; March 2, 1898, p. 7.

[33] McDonnell to Furuseth, Feb. 7, 1898, Furuseth to Wilson, Feb. 2, 1898, Wilson to Furuseth, Feb. 4, June 18, 1898, in SUP, Files.

[34] Bureyson to Furuseth, April 30, 1898, McDonnell to Furuseth, Feb. 3, 1899, in SUP, Files. Bureyson later showed up on the West Coast, presumably paid back the money he had taken, and became an important officer in the union.

[35] Penje to Furuseth, Jan. 20, 1899, in SUP, Files.

[36] *CSJ,* March 15, 1899, p. 6; March 22, 1899, p. 6; April 5, 1899, p. 6.

[37] Minutes of the Shipping Association in Boston (written on stationery of Atlantic Coast Seamen's Union), Jan. 20, 1899, in SUP, Files.

[38] In a letter to Furuseth, n.d., in SUP, Files, McDonnell says that James H. Williams thought crimps should be regarded as "implacable enemies."

[39] William Frazier (N.Y.) to Furuseth, Feb. 22, May 13, 1899, Atkinson (Phila.) to Furuseth, Jan. 20, 1899, in SUP, Files.

[40] ISU, "Proceedings, 1899," in *CSJ,* Jan. 3, 1900, pp. 1–2, 6–7.

[41] For his reports on the Eastern unions, see *CSJ,* Feb. 7, 1900, p. 1; July 11, 1900, pp. 6–7; March 27, 1901, p. 5; April 3, 1901, p. 7.

[42] *CSJ,* March 6, 1901, p. 6.

Notes to Chapter V

FIGHTER

(Pages 57–84)

[1] Principal sources on SUP activities and problems in the first decade of the century are *CSJ;* SUP, Minutes; and SUP, Files.

[2] Quarterly Financial Reports, SUP, Minutes.

[3] Secretary's Report, SUP, Minutes, Dec. 29, 1901.

[4] *San Francisco Call,* May 23, 28, 1899; *CSJ,* April 6, 1899, pp. 6, 7; April 12, 1899, p. 6; April 19, 1899, p. 6; April 26, 1899, pp. 6, 7; May 3, 1899, pp. 6–7; May 17, 1899, p. 7; May 31, 1899, pp. 6, 7; SUP, Minutes, April 4, 10, 17, 24, May 15, 29, July 17, 1899.

[5] Ed Rosenberg to Furuseth, May 29, 1900, in SUP, Files.

[6] Henry Petersen to Furuseth, April 12, 1900, in SUP, Files.

[7] SUP, Minutes, Feb. 12, 26, 1900; unsigned letter to Furuseth, March 9, 1900, Walter Macarthur to Furuseth, May 2, 1900, in SUP, Files.

[8] To prove the loyalty of all factions, a resolution was adopted "that this meeting sends greeting to him [Furuseth] for the noble work he has performed for this union." SUP, Minutes, March 6, 1900.

[9] [Rosenberg] to Furuseth, May 15, 1900, in SUP, Files.

[10] Nicholas Jortall to Furuseth, n.d., in *ibid.*

[11] Best general accounts of this strike are in Ira B. Cross, *A History of the Labor Movement in California* (Berkeley: 1935), pp. 239–245; Thomas W. Page, "The San

Francisco Labor Movement in 1901," *Political Science Quarterly,* XVII (Dec., 1902), 664–688; George Jensen, "The City Front Federation of San Francisco" (unpublished M.A. thesis, University of California, Berkeley, 1912); Robert C. Francis, "A History of Labor on the San Francisco Waterfront" (unpublished Ph.D. thesis, University of California, Berkeley, 1934), pp. 94–117; Robert M. Robinson, "San Francisco Teamsters at the Turn of the Century," *California Historical Society Quarterly,* XXXV (March, 1956), 59–69; (June, 1956), 145–153. Primary sources include the San Francisco newspapers *(Bulletin, Call, Chronicle,* and *Examiner)* as well as union records and *CSJ.*

[12] California Bureau of Labor Statistics, *Annual Report, 1900.*
[13] *San Francisco Examiner,* July 27, 1901.
[14] Other commentators on this period have interpreted the maneuvers of labor as a show to gain favorable public opinion, but it is my opinion that the leadership was sincerely anxious to avoid a fight.
[15] *San Francisco Chronicle,* July 30, 1901.
[16] *Ibid.,* Aug. 25, 1901.
[17] *San Francisco Examiner,* Aug. 6, 1901.
[18] *San Francisco Bulletin,* Aug. 10, 1901; *San Francisco Chronicle,* Aug. 11, 1901; *San Francisco Call,* Aug. 11, 1901.
[19] *San Francisco Examiner,* Sept. 3, 1901.
[20] *San Francisco Bulletin,* Sept. 1, 1901.
[21] *San Francisco Chronicle,* Sept. 28, 1901.
[22] Copy of an affidavit by Furuseth dated Sept. 26, 1901, in James D. Phelan, Correspondence and Papers, Bancroft Library, Berkeley, Calif. Phelan later denied Furuseth's version of the conference. *San Francisco Bulletin,* Nov. 7, 1907.
[23] *San Francisco Examiner,* Sept. 3, 1901.
[24] Letter from S. H. Goff, president, and Ed Rosenberg, secretary, San Francisco Central Labor Council, Aug. 23, 1901, in *CSJ,* Aug. 28, 1901, p. 10.
[25] *CSJ,* Sept. 11, 1901, pp. 2, 3.
[26] Michael to Phelan, July 30, 1901, in *CSJ,* July 31, 1901, pp. 8–9.
[27] *CSJ,* Aug. 14, 1901, p. 11. See also editorial, *CSJ,* Aug. 21, 1901, p. 6; *San Francisco Bulletin,* Aug. 20, 1901.
[28] *San Francisco Call,* Sept. 8, 12, 1901; *San Francisco Examiner,* Sept. 12, 1901; *CSJ,* Sept. 11, 1901, p. 6.
[29] *San Francisco Examiner,* Aug. 8, 1901.
[30] *San Francisco Bulletin,* Aug. 21, 1901.
[31] *San Francisco Chronicle,* Sept. 7, 1901; *San Francisco Bulletin,* Sept. 7, 1901.
[32] *San Francisco Chronicle,* Oct. 3, 1901.
[33] *Ibid.* A search of SUP, Files, failed to reveal any details of the settlement.
[34] Several references are made in SUP, Minutes, to funds being supplied to the longshoremen on September 23 and 30, 1901.
[35] SUP, Minutes, Dec. 28, 1901.
[36] *CSJ,* Oct. 30, 1901, p. 7.
[37] Samuel Gompers, *Seventy Years of Life and Labor* (New York: 1925), I, 349.
[38] *CSJ,* July 23, 1902, p. 6.
[39] *Ibid.*
[40] "I believe," said Furuseth, "that labor organizations...should be free and apart from political organizations...[which are] not one-half as fundamental as the trade union movement." AFL, *Proceedings, 1902,* p. 181.
[41] For this contract, see *CSJ,* April 2, 1902, p. 6; April 9, 1902, p. 17; see also SUP, Minutes, April 14, 1902, and Jan. 29, 1902.
[42] Letters from John Kean, secretary pro tem, to branches, Nov. 19, 1901, Jan. 29, 1902, in SUP, Files; SUP, Minutes, Nov. 11, Dec. 16, 1901.
[43] Furuseth to William Gohl, Aug. 25, 1904, in SUP, Files.

⁴⁴ Accounts of the strike may be found in *CSJ*, Sept. 5, 1906, p. 1; ISU, *Proceedings, 1906*, pp. 14–15, 27, 29.
⁴⁵ E. Ellison to William Frazier, July 25, 1906, and to L. M. Garthe, secretary of Longshoremen's Union, Nome, Alaska, Sept. 18, 1906, in SUP, Files.
⁴⁶ Ellison to Gohl, July 13, 1906, to Frazier, July 25, 1906, and to branches, July 12, 1906, in SUP, Files.
⁴⁷ SUP, Files, contain many copies of such letters. Some of these appear in *CSJ*, July 25, 1906, pp. 1, 2, 10, 11; Aug. 22, 1906, pp. 2, 10.
⁴⁸ AFL, *Proceedings, 1906*, pp. 178–181; testimony of Furuseth before House Committee on Judiciary, March 23, 1904, quoted in *CSJ*, March 30, 1904, pp. 1, 2; Sept. 7, 1904, p. 1.
⁴⁹ Evelyn Wells, *Fremont Older* (New York: 1936), p. 301.
⁵⁰ Ellison to Gohl, Feb. 7, 1907, in SUP, Files.
⁵¹ *CSJ*, Sept. 20, 1905, p. 7 ("If we are the true sons of our fathers who bought our freedom with their blood, we must and will protect it even if it land us in prison for contempt of court"); ISU, *Proceedings, 1908*, p. 58; AFL, *Proceedings, 1908*, pp. 219–221. Furuseth's point of view was not adopted by the AFL convention.
⁵² Furuseth to Gompers, Oct. 11, 1907, in SUP, Files.
⁵³ Ellison to Dan Sullivan, July 13, 1906, in SUP, Files.
⁵⁴ AFL, *Proceedings, 1905*, p. 188.
⁵⁵ *CSJ*, Dec. 7, 1887, p. 1; Dec. 28, 1887, p. 2; CSU, Minutes, Oct. 15, 22, 1888; April 15, Sept. 30, Nov. 9, 1889; Jan. 27, June 23, 30, Aug. 11, Dec. 1, 1890; Jan. 28, March 30, April 13, May 28, June 15, July 13, 1891.
⁵⁶ Furuseth's philosophy on this point is best expressed in *CSJ*, Dec. 24, 1902, pp. 1–2; Jan. 25, 1905; Nov. 1, 1905, p. 1; ISU, *Proceedings, 1902*, pp. 22–25. The best single source of information is three boxes labeled "1905" in SUP, Files, which contain thousands of letters and telegrams on the seamen-longshoremen fight, all the important documents, speeches, and resolutions on the subject, and ILA convention proceedings with notes in the margin by Furuseth.
⁵⁷ ISU, "Proceedings, 1901," in *CSJ*, Jan. 8, 1902, pp. 1–2, 9–10; Jan. 15, 1902, pp. 1–2, 9–10. Previous mild attempts at organization had been made in 1893. *CSJ*, March 8, 1893, p. 8.
⁵⁸ See AFL, *Proceedings, 1901*, p. 243; *1902*, pp. 195–196.
⁵⁹ ISU, *Proceedings, 1902*, p. 13; *1904*, p. 21; *CSJ*, Jan. 1, 1902, p. 6.
⁶⁰ ISU, *Proceedings of the Conference between the I.S.U. and the I.L.A., Erie, Pennsylvania, April 18–20, 1906* (San Francisco: 1906), pp. 98–103.
⁶¹ *San Francisco Chronicle*, July 30, 1903; *San Francisco Examiner*, Aug. 1, 1903; *CSJ*, Aug. 5, 1903, pp. 1–2.
⁶² ISU, "Proceedings, 1899," in *CSJ*, Jan. 3, 1900, pp. 6–7. The Lake Seamen's Union also decided to organize the firemen at their convention on January 15, 1900. *CSJ*, Feb. 7, 1900, p. 4.
⁶³ Penje to Furuseth, Feb. 1, 1899, in SUP, Files.
⁶⁴ Penje to Furuseth, March 13, 1900, in SUP, Files.
⁶⁵ AFL, *Proceedings, 1904*, p. 250.
⁶⁶ *Ibid.*, p. 248.
⁶⁷ Furuseth to branches, June 21, 1904, in SUP, Minutes, June 21, 1904.
⁶⁸ A summary of the ILA-ISU controversy to this point may be found in *CSJ*, July 13, 1904, pp. 1–2, 6.
⁶⁹ *CSJ*, April 19, 1905, pp. 1–2. Hundreds of telegrams and letters (some of them in secret code) cover this period in SUP, Files, 1905.
⁷⁰ ISU, *Proceedings of the Conference between the I.S.U. and the I.L.A.*
⁷¹ AFL, *Proceedings, 1895*, p. 36; *1896*, p. 69; *1899*, p. 139; *1900*, pp. 143–146.
⁷² *CSJ*, July 10, 1907, pp. 1–2, 6.
⁷³ AFL, *Proceedings, 1908*, pp. 77, 151, 255–256, 267.

Notes to Chapter VI

LABOR LEADER

(Pages 85–107)

[1] *CSJ*, March 9, 1910, p. 3.

[2] Very little has been written about Furuseth's personal life. Most of the author's information has been obtained by interviews with people who knew him. Especially helpful was Selim Silver of Oakland, California, who was associated with Furuseth from 1910. Some of the better articles on Furuseth as a person are Alvin S. Johnson, "Andrew Furuseth," *New Republic*, IX (Nov. 11, 1916), 40–42, and some of the eulogies in Silas B. Axtell, comp., *A Symposium on Andrew Furuseth* (New Bedford, Mass.: 1948).

[3] "Andrew Furuseth and His Fifteen Year Siege of Congress," *Current Opinion*, LIX (July, 1915), 18–19.

[4] Victor A. Olander to Jo Davidson, May, 1926, quoted in Axtell, *op. cit.*, pp. 191–192. First photograph appears in ISU, *Proceedings, 1915*, p. 15.

[5] Arthur Ruhl, "The Sailor's Side," *Colliers*, XLVII (July 22, 1911), 18–20.

[6] Personal tributes from men who knew Furuseth may be found in Axtell, *op. cit.*

[7] Furuseth, "Report," Dec. 24, 1912, in SUP, Files.

[8] Fremont Older, *My Own Story* (New York: 1919), pp. 91 ff.

[9] Robert M. La Follette, "The American Sailor a Free Man," *Survey*, XXXIV (May 1, 1915), 116–117, 125–128; Rowland H. Harvey, *Samuel Gompers* (Stanford: 1935), p. 190.

[10] John L. Mathews, "The Coming Ashore of Andrew Furuseth," *Everybody's Magazine*, XXV (July, 1911), 60–71.

[11] He referred to the New York Seaman's Institute as a "crimping" organization in the *San Francisco Call*, Dec. 7, 1909.

[12] Axtell, *op. cit.*, p. 206.

[13] Furuseth, "Labor Day Address," *CSJ*, Sept. 1, 1903, pp. 1–2.

[14] Furuseth, "Is Labor Unionism in All Its Aspects Advantageous to Laboring Men?" *CSJ*, Oct. 16, 1901, pp. 1, 8.

[15] ISU, *Proceedings, 1913*, pp. 119–121. Similar sentiments are expressed in AFL, *Proceedings, 1911*, pp. 312–313.

[16] Nov. 4, 1908, p. 6.

[17] Ellison to P. B. Gill, Feb. 7, 1908, in SUP, Files.

[18] *San Francisco Examiner*, July 27, 1911; interview with Selim Silver.

[19] AFL, *Proceedings, 1914*, pp. 357–358.

[20] *CSJ*, Aug. 10, 1904, p. 6.

[21] May 30, 1906, pp. 1, 6. Walter Macarthur, "San Francisco—A Climax in Civics" (unpublished manuscript, San Francisco, 1905), in Correspondence and Papers, 1890–1945, Bancroft Library, Berkeley, Calif., defended the Union Labor party before it was completely exposed. For the full story of the Union Labor party see Walton Bean, *Boss Ruef's San Francisco* (Berkeley and Los Angeles: 1952).

[22] Furuseth to Harry Olsen, May 10, 1907, in SUP, Files; *CSJ*, March 27, 1907, pp. 1–2, 7; May 15, 1907, pp. 1, 6; May 22, 1907, pp. 1, 7; Older, *op. cit.*, pp. 90–119.

[23] Furuseth to Schmitz, May 17, 1907, in SUP, Files; *CSJ*, May 22, 1907, p. 6; *San Francisco Call*, May 17, 1907; Furuseth to Harry Olsen, May 27, 1907, in SUP, Files.

[24] *CSJ*, July 3, 1907, pp. 6, 7; July 24, 1907, p. 6; July 31, 1907, pp. 1–2.

[25] *San Francisco Call*, Oct. 30, 1907.

[26] *CSJ*, Aug. 2, 1911, pp. 1, 7.

[27] *San Francisco Call*, Sept. 30, 1909; *CSJ*, Oct. 20, 1909, p. 6.

[28] *CSJ*, Nov. 10, 1909, p. 6.

²⁹ *San Francisco Call*, Sept. 20, 22, 1911.
³⁰ *CSJ*, Nov. 8, 1911, pp. 1–2.
³¹ *San Francisco Call*, Sept. 11, 1911; *CSJ*, Oct. 4, 1911, pp. 6–7. The story of the *Times* bombing is best told in Grace H. Stimson, *Rise of the Labor Movement in Los Angeles* (Berkeley and Los Angeles: 1955), pp. 366–419.
³² *CSJ*, Oct. 12, 1904, p. 6; Ellison to J. W. Erickson, Oct. 21, 1908, in SUP, Files; *CSJ*, Sept. 23, 1908, p. 6; Oct. 21, 1908, pp. 1, 6, 7; Oct. 28, 1908, p. 7; Furuseth to J. H. Wilson, Oct. 29, 1910, in SUP, Files.
³³ Furuseth to Frank Morrison, May 11, 1908, in SUP, Files.
³⁴ AFL, *Proceedings, 1902*, p. 181.
³⁵ Ellison to Furuseth, Dec. 18, 1907, Feb. 7, 1908, Furuseth to District Committee, ISU, May 18, 1908, Furuseth to George C. Bodine, Dec. 26, 1908, in SUP, Files. The SUP Files for the period 1907–1909 are particularly rich in materials dealing with contract negotiations. Although the seamen did not agree to lower wages, Furuseth was willing to sacrifice certain working conditions in order to reach an agreement with employers. The firemen and cooks complained that the sacrifices were being made at their expense.
³⁶ Furuseth to members, Oct. 18, 1907, in SUP, Files.
³⁷ Furuseth to members, Aug. 29, 1907, in SUP, Files.
³⁸ Furuseth to A. B. Hammond, April 16, 28, May 8, 1909, and replies, April 12, 23, May 6, 1909, in SUP, Files; *CSJ*, June 9, 1909, pp. 1, 7, 10, 11.
³⁹ Furuseth to Charles Sorenson, [1909], and July 13, 1909, and to P. H. Griffin, April 5, 1909, Ellison to P. B. Gill, Nov. 14, 1907, in SUP, Files.
⁴⁰ Ellison to members, June 10, 1908, in SUP, Files.
⁴¹ *CSJ*, April 3, 1907, pp. 1, 2, 10; Jan. 13, 1909, p. 6; Jan. 27, 1909, pp. 1–2; March 31, 1909, pp. 1, 7; Jan. 18, 1911, p. 6; Feb. 8, 1911, p. 6; March 1, 1911, pp. 1–2. One complete box of correspondence in SUP, Files, titled "1908" contains more than 500 letters on this subject.
⁴² See *CSJ*, Aug. 22, 1894.
⁴³ Furuseth, "Government by Law or by Men," *CSJ*, Aug. 30, 1911, pp. 1, 7; "Labor Is Life, Not Property," *CSJ*, Sept. 7, 1904, p. 1; "Government by Injunction," *CSJ*, Sept. 3, 1902, pp. 2, 6; "Injunction in Labor Disputes," *CSJ*, Sept. 20, 1905, pp. 1, 7 (also in *Organized Labor*, Sept. 9, 1905); "Americans, Wake Up," *American Federationist*, XXIII (Aug., 1916), 653–657; Andrew Furuseth, Walter Macarthur, and I. Wisler, "Report to San Francisco Labor Council on Danbury Hatters Case," *CSJ*, July 19, 1905, p. 1; Andrew Furuseth, James E. Emery, Charles E. Littlefield, and Charles P. Niel, "Use and Abuse of Injunctions in Trade Disputes," *Annals of the American Academy of Political and Social Science*, XXXVI (July, 1910), 87–141 (also in *CSJ*, May 11, 1910, pp. 1, 7); *Hearings on National Anti-Injunction Bill, January 13 to February 26, 1904*, House Committee on Judiciary, 58th Cong., 1st sess. (1904) (also in *CSJ*, March 30, 1904, pp. 1, 3, 7); *Bills to Limit the Meaning of the Word Conspiracy*, Hearings on H.R. 1917 and S. 4233, House Committee on Judiciary, 56th Cong., 2d sess. (1900); *Congressional Record*, 62d Cong., 2d sess., 48:3 (Feb. 29, 1912), 2615. See pages 76–78 on Hammond Lumber Company case in which Furuseth was personally involved; also *Hammond Lumber Co. v. SUP et al.*, No. 13919, U.S. Court of Appeals, in *CSJ*, Feb. 24, 1909, pp. 1–2, 7, 10–11.
⁴⁴ *CSJ*, May 11, 1910, p. 1.
⁴⁵ Furuseth, "Injunctions in Labor Disputes," *CSJ*, Sept. 20, 1905, pp. 1, 7.
⁴⁶ *Ibid.*
⁴⁷ Furuseth to Gompers, [1897], in AFL, Files, Washington, D.C., cited in Harvey, *op. cit.*, pp. 65–66 (in this letter Furuseth advises physical resistance in the Pennsylvania miners' strike); *CSJ*, Sept. 20, 1916, p. 2.
⁴⁸ AFL, *Proceedings, 1908*, pp. 219–222. Furuseth made the same proposal in 1914. AFL, *Proceedings, 1914*, p. 445.

Notes

⁴⁹ AFL, *Proceedings, 1909*, pp. 311–314; *CSJ*, Feb. 5, 1908, pp. 1–2, 6–7; Jan. 6, 1909, p. 7; July 13, 1910, p. 2.

⁵⁰ AFL, *Proceedings, 1912*, pp. 276–308.

⁵¹ Samuel Gompers, *Seventy Years of Life and Labor* (rev. ed.; New York: 1943), pp. 242–243; *CSJ*, April 4, 1906, pp. 1–2, 7.

⁵² AFL, *Proceedings, 1912*, pp. 349–351. There is no contemporary evidence that Furuseth actually opposed the Clayton Act as he later claimed in the 1920's.

⁵³ A. Furuseth and James J. Creamer, "Report of Fraternal Delegates to British Trade Union Congress," AFL, *Proceedings, 1908*, pp. 127–130; also in *CSJ*, Nov. 25, 1908, pp. 1–2, 7–11.

⁵⁴ ISU, *Proceedings, 1907*, pp. 27, 54, 93. The ISU joined the ITW on the motion of Paul Scharrenberg at the 1906 convention. ISU, *Proceedings, 1906*, p. 56. A referendum of the ISU in 1905 on whether to join the ITW had resulted in so few votes being cast that no action was taken. *CSJ*, Aug. 2, 1905, p. 6; ISU, *Proceedings, 1905*, p. 30.

⁵⁵ Furuseth's report on his travels appears in ISU, *Proceedings, 1908*, pp. 32–51, and in *CSJ*, Dec. 30, 1908, pp. 1–2, 7, 9–11. Letters written by Furuseth while en route appear in *CSJ*, Aug. 26, 1908, p. 7; Sept. 2, 1908, p. 7; Sept. 9, 1908, p. 6; Sept. 23, 1908, p. 7.

⁵⁶ Furuseth to *CSJ*, from Nottingham, England, Sept. 5, 1908, in *CSJ*, Sept. 23, 1908, p. 7. For an earlier attack on the European Socialist program for seamen, see the SUP's reply to a legislative questionnaire in *CSJ*, Feb. 25, 1903. Chris Damm, a European labor leader who was not a Socialist, gives his impression of Furuseth in a letter to S. B. Axtell. Axtell, *op. cit.*, p. 230.

⁵⁷ SUP, Files, 1909, especially letters from Furuseth to Frazier in that year; *CSJ*, March 10, 1909, p. 7; Sept. 22, 1909, p. 1

⁵⁸ Furuseth to SUP, from Cardiff, Wales, Aug. 3, 1910, in SUP, Files (also in *CSJ*, Aug. 17, 1910, p. 6). Wilson was a Liberal M.P. who best expressed his bias against British Socialists in letters to Furuseth, Oct. 4, Sept. 2, 9, 1912, in SUP, Files. A good personal description of Wilson when he came to New York in 1909 will be found in *CSJ*, July, 1932, pp. 206–207.

⁵⁹ For an account of the convention, see Furuseth, "Report on Seamen's Conference," in ISU, *Proceedings, 1910*, pp. 93–101 (also in *CSJ*, Sept. 28, 1910, pp. 1–2, 7); and "Talk on a Trip Abroad" (before S.F. Labor Council), *CSJ*, Nov. 2, 1910, p. 11.

⁶⁰ Items on the strike appear in *CSJ* almost every month from January to August, 1911; see also Samuel Gompers, "The Seamen's Successful Uprising," *American Federationist*, XVIII (Sept., 1911), 679–693.

⁶¹ This section is based principally on ISU, *Proceedings*; *CSJ*; and SUP, Files, for these years.

⁶² ISU, "Proceedings, 1900," in *CSJ*, Jan. 16, 1901, p. 1, reported 6,809 members; "Proceedings, 1901," in *CSJ*, Jan. 8, 1902, pp. 1–2, reports 11,123 members; in *Proceedings, 1903*, p. 17, Frazier reported 10,000 new members, which he said was almost a 100 per cent increase.

⁶³ Olander in Axtell, *op. cit.*, pp. 191–192.

⁶⁴ ISU, *Proceedings, 1911*, pp. 33–37.

⁶⁵ *The Seamen's Bill*, Hearings on H.R. 23673, Jan., 1912, House Committee on Merchant Marine and Fisheries, 62d Cong., 2d sess. (1912), pp. 182–184, 198; *CSJ*, Jan. 24, 1912, pp. 1, 7; Jan. 31, 1912, pp. 1, 7.

⁶⁶ Analyses of the seamen's bills by Furuseth, Bodine, and William Denman appear in ISU, *Proceedings, 1911*, pp. 52–68.

⁶⁷ ISU, *Proceedings, 1913*, p. 18; *CSJ*, Feb. 7, 1912, p. 6; Feb. 28, 1912, p. 6.

⁶⁸ Instead, the *Coast Seamen's Journal's* name was changed to *Seamen's Journal* in order to give it a national name. ISU, *Proceedings, 1911*, p. 169. (I will continue to use the abbreviation *CSJ* in this volume.)

⁶⁹ *New York Times*, June 18, 1911; Joseph P. Goldberg, "American Seamen" (Ph.D. thesis, Publication No. 2815, University Microfilms, Ann Arbor, Mich., 1950), pp. 68–70; *CSJ*, June 28, 1911, p. 6; Sept. 13, 1911, pp. 2, 7 (text of agreements).

⁷⁰ Goldberg, *op. cit.*, pp. 70–76.

⁷¹ Furuseth to SUP, April 15, July 8, July 26, 1913, Furuseth, "Report," July 16, 20, 1913, in SUP, Files; Harold L. Varney, "The Story of the I.W.W., Chapter 13," *One Big Union Monthly*, II (April, 1920), 41–44. Weekly attacks on the IWW were made in *CSJ*; one of the best appears in the issue of April 1, 1914, p. 6.

⁷² Furuseth to SUP, April 15, July 6, Aug. 4, 1913, Furuseth, "Report," July 8, 26, 1913, in SUP, Files; *CSJ*, Oct. 1, 1913, p. 1; Feb. 4, 1914, p. 6. Furuseth further charged that Bodine used union funds for personal gain.

⁷³ ISU, *Proceedings, 1914*, pp. 18–25. In letters to Thomas Hanson, Sept. 15, 16, 1913, in SUP, Files, Furuseth reported that Atlantic seamen were confused and were not paying dues to either organization.

⁷⁴ "Report," Dec. 24, 1912, in SUP, Files.

⁷⁵ The firemen, formerly with the ILA, joined the ISU in 1907.

⁷⁶ For different views on the Welfare Plan, see Paul F. Brissenden, *Employment System of the Lake Carriers' Association*, U.S. Bureau of Labor Statistics, Bull. no. 235 (Washington: 1918), pp. 1–33; *Annual Report, 1909*, Lake Carriers' Association (Detroit: 1910); ISU, *Proceedings, 1909*, pp. 12–16, 116–120; Furuseth, "The Welfare Plan," *CSJ*, Jan. 26, 1910, p. 7; Henry E. Hoagland, *Wage Bargaining on the Vessels of the Great Lakes* (Urbana, Ill.: 1917).

⁷⁷ Furuseth to Olander, May 6, 1909, in SUP, Files.

⁷⁸ *CSJ*, April 28, 1909, p. 6; May 5, 1909, p. 6; July 14, 1909, p. 1; AFL, *Proceedings, 1909*, p. 248.

⁷⁹ Furuseth to Frazier, Oct. 21, 1909, in SUP, Files.

⁸⁰ The *CSJ* published articles on the strike almost weekly and a special edition on March 15, 1911. See also "The Lake Seamen's Struggle for Liberty," *American Federationist*, XVII (May, 1910), 413–415.

⁸¹ AFL, *Proceedings, 1909*, p. 63.

⁸² ISU, *Proceedings, 1915*, pp. 16–26.

Notes to Chapter VII

THE SEAMEN'S ACT

(Pages 108–132)

¹ Furuseth to Mrs. J. H. Archibald, Aug. 20, 1907, in SUP, Files.

² *Congressional Record*, 58th Cong., 2d sess., 38:3 (Feb. 19, 1904), 2094.

³ "The Dawn of Another Day," *American Federationist*, XXII (Sept., 1915), 717–722.

⁴ In 1800 vessels carried 50 tons per man; in 1900 they carried 600 tons per man. *CSJ*, Dec. 26, 1900, p. 6.

⁵ U.S. Industrial Commission, *Report* (Washington: 1901), IV, 690–691, 695. This report is a principal source for the description of conditions aboard ship. Among others are James H. Williams, "How We Live to Make Her Go," *Independent*, LVI (Jan. 7, 1904), 18–22; *Report of the Merchant Marine Commission and Hearings*, Senate Committee on Commerce, 58th Cong., 3d sess., S. Rept. 2755 (1905); Arthur Ruhl, "The Sailor's Side," *Collier's*, XLVII (July 22, 1911), 18–20; George M. Hunter, "The Revolution on the Sea," *Survey*, XXVIII (May 4, 1912), 199–205; Ernest J. Hopkins, "Changing the Life in the Forecastle," *Survey*, XXVIII (July 6, 1912), 495-496; Atlanticus, "Unionism Afloat," *Atlantic Monthly*, CXVI (July, 1915), 50–56. Typical of the shipowner's view of the sailor is an article by a member of the U.S. Shipping Board, John A. Donald, "The Sea Calls Again," *Saint Nicholas*, XLIV (Sept., 1917), 973–975.

⁶ *CSJ*, Jan. 18, 1905, p. 6.
⁷ Furuseth to Harry Olsen, July 16, 1907, in SUP, Files.
⁸ *CSJ*, Aug. 16, 1911, p. 7.
⁹ Material in this section is drawn mainly from *CSJ;* ISU, *Proceedings;* AFL, *Proceedings; Congressional Record,* 57th Cong., 2d sess., 36:3 (Feb. 25, 1903); 58th Cong., 3d sess., 39:3 (Feb. 11, 1905); and 59th Cong., 1st sess., 42:4 (March 16, 1908); and Walter Macarthur, "Efficiency of Ships' Crews," *Charities and the Commons,* XVI (May 19, 1906), 250–252.
¹⁰ *CSJ*, May 10, 1911, p. 6. Furuseth brought civil suit against the Pacific Mail Steamship Company for violation of the Chinese Exclusion and Alien Contract Labor laws.
¹¹ Furuseth to T. Liddy, Sept. 27, 1907, in SUP, Files.
¹² ISU, *Proceedings, 1916,* pp. 13–17; letter from Indian seamen's union to SUP, Feb., 1938, in possession of Selim Silver, Oakland, California.
¹³ See, for example, *CSJ*, Jan. 17, 1906, p. 6; Dec. 18, 1906, p. 6; Jan. 2, 1907; Samuel Gompers, *Seventy Years of Life and Labor* (New York: 1925), I, 165–166.
¹⁴ *CSJ*, Dec. 12, 1900, p. 7.
¹⁵ This account of the evolution of the seamen's bill is based on *CSJ;* ISU, *Proceedings;* AFL, *Proceedings; Congressional Record,* 58th Cong., 2d sess., 38:3 (Feb. 19, 1904); *Petition of Seamen,* Senate Committee on Commerce, 61st Cong., 2d sess., S. Doc. 379 (1910); *American Seamen,* Hearings on H.R. 11193, House Committee on Merchant Marine and Fisheries, 61st Cong., 1st sess. (1910); *Hearings on H.R. 11372,* House Committee on Merchant Marine and Fisheries, 62d Cong., 2d sess. (1912); *The Decay of Seamanship, by Andrew Furuseth,* Senate Committee on Commerce, 63d Cong., 1st sess., S. Doc. 216 (1913).
¹⁶ *CSJ*, June 28, 1911, pp. 1, 7.
¹⁷ *Legal Status of Seamen,* Senate Committee on Commerce, 61st Cong., 2d sess., S. Doc. 552 (1910); Furuseth, "Peonage and Wages," *CSJ*, June 14, 1911, pp. 1–2, and "Status of Seamen in Late Colonial Times and Since," *CSJ*, Oct., 1935, pp. 175–176.
¹⁸ *CSJ*, Dec. 30, 1908, p. 10.
¹⁹ AFL, *Proceedings, 1902,* p. 70; *1903,* p. 108. Compare with *CSJ*, May 16, 1900, p. 6, which editorially asks that desertion of foreign seamen in American ports be stopped.
²⁰ Furuseth to J. W. Alexander, chairman of House Committee on Merchant Marine and Fisheries, April, 1912, in *CSJ*, April 10, 1912, p. 1; Furuseth to Woodrow Wilson, June 26, 1913, in SUP, Files.
²¹ ISU, *Proceedings, 1910,* p. 5.
²² *CSJ*, July 13, 1910, pp. 1, 7; Aug. 17, 1910, p. 6; ISU, *Proceedings, 1910,* pp. 5–8; Furuseth, "Supplemental Report," July 8, 1910, bound with *Hearings on Spight Seamen's Bill* (special edition in International Longshoremen's Union Library, San Francisco).
²³ Furuseth to Raymond Robbins, Chicago, July 18, 1909, in SUP, Files.
²⁴ *CSJ*, June 22, 1910, p. 6.
²⁵ In addition to the basic union sources cited earlier, see *Hearings on H.R. 11372; The Seamen's Bill,* Hearings on H.R. 23673, House Committee on Merchant Marine and Fisheries, 62d Cong., 2d sess. (1911–1912); *The Seamen's Bill,* Hearings on S. 136, House Committee on Merchant Marine and Fisheries, 63d Cong., 2d sess. (1913–1914); *Involuntary Servitude Imposed upon Seamen,* Hearings on H.R. 23673, Senate Committee on Commerce, 62d Cong., 3d sess. (1912–1913); *The Seamen's Bill,* Hearings on S. 136, Senate Committee on Commerce, 63d Cong., 2d sess. (1914).
²⁶ Oct. 10, 1888, p. 1.
²⁷ William S. Benson, *The Merchant Marine* (New York: 1923).
²⁸ *Development of American Merchant Marine,* H. Rept. 4136 on H.R. 17098, House Committee on Merchant Marine and Fisheries, 58th Cong., 3d sess. (Feb. 1, 1905), p. 27.
²⁹ ISU, *Proceedings, 1906,* pp. 51–52.
³⁰ *San Francisco Bulletin,* Aug. 20, 1909; AFL, *Proceedings, 1910,* p. 178.

³¹ *CSJ*, May 29, 1912, p. 6; Aug. 14, 1912, pp. 1, 6, 7; James Rolph to President Wilson, July 25, 1914, in SUP, Files.

³² Rudolph Spreckles, *An Answer to the Printed Attack of Mr. R. P. Schwerin* (San Francisco: n.d.).

³³ *Congressional Record*, 58th Cong., 3d sess., 39:3 (Feb. 11, 1905), 2411.

³⁴ Feb. 1, 1911, pp. 1, 7.

³⁵ Furuseth to House Committee on Merchant Marine and Fisheries, April 5, 1912, in SUP, Files.

³⁶ *CSJ*, May 1, 1912, pp. 1, 7; Aug. 27, 1913, pp. 1, 10; *San Francisco Call*, April 17, 1912; George M. Hunter, "Law Making by Landsmen for Seamen," *Survey*, XXVIII (May 18, 1912), 292–294; Samuel Gompers, "The Titanic Disaster," *American Federationist*, XIX (July, 1912), 545–548; James H. Williams, "Manning Our Merchant Marine," *Independent*, XCI (Sept. 22, 1917), 469, 483; *New York Times*, April 14, 20, 1913.

³⁷ *The Seamen's Bill*, House Committee on Merchant Marine and Fisheries, 62d Cong., 2d sess., H. Rept. 645, Pt. 2, *Free and Efficient Seamen* (1912).

³⁸ *CSJ*, July 10, 1912, p. 6.

³⁹ Furuseth, "Report," Dec. 21, 1912, in SUP, Files.

⁴⁰ *CSJ*, Feb. 26, 1913, p. 1; March 19, 1913, pp. 1–2; Furuseth to SUP, Feb. 23, 1913, in SUP, Files.

⁴¹ *Congressional Record*, 62d Cong., 3d sess., 49:5 (March 2, 1913), 4563–4588; *New York Times*, March 3, 1913; Furuseth to SUP, March 3, 1913, in SUP, Files.

⁴² *CSJ*, March 12, 1913, p. 1; *New York Times*, March 4, 5, 1913.

⁴³ Principal sources on the fortunes of the seamen's bill in the Senate are Furuseth's reports to the SUP in SUP, Files; *Congressional Record*, 63d Cong., 1st sess., 50:6 (Oct., 1913); and *New York Times*.

⁴⁴ Furuseth, "Report," April 15, July 6, 8, 16, 18, 20, 26, Aug. 4, Sept. 16, 1913, Furuseth to E. Ellison, July 26, 1913, Furuseth to Thomas A. Hanson, Sept. 15, 1913, in SUP, Files.

⁴⁵ *Joint Letter from Secretary of Commerce and Secretary of Labor on S. 4...*, Senate Committee on Commerce, 63d Cong., 1st sess., S. Doc. 211 (1913).

⁴⁶ Furuseth to Ellison, June 19, 1913, in SUP, Files.

⁴⁷ *CSJ*, Sept. 10, 1913, p. 1; *Washington Times*, Aug. 21, 1913.

⁴⁸ *New York Times*, Oct. 12, 17, 1913; "Editorial," *Survey*, XXXI (Nov. 8, 1913), 163–164; "Why We Need a Shipping Bill," *Outlook*, CV (Nov. 8, 1913), 503–504; Florence Kelly, "Seamanship and Safety," *Survey*, XXXI (Nov. 8, 1913), 154–155, and "Safety at Sea and the Consumers' League," *Survey*, XXXII (May 2, 1914), 112.

⁴⁹ *Congressional Record*, 63d Cong., 1st sess., 50:6 (Oct. 21, 1913), 5715.

⁵⁰ Robert La Follette to Robert La Follette, Jr., Oct. 24, 1913, cited in Belle C. La Follette, *Robert M. La Follette* (New York: 1953), I, 531

⁵¹ Main sources on this conference are Furuseth's reports and letters to the SUP in SUP, Files; *CSJ*; ISU, *Proceedings*; *Welfare of American Seamen, Memorial of International Seamen's Union on International Conference on Safety of Life at Sea*, Senate Committee on Foreign Relations, 63d Cong., 2d sess., S. Rept. 452 (1914); *Message and Documents on International Conference on Safety of Life at Sea*, Senate Committee on Foreign Relations, 63d Cong., 2d sess., S. Doc. 463 (1914).

⁵² *CSJ*, Aug. 5, 1908, pp. 1, 7; Sept. 30, 1908, pp. 1, 7; March 10, 1909, p. 1; ISU, *Proceedings, 1908*, pp. 20–23; *Better Security of Life at Sea; Commission on Revision of Laws Relating to Safety of Life at Sea*, Senate Committee on Commerce, 60th Cong., 2d sess., S. Doc. 701 (1909).

⁵³ Furuseth to W. C. Redfield, Oct. 6, 1913, in SUP, Files; *CSJ*, Nov. 5, 1913, pp. 1, 2. Woodrow Wilson believed that Congress should not act until after the London conference. See letter from Wilson to Redfield, Oct. 20, 1913 (Wilson Papers, Library of

Congress), cited in Joseph P. Goldberg, "American Seamen" (Ph.D. thesis, Publication No. 2815, University Microfilms, Ann Arbor, Mich., 1950), p. 119

[54] Telegram from Furuseth to John Tennison, Oct. 4, 1913, in SUP, Files.

[55] Furuseth, "Report," Oct. 11, 1913, in SUP, Files.

[56] Furuseth to Tennison, Oct. 27, 1913, Furuseth, "Report," Oct. 29, 1913, in SUP, Files.

[57] Furuseth to Tennison, Nov. 28, 1913, in SUP, Files. J. Havelock Wilson, present as a British technical adviser, wrote to SUP, Dec. 18, 1913: "It is a perfect treat to hear Andy talk to the International shipowners and representatives of the Board of Trade from other countries." SUP, Files.

[58] Furuseth to SUP, Nov. 16, 1913, in SUP, Files.

[59] *New York Times*, Dec. 27, 1913; *San Francisco Examiner*, Dec. 25, 26, 1913; Furuseth to President Wilson, Jan. 12, 1914, in SUP, Files.

[60] Furuseth, "Report," Jan. 10, May 23, 1914, in SUP, Files; Redfield to Woodrow Wilson, Feb. 2, 1914 (Wilson Papers), cited in Goldberg, *op. cit.*, p. 110.

[61] *San Francisco Examiner*, Dec. 21, 1913; *New York Times*, Oct. 25, 26, Nov. 22, 24, 30, Dec. 10, 16, 1913; Jan. 10, 15, 17, 19, April 2, 1914; letter to shipowners on Pacific Coast, June 18, 1914, in John Kentfield and Company, Business Records, 1853–1923, Box 10, Folder 1, Bancroft Library, Berkeley, Calif.; "An Ill-considered and Pernicious Bill," *Scientific American*, CX (Jan. 31, 1914), 94; "Finding Flaws in the Seamen's Bill," *Literary Digest*, XLVII (Nov. 8, 1913), 860.

[62] Officer of the Inland Marine, "Our National Waterways and the La Follette Seamen's Bill," *Survey*, XXXIII (Dec. 12, 1914), 282–283; Herbert C. Sadler, "The Seamen's Bill," *Nation*, XCVIII (Jan. 15, 1914), 57; George W. White, "The La Follette Seamen's Bill," *Outlook*, CV (Nov. 29, 1913), 713; "Safety at Sea," *Survey*, XXXII (June 27, 1914), 349–351.

[63] "Report," March 14, 1914, in SUP, Files. This section is based largely on Furuseth's reports to the SUP and the *CSJ*; see also *Hearings on International Conference on Safety of Life at Sea*, Senate Committee on Foreign Relations, 63d Cong., 2d sess. (1914); *Welfare of American Seamen*, House Committee on Merchant Marine and Fisheries, 63d Cong., 2d sess., H. Rept. 852 (1914); *Conference Report on Seamen's Bill, S. 136*, House Committee on Merchant Marine and Fisheries, 63d Cong., 3d sess., H. Rept. 1439 (1915); *Congressional Record*, 63d Cong., 3d sess., 50:14 (Aug. 27, 1914), and 52:5 (Feb. 25, 1915).

[64] *New York Times*, Dec. 16, 17, 1918. The treaty did not go into effect because no official action was taken owing to the war.

[65] One explanation for passage of the bill at this time was that Congress wanted to encourage registration of foreign ships under the U.S. flag and it was necessary to clear up any uncertainties. "Modified Seamen's Bill Passes the House," *Survey*, XXXII (Sept. 5, 1914), 555–556.

[66] Furuseth, "Report," Oct. 17, 1914, in SUP, Files.

[67] Gompers to Senator Thomas A. Martin, Oct. 6, 1914, in SUP, Files; *CSJ*, Oct. 21, 1914, p. 6; Oct. 28, 1914, p. 6.

[68] Furuseth to Tennison, Oct. 10, 1914, Furuseth, "Report," Oct. 23, 1914, in SUP, Files. See earlier attack on Chamberlain and Uhler in *CSJ*, April 22, 1914, p. 3; June 10, 1914, pp. 1–2.

[69] Furuseth to T. A. Hanson, Dec. 5, 1914, in SUP, Files.

[70] Furuseth to Hanson, Oct. 31, Nov. 17, 21, 28, Dec. 5, 1914, in SUP, Files.

[71] Furuseth, "Report," March 5, 1915, in SUP, Files; *New York Times*, Feb. 28, 1915.

[72] For an explanation of the Seamen's Act, see Robert M. La Follette, "The American Sailor a Free Man," *Survey*, XXXIV (May 1, 1915), 116–117, 125–128. Full text is in *Congressional Record*, 63d Cong., 3d sess., 52:5 (Feb. 25, 1915), 4560–4568.

[73] John Bassett Moore to Woodrow Wilson, Oct. 16, 1913 (Wilson Papers), cited in Goldberg, *op. cit.*, p. 115.

⁷⁴ Woodrow Wilson to Furuseth, March 2, 1915 (Wilson Papers), cited in Goldberg, *op. cit.*, p. 121.

⁷⁵ Bryan to Wilson, Feb. 27, 1915 (Bryan Papers), cited in Arthur S. Link, *Woodrow Wilson and the Progressive Era, 1910–1917* (New York: 1954), p. 63.

⁷⁶ Furuseth said in "Report," March 5, 1915, that Bryan sent the synopsis of the conversation without comment. Link, *op. cit.*, p. 63, cites a letter from Bryan to Wilson, March 2, 1915 (Wilson Papers), as authority for saying that Bryan reversed his previous position. I agree, however, with Belle La Follette, *op. cit.*, pp. 534–535, who cites the same letter to say that Bryan opposed the bill.

⁷⁷ Furuseth, "Report," March 5, 1915. Belle La Follette, *op. cit.*, p. 535, gives an account of this interview based on the recollections of Robert La Follette and Gilbert Roe many years after the event. Furuseth, according to La Follette, got down on his knees to plead for the freedom of the seamen. This version seems out of character. Furuseth was not an actor and he never begged for favors.

⁷⁸ Wilson to Baker, March 5, 1915 (Wilson Papers), cited in Goldberg, *op. cit.*, p. 129, and in Link, *op. cit.*, p. 63.

⁷⁹ La Follette to SUP, March 6, 1915, in SUP, Files.

⁸⁰ Furuseth to SUP, March 5, 1915, in SUP, Files.

Notes to Chapter VIII

USING THE SEAMEN'S ACT

(Pages 133–142)

¹ This chapter is based largely upon the extensive correspondence available in SUP, Files, upon the proceedings and reports contained in the annual ISU *Proceedings* and AFL *Proceedings*, and upon an examination of the *New York Times*, *Literary Digest*, and *CSJ*. The best of the many articles attacking the Seamen's Act may be found in the editorials of the *New York Times*, March 16, 27, April 10, 24, June 12, 13, 27, July 1, 8, 19, 24, Aug. 16, Sept. 15, 29, Oct. 2, 18, Nov. 6, 11, 14, Dec. 7, 1915. Statements by shipowners may also be found in the *New York Times*, April 8, May 12, July 5, 7, 9, 10, Oct. 11, 23, 28, 29, 31, 1915.

² The extensive debate on the alleged bankruptcy of the Pacific Mail Steamship Company can be found in Furuseth, "The Campaign Against the La Follette Bill," *Survey*, XXXIV (July 31, 1915), 396–400; William B. Wilson, "The Seamen's Act," *Harper's Weekly*, LXII (April 22, 1916), 426–427; Gerard Henderson, "Economics of American Shipping," *New Republic*, IV (Oct. 16, 1915), 279–281; ISU, *Proceedings, 1915*, pp. 110–115; William B. Wilson to Furuseth, April 21, 1915, and to Fred Gannett, April 23, 1915, in SUP, Files; *New York Times*, June 11, 20, 27, July 9, 21, Aug. 7, 15, 17, Sept. 10, 13, 23, Oct. 2, 10, 18, Nov. 9, 1915; May 18, 27, Aug. 19, 28, 1916; *CSJ*, March 17, 1915, p. 6; June 30, 1915; Nov. 10, 1915, pp. 7, 11.

³ Chamber of Commerce of the United States, *Referendum Number 12 on the Report of the Special Committee on the Seamen's Act* (Washington, D.C.: 1916); Furuseth, "The Campaign Against the La Follette Bill"; "Latest Score in the Seamen's Law Fight," *Everybody's Magazine*, XXXIV (May, 1916), 655–657; San Francisco Chamber of Commerce, *The Seamen's Bill* (San Francisco: 1915); Daniel Hawthorne, "The Life of the American Sailor," *Outlook*, CXIII (Aug. 9, 1916), 858–862 (showing that the lot of the American sailor was satisfactory); Henderson, *op. cit.*, *New Republic*, IV (Oct. 9, 1915), 254–256 (an excellent discussion of the desertion and language features of the bill); *New York Times*, July 5, 20, 1915; *CSJ*, April 28, 1915, pp. 7, 10; Aug. 25, 1915, p. 6; April 5, 1916, pp. 1–2.

⁴ Typical of the personal letters that Furuseth wrote to journalists are those to Chester Rowell, Aug. 30, Oct. 5, 1915, in Chester H. Rowell Collection, Carton 6,

Bancroft Library, Berkeley, Calif. Furuseth's activities are summarized in ISU, *Proceedings, 1915,* pp. 38–41; *1916,* pp. 38–47; *1917,* pp. 7–42.

[5] *CSJ,* Sept. 1, 1915, p. 6; Sept. 15, 1915, pp. 1–2.

[6] Furuseth, "Letter to Argonaut," May 28, 1915, *CSJ,* June 2, 1915, pp. 7, 11; Furuseth, "Address before Economic Club of Boston, Feb. 23, 1916," *CSJ,* Feb. 23, 1916, pp. 1–2, 11; Furuseth, "The Seamen's Law and Its Critics," *American Labor Legislation Review,* VI (March, 1916), 61–68; Furuseth, "The Plain Truth," *CSJ,* April 14, 1915, pp. 7, 10; Furuseth to William B. Wilson and to John J. Hannon, April 15, 1915, in SUP, Files; *San Francisco Examiner,* Aug. 20, Sept. 9, Nov. 7, 1915.

[7] *Amendment of the Seamen's Act,* Hearings on H.R. 10026, House Committee on Merchant Marine and Fisheries, 64th Cong., 1st sess. (1916).

[8] *The Seamen's Act, by Andrew Furuseth,* 64th Cong., 2d sess., S. Doc. 694 (1917); ISU, *Proceedings, 1917,* pp. 15–16; U.S. Department of Commerce, "Circular 265," 1915, in SUP, Files; Furuseth, "Report," Dec. 31, 1915, Jan. 8, July 24, 1916, Furuseth to J. Tennison, July 15, Dec. 31, 1915, Furuseth to A. L. Thurman, Jan. 19, 1916, Thurman to Furuseth, Jan. 17, 1916, in SUP, Files; Philip B. Kennedy, "The Seamen's Act," *Annals of the American Academy of Political and Social Science,* XLIII (Jan., 1916), 240.

[9] The U.S. Department of Commerce interpretation of this provision is contained in "Circular 264," Sept. 15, 1915. Furuseth's attitude toward this construction may be found in Furuseth, "Report," Dec. 24, 1915, and in his letters to J. Tennison, Dec. 4, 15, 23, 1915, and to A. L. Thurman, Jan. 3, 1916, in SUP, Files.

[10] Furuseth to P. Pryor, April 22, 1915, in SUP, Files.

[11] Furuseth, "Report," Dec. 24, 1915, Jan. 8, May 22, Aug. 19, 1916, Furuseth to Tennison, Dec. 23, 1915, July 15, 1916, in SUP, Files.

[12] Furuseth, "Report," April 10, 1916, in SUP, Files; *Watch-and-Watch at Sea, by Andrew Furuseth,* 64th Cong., 2d sess., S. Doc. 693 (1917).

[13] Furuseth, "Report," Feb. 12, 1916, Furuseth to T. A. Hanson, July 10, 1915, in SUP, Files; Furuseth, "The Dawn of Another Day," *American Federationist,* XXII (Sept., 1915), 722; "The Unworkable Seamen's Act," *World's Work,* XXX (Oct., 1915), 635–636; *New York Times,* June 12, 13, Aug. 10, 12, 27, Sept. 8, 1915.

[14] Furuseth, "The Fight for Justice and Safety at Sea," *American Federationist,* XXX (April, 1923), 310.

[15] William C. Redfield, *With Congress and Cabinet* (Garden City, N.Y.: 1924), pp. 246–248; "Editorial," *Survey,* XXXIV (Aug. 7, 1915), 428–429; Mary E. Dreier, *Margaret Dreier Robins* (New York: 1950), pp. 119–121; *CSJ,* Aug. 4, 1915, pp. 1–2.

[16] Samuel Gompers to President Wilson, Jan. 7, 1916, in SUP, Files.

[17] Redfield to Furuseth, Jan. 13, 1916, Redfield to Gompers, March 7, 1916, in SUP, Files; Furuseth, "International Seamen's Union," *American Federationist,* XXIII (Sept., 1916), 802–805; Furuseth to Redfield, Jan. 13, 1916, Furuseth, "Report," Jan. 15, Aug. 5, 1916, in SUP, Files.

[18] Furuseth, "Report," Jan. 31, 1916, in SUP, Files.

[19] *Paul Scharrenberg v. Dollar Steamship Company,* 242 U.S. 642 (1916) (violation of Alien Contract Labor Act), cited in *CSJ,* Nov. 21, 1917, pp. 7, 10; Nov. 28, 1917, pp. 1–2; *Neilson v. Rhine Shipping Company,* 248 U.S. 205 (1918) (illegal advance to foreign seamen), brief for union cited in *CSJ,* March 6, 1918, pp. 1–2; *Sandberg v. McDonald* (often referred to as *Talus* case), 248 U.S. 145 (1918) (illegal advance in foreign ports), cited in *CSJ,* Jan. 15, 1918, pp. 1–2, 9.

[20] Furuseth, "International Seamen's Union," pp. 802–805; Furuseth, "Report," May 15, 1916, in SUP, Files.

[21] ISU, *Proceedings, 1917,* pp. 7–8.

[22] *CSJ,* Nov. 11, 1914, p. 6; Feb. 17, 1915, p. 6; Furuseth to SUP, Feb. 9, 1914, in SUP, Files.

[23] Furuseth to Tennison, Feb. 9, 1914, in SUP, Files.

²⁴ Furuseth to Tennison, May 4, 1914, Furuseth to Gompers, April 26, 1915, in SUP, Files.
²⁵ Furuseth to SUP, Feb. 11, Nov. 17, 1914, and to Tennison, Nov. 21, Dec. 22, 1914, in SUP, Files.
²⁶ *CSJ*, July 29, 1914, p. 2.
²⁷ Furuseth to William B. Wilson, April 28, 1915, in SUP, Files.
²⁸ Furuseth to W. J. Maloney, Master, *S.S. Cricket,* April 21, 1915, to J. H. Wilson, April 23, 1915, and to Gompers, April 26, 29, 1915, in *ibid.*
²⁹ Furuseth to Percy Pryor, April 19, 1915, Pryor to Furuseth, April 22, 1915, in *ibid.*
³⁰ John S. Hannon to Robert La Follette, June 14, 1915, E. H. Foley, secretary of Stevedores and Riggers Union, San Francisco, to Furuseth, May 19, 1915, Furuseth to Foley, May 14, 22, 1915, in *ibid.;* Minutes, District Committee, ISU, San Francisco, May 14, 1915, in *ibid.*
³¹ *CSJ*, Sept. 20, 1916, p. 2; Oct. 18, 1916, p. 7; SUP, Minutes, Oct. 16, 1916; J. A. Madsen, president of Pacific Coast District, ILA, to Furuseth, Sept. 26, 1916, Furuseth to Madsen, Oct. 3, 1916, Furuseth to Tennison, July 11, 1916, Furuseth to SUP [Sept., 1916], Furuseth to T. A. Hanson, Sept. 15, 1916, in SUP, Files; *San Francisco Examiner*, Sept. 14, 1916.
³² *San Francisco Examiner,* Oct. 20, 27, 1917; April 10, 1918; *CSJ,* Oct. 24, 1917, p. 6; Dec. 5, 1917, p. 6; Edward H. Nockles, secretary of Chicago AFL, and Andrew Furuseth to Fremont Older, May 30, 1917, Congressman John I. Nolan to Paul Scharrenberg (and others), May 30, 1917, Furuseth to William D. Stephens, Governor of California, April 4, 1918, in Miscellaneous Correspondence, 1918–1928, Francis Gates residence, Berkeley, Calif.; interview with Selim Silver; AFL, *Proceedings, 1918,* p. 325.
³³ A trip to San Francisco in February, 1917, was also inspired, in part at least, by attempts of the ILA to involve the seamen in another strike. John Kean, president of Pacific Coast District, ILA, to SUP, Feb. 10, 1917, in SUP, Files.
³⁴ ISU, *Proceedings, 1915,* pp. 33–34; Furuseth to T. A. Hanson, April 15, 1915, in SUP, Files.
³⁵ ISU, *Proceedings, 1915,* pp. 34–35; Furuseth to Tennison, June 13, 1915, Furuseth to Hanson, June 19, 25, July 1, 10, 1915, in SUP, Files.
³⁶ Furuseth to Thomas Chambers, secretary of the British seamen's union, July 21, 1915, in SUP, Files.
³⁷ ISU, *Proceedings, 1915,* p. 37.
³⁸ Furuseth to Hanson, July 17, 1915, in SUP, Files.
³⁹ A brief summary of the strike may be found in ISU, *Proceedings, 1916,* pp. 20–21; *CSJ,* Jan. 19, 1916; and in Furuseth, "On the Crest of the Wave," *American Federationist,* XXIII (May, 1916), 372–373. Events leading up to the strike are reported in letters from Furuseth to Hanson, Dec. 28, 1915, and to Tennison, Jan. 22, April 18, 1915, and in Furuseth, "Report," Jan. 22, April 22, May 15, Aug. 5, 1915, in SUP, Files. The *New York Times* is the best source for daily reports of the strike.
⁴⁰ Furuseth to P. B. Gill, May 28, 1915, Furuseth, "Report," Jan. 31, Feb. 5, July 28, Aug. 5, 1915, in SUP, Files.
⁴¹ *CSJ,* April 19, 1916, p. 6; May 3, 1916, p. 1; May 10, 1916, p. 6; *San Francisco Examiner,* April 25, 29, 1916; Furuseth, "Report," Sept., 1916, in SUP, Files.
⁴² ISU, *Proceedings, 1922,* pp. 32–33 (complete membership figures, 1912–1921); *1923,* pp. 21–37; *CSJ,* March 28, 1917, p. 7; SUP, Minutes, March 26, 1917. To compare the growth of the ISU with that of other unions, see Leo Wolman, *Ebb and Flow of Trade Unionism* (New York: 1936), p. 30.

Notes to Chapter IX

WORLD WAR I

(Pages 143–154)

[1] AFL, *Proceedings, 1917*, pp. 73–74

[2] AFL, *Proceedings, 1919*, p. 413.

[3] Except as otherwise noted, Furuseth's views presented in this section are drawn from AFL, *Proceedings*, 1893–1903, and from *CSJ* for the relevant period.

[4] Walter Macarthur to Furuseth, Jan. 22, 1898, in SUP, Files.

[5] A. M. McDonnell to Furuseth, April 7, 1898, in *ibid*.

[6] AFL, *Proceedings, 1900*, p. 113.

[7] AFL, *Proceedings, 1914*, pp. 473–475. See Rowland H. Harvey, *Samuel Gompers* (Stanford: 1935), p. 193.

[8] Furuseth to T. A. Hanson, May 6, 1915, in SUP, Files.

[9] Furuseth to William B. Wilson, May 8, 1915, and to Thomas Chambers, May 10, 1915, in *ibid.; CSJ*, May 19, 1915, p. 6.

[10] Furuseth to John Tennison, Feb. 15, 1915, in SUP, Files; Belle C. La Follette, *Robert M. La Follette* (New York: 1953), I, 566–567.

[11] La Follette, *op. cit.*, I, 603–625.

[12] Jan. 19, 1916, p. 6.

[13] SUP, Minutes, May 22, 1916.

[14] AFL, *Proceedings, 1917*, pp. 283–308. Furuseth voted with Gompers on the war issue. ISU, *Proceedings, 1917*, p. 22; *CSJ*, April 4, 1917, pp. 6, 7. The main sources on Furuseth's attitude toward and his participation in the war effort are ISU, *Proceedings; CSJ*; and his reports to the SUP during these years. See also *Creating a Shipping Board, a Naval Auxiliary, and a Merchant Marine*, Hearings on H.R. 10500, House Committee on Merchant Marine and Fisheries, 64th Cong., 1st sess. (1916); *American Sea Power and the Seamen's Act, by Andrew Furuseth*, 65th Cong., 2d sess., S. Doc. 228 (1918); *U.S. Shipping Board Emergency Fleet Corp.*, Hearings on S. Res. 170, Senate Committee on Commerce, 65th Cong., 2d sess. (1918); Furuseth to Josephus Daniels, secretary of navy, Feb. 18, March 31, 1916, Dec. 6, 1917, in SUP, Files; Furuseth, "Naval vs. Merchant Seamen," *CSJ*, Jan. 30, 1918, pp. 1–2, 11; May 8, 1918, p. 6; Furuseth, "Sea Service," *American Federationist*, XXV (Feb., 1918), 133–140.

[15] ISU, *Proceedings, 1917*, p. 42. See also *CSJ*, Oct. 24, 1917, pp. 6–7; Jan. 2, 1918, p. 6; *New York Times*, Aug. 18, 19, 1917; "Sea Justice," *Living Age*, CCXCVIII (Aug. 10, 1918), 364–365.

[16] George P. West in *CSJ*, Aug. 15, 1917, pp. 1–2; Samuel Gompers in *CSJ*, Sept. 12, 1917, pp. 1–2, 10; *CSJ*, Nov. 21, 1917, p. 8. For a discussion of the results of Gompers' wage policies, see George E. Barnett, "American Trade Unions and the Standardization of Wages During the War," *Journal of Political Economy*, XXVII (Oct., 1919), 670–693.

[17] Sept. 12, 1917, p. 6.

[18] ISU, *Proceedings, 1917*, pp. 20–22; *CSJ*, Sept.–Oct., 1917.

[19] ISU, *Proceedings, 1917*, pp. 31–32.

[20] *Ibid.*, pp. 20–36, 52, 60; Paul F. Brissenden, *Employment System of the Lake Carriers' Association*, U.S. Bureau of Labor Statistics, Bull. no. 235 (Washington: 1918); *CSJ*, Oct. 10, 1917, p. 6; Furuseth, "Report," May 25, July 13, Aug. 3, 1918, in SUP, Files; Furuseth, "Sea Service," pp. 133–140; "New Slogan, 'Back to the Sea,' " *Survey*, XXXVIII (Aug. 18, 1917), 443.

[21] *CSJ*, July 10, 1918, pp. 6–7, 10.

[22] *New York Times*, July 26, 28, 29, Aug. 2, 1918; ISU, *Proceedings, 1919*, pp. 25–43.

[23] ISU, *Proceedings, 1919*, pp. 20-22; Furuseth, "Report," April 20, May 20, 1918, in SUP, Files.

[24] *CSJ*, May 29, 1918, p. 6.

[25] A most interesting eight-page letter on this topic was written by Frank P. Merriweather, a minister, to the secretary of the ISU in Boston, Oct. 21, 1918. SUP, Files.

[26] *New York Times*, July 7, 1918; "Alien Crews on Our Merchant Ships," *Scientific American*, CXVIII (Feb. 23, 1918), 162; "Manning Our Ships," *Public*, XXI (March 16, 1918), 329-330.

[27] Furuseth to Woodrow Wilson, Feb. 11, 1918, in SUP, Files; Woodrow Wilson, "Message to Seamen," in ISU, *Proceedings, 1919*, pp. 112-113; Furuseth, "Report," April 3, July 6, Sept. 14, 23, 1918, in SUP, Files. The quotation is from Furuseth's report of September 23.

[28] Furuseth to Lieut. R. T. Merrill, April 25, 1917, Furuseth, "Report," May 4, 18, June 1, July 27, Sept. 7, 28, 1918, in SUP, Files.

[29] *CSJ*, Sept. 19, 1917, p. 2.

[30] Furuseth, "Report," Oct. 5, 1918, in SUP, Files.

[31] *Ibid.*, Aug. 24, 1918, in *ibid*.

[32] Furuseth to Charles R. Page, Nov. 4, 1918, in *ibid*.

[33] Furuseth to John Tennison, Oct. 19, 1918, in *ibid*.

[34] Furuseth, "Report," Nov. 16, 1918, in *ibid*.

[35] When the Shipping Board was first created in December, 1916, the seamen were pleased with the appointment of William Denman, a former attorney for the SUP, as chairman (*CSJ*, Dec. 27, 1916, p. 6); but they were displeased with the other four appointments because they represented the interests of shipowners (*CSJ*, Jan. 24, 1917, pp. 1-2). For a more thorough discussion of ISU relations with the Shipping Board, see U.S. Shipping Board, *Marine and Dock Labor* (Washington: 1919), especially chapters 1, 10, and 12; Horace B. Drury, "The Labor Policy of the Shipping Board," *Journal of Political Economy*, XXIX (Jan., 1921), 3.

[36] ISU, *Proceedings, 1922*, pp. 32-33.

[37] *New York Times*, Nov. 19, 1918; Furuseth, "Report," Nov. 25, 1918, in SUP, Files; *CSJ*, Nov. 27, 1918, p. 6; Dec. 4, 1918, p. 8. It is significant that during Furuseth's absence in Europe, the *CSJ* printed several articles favorable to the proposed League of Nations. Dec. 4, 1918, p. 6; Feb. 19, 1919, p. 1; March 5, 1919, pp. 6, 10. This position was reversed after Furuseth's visit to San Francisco in May, 1919. *CSJ*, June 11, 1919, p. 7.

[38] Furuseth, "Report," Nov. 16, 1918, in SUP, Files.

[39] *Ibid.*; Conference of ISU Officers in New York, Minutes, Nov. 17, 1918, in SUP, Files.

[40] Furuseth to Woodrow Wilson, Nov. 16, 1918, in SUP, Files; Woodrow Wilson to Furuseth, Nov. 18, 1918 (Wilson Papers), cited in Joseph P. Goldberg, "American Seamen" (Ph.D. thesis, Publication No. 2815, University Microfilms, Ann Arbor, Mich., 1950), p. 141.

[41] Furuseth, "Report," Nov. 25, 1918, in SUP, Files.

[42] *Ibid.*, Nov. 30, 1918, in SUP, Files. Furuseth actually considered calling a strike of all seamen should the decision at the Peace Conference threaten the Seamen's Act. Meeting of ISU Officers, Minutes, Dec. 4, 1918, in SUP, Files

[43] Furuseth, "Report," Nov. 25, 1918, in SUP, Files.

[44] Originally the ISF was called together by J. Havelock Wilson because the headquarters of the International Transport Workers' Federation was in Berlin. See ISU, *Proceedings, 1919*, p. 98.

[45] All official reports on Furuseth's European tour appear in *CSJ*, May 7, 1919, pp. 1-2, 9; May 14, 1919, pp. 1-2, 9; May 28, 1919, pp. 1-2; ISU, *Proceedings, 1920*, pp. 212-229. Furuseth spoke at a meeting in San Francisco on May 7, 1919, reported in *CSJ*, May 28, 1919, pp. 6-7; June 11, 1919, p. 7; other reports can be found in

Notes 227

New York Times, March 2, 1919; *San Francisco Chronicle*, Dec. 4, 1918, March 4, May 11, 21, 1919; Samuel Gompers, *Seventy Years of Life and Labor* (New York: 1925), I, 473–500; "Annual Convention of I.S.U. of A., January, 1920," *Monthly Labor Review*, X (March, 1920), 797–799. Many letters cover this subject; the best are Furuseth to T. A. Hanson, Jan. 8, March 7, 16, 29, May 7, 1919, in SUP, Files.

[46] The information on the attitude of AFL leaders toward the League of Nations and the Peace Conference and the quotations that follow are from AFL, *Proceedings, 1919*, pp. 18, 399–416. Additional information may be found in the references cited in note 45, and in a speech by La Follette in *Congressional Record*, 66th Cong., 1st sess., 58:8 (Oct. 29, 1919), 7669–7677.

Notes to Chapter X

CHANGING FORTUNES

(Pages 155–163)

[1] The 1919 strike is discussed in Horace B. Drury, "The Labor Policy of the Shipping Board," *Journal of Political Economy*, XXIX (Jan., 1921), 1–28; Robert W. Bruere and Heber Blankenhorn, "For an American Manned Merchant Marine," *New Republic*, XX (Aug. 27, 1919), 116–119; *New York Times*, July 11–29, 1919; *CSJ*, July 23, 1919, p. 6; Aug. 13, 1919, p. 6; ISU, *Proceedings, 1920*, pp. 28–29; Joint Shipping Industrial Conference, Ocean Marine Conference, "Minutes," July 2, 1919, in SUP, Files.

[2] Darrell H. Smith and Paul V. Betters, *The United States Shipping Board* (Washington, D.C.: 1931), pp. 46–48. This book is the best work on the history and operation of the Shipping Board.

[3] Furuseth to John Tennison, July 19, 1919, in SUP, Files; *CSJ*, Aug. 20, 1919, p. 1.

[4] Furuseth, "Report," July 18, 1919, in SUP, Files.

[5] Furuseth to P. B. Gill, Tennison, and others, June 7, 1919, Furuseth to T. A. Hanson, July 12, 1919, Furuseth, "Report," July 19, 1919, in SUP, Files. Furuseth was also conveniently in Europe during the 1920 Atlantic negotiations.

[6] *CSJ*, Nov. 12, 1919, pp. 1–2. An excellent summary of laws and working conditions at this time can be found in a report prepared by the U.S. Department of Labor for the ILO, "Laws and Agreements Governing Working Conditions among American Seamen," *Monthly Labor Review*, X (May, 1920), 1075–1094.

[7] The account of the destruction of the union is based on ISU, *Proceedings*; ISU, *Statement of Facts Concerning the Present Lockout in the Merchant Marine* (Washington, D.C.: 1921); and *CSJ*, in addition to the specific sources cited.

[8] *CSJ*, Jan., 1926, pp. 3–4.

[9] *New York Times*, Jan. 19, April 7, 1921; Furuseth to Ed Rosenberg, Dec. 3, 1920, in SUP, Files.

[10] AFL, *Proceedings, 1921*, pp. 208, 263–264.

[11] After the lockout began, the union proposed preferential hiring of American citizens without any preference for union members. The owners rejected this proposal.

[12] *To Amend Merchant Marine Act of 1920*, Joint Hearings on S. 3217 and H.R. 10644, Senate Committee on Commerce and House Committee on Merchant Marine and Fisheries, 67th Cong., 1st sess. (1922), II, 1309–1320; Drury, *op. cit.*, p. 3; Smith and Betters, *op. cit.*, pp. 46–48, 83; Furuseth, "Mastery of the Sea," *New Republic*, XXVII (July 20, 1921), 208–210; *New York Times*, Jan. 21–May 1, 1921.

[13] *New York Times*, May 1–15, June 22, 1921.

[14] Ed Rosenberg to J. C. Rolph, Nov. 18, 1920, in SUP, Files.

[15] Furuseth to Rosenberg, Dec. 3, 1920, in *ibid*.

[16] Robert J. Lampman, "Collective Bargaining of West Coast Sailors, 1885–1947" (unpublished Ph.D. thesis, University of Wisconsin, 1950), p. 148.

[17] ISU, *Proceedings, 1922*, pp. 32–33; Leo Wolman, *Ebb and Flow of Trade Unionism* (New York: 1936), p. 30.

[18] Furuseth to George Larsen, Jan. 30, 31, 1922, Furuseth to R. Ingwardsen, Feb. 8, March 20, 1922, unsigned letter to Furuseth, Feb. 10, 1922, Furuseth, "Report," March 4, 11, 18, 25, May 27, 1922, in SUP, Files.

[19] George Larsen to Joseph Faltus, June 29, 1922, in "Letter-book, Honolulu Branch," in *ibid*.

[20] Furuseth, "The One Big Union Fallacy," *American Federationist*, XXX (Sept., 1923), 724–726.

[21] John Sandgren, "An International Conference of Marine Transport Workers," *One Big Union Monthly*, I (March, 1919), 53; Upton Hold, "Salting Down the Marine Workers," *Industrial Pioneer*, I (Oct., 1921), 34–38.

[22] Furuseth to SUP, Nov. 26, 1918, Nov. 27, 1919, Furuseth to Tennison, Dec. 1, 1919, in SUP, Files.

[23] *New York Times*, Aug. 7, 1921; P. O'Brien, "Report," Sept. 17, 1921, Furuseth, "Report," March 11, April 1, 1922, in SUP, Files.

[24] George P. West, "Andrew Furuseth and the Radicals," *Survey*, XLVII (Nov. 5, 1921), 207–209; SUP, Minutes, July 11, 1921.

[25] George P. West, "Andrew Furuseth Stands Pat," *Survey*, LI (Oct. 15, 1923), 86–90; SUP, Minutes, July 29, 1921.

[26] Furuseth to President Harding, April 26, 1923, in ISU, *Proceedings, 1924*, pp. 127–128.

[27] Furuseth, *Circular No. 2* (Washington, D.C.: 1921); Furuseth, *A Sound Warning* (Washington, D.C.: 1921); Furuseth, *Shipowners' Queer Policies* (Washington, D.C.: 1921); *To Amend Merchant Marine Act of 1920*, Joint Hearings on S. 3217 and H.R. 10644, II, 1430–1485; *To Inquire into Operations, Policies, and Affairs of the United States Shipping Board and United States Emergency Fleet Corporation*, Hearings on H.R. 186, House Select Committee on U.S. Shipping Board, 68th Cong., 1st sess. (1925), pp. 2518–2526; *San Francisco Examiner*, Sept. 1, 10, Oct. 22, Dec. 15, 1921; *New York Times*, May 5, 1922; George Siddon, "Affidavit," San Francisco, Sept. 25, 1922, in SUP, Files; West, "Andrew Furuseth Stands Pat"; Furuseth, "Report," Feb. 25, May 27, 1922, in SUP, Files; AFL, *Proceedings, 1923*, pp. 334–336.

[28] Marine Transport Workers' Industrial Union No. 510, IWW, *Exposed* (Chicago: 1923) and *The Marine Worker* (n.p.: 1922–23); *Industrial Solidarity* (Chicago: 1921–23); *Industrial Worker* (Seattle: 1921–23); MTWIU No. 510, IWW, "Strike Bulletin," Oct. 29, 1922; an IWW leaflet collection of material relating to maritime affairs in File No. 3, "Historical Chronicle," in SUP, Files; Tom Barker, "The Future of the Marine Transport Industry," *One Big Union Monthly*, II (Dec., 1920), 29–30; Tom Barker, "Panama and Marine Transport Workers," *Industrial Pioneer*, I (Nov., 1921), 7–8; *CSJ*, Nov. 23, 1921, p. 7; Nov. 30, 1921, p. 7; March 15, 1922, p. 7; SUP, Minutes, Nov. 21, 1921.

[29] IWW leaflets and strike bulletins in Paul S. Taylor, Strikes in California, 1933–1939, Carton 2, Bancroft Library, Berkeley, Calif.; Hyman Weintraub, "The I.W.W. in California, 1905–1931" (unpublished M.A. thesis, University of California, Los Angeles, 1947), pp. 216–246.

[30] Furuseth to A. D. Lasker, chairman of U.S. Shipping Board, Jan. 11, 1923, in ISU, *Proceedings, 1922*, pp. 69–70; West, "Andrew Furuseth Stands Pat"; *San Francisco Examiner*, April 24, May 1–13, 27, 1923; *New York Times*, April 24–30, May 3–16, 1923; *To Inquire into Operations, Policies, and Affairs of the ... Shipping Board ...*, Hearings on H.R. 186, pp. 2537–2544.

Notes to Chapter XI

DEFENDER OF THE SEAMEN'S ACT
(Pages 164–176)

[1] In addition to the specific sources cited in this chapter, there is voluminous material in *CSJ*; ISU, *Proceedings*; AFL, *Proceedings*; Furuseth's "Reports"; *New York Times*; and *Congressional Record*.

[2] In nine years, beginning in 1915, the national organization alone spent $40,000 on litigation, $35,000 on legislation, and another $25,000 on literature to influence legislation. ISU, *Proceedings, 1922*, pp. 34–35.

[3] *Dillon v. Strathearn*, 252 U.S. 348 (1920); *O'Hara v. Luckenbach Steamship Co.*, 269 U.S. 463 (1926); *Nielsen v. Rhine*, 248 U.S. 205 (1918); *Sandberg v. McDonald*, 248 U.S. 185 (1918); *Hardy et al. v. Shephard and Morse Lumber Co.*, 248 U.S. 205 (1918); *Jackson et al. v. S. S. Archimedes*, 275 U.S. 463 (1928); *E. Hamilton et al. v. United States*, 249 U.S. 610 (1919), 254 U.S. 645 (1920); and *Nelleman v. London* in District Court, Philadelphia, cited in ISU, *Proceedings, 1917*, pp. 10–11.

[4] Victor Olander to George Larsen and to Furuseth, Oct. 27, 1926, in SUP, Files.

[5] *Scharrenberg v. Dollar Steamship Co.*, 242 U.S. 642 (1916); ISU, *Proceedings, 1917*, pp. 36–37; *CSJ*, Nov. 7, 1917, p. 6; Nov. 21, 1917, pp. 7, 10; Nov. 28, 1917, pp. 1–2.

[6] *Street v. Shipowners Association of Pacific Coast*, 263, U.S. 334 (1923), 266 U.S. 611 (1924); *Cornelius Anderson v. Shipowners Association of Pacific Coast*, 269 U.S. 581 (1925), 271 U.S. 652 (1926), 272 U.S. 359 (1926), 279 U.S. 864 (1929); Furuseth, *Memorial ... Relating to the Shipowners' Monopoly* (San Francisco: 1923); *New York Times*, Oct. 29, 1926; *To Inquire into Operations, Policies, and Affairs of United States Shipping Board and United States Emergency Fleet Corporation*, Hearings on H.R. 186, House Select Committee on U.S. Shipping Board, 68th Cong., 1st sess. (1925), pp. 2534–2537; "Employment Registry as Violation of Anti-Trust Act," *Monthly Labor Review*, XXIV (Jan., 1927), 132–134; *San Francisco Chronicle*, Dec. 28, 1923; June 23, 1925; Nov. 22, 1926; William S. Hopkins, "Employment Exchanges for Seamen," *American Economic Review*, XXV (June, 1935), 250–258; Furuseth to Patrick Flynn, Nov. 27, 1926, to George Larsen, Feb. 24, March 3, 12, 1927, March 21, 1929, to H. W. Hutton, March 21, 1929, Larsen to Furuseth, Feb. 17, 1927, March 3, 1928, in SUP, Files.

[7] Furuseth to J. C. Jenkins, Dec. 17, 1923, in SUP, Files; ISU, *Proceedings, 1924*, pp. 170–171. In 1930 Furuseth warned shipowners that the ISU would undertake a legislative campaign to seek repeal of special privilege legislation for shipowners unless they consented to negotiate with the union. ISU, *Proceedings, 1930*, p. 130; Furuseth to Larsen, Feb. 17, 1930, in SUP, Files.

[8] 275 U.S. 463 (1928); *New York Times*, Dec. 24, 1927.

[9] *U.S. Statutes*, Public Law 261, 66th Cong., 2d sess. (June 5, 1920); *Hearings Relative to the Establishment of a Merchant Marine*, Senate Committee on Commerce, 66th Cong., 1st sess. (1919–1920); *Promotion and Maintenance of the American Merchant Marine*, S. Rept. 573 on H.R. 10378, Senate Committee on Commerce, 66th Cong., 2d sess. (1920); *New York Times*, Feb. 26, 1920.

[10] *CSJ*, March, 1930, p. 67.

[11] AFL, *Proceedings, 1926*, p. 203.

[12] Furuseth, "Memorandum on *Vestris*," in SUP, Files. The *Morro Castle* disaster also served as a springboard for agitation to enforce the Seamen's Act. See M. R. Bendiner, "Is It Safe To Go to Sea?" *Nation*, CXLII (April 29, 1936), 542–544.

[13] Furuseth to Martin B. Madden, Jan. 2, 1928, in SUP, Files; Furuseth, *Memorial from the Seamen on the Sea Service Bureau—Crimping System vs. Shipping Commis-*

sioners' Offices (Washington, D.C.: 1930); Furuseth to President Franklin D. Roosevelt, July 11, 1935, and to Wilbur J. Carr, Aug. 2, 1935, in SUP, Files.

[14] S. 4093 (1922), S. 1079 (1926), S. 2945 (1928), S. 5089 (1929), S. 202, S. 314 (1930); N. Sparks, *The Struggle of the Marine Workers* (New York: 1930), p. 27; *Continuous Discharge Books for American Seamen*, Hearings on S. 1079, Senate Committee on Commerce, 69th Cong., 1st sess. (1926).

[15] Furuseth, "Lest We Forget," *American Federationist*, XLII (May, 1935, supplement).

[16] AFL, *Proceedings, 1919*, p. 366; ISU, *Proceedings, 1924*, pp. 137–139; *CSJ*, June, 1924, p. 177; Furuseth, "Scientific Legislation," *American Federationist*, XXXI (March, 1924), 300–302.

[17] H.R. 12169 (1922); S. 3574 (1926); S. 717 (1929); S. 202, H.R. 7763 (1930); S. 7 (1932); S. 379 (1935); H.R. 5380 (1935).

[18] Practically every issue of *CSJ*, every "Report" that Furuseth made to his union, and every ISU and AFL *Proceedings* for this period contain material on this subject. See also *Congressional Record*, 68th Cong., 1st sess., 65:8 (May 9, 1924), 8250; House Committee on Immigration: *Restriction of Immigration*, Hearings on H.R. 5 and H.R. 101, 68th Cong., 1st sess. (1924); *Deportation of Alien Seamen*, Hearings on Amendments to H.R. 11796, 68th Cong., 2d sess. (1925); *Deportation of Deserting Alien Seamen*, Hearings on S. 3574, 69th Cong., 2d sess. (1927); *Deportation of Alien Seamen*, Hearings on S. 202, 71st Cong., 3d sess. (1931); *Deportation of Alien Seamen*, H. Rept. 1924 on H.R. 12173, 72d Cong., 2d sess. (1933); *Deportation of Certain Alien Seamen*, Hearings on S. 379, 74th Cong., 1st sess. (1935); Senate Committee on Immigration: *Deportation of Certain Alien Seamen*, Hearings on S. 3574, 69th Cong., 1st sess. (1926); *Deportation of Alien Seamen*, S. Rept. 1037 on S. 717, 70th Cong., 1st sess. (1928); *Deportation of Certain Alien Seamen*, Hearings on S. 202, 71st Cong., 2d sess. (1930); *Deportation of Certain Alien Seamen*, S. Rept. 677 on S. 7, 72d Cong., 1st sess. (1932); *Deportation of Alien Seamen*, Hearings on S. 868, 73d Cong., 2d sess. (1934); *San Francisco Chronicle*, Feb. 27, 28, 1923; *New York Times*, Aug. 6, 7, Nov. 8, 1921; Feb. 27, 28, 1923; Feb. 17, 1924; Aug. 30, 1925; Feb. 7, 1927; Furuseth to George Larsen, March 22, 1924, Jan. 27, Apr. 4, 13, 1931, to Robe C. White, Nov. 2, 1926, to Hiram Bingham, May 21, 1928, to Royal S. Copeland, July 11, 1935, and to Cordell Hull, July 18, 1935, in SUP, Files.

[19] See *CSJ*, Nov., 1929, for an example of antiforeign comment.

[20] *Exclusion of Immigration from the Philippine Islands*, Hearings on H.R. 80708, House Committee on Immigration and Naturalization, 71st Cong., 2d sess. (1930), p. 235. It is worth noting that from Furuseth's own estimates, the number of Filipinos in the U.S. merchant marine at that time was about 18,000—at least three times as large as the total membership of the ISU. The Communists made sure that the Philippine sailors knew how the leaders of the ISU felt toward them. See also Furuseth to T. V. O'Connor, March 7, 1924, in SUP, Files.

[21] Furuseth, "Report," Sept. 13, Oct. 4, 9, 17, Nov. 1, 15, 1919, Feb. 14, 28, 1920, in SUP, Files.

[22] Furuseth reported on his role in the commissions to revise the navigation codes at ISU conventions, in *CSJ*, and in his "Reports." Extensive excerpts are available from these sources. In addition see *To Inquire into Operations, Policies, and Affairs of the United States Shipping Board and United States Emergency Fleet Corporation*, Hearings on H.R. 186, House Select Committee on U.S. Shipping Board, 68th Cong., 1st sess. (1925).

[23] U.S. Chamber of Commerce, *National Merchant Marine Conference, Nov. 16–17, 1925, Washington, D.C.* (Washington, D.C.: 1925), I, 169–170.

[24] ISU, *The Seamen's View* (San Francisco: 1927); Paul Scharrenberg, "The Advantages of the La Follette Seamen's Act," *American Federationist*, XXX (Feb., 1933),

Notes

134–138; U.S. Shipping Board, Division of Industrial Relations, *Operation of La Follette Act* (Washington, D.C.: 1919).

[25] ISU, *The Seamen's View*, p. 5.

[26] A typical example out of hundreds is American Bureau of Shipping, *The American Merchant Marine* (New York: 1933). Both sides of the subsidy issue are briefly stated in *United States Maritime Commission*, S. Rept. 1721 to accompany S. 3500, Senate Committee on Commerce, 74th Cong., 2d sess. (1936). Full hearings were held. *Merchant Marine Act*, Hearings on S. 3500, S. 4110, and S. 4111, Senate Committee on Commerce, 74th Cong., 2d sess. (1936).

[27] "Our Merchant Marine's Wage Burden," *Literary Digest*, LXXXII (Sept. 6, 1924), 70–72; Edward N. Hurley, *The New Merchant Marine* (New York: 1920), p. 256.

[28] ISU, *Proceedings, 1926*, pp. 55, 77–78, 93–111, 117–122; *CSJ*, Jan., 1927, pp. 9–10.

[29] U.S. Shipping Board, *Proceedings of the National Conference on the Merchant Marine, January 4–5, 1933* (Washington, D.C.: 1933), pp. 66–73. See also Furuseth, "Lest We Forget," *American Federationist*, XLII (May, 1935, supplement); *New York Times*, Aug. 28, 30, 1925; "The Last Serfs," *Nation*, CXXIV (Feb. 2, 1927), 107–108.

[30] Furuseth, "Report," June 28, 1935, in SUP, Files; see also "Analysis of S. 2582," May 17, 1935, in *ibid*.

[31] Furuseth to Larsen, May 22, 1935, in *ibid*.

[32] "The Illusive American Seaman," *Nation*, CXIV (March 29, 1922), 361.

[33] Furuseth to Calvin Coolidge, May 28, 1925, in SUP, Files.

[34] *New York Times*, April 19, 28, 1922; May 11, 12, 1925; *To Amend Merchant Marine Act of 1920*, Joint Hearings on S. 3217 and H.R. 10644, Senate Committee on Commerce and House Committee on Merchant Marine and Fisheries, 67th Cong., 1st sess. (1922).

[35] *Sea Power and Its Development* (Washington, D.C.: 1925), pp. 1–2. More specific proposals for training seamen can be found in *CSJ*, July, 1930, pp. 319–320; March, 1931, pp. 68, 75–76. Similar thoughts are expressed in Furuseth, "Mastery of the Sea," *New Republic*, XXVII (July 20, 1921), 208–210.

[36] The best single attempt to evaluate the Seamen's Act is Paul S. Taylor, "Eight Years of the Seamen's Act," *American Labor Legislation Review*, XV (March, 1925), 52–63. Taylor's statistics are presented so as to give the most favorable view of the effectiveness of the act.

[37] A typical article is Furuseth, "The Fight for Justice and Safety at Sea," *American Federationist*, XXX (April, 1923), 310–312. Interesting, because Furuseth's views on the act are expressed after twenty years' experience, is *Merchant Marine Act*, Hearings on S. 3500, S. 4110, and S. 4111, pp. 197–235.

[38] American Bureau of Shipping, *op. cit.*, pp. 109–110; William W. Bates, *American Marine* (Boston: 1892), p. 357. The authority cited most often by Furuseth was Robert P. Bass (director of the Marine and Dock Industrial Relations Division), *Marine and Dock Labor* (Washington, D.C.: 1919). Bass merely points out, however, that wages were equalized, not that the Seamen's Act was the cause of equalization. *CSJ*, Nov. 12, 1919, pp. 1–2; Scharrenberg, *op. cit.*, pp. 134–138; "The Seamen's Act," *New Republic*, XIX (May 3, 1919), 8–9; Furuseth, "International Seamen's Union," *American Federationist*, XXIII (Sept., 1916), 802–805; Joseph P. Goldberg, "American Seamen" (Ph.D. thesis, Publication No. 2815, University Microfilms, Ann Arbor, Mich., 1950), p. 135; ILO, *Maritime Statistical Handbook* (Geneva: 1936). Articles comparing U.S. and foreign wage rates appear in *Monthly Labor Review*, XVI (Feb., 1923), 358–364; XXIV (April, 1927), 738–740; XXVI (May, 1928), 1004–1006; XXX (March, 1930), 637–639; XXXVI (Jan., 1933), 176–178.

[39] ISU, *Proceedings, 1921*, pp. 377–380; *New York Times*, June 17, July 7, 13, 1923; June 11, 1924; Aug. 30, 1925; Rudolph W. Wissman, *The Maritime Industry* (New York: 1942), p. 376.

⁴⁰ *CSJ*, Sept. 10, 1919, p. 6; American Bureau of Shipping, *op. cit.*, p. 107; "Nationality of Members of the International Seamen's Union of America," *Monthly Labor Review*, XI (Feb., 1921), 430–431; *To Amend Merchant Marine Act of 1920*, Joint Hearings on S. 3217 and H.R. 10644, II, 1263–1264, 1267–1268.

⁴¹ *Monthly Labor Review*, XXXVIII (Feb., 1934), 379–380; XLII (April, 1936), 1059–1060. U.S. Department of Commerce, Bureau of Marine Inspection and Navigation, *Merchant Marine Statistics*, gives yearly reports on wages for seamen.

Notes to Chapter XII

LONELY WARRIOR
(Pages 177–200)

¹ *San Francisco Examiner*, May 12, 1920; *New York Times*, May 24, June 6, 7, 15, 16, 1920; International Seafarers' Federation, *Minutes of Proceedings of an International Conference of Seafarers, Genoa, Italy, June 11–14, 1920* (London, 1920). Additional material on the ISF and the ITWF may be found in "Annual Convention of the I.S.U. of A., January, 1920," *Monthly Labor Review*, X (March, 1920), 797–798; Furuseth, "Report," March 13, 1920, in SUP, Files; International Seafarers' Federation, *Rules and Constitution, 1920* (Antwerp: 1920); A. Zacharissen, "History of the Norwegian Seamen's Union" (unpublished manuscript, n.d.), Bancroft Library, Berkeley, Calif., p. 34; H. Nathans, *The International Transport Workers' Federation* (Amsterdam: 1922); *CSJ*, May, 1923, p. 3.

² International Labor Organization, *Proceedings, International Labor Conference, Genoa, 1920* (Geneva: 1920), pp. 99–100.

³ ILO, *Daily Bulletin*, June–July, 1920; *New York Times*, June 20, 27, July 10, 14, 18, 1920; "The Seamen's Conference at Genoa," *The New Europe*, XVI (July 22, 1920), 38–41; "Protection for Seamen," *American Labor Legislation Review*, X (Sept., 1920), 211–216; "The Genoa Conference," *New Statesman*, XV (June 12, 1920), 271–272.

⁴ For the period from July, 1920, to October, 1922, there are very complete reports on the international unions for seamen in ISU, *Proceedings*; *CSJ*; Furuseth's reports; and Zacharissen, *op. cit.*, p. 37. Primary sources include ISF, *Minutes of Proceedings at Secretariat Meeting and International Seafarers' Conference, Brussels, Belgium, August 5, 1920* (London: 1920); ISF, *Meeting with M. Albert Thomas, Sept. 3, 1920* (London: 1920); ISF, *Minutes of Meeting between ISF and ITWF, Oct. 15, 1920* (London: 1920); International Transport Workers' Federation, *Report of I.T.W. Congress, Vienna, Oct. 2–6, 1922* (Amsterdam: 1923).

⁵ *CSJ*, Jan. 12, 1921, p. 10.

⁶ Furuseth to Edo Fimmen, secretary of ITWF, Dec. 21, 1921, in ISU, *Proceedings, 1922*, p. 108.

⁷ Furuseth to William Green, Jan. 6, 1926, in ISU, *Proceedings, 1926*, p. 170. See also Walter Macarthur to J. O. Randall, Nov. 2, 1922, in Macarthur, Correspondence and Papers, 1890–1945, Box 1, Bancroft Library, Berkeley, Calif.; Furuseth, "Report," Aug. 12, 26, 1922, in SUP, Files.

⁸ Furuseth to Albert M. Thomas, Oct. 3, 1924, in SUP, Files. See also *Congressional Record*, Senate Appendix, 68th Cong., 1st sess., 65:7 (April 26, 1924), 7232–7240.

⁹ *San Francisco Chronicle*, Sept. 23, 1925; *San Francisco Examiner*, Sept. 23, 1925; Furuseth, *Report upon International Code for Seamen* (Washington, D.C.: 1925); ILO, *International Codification of the Rules Relating to Seamen's Articles of Agreement, 1925* (Geneva: 1925); Furuseth to Victor Olander, July 10, 14, 1925, Furuseth, "Report," Feb. 6, 1926, in SUP, Files.

¹⁰ *San Francisco Chronicle*, June 8, 1926; ILO, *International Labor Conference, Geneva, 1926* (Geneva: 1926), pp. 401–407; ILO, *Protection of the Health of Seamen*

Against Venereal Disease (Geneva: 1926); ILO, *Report on the International Codification of the Rules Relating to Seamen's Articles of Agreement* (Geneva: 1926); ILO, *Report on General Principles for the Inspection of the Conditions of Work of Seamen* (Geneva: 1926); ILO, *Seamen's Articles of Agreement* (Geneva: 1926); Furuseth to George Larsen, June 11, 1926, in SUP, Files.

[11] ISU, *Proceedings, 1927*, p. 140.

[12] For a brief history of the ILO and the seamen, see Elmo P. Hohman, *The International Labor Organization and the Seamen* (Geneva: 1937). A more scholarly history and description of the operation of the ILO is in William G. Rice and W. Ellison Chalmers, "Improvement of Labor Conditions on Ships by International Action," *Monthly Labor Review*, XLII (May, 1936), 1181-1203.

[13] Furuseth, "Report," April 14, May 27, June 25, 1929, Furuseth to Olander, April 25, June 19, 1929, and to Larsen, June 2, 27, 1929, in SUP, Files.

[14] Furuseth, "Report," Dec. 13, 1929, Aug. 2, 1935, in SUP, Files; Furuseth, "Safety of Life at Sea—Proposed Treaty," *American Federationist*, XLII (Feb., 1935), 134-136; U.S. Shipping Board, *Proceedings of the National Conference on Merchant Marine, Jan. 27-28, 1932* (Washington, D.C.: 1932), pp. 129-132; *Ibid., Jan. 4-5, 1933*, pp. 66-73, 105, 124-136.

[15] U.S. Shipping Board, *Proceedings of the National Conference on Merchant Marine, Jan. 4-5, 1933*, p. 127.

[16] ISU, *Proceedings, 1921*, p. 45.

[17] Zacharissen, *op. cit.*, p. 41; Furuseth, "Report," June 7, July 19, Aug. 22, Oct. 25, 1935, Furuseth to Larsen, Oct. 28, 1935, in SUP, Files; AFL, *Proceedings, 1929*, p. 369 (shows that Furuseth opposed sending unofficial delegates to ILO); ILO, *Brief Report on the Maritime Work, 1929-1936* (Geneva: 1936); ILO, *Report and Record of the Meeting of the Principal Maritime Countries* (Geneva: 1935).

[18] Smith Simpson, "The I.L.O. Month by Month," *American Federationist*, XLIII (Dec., 1936), 1309-1313; "The Twenty-first and Twenty-second (Maritime) Sessions of the International Labor Conference," *International Labor Review*, XXXV (Jan., 1937), 3-30; (Feb., 1937), 141-176; Carter Goodrich, "Maritime Labor Treaties of 1936," *Monthly Labor Review*, XLII (Feb., 1937), 349-355.

[19] Interview with Harry Lang, Los Angeles, California.

[20] AFL, *Proceedings, 1926*, pp. 202-203, 353. Unless otherwise noted, the views discussed here have been taken from AFL, *Proceedings*.

[21] Aside from his union membership, Furuseth is not known to have joined any other organization. He said the ACLU used his name without permission. This information is based on interviews with Selim Silver, Paul Scharrenberg, and Selma Borschardt.

[22] ISU, *Proceedings, 1927*, pp. 107-108. Furuseth's views on government ownership of the merchant marine are expressed in AFL, *Proceedings, 1921*, p. 365; *1922*, p. 173; *CSJ*, Feb. 25, 1920, pp. 8-9; March 10, 1920, p. 6.

[23] AFL, *Proceedings, 1929*, p. 268; *1932*, pp. 243-244, 266-267.

[24] *Ibid., 1930*, pp. 267, 322-323. Furuseth did not object to a campaign for a shorter workweek to be achieved by union action. *Ibid., 1932*, pp. 293-295.

[25] Furuseth, "Work Is Worship," *American Federationist*, XXXV (Jan., 1928), 25-30.

[26] *CSJ*, Sept., 1923, pp. 3-5. George P. West, "Andrew Furuseth Stands Pat," *Survey*, LI (Oct. 15, 1923), 90, has some interesting conclusions on Furuseth's labor philosophy.

[27] AFL, *Proceedings, 1932*, p. 336.

[28] *Ibid., 1929*, pp. 260-261.

[29] *Ibid.*, pp. 374-375.

[30] *Ibid., 1922*, pp. 136-137; West, *op. cit.*, pp. 86-90.

[31] AFL, *Proceedings, 1934*, pp. 332-333; Thomas L. Dabney, "Organized Labor's Attitude toward Negro Workers," *The Southern Workman*, LVII (Aug., 1928), 323-330.

[32] From 1917 until Furuseth's death the issue of workmen's compensation was discussed at every ISU convention, in the columns of the *CSJ*, and in Furuseth's reports. In addition to these sources, Furuseth's viewpoint is best expressed in his article "Harbor Workers Are Not Seamen," *American Labor Legislation Review*, XI (June, 1921), 139–142; Furuseth to Silas B. Axtell, Nov. 30, 1925, cited in Axtell, *Merchant Seamen's Law* (2d ed.; New York: 1945), pp. 75–78; Furuseth to Larsen, Dec. 17, 1926, Furuseth to Otto Wahrenberg, March 6, 1926 (in 1928 file), Silas B. Axtell to Furuseth, Jan. 4, 1935, in SUP, Files. Other important articles on this subject are Frederick Hoffman, "Occupational Hazards in the American Merchant Marine," *American Labor Legislation Review*, VI (March, 1916), 69–73; "Liability of Emergency Fleet Corporation for Injury to Seamen," *Monthly Labor Review*, XXI (July, 1925), 163–165; Mortier W. LaFever, *Settlement for Accidents to American Seamen*, U.S. Bureau of Labor Statistics, Bull. no. 466 (Washington: 1928); "Can Workmen's Compensation Benefit Seamen?" *American Labor Legislation Review*, XVIII (Sept., 1928), 268–269; "Injured Seamen Allowed Maintenance, Cure, and Wages in Addition to Damages," *Monthly Labor Review*, XXVIII (Feb., 1929), 270–271; also Walter MacArthur to Walter F. Dodd, July 16, 1929, in Macarthur, Correspondence and Papers, Box 1.

[33] S. 4342 (1918), S. 4607 and S. 4708 (1920), S. 3076 (1920), S. 746 (1921), S. 4730 (1926), H.R. 9498 (1926), S. 1549 (1930).

[34] *CSJ*, April, 1932, p. 111.

[35] AFL, *Proceedings, 1912*, pp. 287–290. See above, pp. 95–98. Furuseth in the 1920's kept repeating that he had vigorously opposed the Clayton Act, but he was chairman of the 1912 committee that gave the bill qualified endorsement.

[36] AFL, *Proceedings, 1921*, pp. 56–65. Furuseth's views about this time are expressed in articles in *CSJ*, Dec. 24, 1919, pp. 1–2; July 14, 1920, pp. 1–2, 7, 11; June 19, 1921, p. 10; ISU, *Proceedings, 1921*, pp. 400–401.

[37] AFL, *Proceedings, 1929*, p. 261.

[38] S. 5829 (1926), S. 1482 (1927); AFL, *Proceedings, 1925*, pp. 233–234; *1926*, pp. 307–316.

[39] *Hearings before Subcommittee on Shipstead Bill, S. 1482*, Senate Committee on Judiciary, 70th Cong., 1st sess. (1928); Furuseth, "Extension and Misuse of Equity Power," *American Federationist*, XXXVI (Jan., 1929), 83–90; Furuseth, "Labor Injunctions Traced to Days of Ancient Rome," *CSJ*, June, 1927, pp. 171–172; Furuseth, "Equity Power and Its Abuse," *American Federationist*, XXXIV (Dec., 1927), 1435–1444. Reactions to Furuseth's views on the injunction may also be found in AFL, *Proceedings, 1928*, pp. 109–113, 250–253; Fiorello La Guardia cited in Silas B. Axtell, comp., *A Symposium on Andrew Furuseth* (New Bedford, Mass.: 1948), p. 228; Felix Frankfurter and N. Greene, *The Labor Injunction* (New York: 1930), pp. 206–208; Edwin E. Witte, *The Government in Labor Disputes* (New York: 1932), pp. 104–108.

[40] AFL, *Proceedings, 1929*, p. 342. The Civic Federation was an organization of labor leaders and wealthy businessmen for the purpose of achieving industrial peace. It had, however, acquired a very unsavory reputation among liberals and Socialists.

[41] The principal arguments pro and con are presented in AFL, *Proceedings, 1929*, pp. 317–352; *1930*, pp. 357–365; *1931*, pp. 452–461. Furuseth's report on the 1929 AFL convention debate is told in a personal letter to George Larsen, Oct. 23, 1929, in SUP, Files. Furuseth wrote an interesting letter on the Shipstead bill to Victor Olander, Sept. 20, 1929, in SUP, Files, but he failed to convince his friend.

[42] AFL, *Proceedings, 1935*, p. 449.

[43] Furuseth, "Report," April 1, 1916, in SUP, Files.

[44] *New York Times*, July 6, 1924; *CSJ*, May 19, 1920, p. 8; Aug., 1924, pp. 227–228; Sept., 1924, pp. 267–268; Oct., 1924, pp. 291–292; Nov., 1924, p. 324; Belle C. La Follette, *Robert M. La Follette* (New York: 1953), II, 1114; Furuseth to Joseph Faltus, Oct. 15, 1924, in SUP, Files (predicts defeat of Coolidge and victory for La Follette

in all Western states, and perhaps even a landslide). The following year Furuseth told the AFL convention that the electoral college system made the election of a third-party candidate a virtual impossibility. He welcomed the return to nonpartisan politics. AFL, *Proceedings, 1925*, pp. 278, 298–299.

[45] ISU, *Proceedings, 1925*, pp. 23–25.

[46] See *Industrial Worker* for 1923 and 1926; ISU, *Proceedings, 1926*, p. 8; *New York Times*, May 10, 12, 1923.

[47] *CSJ*, Nov., 1931, p. 326.

[48] W. E. Shutz, secretary of Masters, Mates and Pilots of the Pacific, to James S. Davis, secretary of labor (1929), in SUP, Files; *CSJ*, every issue, but see, for example, May, 1922, p. 3; Oct., 1926, p. 302; July, 1928, p. 202.

[49] *Continuous Discharge Books for American Seamen*, Hearings on S. 1079, Senate Committee on Commerce, 69th Cong., 1st sess. (1926), Pt. 2, p. 151; *New York Times*, Dec. 28, 1924; Richard O. Boyer, *The Dark Ship* (Boston: 1947), pp. 69–71.

[50] ISU, *Proceedings, 1926*, p. 17.

[51] *Ibid., 1929*, p. 169. See letter from Martin Wilhelmsen to Furuseth, Dec. 3, 1922, and reply, Dec. 7, 1922 (in which Furuseth explains why SUP cannot continue paying one dollar per week to members in the hospital), in SUP, Files.

[52] In addition to the sources cited, this account of the decline of the union is based on ISU, *Proceedings; CSJ;* and Furuseth's reports.

[53] Furuseth, "Message," *CSJ*, April, 1925, pp. 99–100; Furuseth to K. B. Nolan, Nov. 10, 1923, Furuseth, "Report," March 21, 1925, Furuseth to Larsen, April 8, 1927, in SUP, Files.

[54] "When we shall again have proved that we are capable of obtaining some of the important things for which we are struggling without any assistance from shipowners or the Shipping Board, we shall receive it without begging." Furuseth, "Report," Feb. 28, 1925, in SUP, Files.

[55] AFL, *Proceedings, 1927*, p. 351; see also Furuseth to Gompers, Jan. 8, 1924, in ISU, *Proceedings, 1924*, pp. 97–99.

[56] ISU, *Proceedings, 1930*, p. 98.

[57] *Ibid., 1929*, p. 131.

[58] Boyer, *op. cit.*, pp. 194–196; William L. Standard, *Merchant Seamen* (New York: 1947), pp. 49–53.

[59] Furuseth to Ed Rosenberg, Dec. 3, 1920, in SUP, Files.

[60] Scharrenberg to Olander, Oct. 15, 1928, in Miscellaneous Correspondence, 1918–1928, Francis Gates residence, Berkeley, Calif.

[61] Furuseth to Faltus, Oct. 7, 1924, in SUP, Files.

[62] Typical of congressional opinion of Furuseth is the dialogue reported in *CSJ*, June, 1924, p. 171; see also letter from Mae Waggaman to Silas B. Axtell, Feb. 25, 1947, in Axtell, *A Symposium on Andrew Furuseth*, pp. 35–37.

[63] *CSJ*, Oct. 23, 1918, p. 6.

[64] Furuseth to Larsen, March 28, July 1, Nov. 11, 1929, in SUP, Files.

[65] Furuseth to Larsen, March 28, 1929, in *ibid.*

[66] Furuseth to Larsen, Nov. 4, 1929, in *ibid.;* see also Furuseth to Larsen, Oct. 28, 1929, in *ibid.*

[67] Larsen to Furuseth, Nov. 7, 20, 1929, in *ibid*. In 1935 Furuseth again asked the union to take up a collection, but there was no response. Furuseth to Larsen, March 14, April 3, 1935, and reply, April 18, 1935, in *ibid.*

[68] *San Francisco Chronicle*, March 13, 1935; Patrick O'Brien, "Report," March 15, 1935, in SUP, Files. An earlier illness, cancer of the lip, is mentioned in Furuseth to Olander, April 2, 1928, in SUP, Files. The cure left a permanent scar on his upper lip.

[69] AFL, *Proceedings, 1934*, p. 231.

⁷⁰ Furuseth was appointed to the California State Recovery Board of the NIRA but he does not appear to have attended any meetings (*CSJ*, Sept., 1933, p. 136).

⁷¹ Sam Darcy, "The Great West Coast Strike," *The Communist*, XIII (July, 1934), 664–686.

⁷² Larsen to Furuseth, Nov. 7, Dec. 2, 7, 1929, March 28, 1930, Furuseth to Larsen, Nov. 4, 11, 25, 1929, March 10, 1931, Furuseth to Patrick Flynn, Dec. 22, 1929, in SUP, Files.

⁷³ Furuseth to Larsen, Nov. 4, 11, 1929, Feb. 4, June 28, 1935, Furuseth, "Report," May 5, 1931, in *ibid*.

⁷⁴ Some accounts of the 1934 maritime strike in San Francisco can be found in Mike Quin, *The Big Strike* (Olema, Calif.: 1949); Ira B. Cross, *A History of the Labor Movement in California* (Berkeley: 1935), pp. 254–262; Darcy, *op. cit.*; Sam Darcy, "The San Francisco Bay Area," *The Communist*, XIII (Oct., 1934), 985–1004; William F. Dunne, *The Great San Francisco Strike* (New York: 1934); *CSJ*, July, 1934, pp. 97–98; Aug., 1934, pp. 115–116; Nov., 1934, p. 162.

⁷⁵ Marine Workers' Industrial Union, *Foc'sle Head*, June 24, 28, 29, 30, July 4, 5, 10, 11, 30, 1934. Assessing Furuseth's influence, Mike Quin, *op. cit.*, p. 140, says: "... he merely cluttered up the scene, created confusion in the public mind, and agitated himself into a nervous breakdown."

⁷⁶ MWIU, *Foc'sle Head*, June 28, 29, 30, July 4, 5, 1934; *San Francisco Chronicle*, June 30, 1934; *San Francisco Call Bulletin*, June 27, 1934; *San Francisco News*, June 28, 1934; *San Francisco Examiner*, June 30, 1934.

⁷⁷ MWIU, *Foc'sle Head*, July 30, 1934; Furuseth to George Larsen, May 29, 1935, in SUP, Files.

⁷⁸ *CSJ*, Feb.–Aug., 1935.

⁷⁹ July 1, 1935, in SUP, Files.

⁸⁰ Furuseth to Larsen, Feb. 4, 7, April 18, May 22, June 28, July 2, 19, Oct. 25, 1935, Larsen to Furuseth, Feb. 1, 19, July 5, 19, Aug. 2, Oct. 22, 1935, telegrams from Furuseth to Larsen, May 19, June 10, 26, 28, July 1, 8, 22, 1935, Furuseth to P. B. Gill, Nov. 1, 1935, Furuseth to officers and members of ISU on Pacific, May 9, 1935, Furuseth, "Report," June 7, 1935, in *ibid.*; *CSJ*, July, 1935, pp. 113–114, 125; Nov., 1935, p. 193.

⁸¹ *Voice of the Federation* (San Francisco), Feb. 13, 1936, pp. 1, 6.

⁸² Furuseth to Larsen, May 19, July 2, 1935, in SUP, Files. To follow what was happening on the East Coast, see ISU, *Pilot* (New York).

⁸³ *CSJ*, July, 1935, pp. 113–114, 125.

⁸⁴ Furuseth, "Report," June 7, 1935, in SUP, Files.

⁸⁵ *Voice of the Federation*, 1935–1938.

⁸⁶ ISU, "Proceedings, 1936," in *CSJ*, April, 1936, p. 136.

⁸⁷ Furuseth to Larsen, May 29, 1935, in SUP, Files.

⁸⁸ Paul Scharrenberg, "Furuseth," *American Federationist*, LII, (Sept., 1945), 24–26; *West Coast Sailor*, Sept. 10, 1937, p. 2; Oct. 29, 1937, p. 1. A few of the obituary notices and articles on Furuseth were in *West Coast Sailor*, Jan. 28, 1938, p. 1; *San Francisco News*, Jan., 1938; *San Francisco Chronicle*, Jan. 23–27, 30, March 11, 1938; *Congressional Record*, Jan. 28, 1938; "Portrait of Andrew Furuseth," *Survey Graphic*, XXVII (March, 1938), 134; *New York Times*, Jan. 24, 25, March 11, 1938; "Andrew Furuseth," *American Federationist*, XLV (Feb., 1938), 129. Honors accorded Furuseth are recorded in *San Francisco Chronicle*, Oct. 4, 1940; April 10, Aug. 8, 29, Sept. 2, 1941; Oct. 16, 1942; March 11, 1954.

BIBLIOGRAPHY

BIBLIOGRAPHY

Manuscripts

Book of Ritual for the Invisible Republic, 1882. 2 vols. Bancroft Library, University of California, Berkeley, Calif.

Coast Seamen's Union of the Pacific Coast. Minutes, 1886–1891. Headquarters, Sailors' Union of the Pacific, San Francisco, Calif.

———. Treasurer's Ledger, 1885/1887. Bancroft Library, University of California, Berkeley, Calif.

Cross, Ira B. California Labor Notes, 1847–1896. Bancroft Library, University of California, Berkeley, Calif.

Ferryboatmen's Union of California vs. Atchison, Topeka and Santa Fe Railway, Arbitration Proceedings, Brief for the Union, San Francisco, 1927. National Labor Bureau, San Francisco, Calif.

Gill, Peter B. "The Sailors' Union of the Pacific from 1885–1929." 1942. Bancroft Library, University of California, Berkeley, Calif.

Haskell, Burnette G. Notes and Reminiscences, 1879–1893. Bancroft Library, University of California, Berkeley, Calif.

International Seamen's Union of America. Arbitration between I.S.U. et al. and American Mail Lines et al., San Francisco, March 18–19, 1936. University of California Library, Berkeley, Calif.

———. Arbitration Proceedings between I.S.U. et al. and Pacific Coast and American Mail Lines. 19 vols. 1935. University of California Library, Berkeley, Calif.

———. Arbitration Proceedings between I.S.U. et al. and Shipowners' Association of the Pacific Coast. 5 vols. 1935. University of California Library, Berkeley, Calif.

Kaweah Cooperative Colony Records, 1885–1891. Bancroft Library, University of California, Berkeley, Calif.

Kentfield, John, and Company. Business Records, 1853–1923. Bancroft Library, University of California, Berkeley, Calif.

Macarthur, Walter. Correspondence and Papers, 1890–1945. Bancroft Library, University of California, Berkeley, Calif.

Minute Book of the International Workingmen's Association, San Francisco, Central Committee, 1884–6. Bancroft Library, University of California, Berkeley, Calif.

Miscellaneous Correspondence, 1918–1928. Francis Gates residence, Berkeley, Calif.

Phelan, James D. Correspondence and Papers. Bancroft Library, University of California, Berkeley, Calif.

Rowell, Chester H. Collection. Carton 6. Bancroft Library, University of California, Berkeley, Calif.

Sailors' Union of the Pacific. Correspondence, Letter Books, Files, 1885–1938. Headquarters, Sailors' Union of the Pacific, San Francisco, Calif.

This material stored in the headquarters of the union occupies an entire room. It consists of all incoming correspondence to the SUP; letter books for short periods, especially 1906–1911; all outgoing correspondence; copies of letters sent out for other periods; reports of all committees; and complete financial records. There are large gaps in materials for Furuseth, but there are at least 10,000 letters from Furuseth and many more addressed to him. Most of them concern purely administrative details. The period from 1898 to 1906 includes the correspondence which Furuseth kept in Washington, D.C., and which was transferred to the SUP files. The correspondence that arrived in Washington, D.C., for the later period was either (1) given to the ISU headquarters and lost, (2) burned in a hotel fire, or (3) turned over to V. A. Olander, who gave it to Paul Scharrenberg. Copies or originals of most of Furuseth's correspondence can be found in this file. This collection is not open to public inspection.

Sailors' Union of the Pacific. Minutes, 1891–1932. Headquarters, Sailors' Union of the Pacific, San Francisco, Calif.

Taylor, Paul S. "Chapters from the Early History of the Seamen of the Pacific Coast." 1920. Bancroft Library, University of California, Berkeley, Calif.

———. "Strikes in California, 1933–1939." Bancroft Library, University of California, Berkeley, Calif.

United States Maritime Commission. Hearings on Minimum Manning Scales, Minimum Wage Scales and Reasonable Working Conditions, 1937. University of California Library, Berkeley, Calif.

———. Investigation, 1936. University of California Library, Berkeley, Calif.

United States National Longshoremen's Board. Proceedings and the Arbitrator's Award. 8 vols. 1934. University of California Library, Berkeley, Calif.

Zacharissen, A. "History of the Norwegian Seamen's Union." N.d. Bancroft Library, University of California, Berkeley, Calif.

Theses

Francis, Robert C. "A History of Labor on the San Francisco Waterfront." Unpublished Ph.D. thesis, University of California, Berkeley, 1934.

Goldberg, Joseph P. "American Seamen." Ph.D. thesis, Publication No. 2815, University Microfilms, Ann Arbor, Michigan, 1950.

Hollingsworth, J. B. "The Labor Problem as a Factor in American Shipping." Unpublished thesis, University of Southern California, 1923.

Jensen, George C. "The City Front Federation of San Francisco." Unpublished M.A. thesis, University of California, Berkeley, 1912.

Lampman, Robert J. "Collective Bargaining of West Coast Sailors, 1885–1947." Unpublished Ph.D. thesis, University of Wisconsin, 1950.

Palmer, Dwight L. "Pacific Coast Maritime Labor." Unpublished Ph.D. thesis, Stanford University, 1935.

Robinson, R. M. "Maritime Labor in San Francisco, 1933–1937." Unpublished M.A. thesis, University of California, Berkeley, 1937.

Weintraub, Hyman. "The I.W.W. in California, 1905–1931." Unpublished M.A. thesis, University of California, Los Angeles, 1947.

Interviews

Borschardt, Selma, Washington, D.C.
Cross, Ira B., Berkeley, Calif.
Curran, Joseph P., New York, N.Y.

Lang, Harry, Los Angeles, Calif.
Lundeberg, Harry, San Francisco, Calif.
McDevitt, William, San Francisco, Calif.
McDonald, Jack, San Francisco, Calif.
Melnikow, Henry P., Los Angeles, Calif.
Scharrenberg, Paul, San Francisco, Calif.
Shipley, Mrs. Maynard, San Francisco, Calif.
Silver, Selim, Oakland, Calif.
Tennison, John, San Francisco, Calif.

GOVERNMENT PUBLICATIONS

CALIFORNIA

California Bureau of Labor Statistics. *Annual Report*, 1883–1928. Sacramento: 1883–1928.
———. *Investigation into Condition of Men Working on the Waterfront and on Board Pacific Coast Vessels, San Francisco, June 29–July 10, 1887*. Sacramento: 1887.

INTERNATIONAL

International Conference on Safety of Life at Sea, London, 1913–1914. *Text of Convention*. London: 1914.
International Labor Conference. *The International Seamen's Code*. Montreal: International Labor Conference, 1942.
International Labor Office:
 Brief Report on the Maritime Work, 1929–1936. Geneva: 1936.
 Continuous Employment. Montreal: 1945, 1946.
 Daily Bulletin. Genoa: June–July, 1920.
 Holidays with Pay for Seamen. Geneva: 1935, 1936.
 Hours of Work on Board Ship. Geneva: 1929.
 International Labor Conference, Geneva, 1926. Geneva: 1926. Pp. 401–407.
 International Labor Conference, Genoa, 1920. Geneva: 1920.
 International Labor Office and Seafarers. Montreal: 1946.
 Maritime Statistical Handbook. Geneva: 1936.
 Partial Revision of Minimum Age Convention, 1920. Geneva: 1936.
 Promotion of Seamen's Welfare in Port. Geneva: 1929, 1931.
 Protection of Seamen in Case of Sickness. Geneva: 1929, 1931.
 Protection of the Health of Seamen Against Venereal Disease. Geneva: 1926.
 Recognition of Seafarers' Organizations. Montreal: 1945, 1946.
 Regulation of Hours of Work on Board Ship. Geneva: 1929, 1931.
 Report and Record of the Meeting of the Principal Maritime Countries. Geneva: 1935.
 Report of the Governing Body of the International Labor Office upon the Working of the Convention, Number 22. Geneva: 1938.
 Report of the Governing Body of the International Labor Office upon the Working of the Convention, Number 23. Geneva: 1938.
 Report of the Governing Body of the International Labor Office upon the Working of the Convention Concerning Unemployment Indemnity. Geneva: 1933.

Report of the Governing Body of the International Labor Office upon the Working of the Convention for Establishing Facilities for Finding Employment for Seamen. Geneva: 1930.
Report on General Principles for the Inspection of the Conditions of Work of Seamen. Geneva: 1926.
Report on the International Codification of the Rules Relating to Seamen's Articles of Agreement. Geneva: 1926.
Seamen's Articles of Agreement. Geneva: 1926.

UNITED STATES, BUREAUS

Bureau of the Census. *Transportation by Water,* 1906, 1916, 1926. Washington: 1906, 1916, 1926.
Bureau of Immigration. *Annual Report of Commissioner General to Secretary of Labor,* 1924–1929. Washington: 1924–1929.
Bureau of Marine Inspection and Navigation. *Merchant Marine Statistics,* nos. 1–13. Washington: 1925–1936.
Bureau of Navigation, Department of Commerce. *Annual Report of Commission of Navigation,* 1883–1932. Washington: 1884–1932.
———. *Merchant Marine Statistics,* 1924–1941. Washington: 1924–1941.
———. *Merchant Vessels of the United States,* 1867–1940. Washington: 1867–1940.
———. *Navigation Laws of the United States,* 1899, 1935, 1940. Washington: 1899, 1935, 1940.

UNITED STATES, CONGRESS

Congressional Record, 1890–1938.
FIFTY-FIRST CONGRESS
House Committee on Merchant Marine and Fisheries:
The Tonnage Bill, Hearings on H.R. 4663. 1st sess., 1890.
American Merchant Marine in the Foreign Trade, H. Rept. 1210 on H.R. 4663. 1st sess., 1890.
International Marine Conference Proceedings, October 16 to December 31, 1889, S. Exec. Doc. 53. 1st sess., 1890. 3 vols.
FIFTY-FOURTH CONGRESS
House Committee on Merchant Marine and Fisheries:
Hearings on Bills Regulating Allotment of Seamen's Wages. 1st sess., 1896.
Hearings on Bills Relating to Rights and Duties of Seamen. 1st sess., 1896.
To Amend the Laws Relating to Navigation, H. Rept. 1660 on H.R. 2663. 1st sess., 1896.
Laws Relating to American Seamen, H. Rept. 1868 on H.R. 6399. 1st sess., 1896.
FIFTY-FIFTH CONGRESS
House Committee on Merchant Marine and Fisheries:
Laws Relating to American Seamen, H. Rept. 1657 on S. 95. 2d sess., 1898.
FIFTY-SIXTH CONGRESS
House Committee on Judiciary:
Bills To Limit the Meaning of the Word Conspiracy, Hearings on H.R. 1917 and S. 4233. 2d sess., 1900.

Bibliography

FIFTY-SEVENTH CONGRESS
Employment of Chinese on Vessels Flying American Flag, S. Exec. Doc. 254. 1st sess., 1902.
Chinese Exclusion, S. Rept. 776. 1st sess., 1902.

FIFTY-EIGHTH CONGRESS
House Committee on Judiciary:
Hearings on National Anti-injunction Bill, January 13 to February 26, 1904. 1st sess., 1904.
House Committee on Merchant Marine and Fisheries:
Development of American Merchant Marine, H. Rept. 4136 on H.R. 17098. 3d sess., 1905.
Senate Committee on Commerce:
Development of the American Merchant Marine and American Commerce, S. Rept. 10 on S. 529. 3d sess., 1905.
Report of the Merchant Marine Commission and Hearings, S. Rept. 2755. 3d sess., 1905.

FIFTY-NINTH CONGRESS
House Committee on Judiciary:
Anti-injunction Bill, Hearings on H.R. 4445. 2d sess., 1906.

SIXTIETH CONGRESS
Senate Committee on Commerce:
Better Security of Life at Sea; Commission on Revision of Laws Relating to Safety of Life at Sea, S. Doc. 701. 2d sess., 1909.
House Committee on Merchant Marine and Fisheries:
Better Security of Lives of Passengers and Crews, Hearings on H.R. 12351 and 18682. 2d sess., 1910.

SIXTY-FIRST CONGRESS
House Committee on Merchant Marine and Fisheries:
American Seamen, Hearings on H.R. 11193. 1st sess., 1910.
Senate Committee on Commerce:
Petition of Seamen, S. Doc. 379. 2d sess., 1910.
Legal Status of Seamen, S. Doc. 552. 2d sess., 1910.

SIXTY-SECOND CONGRESS
House Committee on Merchant Marine and Fisheries:
The Seamen's Bill, Hearings on H.R. 23673. 2d sess., 1911–1912.
Hearings on H.R. 11372, et al. 2d sess., 1912.
The Seamen's Bill, H. Rept. 645 on H.R. 23673. 2d sess., 1912.
Senate Committee on Commerce:
Desertion of Seamen from United States Vessels, S. Rept. 482. 2d sess., 1912.
Desertion of Seamen from United States Vessels, S. Rept. 5757. 2d sess., 1912.
Hearings on Titanic, S. Doc. 726. 2d sess., 1912.
Involuntary Servitude Imposed upon Seamen, Hearings on H.R. 23673. 3d sess., 1912–1913.

SIXTY-THIRD CONGRESS
House Committee on Merchant Marine and Fisheries:
The Seamen's Bill, Hearings on S. 136. 2d sess., 1913–1914.
Welfare of American Seamen, H. Rept. 852 to accompany S. 136. 2d sess., 1914.
Conference Report on Seamen's Bill, S. 136, H. Rept. 1439 on S. 136. 3d sess., 1915.

Senate Committee on Commerce:
: *Joint Letter from Secretary of Commerce and Secretary of Labor on S. 4, Involuntary Servitude Imposed upon Seamen*, S. Doc. 211. 1st sess., 1913.
: *The Decay of Seamanship*, by Andrew Furuseth, S. Doc. 216. 1st sess., 1913.
: *The Seamen's Bill*, Hearings on S. 136. 2d sess., 1914.

Senate Committee on Foreign Affairs:
: *Safety of Life at Sea*, by Andrew Furuseth, S. Doc. 476. 2d sess., 1914.

Senate Committee on Foreign Relations:
: *Hearings on International Conference on Safety of Life at Sea*. 2d sess., 1914.
: *Message and Documents on International Conference on Safety of Life at Sea*, S. Doc. 463. 2d sess., 1914.
: *Welfare of American Seamen, Memorial of International Seamen's Union on International Conference on Safety of Life at Sea*, S. Rept. 452. 2d sess., 1914.

SIXTY-FOURTH CONGRESS

House Committee on Merchant Marine and Fisheries:
: *Amendment of the Seamen's Act*, Hearings on H.R. 10026. 1st sess., 1916.
: *Creating a Shipping Board, a Naval Auxiliary, and a Merchant Marine*, Hearings on H.R. 10500. 1st sess., 1916.

Senate Committee on Commerce:
: *Creating a Shipping Board...*, Hearings on H.R. 15455. 1st sess., 1916.

Senate Committee on Printing:
: *Watch-and-Watch at Sea*, by Andrew Furuseth, S. Doc. 693. 2d sess., 1917.
: *The Seamen's Act*, by Andrew Furuseth, S. Doc. 694. 2d sess., 1917.

SIXTY-FIFTH CONGRESS

: *American Sea Power and the Seamen's Act*, by Andrew Furuseth, S. Doc. 228. 2d sess., 1918.

SIXTY-SIXTH CONGRESS

House Committee on Immigration and Naturalization:
: *Hearings on Japanese Immigration, July 12–14, 1920 (San Francisco and Sacramento)*. 2d sess., 1921.

House Committee on Merchant Marine and Fisheries:
: *Inquiry into Operations of the United States Shipping Board*. 1st sess., 1919.
: *Welfare of American Seamen*, Hearings on H.R. 8069. 1st sess., 1919.

Senate Committee on Commerce:
: *Hearings Relative to the Establishment of a Merchant Marine*. 1st sess., 1919–1920.
: *Promotion and Maintenance of the American Merchant Marine*, S. Rept. 573 on H.R. 10378. 2d sess., 1920.

Senate Committee on Interstate Commerce:
: *To Prohibit Interference with Commerce*, S. Rept. 644 on S. 4204. 2d sess., 1920.

SIXTY-SEVENTH CONGRESS

Senate Committee on Commerce:
: *Report on United States Shipping Board, 1921*, S. Doc. 38. 1st sess., 1921.

Senate Committee on Commerce and House Committee on Merchant Marine and Fisheries:
: *To Amend Merchant Marine Act of 1920*, Joint Hearings on S. 3217 and H.R. 10644. 1st sess., 1922. 2 vols.

Bibliography 245

SIXTY-EIGHTH CONGRESS
House Committee on Immigration:
  Restriction of Immigration, Hearings on H.R. 5, H.R. 101, and H.R. 561. 1st sess., 1924. 2 vols.
House Committee on Merchant Marine and Fisheries:
  To Amend Section 28 of Merchant Marine Act of 1920, Hearings on H.R. 8091. 1st sess., 1924.
House Select Committee on United States Shipping Board:
  To Inquire into Operations, Policies, and Affairs of the United States Shipping Board and United States Emergency Fleet Corporation, Hearings on H.R. 186. 1st sess., 1925.
SIXTY-NINTH CONGRESS
House Committee on Immigration and Naturalization:
  Hearings on Deportation of Alien Seamen. 1st sess., 1926.
  Deportation of Deserting Alien Seamen, Hearings on S. 3574. 2d sess., 1927.
  Report on Matters Affecting American Merchant Marine, by Harold N. Lowrie, S. Doc. 85. 1st sess., 1926.
Senate Committee on Commerce:
  Continuous Discharge Books for American Seamen, Hearings on S. 1079. 1st sess., 1926.
  Requesting Shipping Board to Postpone Sale of Certain Ships, Hearings on S. Res. 294. 2d sess., 1926–1927.
  Further Development of the American Merchant Marine, S. Rept. 1696 on S. 5792. 2d sess., 1927.
Senate Committee on Immigration:
  Deportation of Certain Alien Seamen, Hearings on S. 3574. 1st sess., 1926.
SEVENTIETH CONGRESS
House Committee on Merchant Marine and Fisheries:
  Hearings on the Merchant Marine. 1st sess., 1928.
Senate Committee on Commerce:
  Payment of Seamen on Foreign Vessels, S. Rept. 833 on S. 2945. 1st sess., 1928.
Senate Committee on Immigration:
  Deportation of Alien Seamen, S. Rept. 1037 on S. 717. 1st sess., 1928.
Senate Committee on Judiciary:
  Hearings before Subcommittee on Shipstead Bill, S. 1482. 1st sess., 1928.
SEVENTY-FIRST CONGRESS
House Committee on Immigration and Naturalization:
  Exclusion of Immigration from the Philippine Islands, Hearings on H.R. 80708. 2d sess., 1930.
  Deportation of Alien Seamen, Hearings on S. 202. 3d sess., 1931.
House Committee on Merchant Marine and Fisheries:
  Payment on Seamen's Wages, Hearings on H.R. 6789. 2d sess., 1930.
Senate Committee on Commerce:
  To Amend Certain Laws Relating to Seamen, Hearings on S. 306 and S. 314. 2d sess., 1930.
Senate Committee on Immigration:
  Deportation of Certain Alien Seamen, Hearings on S. 202. 2d sess., 1930.

SEVENTY-SECOND CONGRESS
House Committee on Immigration and Naturalization:
 Deportation of Alien Seamen, H. Rept. 1924 to accompany H.R. 12173. 2d sess., 1933.
Senate Committee on Immigration:
 Deportation of Certain Alien Seamen, S. Rept. 677 on S. 7. 1st sess., 1932.
SEVENTY-THIRD CONGRESS
House Committee on Merchant Marine and Fisheries:
 Regulating Licensed Officers and Hours of Labor on Vessels of Certain Tonnage, Hearings on H.R. 3348 and H.R. 7979. 2d sess., 1934.
Senate Committee on Immigration:
 Deportation of Alien Seamen, Hearings on S. 868. 2d sess., 1934.
SEVENTY-FOURTH CONGRESS
House Committee on Merchant Marine and Fisheries:
 Safety of Life and Property at Sea, Hearings on H.R. 6039, H.R. 6040, and H.R. 6041. Pt. 3. 1st sess., 1935.
 To Develop an American Merchant Marine, Hearings on H.R. 7521. 1st sess., 1935.
 Message of the President of the United States on Subject of Adequate Merchant Marine, H. Doc. 118. 1st sess., 1935.
 The Merchant Marine Bill, 1935, H. Rept. 1277 on H.R. 8555. 1st sess., 1935.
 Seamen's Legislation, H. Rept. 1322 on H.R. 8597. 1st sess., 1935.
 Hearings on H.R. 6189, H.R. 6202, H.R. 6203, H.R. 7319, and H.R. 10000. 2d sess., 1936.
 Amend Section 13 of Act To Promote Safety at Sea, Conf. Rept. 3041 on H.R. 8597. 2d sess., 1936.
Senate Committee on Commerce:
 Merchant Marine Act, Hearings on S. 2582. 1st sess., 1935.
 Memorandum on France, Germany, Great Britain, etc., Prepared by United States Bureau of Foreign and Domestic Commerce, S. Doc. 60 for consideration of S. 2582. 1st sess., 1935.
 Welfare of American Seamen, S. Rept. 1461 on S. 2003. 1st sess., 1935.
 Merchant Marine Act, Hearings on S. 3500, S. 4110, and S. 4111. 2d sess., 1936.
 United States Maritime Commission, S. Rept. 1721 to accompany S. 3500. 2d sess., 1936.
Senate Committee on Education and Labor:
 Special Committee To Investigate Air and Ocean Mail Contracts, Preliminary Report, S. Rept. 898. 1st sess., 1935.
Senate Committee on Immigration:
 Deportation of Certain Alien Seamen, Hearings on S. 379. 1st sess., 1935.
SEVENTY-FIFTH CONGRESS
House Committee on Merchant Marine and Fisheries:
 Maritime Labor Bill, Hearings on H.R. 5193. 1st sess., 1937.
 Rights of Appeal from Suspension of Licenses and Certificates of Service, Hearings on H.R. 7017. 1st sess., 1937.
 Continuous Discharge Books for Seamen, Hearings on H. Res. 121 and J. Res. 143. 1st sess., 1937.
 School Ship Graduates, Hearings on S. 2084, et al. 1st sess., 1937.

Bibliography

    Graduates of Approved School Ships, H. Rept. 784 on S. 2084. 1st sess., 1937.
    Amending Merchant Marine Act of 1936, Hearings on H.R. 8532. 2d sess., 1937–1938.
    Eight Hour Day for Seamen, Hearings on H.R. 6745, et al. 3d sess., 1938.
    Amendments to the Merchant Marine Act of 1936, Conf. Rept. 2582 to accompany H.R. 10315. 3d sess., 1938.
House Special Committee on Un-American Activities:
    Investigation of Un-American Propaganda Activities in the United States. 3d sess., 1938.
Senate Committee on Commerce:
    Hearings on Presentation of Demands of Striking "Rank and File" Seamen Relative to Continuous Discharge Book. 1st sess., 1937.
    "Morro Castle" and "Mohawk" Investigation, S. Rept. 184. Pt. 4. 1st sess., 1937.
    S. Rept. 200 to accompany H.R. 5487. 1st sess., 1937.
    Amending Merchant Marine Act of 1936, S. Rept. 1618 on S. 3078. 3d sess., 1938.
Senate Subcommittee on Commerce:
    Hearings on Maritime Commission Nomination. 1st sess., 1937.
Senate Committee on Commerce and Senate Committee on Education and Labor:
    Amending Merchant Marine Act of 1936, Hearings on S. 3078. 2d sess., 1937–1938.
SEVENTY-SIXTH CONGRESS
House Committee on Merchant Marine and Fisheries:
    Hiring of Seamen, Hearings on H.R. 4051. 1st sess., 1939.
    Economic Survey of Coastwise and Intercoastal Shipping by United States Maritime Commission, H. Rept. 209. 1st sess., 1939.
Senate Committee on Education and Labor:
    Hearings on Violation of Free Speech and Labor. Pts. 60, 61. 3d sess., 1940.
SEVENTY-SEVENTH CONGRESS
Senate Committee on Education and Labor:
    To Investigate Violations of the Right of Free Speech and Assembly, S. Rept. 1150 on S. Res. 266. 2d sess., 1942.
SEVENTY-EIGHTH CONGRESS
Senate Committee on Education and Labor:
    To Investigate Violations of the Right of Free Speech and Assembly, S. Rept. 398 on S. Res. 266. 2d sess., 1944.
EIGHTIETH CONGRESS
House Committee on Education and Labor:
    Hearings on Amendments to National Labor Relations Act. 1st sess., 1947.
    Hearings on Investigation of Steamship Unions. 1st sess., 1948.

UNITED STATES, MISCELLANEOUS

Delegation to International Conference on Safety of Life at Sea. *Report of Delegation of the United States.* Washington: 1929.
Department of Commerce. *American Ships in Foreign Trade.* Washington: 1936.

———. *Advisory Conference on the Subject of Making Passenger Vessels More Secure from Destruction by Fire, May 3, 1916.* Washington: 1916.
Department of State. *Digest of Consular Regulations Relating to Vessels and Seamen.* Washington: 1921.
Industrial Commission. *Report.* Vols. IV, IX, 1900–1901. Washington: 1901.
Maritime Commission. *Reports,* 1936, 1948/1949. Washington: 1936, 1948/-1949.
Office of Federal Coordinator of Transportation. *Hours, Wages and Working Conditions in Domestic Water Transportation.* Washington: 1936.
Secretary of Labor. *Annual Report,* 1917–1922.
Shipping Board. *Annual Report,* 1916/1917–1932/1933. Washington: 1917–1933.
———. *Proceedings of the National Conference on Merchant Marine,* 1932, 1933. Washington: 1932, 1933.
———. *Report,* 1921. Washington: 1921.
———. *Trade Routes and Shipping Services.* Washington: 1927.

Newspapers and Periodicals

American Federationist. Vols. I–XLV. Washington: American Federation of Labor, 1889–1938.
Coast Seamen's Journal. San Francisco, 1887–1937 (published as *Seamen's Journal,* 1918–1937).
The Foc'sle Head. San Francisco, May–Sept., 1934.
General Strike Bulletin. IWW Strike Committee, Marine Transport Workers' Industrial Union, No. 510. San Francisco, April 25, 26, 28, 30, May 1, 1923.
Industrial Solidarity. Chicago, 1911–1917, 1920–1931.
Industrial Worker. Seattle, 1916–1935.
I.S.U. Pilot. New York, 1935–1937.
Labor Clarion. San Francisco, 1902–1914.
Marine Worker. [San Francisco], 1920–1922.
New York Times. 1914–1938.
Organized Labor. San Francisco, 1900–1901, 1902–1905.
Pacific Marine Review. San Francisco, 1913–1936.
San Francisco Call. 1885–1939.
San Francisco Chronicle. 1885–1939.
San Francisco Examiner. 1885–1939.
The Seaman. London, 1913–1939.
Voice of the Federation. San Francisco, 1935–1939.
West Coast Sailors. San Francisco, 1937–1941.

Books

Abbot, Willis J. *American Merchant Ships and Sailors.* New York: Dodd, Mead, 1902.
Adamic, Louis. *Dynamite.* Rev. ed. New York: Viking, 1934.
American Bureau of Shipping. *The American Merchant Marine.* New York: American Bureau of Shipping, 1933.
American Federation of Labor. *History, Encyclopedia, Reference Book,* 1919, 1924. Washington: American Federation of Labor, 1919, 1924.

Bibliography

———. *Legislative Achievements of the A.F.L.* Washington: American Federation of Labor, 1916.
———. *Proceedings of the Annual Convention, 1886–1938.* Washington: American Federation of Labor, 1886–1938.
Asiatic Exclusion League. *First International Convention, Proceedings, February 3–5, 1908.* San Francisco, 1908.
———. *Proceedings, 1907–1912.* San Francisco, 1907–1912.
Axtell, Silas B. *Merchant Seamen's Law.* 2d ed. New York: Consumers Book Cooperative, 1945.
———, comp. *A Symposium on Andrew Furuseth.* New Bedford, Mass.: Darwin Press, 1948.
Babcock, Kendrick Charles. *Scandinavian Element in the United States.* Studies in Social Science, Vol. III, no. 3. Urbana: University of Illinois Press, 1914.
Bancroft, Hubert H. *History of California.* Vol. VII. San Francisco: The History Company, 1890.
Bankers Trust Company. *America's Merchant Marine.* New York: Bankers Trust Company, 1920.
Bates, William W. *American Marine.* Boston: Houghton, Mifflin, 1892.
———. *American Navigation.* Boston: Houghton, Mifflin, 1902.
Bean, Walton. *Boss Ruef's San Francisco.* Berkeley and Los Angeles: University of California Press, 1952.
Benson, William S. *The Merchant Marine.* New York: Macmillan, 1923.
Berman, Edward. *Labor and the Sherman Act.* New York: Harper, 1931.
Boyer, Richard O. *The Dark Ship.* Boston: Little, Brown, 1947.
Brissenden, Paul F. *History of the I.W.W.* 2d ed. New York: Longmans, Green, 1920.
Brooks, Elbridge S. *The Story of the American Sailor.* Boston: D. Lathrop, 1888.
Brown, Charles W. *My Ditty Bag.* Boston: Small, Maynard, 1925.
Bullen, Frank T. *The Men of the Merchant Service.* New York: Frederick A. Stokes, 1900.
Camp, William M. *San Francisco: Port of Gold.* Garden City, N.Y.: Doubleday, 1947.
Caughey, John W. *California.* 2d ed. New York: Prentice-Hall, 1953.
Chamber of Commerce of the United States. *National Merchant Marine Conference, November 16–17, 1925.* Washington: 1925.
———. *Referendum Number 12 on the Report of the Special Committee on the Seamen's Act.* Washington: 1916.
Chaplin, Ralph. *Wobbly.* Chicago: University of Chicago Press, 1948.
Chappelle, Howard I. *The History of American Sailing Ships.* New York: Norton, 1935.
Cleland, Robert G. *A History of California: The American Period.* New York: Macmillan, 1922.
Codman, John. *Free Ships.* New York: Putnam, 1881.
Commons, John R., and others. *History of Labor in the United States.* New York: Macmillan, 1921–1935. 4 vols.
Coolidge, Mary. *Chinese Immigration.* New York: Henry Holt, 1909.

Cronin, Bernard C. *Father Yorke and the Labor Movement in San Francisco, 1900–1910*. Washington: The Catholic University Press, 1943.

Cross, Ira B. *A History of the Labor Movement in California*. Berkeley: University of California Press, 1935.

Dana, Richard Henry. *Two Years Before the Mast*. New York: Harper, 1841.

Denison, Archibald C. *America's Maritime History*. New York: Putnam, 1944.

Denman, William. *Chinese Crews and the Wrecking of the Rio*. San Francisco: The Star Press, 1903.

Dreier, Mary E. *Margaret Dreier Robins*. New York: Island Press Cooperative, Inc., 1950.

Dulles, Foster Rhea. *Labor in America*. New York: Crowell, 1949.

Dunne, William F. *The Great San Francisco Strike*. New York: Workers Library Publishers, 1934.

Eaves, Lucile. *A History of California Labor Legislation*. Berkeley: The University Press, 1910.

Eliel, Paul. *The Waterfront and General Strikes*. San Francisco: Hooper Printing Company, 1934.

Faulkner, Harold U. *The Quest for Social Justice, 1898–1914*. History of American Life Series, Vol. XI. New York: Macmillan, 1931.

Fell, James. *British Merchant Seamen in San Francisco, 1892–1898*. London: E. Arnold, 1899.

Fine, Nathan. *Labor and Farmer Parties in the United States, 1828–1928*. New York: Rand School of Social Science, 1928.

Foster, William Z. *From Bryan to Stalin*. New York: International Publishers, 1937.

Frankfurter, Felix, and N. Greene. *The Labor Injunction*. New York: Macmillan, 1930.

Furuseth, Andrew. *Labor and Freedom: An Address of Andrew Furuseth before the Convention of the Whole Constitutional Convention of Illinois, April 7, 1920*. Illinois State Federation of Labor, Bull. no. 3. Chicago: Illinois Federation of Labor, 1920.

———. *The Open Shop: A Debate*. New York: League for Industrial Rights, 1921.

Galenson, Walter. *Labor in Norway*. Cambridge: Harvard University Press, 1947.

Gambs, John S. *Decline of the I.W.W.* New York: Columbia University Press, 1932.

Ginzberg, Eli. *The Labor Leader*. New York: Macmillan, 1948.

Gjerset, Knut. *Norwegian Sailors in American Waters*. Northfield, Minn.: Norwegian-American Historical Association, 1933.

———. *Norwegian Sailors on the Great Lakes*. Northfield, Minn.: Norwegian-American Historical Association, 1928.

Gompers, Samuel. *Seventy Years of Life and Labor*. New York: Dutton, 1925. 2 vols. Rev. ed., 1943.

Gorter, Wytze, and George H. Hildebrand. *The Pacific Coast Maritime Shipping Industry, 1930–1948*. Berkeley and Los Angeles: University of California Press, 1952, 1954. 2 vols.

Grafton Foundation. *Memorandum on Industrial Situation after the War*. Philadelphia: United States Shipping Board, 1918.

Great Britain Board of Trade. *Safety of Life at Sea.* London: H.M.S.O., 1927.
Hannoy, David. *The Sea Trader.* London: Harper, 1912.
Harrison, Gregory. *Maritime Strikes on the Pacific Coast, Statement on Behalf of Coast Committee of Shipowners before the United States Maritime Commission, San Francisco, California, November 2, 1912.* San Francisco: Waterfront Employers Association, November 20, 1936.
Harvey, Rowland H. *Samuel Gompers.* Stanford: Stanford University Press, 1935.
Healey, James C. *Foc'sle and Glory Hole.* New York: Merchant Marine Publishing Association, 1936.
Hittell, Theodore H. *History of California.* San Francisco: Pacific Press Publishing House, 1885–1897. 4 vols.
Hoagland, Henry E. *Wage Bargaining on the Vessels of the Great Lakes.* Urbana: University of Illinois Press, 1917.
Hohman, Elmo P. *History of American Merchant Seamen.* Hamden, Conn.: Shoe String Press, 1956.
———. *The International Labor Organization and the Seamen.* Geneva: Geneva Research Center, 1937.
———. *Seaman Ashore.* New Haven: Yale University Press, 1952.
Hoxie, Robert F. *Trade Unionism in the United States.* 2d ed. New York: Appleton-Century, 1936.
Hurley, Edward N. *The New Merchant Marine.* New York: Century, 1920.
Hutchins, John G. B. *The American Maritime Industries and Public Policy, 1789–1914.* Cambridge: Harvard University Press, 1941.
Hutton, H. W. *Objections to Ratification by the United States Senate of Proposed Treaty on Safety of Life at Sea, 1929.* San Francisco: International Seamen's Union, n.d.
International Seamen's Union of America. *Proceedings of the Annual Convention.* Vols. I–XXXIII. San Francisco, 1893–1936.
———. *Proceedings of the Conference between the I.S.U. and the I.L.A., Erie, Pennsylvania, April 18–20, 1906.* San Francisco: International Seamen's Union, 1906.
———. *Red Record.* San Francisco: Coast Seamen's Journal, 1895.
———. *Statement of Facts Concerning the Present Lockout in the Merchant Marine.* Washington: International Seamen's Union, 1921.
Jewell, J. Gray. *Among Our Sailors.* New York: Harper, 1874.
Keim, Karl. *Das Internationale Arbeitsrecht im der Seeschiffahrt.* Berlin: F. Dummler, 1925.
King, Stanton H. *Dog Watches at Sea.* Boston: Houghton, Mifflin, 1901.
La Follette, Belle C. *Robert M. La Follette.* New York: Macmillan, 1953. 2 vols.
La Follette, Robert M. *La Follette's Autobiography.* Madison, Wis.: Robert La Follette Company, 1913.
Lake Carriers' Association. *Annual Report, 1909.* Detroit: Lake Carriers' Association, 1910.
Lang, Frederick J. *Maritime; a Historical Sketch and a Workers' Program.* New York: Pioneer Press, 1943.
Lawson, Will. *Pacific Steamers.* Glasgow: Brown, Son and Ferguson, Ltd., 1927.
Lescohier, Don D., and Elizabeth Brandeis. *History of Labor in the United States, 1896–1932.* New York: Macmillan, 1935.

Link, Arthur S. *Woodrow Wilson and the Progressive Era, 1910–1917.* New York: Harper, 1954.
Lorwin, Lewis L. *The American Federation of Labor.* Washington: The Brookings Institution, 1933.
Lubbock, Basil. *The Down Easters: American Deep-water Sailing Ships, 1869–1929.* Boston: Charles E. Lauriat Company, 1929.
———. *The Last of the Windjammers.* Boston: Charles E. Lauriat Company, 1927, 1929. 2 vols.
Macarthur, Walter. *Last Days of Sail on the West Coast.* San Francisco: James H. Barry, 1929.
———. *The Seamen's Contract, 1790–1918.* San Francisco: James H. Barry, 1919.
McNairn, Jack, and Jerry McMullen. *Ships of the Redwood Coast.* Stanford: Stanford University Press, 1945.
Marine Engineers Beneficial Association, No. 335, San Francisco. *Souvenir Manual and Directory of Members, 1895.* San Francisco: 1895.
Mears, Eliot G. *Maritime Trade of the Western United States.* Stanford: Stanford University Press, 1935.
Missions to Seamen. *From the Bristol Channel to the Seven Seas.* London: Missions to Seamen, 1935.
Mowry, George E. *The California Progressives.* Berkeley and Los Angeles: University of California Press, 1951.
National Industrial Conference Board. *The American Merchant Marine Problem.* New York: National Industrial Conference Board, 1929.
National Maritime Union of America. *Proceedings of the National Convention,* I–IV. New York: National Maritime Union of America, 1937–1941.
Nevins, Allan. *Sail On.* New York: United States Lines Company, 1946.
Nordhoff, Charles. *Nine Years a Sailor.* Cincinnati: Moore, Wilstach, and Baldwin, 1866.
Older, Fremont. *My Own Story.* New York: Macmillan, 1919.
Paine, Ralph D. *The Old Merchant Marine.* Chronicles of America Series, Vol. XXXVI. New Haven: Yale University Press, 1921.
Perlman, Selig. *A History of Trade Unionism in the United States.* New York: Macmillan, 1923.
Peterson, Walter J. *Marine Labor Union Leadership.* San Francisco: 1925.
Plimsoll, Samuel. *Our Seamen.* London: Virtue and Company, 1873.
Quin, Mike. *The Big Strike.* Olema, Calif.: Olema Publishing Company, 1949.
Redfield, William C. *With Congress and Cabinet.* Garden City: Doubleday, Page, 1924.
Reed, Louis B. *The Labor Philosophy of Samuel Gompers.* New York: Columbia University Press, 1930.
Riesenberg, Felix. *Under Sail.* New York: Macmillan, 1918.
Riesenberg, Felix, Jr. *Golden Gate, the Story of San Francisco Harbor.* New York: Knopf, 1940.
Roney, Frank. *Frank Roney, Irish Rebel and California Labor Leader. An Autobiography.* Ed. Ira B. Cross. Berkeley: University of California Press, 1931.
Rydell, Raymond A. *Cape Horn to the Pacific.* Berkeley and Los Angeles: University of California Press, 1952.

Bibliography

San Francisco Chamber of Commerce. *Law and Order in San Francisco, 1916.* San Francisco: Chamber of Commerce, 1916.
Saposs, David J. *Left Wing Unionism.* New York: International Publishers, 1926.
Schlesinger, Arthur M. *The Rise of the City, 1878–1898.* History of American Life Series, Vol. X. New York: Macmillan, 1933.
Schneiderman, William. *The Pacific Coast Maritime Strike.* San Francisco: Western Worker Publishers, 1937.
Smith, Darrell H., and Paul V. Betters. *The United States Shipping Board.* Washington: The Brookings Institution, 1931.
Sparks, N. *The Struggle of the Marine Workers.* New York: International Pamphlets, 1930.
Spears, John R. *The Story of the American Merchant Marine.* New York: Macmillan, 1910.
Standard, William L. *Merchant Seamen.* New York: International Publishers, 1947.
Steffens, Lincoln. *The Autobiography of Lincoln Steffens.* New York: Harcourt, Brace, 1931.
Stimson, Grace Heilman. *Rise of the Labor Movement in Los Angeles.* Berkeley and Los Angeles: University of California Press, 1955.
Straus, Robert. *Medical Care for Seamen.* New Haven: Yale University Press, 1950.
Taylor, Paul S. *The Sailors' Union of the Pacific.* New York: Ronald Press, 1923.
Tupper, Edward. *Seamen's Torch.* London: Hutchinson, 1938.
Van Metre, Thurman W. "The Coastwise Trade," in Emery R. Johnson and others, *History of the Domestic and Foreign Commerce of the United States.* Washington: Carnegie Institute of Washington, 1922. 2 vols.
Ware, Norman J. *The Labor Movement in the United States, 1860–1895.* New York: Appleton, 1929.
Watkins, Gordon S. *Labor Problems and Labor Administration in the United States during the World War.* Urbana: University of Illinois Press, 1920.
Weiss, George. *America's Maritime Progress.* New York: New York Marine News Company, 1920.
Wells, David Ames. *Our Merchant Marine.* New York: Putnam, 1882.
Wells, Evelyn. *Champagne Days of San Francisco.* New York: Doubleday, 1947.
———. *Fremont Older.* New York: Appleton-Century, 1936.
Whidden, John D. *Ocean Life in the Old Sailing Ship Days.* Boston: Little, Brown, 1912.
Wissman, Rudolph W. *The Maritime Industry.* New York: Cornell Maritime Press, 1942.
Witte, Edwin E. *The Government in Labor Disputes.* New York: McGraw-Hill, 1932.
Woehlke, Walter V. *Union Labor in Peace and War.* San Francisco: Sunset Publishing House, 1918.
Wolman, Leo. *Ebb and Flow of Trade Unionism.* New York: National Bureau of Economic Research, 1936.
———. *The Growth of American Trade Unions.* New York: National Bureau of Economic Research, 1924.

Wright, Benjamin C. *San Francisco's Ocean Trade, Past and Future*. San Francisco: A. Carlisle, 1911.
Wright, E. W., ed. *Lewis and Dryden's Marine History of the Pacific Northwest*. Portland: The Lewis and Dryden Printing Company, 1895.
Zeis, Paul M. *American Shipping Policy*. Princeton: Princeton University Press, 1938.

Pamphlets and Leaflets

Pamphlets and leaflets, 1887–1938, published by the Sailors' Union of the Pacific, the International Seamen's Union, the Marine Transport Workers' Industrial Union, the International Longshoremen's Association, the Marine Workers' Industrial Union, the Industrial Workers of the World, and many other organizations, can be found principally in Sailors' Union of the Pacific Headquarters, San Francisco, California; University of California Library, Berkeley, California; and in Paul S. Taylor, "Strikes in California, 1933–1939," Bancroft Library, University of California, Berkeley, California.

Thousands of such items make it impractical to list them separately.

Articles

"Agreement and Arbitration Award in Shipping Industry on Pacific Coast," *Monthly Labor Review*, XLI (July, 1935), 107–109.
"Alien Crews on Our Merchant Ships," *Scientific American*, CXVIII (Feb. 23, 1918), 162.
"America to Benefit by Seamen Deserting," *Everybody's Magazine*, XXXIV (Jan., 1916), 143.
"American Foreign Trade Relations," *Proceedings of the Academy of Political Science in the City of New York*, IX (Feb., 1921).
"American Mariners for American Ships," *Outlook*, CXII (March 1, 1916), 509–511.
"American Ships and Shipping," *Current Opinion*, LIX (Oct., 1915), 276–283.
"Andrew Furuseth and His Fifteen Year Siege of Congress," *Current Opinion*, LIX (July, 1915), 18–19.
Andrews, John B. "Hours and Manning Convention Should Be Ratified Now," *American Labor Legislation Review*, XXVI (Dec., 1936), 153–154.
"Annual Convention of the I.S.U. of A., January, 1920," *Monthly Labor Review*, X (March, 1920), 797–799.
Atlanticus. "Unionism Afloat," *Atlantic Monthly*, CXVI (July, 1915), 50–56.
Barker, Tom. "The Future of the Marine Transport Industry," *One Big Union Monthly*, II (Dec., 1920), 29–30.
———. "Panama and Marine Transport Workers," *Industrial Pioneer*, I (Nov., 1921), 7–8.
———. "The Story of the Sea," *One Big Union Monthly*, III (Jan., 1921), 17–25; *Industrial Pioneer*, I (Feb., 1921), 52–58; (March, 1921), 40–44; (April, 1921), 49–52; (May, 1921), 44–46; (July, 1921), 50–52; (Aug., 1921), 36–43.
Barnett, George E. "American Trade Unions and the Standardization of Wages during the War," *Journal of Political Economy*, XXVII (Oct., 1919), 670–693.

Bibliography

Bendiner, M. R. "Is It Safe To Go to Sea?" *Nation*, CXLII (April 29, 1936), 542–544.
Brassy, Thomas. "Tyrants of the Sea," *Contemporary Review*, XLIX (March, 1886), 403–412.
British Marine Officer. "Can America Produce Merchant Seamen?" *Atlantic Monthly*, CIV (Dec., 1909), 798–807.
Bruere, Robert W., and Heber Blankenhorn. "For an American Manned Merchant Marine," *New Republic*, XX (Aug. 27, 1919), 116–119.
———. "I.L.O. Maritime Conferences," *American Labor Legislation Review*, XXVI (Dec., 1936), 150–152.
Buell, Katherine. "Your Chance of Drowning," *Harper's Weekly*, LIX (July 4, 1914), 4–6.
Campbell, Spencer. "The Peril Afloat," *Fortnightly*, XCVII (April, 1912), 747–757.
"Can Workmen's Compensation Benefit Seamen?" *American Labor Legislation Review*, XVIII (Sept., 1928), 268–269.
Carlson, Oliver. "The San Francisco Waterfront," *Nation*, CXLII (Jan. 22, 1936), 105–106.
"Congress, the Seamen's Bill," *Outlook*, CIX (March 10, 1915), 547–548.
Crochatt, Peter C. "The Degradation of Seamen," *Survey*, XLV (March 19, 1921), 894–895.
Dabney, Thomas L. "Organized Labor's Attitude toward Negro Workers," *The Southern Workman*, LVII (Aug., 1928), 323–330.
Daniel, Hawthorne. "The Life of the American Sailor," *Outlook*, CXIII (Aug. 9, 1916), 858–862.
"Danish Seamen's Law of May 1, 1923," *Monthly Labor Review*, XVII (Aug., 1923), 480–482.
Darcy, Sam. "The Great West Coast Strike," *The Communist*, XIII (July, 1934), 664–686.
———. "The San Francisco Bay Area," *The Communist*, XIII (Oct., 1934), 985–1004.
"Doubtful 'Welfare' for Seamen," *Literary Digest*, L (June 26, 1915), 1523–1524.
"Drastic Seamen's Legislation," *Journal of Political Economy*, XXIII (April, 1915), 397–398.
Drury, Horace B. "The Labor Policy of the Shipping Board," *Journal of Political Economy*, XXIX (Jan., 1921), 1–28.
Eaves, Lucile. "When San Francisco Was Sorest Struck," *Charities and the Commons* (May 5, 1906).
"Editorial," *Survey*, XXXI (Nov. 8, 1913), 163–164.
"Editorial," *Survey*, XXXIV (Aug. 7, 1915), 428–429.
"Employment Registry as Violation of Anti-trust Act," *Monthly Labor Review*, XXIV (Jan., 1927), 132–134.
Farnham, Henry W. "The Seamen's Act of 1915," *American Labor Legislation Review*, VI (March, 1916), 41–60.
"Finding Flaws in the Seamen's Bill," *Literary Digest*, XLVII (Nov. 8, 1913), 860.
Forsyth, Ralph Kendall. "The Wage Scale Agreements of the Maritime Unions," *Annals of the American Academy of Political and Social Science*, XXXVI (July, 1910), 349–365.

"The 'Full Crew' Seamen's Law," *Literary Digest*, L (March 20, 1915), 596–597.

Furuseth, Andrew. "The American Plan," *American Federationist*, XXX (Sept., 1923), 736–739.

———. "American Seamen's Act Upheld," *American Labor Legislation Review*, X (June, 1920), 123–124.

———. "Americans, Wake Up," *American Federationist*, XXIII (Aug., 1916), 653–657.

———. "The Campaign against the La Follette Bill," *Survey*, XXXIV (July 31, 1915), 396–400.

———. "Company Unions," *American Federationist*, XXXV (May, 1928), 541–545.

———. "The Dawn of Another Day," *American Federationist*, XXII (Sept., 1915), 717–722.

———. "The Deadly Parallels," *American Federationist*, XLI (April, 1935), 370–372.

———. "Equity Power and Its Abuse," *American Federationist*, XXXIV (Dec., 1927), 1435–1444.

———. "Extension and Misuse of Equity Power," *American Federationist*, XXXVI (Jan., 1929), 83–90.

———. "The Fight for Justice and Safety at Sea," *American Federationist*, XXX (April, 1923), 310–312.

———. "Harbor Workers Are Not Seamen," *American Labor Legislation Review*, XI (June, 1921), 139–142.

———. "A Historic Labor Review," *American Federationist*, XXVIII (May, 1921), 395–400.

———. "International Seamen's Union," *American Federationist*, XXIII (Sept., 1916), 802–805.

———. "Lest We Forget," *American Federationist*, XLII (May, 1935, supplement).

———. "Mastery of the Sea," *New Republic*, XXVII (July 20, 1921), 208–210.

———. "On the Crest of the Wave," *American Federationist*, XXIII (May, 1916), 372–373.

———. "The One Big Union Fallacy," *American Federationist*, XXX (Sept., 1923), 724–726.

———. "An Open Letter to Senator Wagner," *American Federationist*, XLII (June, 1935), 601–605.

———. "Safety of Life at Sea—Proposed Treaty," *American Federationist*, XLII (Feb., 1935), 134–136.

———. "Scientific Legislation," *American Federationist*, XXXI (March, 1924), 300–302.

———. "Sea Service," *American Federationist*, XXV (Feb., 1918), 133–140.

———. "The Seamen's Law and Its Critics," *American Labor Legislation Review*, VI (March, 1916), 61–68.

———. "Work Is Worship," *American Federationist*, XXXV (Jan., 1928), 25–30.

Furuseth, Andrew, James A. Emery, Charles E. Littlefield, and Charles P. Neal. "Use and Abuse of Injunctions in Trade Disputes," *Annals of the American Academy of Political and Social Science*, XXXVI (July, 1910), 87–141.

Bibliography

"The Genoa Conference," *New Statesman,* XV (June 12, 1920), 271–272.
Gompers, Samuel. "Free and Skilled Seamen Insure Safety at Sea," *American Federationist,* XX (Dec., 1913), 1036–1039.
———. "The Seamen's Successful Uprising," *American Federationist,* XVIII (Sept., 1911), 679–693.
———. "The Titanic Disaster," *American Federationist,* XIX (July, 1912), 545–548.
Goodrich, Carter. "Maritime Labor Treaties of 1936," *Monthly Labor Review,* XLII (Feb., 1937), 349–355.
"The Government, the Unions, and Safety at Sea," *Scientific American,* CVI (May 18, 1912), 447.
"The Great Nautical Experiment," *Sunset Magazine,* XXXV (Oct., 1915), 656–657.
"The Hard Lot of the Sailor," *Survey,* XXVI (May 13, 1911), 266–267.
Henderson, Gerard. "Economics of American Shipping," *New Republic,* IV (Oct. 2, 1915), 225–227; (Oct. 9, 1915), 254–256; (Oct. 16, 1915), 279–281.
Hoffman, Frederick. "Occupational Hazards in the American Merchant Marine," *American Labor Legislation Review,* VI (March, 1916), 69–73.
Hohman, Elmo P. "Maritime Labor in the United States," *International Labor Review,* XXXVIII (Aug., 1938), 200.
Hold, Upton. "Salting Down the Marine Workers," *Industrial Pioneer,* I (Oct., 1921), 34–38.
Hopkins, Ernest J. "The Seamen's Act—Blessing or Boomerang," *Sunset,* XXXV (Sept., 1915), 478–480.
Hopkins, William S. "Employment Exchanges for Seamen," *American Economic Review,* XXV (June, 1935), 250–258.
Hunter, George McPherson. "Changing the Life in the Forecastle," *Survey,* XXVIII (July 6, 1912), 495–496.
———. "Destitution among Seamen," *Survey,* XXVIII (Aug. 3, 1912), 610–618.
———. "Law Making by Landsmen for Seamen," *Survey,* XXVIII (May 18, 1912), 292–294.
———. "The Revolution on the Sea," *Survey,* XXVIII (May 4, 1912), 199–205.
"An Ill-Considered and Pernicious Bill," *Scientific American,* CX (Jan. 31, 1914), 94.
"The Illusive American Seaman," *Nation,* CXIV (March 29, 1922), 361.
"Injured Seamen Allowed Maintenance, Cure, and Wages in Addition to Damages," *Monthly Labor Review,* XXVIII (Feb., 1929), 270–271.
Johnson, Alvin S. "Andrew Furuseth," *New Republic,* IX (Nov. 11, 1916), 40–42.
Keay, Frances Anne. "Oyster Boats on the Chesapeake," *Charities and the Commons,* XVII (Jan., 1908), 630–633.
———. "The Sailor in Port: Philadelphia," *Charities and the Commons,* XVII (Jan., 1908), 712–716.
———. "The Wages of Seamen," *Charities and the Commons,* XVII (Feb. 2, 1908), 845–848.
Kelly, Florence. "Safety at Sea and the Consumers' League," *Survey,* XXXII (May 2, 1914), 112.
———. "Seamanship and Safety," *Survey,* XXXI (Nov. 8, 1913), 154–155.

Kennedy, Philip B. "The Seamen's Act," *Annals of the American Academy of Political and Social Science,* XLIII (Jan., 1916), 232-243.
"Knives Out for the Seamen's Law," *Literary Digest,* LI (Oct. 4, 1915), 1269-1270.
Kyne, P. B. "Saint Andrew the Sailor," *Readers Digest,* XXXV (Dec., 1939), 9-14.
La Follette, Robert M. "The American Sailor a Free Man," *Survey,* XXXIV (May 1, 1915), 116-117, 125-128.
"The Lake Seamen's Struggle for Liberty," *American Federationist,* XVII (May, 1910), 413-415.
"The Last Serfs," *Nation,* CXXIV (Feb. 2, 1927), 107-108.
"Latest Score in the Seamen's Law Fight," *Everybody's Magazine,* XXXIV (May, 1916), 655-657.
"Laws and Agreements Governing Working Conditions among American Seamen," *Monthly Labor Review,* X (May, 1920), 1075-1094.
"Leave It to Furuseth, He'll Get the Sailors," *Literary Digest,* LV (Nov. 24, 1917), 70.
"Legislating for the Sailor," *Sunset Magazine,* XXXV (Sept., 1915), 445-446.
"Liability of Emergency Fleet Corporation for Injury to Seamen," *Monthly Labor Review,* XXI (July, 1925), 163-165.
"Light on the Seamen's Bill," *Scientific American,* CXIII (July 17, 1915), 58.
Longford, Joseph H. "Manning of Our Merchant Marine," *Nineteenth Century,* LXXII (Dec., 1912), 1114-1130.
Macarthur, Walter. "The American Seaman under the Law," *Forum,* XXVI (Feb., 1899), 718-731.
———. "Efficiency of Ships' Crews," *Charities and the Commons,* XVI (May 19, 1906), 250-252.
"Manning Our Ships," *Public,* XXI (March 16, 1918), 329-330.
"The Market Place," *Independent,* LXXXII (June 21, 1915), 516.
Mathews, John L. "The Coming Ashore of Andrew Furuseth," *Everybody's Magazine,* XXV (July, 1911), 60-71.
"The Men of the Merchant Service," *The Atheneum,* II (Oct. 27, 1900), 543-544.
"Minimum Wage for Japanese Seamen," *Monthly Labor Review,* XXVII (Nov., 1928), 1009-1010.
"Modified Seamen's Bill Passes the House," *Survey,* XXXII (Sept. 5, 1914), 555-556.
"Nationality of Members of the International Seamen's Union of America," *Monthly Labor Review,* XI (Feb., 1921), 430-431.
"New Slogan, 'Back to the Sea,'" *Survey,* XXXVIII (Aug. 18, 1917), 443.
"Our Merchant Marine's Wage Burden," *Literary Digest,* LXXXII (Sept. 6, 1924), 70-72.
"Our Natural Waterways and the La Follette Seamen's Bill," *Survey,* XXXIII (Dec. 12, 1914), 282-283; rejoinder by Andrew Furuseth (Dec. 19, 1914), 311-312; reply by officer (Dec. 26, 1914), 344-345.
Page, Thomas Walker. "The San Francisco Labor Movement in 1901," *Political Science Quarterly,* XVII (Dec., 1902), 664-688.
"Proceedings of the American Seamen's Convention, 1926," *Monthly Labor Review,* XXIII (Aug., 1926), 289.

Bibliography

"Productivity of Labor of Seamen," *Monthly Labor Review*, XXV (Nov., 1927), 980–981.
"Protection for Seamen," *American Labor Legislation Review*, X (Sept., 1920), 211–216.
Pullman, Raymond W. "Fate of Seamen's Bill Hanging in the Balance," *Survey*, XXXIII (Dec. 26, 1914), 332.
———. "The Seamen's Bill a Law after Twenty Years' Fight," *Survey*, XXXIV (March 13, 1915), 645.
Rice, William G., and W. Ellison Chalmers. "Improvement of Labor Conditions on Ships by International Action," *Monthly Labor Review*, XLII (May, 1936), 1181–1203.
Robinson, Robert M. "San Francisco Teamsters at the Turn of the Century," *California Historical Society Quarterly*, XXXV (March, 1956), 59–69; (June, 1956), 145–153.
Rothschild, V. H., II. "The Legal Implications of a Strike by Seamen," *Yale Law Journal*, XLV (May, 1936), 1181–1200.
Ruhl, Arthur. "The Sailor's Side," *Colliers*, XLVII (July 22, 1911), 18–20.
Russel, W. Clark. "The Life of the Merchant Sailor," *Scribner's Magazine*, XIV (July, 1893), 1–19.
"Sabotage at Sea," *New Republic*, LXXXVI (April 22, 1936), 301.
Sadler, Herbert C. "The Seamen's Bill," *Nation*, XCVIII (Jan. 15, 1914), 57.
"Safety at Sea," *Survey*, XXXII (June 27, 1914), 349–351.
"Safety-at-Sea in Danger of Congress," *Survey*, XXXII (July 4, 1915), 355–356.
Sandgren, John. "An International Conference of Marine Transport Workers," *One Big Union Monthly*, I (March, 1919), 53.
Scharrenberg, Paul. "The Advantages of the La Follette Seamen's Act," *American Federationist*, XXX (Feb., 1933), 134–138.
"Sea Justice," *Living Age*, CCXCVIII (Aug. 10, 1918), 364–365.
"The Seamen's Act," *New Republic*, XIX (May 3, 1919), 8–9.
"The Seamen's Bill," *Outlook*, CIX (March 17, 1915), 601–602.
"The Seamen's Bill," *Survey*, XXXI (Nov. 22, 1913), 205–206.
"The Seamen's Bill and American Shipping," *Outlook*, CX (June 23, 1915), 406–407.
"The Seamen's Conference at Genoa," *The New Europe*, XVI (July 22, 1920), 38–41.
Simpson, Smith. "The I.L.O. Month by Month," *American Federationist*, XLIII (Dec., 1936), 1309–1313.
Slocum (pseud.). "Land-locked Disaster," *Survey*, XXXII (June 6, 1914), 253–256.
Smith, E. Hinton. "Seamen's Hours of Work," *Contemporary Review*, CXXXVIII (Aug., 1930), 225–230.
"The Spectator," *Outlook*, CV (Dec. 20, 1913), 854–856.
Taylor, Paul S. "Eight Years of the Seamen's Act," *American Labor Legislation Review*, XV (March, 1925), 52–63.
Thompson, Laura A. "Injunctions in Labor Disputes, Select List of Recent References," *Monthly Labor Review*, XXVII (Sept., 1928), 201–220.
"The Twenty-first and Twenty-second (Maritime) Sessions of the International Labor Conference," *International Labor Review*, XXXV (Jan., 1937), 3–30; (Feb., 1937), 141–176.

"Union of Sailors," *Survey,* XXVI (May 27, 1911), 324.
"The Unworkable Seamen's Act," *World's Work,* XXX (Oct., 1915).
"U.S. Shipping," *Fortune,* XVI (Sept., 1937).
Varney, Harold Lord. "The Story of the I.W.W., Chapter 13," *One Big Union Monthly,* II (April, 1920), 41–44.
"Wage Agreements and Working Conditions in the German Merchant Marine," *Monthly Labor Review,* XVII (Aug., 1923), 134–142.
"Wage Rates on American and Foreign Cargo Steamships, 1922," *Monthly Labor Review,* XVI (Feb., 1923), 358–364.
"Wages of Seamen, 1926," *Monthly Labor Review,* XXIV (May, 1927), 738–740.
"Wages of Seamen, 1927," *Monthly Labor Review,* XXVI (May, 1928), 1004–1006.
"Wages of Seamen, 1929," *Monthly Labor Review,* XXX (March, 1930), 637–639.
"Wages of Seamen, 1932," *Monthly Labor Review,* XXXVI (Jan., 1933), 176–178.
"Wages of Seamen, 1929 to 1935," *Monthly Labor Review,* XLII (April, 1936), 1059–1060.
"Watches and Wages of Seamen," *Monthly Labor Review,* XXIV (April, 1927), 719–720.
West, George P. "Andrew Furuseth and the Radicals," *Survey,* XLVII (Nov. 5, 1921), 207–209.
———. "Andrew Furuseth Stands Pat," *Survey,* LI (Oct. 15, 1923), 86–90.
Wetjen, Albert Richard. "Ships and Men and the Sea," *Colliers,* LXXV (March 7, 1925), 24–25.
White, George W. "The La Follette Seamen's Bill," *Outlook,* CV (Nov. 29, 1913), 713.
"Why We Need a Shipping Bill," *Outlook,* CV (Nov. 8, 1913), 503–504.
Williams, James H. "The Autobiography of a Labor Leader," *Independent,* LIV (Nov. 6, 1902), 2634–2638.
———. "Betrayed," *Independent,* LXV (Aug. 20, 1908), 407–413; (Aug. 27, 1908), 470–475.
———. "A Better Berth for Jack Tar," *Independent,* XCI (Sept. 29, 1917), 502–503, 515.
———. "How We Live To Keep Her Going," *Independent,* LVI (March 24, 1904), 653–661.
———. "How We Live To Make Her Go," *Independent,* LVI (Jan. 7, 1904), 18–22.
———. "Manning Our Merchant Marine," *Independent,* XCI (Sept. 22, 1917), 469, 483.
———. "The Sailor and the Law," *Independent,* LII (Nov. 15, 1900), 2733–2737.
———. "Shanghaied," *Independent,* LV (Dec. 31, 1903), 3102–3107.
Wilson, William B. "The Seamen's Act," *Harper's Weekly,* LXII (April 22, 1916), 426–427.
"Workmen's Compensation for Seamen in Belgium," *Monthly Labor Review,* XXX (June, 1930), 1299–1300; XXXI (Oct., 1930), 941–942.

INDEX

INDEX

Advance and allotment: defined, 5; legislation on, 29, 31, 34, 39, 42–43, 111, 130–131, 134, 165; court decisions on, 165–166, 223

Alexander, J. W., 120, 122–125, 127, 128

Allotment. *See* Advance and allotment

American Federation of Labor, 34, 43, 48–51, 62, 78, 80–83, 143; legislative interests of, 51, 111; on injunctions, 97, 187–189; on League of Nations, 151–154

American-Hawaiian Line, 95

American Seamen's Friend Society, 36, 40

American Steamship Owners Association, 156

Anderson, Edward, 18, 58, 59, 103

Ark, Henry, 21, 22

Association of Passenger Steamboat Lines, 126

Atlantic Coast seamen's unions, 52, 54, 56, 101–105, 140–142, 149, 155–158, 160–161, 190, 198, 211

Axtell, Silas B., 137, 192

Bacon, Augustus, 123
Baker, Newton D., 132
Barry, James H., 42, 58
Barter, H. C., 83
Bell, John R., 33
Benson, Fred, 101, 102
Benson, William S., 156–158
Berengher, José, 102
Bingham, Henry H., 33
Boardinghouses, sailors', 4–7
Bodine, George C., 102–105, 117
Bolton, George, 31
Bradley, John, 35
Brewery workers, 15, 48, 62
Bridges, Harry, 197
British seamen, 20, 53–54, 98–100, 150, 154, 177–178, 179, 181, 190
Brouillet, A. W., 139, 140
Brown, G. H., 191
Brown, Vernon C., 36
Bruge, Secundino, 102
Bryan, William J., 131, 222
Building trades workers, 67
Bureyson, F. H., 54, 212
Burton, Theodore H., 121, 123, 129
Bushnell, W. A., 21, 45
Butchers, 62

Calhoun, Patrick, 92

California State Federation of Labor, 60–61, 74

Cannon, Joseph, 94

Carlson, Oscar, 103, 105, 177

Carriage and wagon workers, 61

Chamberlain, Eugene T., 36, 41, 125, 128

Chambers, Thomas, 102

Chinese issue. *See* Oriental issue

City Front Federation, 60, 63–64, 69, 75, 106

Clarke, James P., 122, 128

Clayton Act, 97–98, 187

Cleveland, Grover, 34

Coast Seamen's Journal: established, 16; conflicts over, 33–34, 58–60, 160–161; on Union Labor party, 71, 92, 93

Coast Seamen's Union, 11–22, 29–30

Communists, 195–199, 230

Competition, foreign, 20, 115–116. *See also* Merchant marine, American

Conditions aboard ship, 3–4, 37–38, 108–111

Cooks and stewards, 19, 56, 73, 75, 79–80, 104

Coolidge, Calvin, 173

Crangle, Edward, 12, 20, 22, 31

Crimping system: description of, 4–7; Furuseth on, 10, 39, 55–56; union struggles against, 12–13, 22–27, 34, 60–71, 72–73, 94–95; legislation on, 29–30, 31, 39, 42–44. *See also* Advance and allotment

Cummins, Albert B., 123

Curtin, Johnny, 26

Dana, Richard Henry, 3
Danielwicz, Sigismund, 11
Davidson, Jo, 193
Denman, William, 86, 226
Deportation bills, 168–169
Desert, freedom to, 34, 42–43, 95, 111, 113–115, 119, 130–131, 134, 170; *Arago* decision, 35
Dingley, Nelson, 33
Dingley Act, 29
Discharge book. *See* Grade book
Dollar, Robert, 133, 134
Dollar Steamship Co., 165

Elderkin, T. J., 33, 52, 53, 212
Ellison, E., 77, 106

[263]

Fickert, Charles M., 93, 139
Finnerty, Thomas, 53
Firemen, 19, 56, 60, 75, 81–82, 84, 101–105, 140, 142, 155
Fletcher, Duncan U., 123, 129
Flynn Patrick, 140, 141
Frankfurter, Felix, 188
Frazier, William H., 56, 101, 103–105, 116
Free, Arthur M., 170
Frey, John P., 86, 188
Frye, William P., 32, 41
Fuhrman, Alfred, 18, 45, 48, 52
Furuseth, Andrew: sea experience, 2–3, 7–10; character, 10, 73–74, 85–92, 95, 154, 192; union offices, 14, 21–22, 53, 101; international activities, 20, 98–100, 150–151, 177–182; on hiring hall, 22, 73, 160, 194; legislative activities, 32–44, 51, 95, 111–132, 165–169; and politics, 32, 34, 71, 92–94, 189, 213, 235; as speaker, 45–47; philosophy, 47–48, 50–51, 79, 88–89, 113–114, 182 ff.; at AFL conventions, 48–50, 183; on arbitration, 50, 83, 157, 196; on minorities, 112–113; on subsidies, 112, 117–118, 171–173; on war, 143–145; on social legislation, 183–186. For Furuseth's position on other matters, see particular subjects

Gage, Henry T., 66, 70
Gary, Elbert H., 106
Goff, S. H., 68
Gohl, William, 73
Gompers, Samuel, 32, 52, 78, 80, 87, 106, 211; and politics, 40, 94; and seamen's legislation, 43, 116, 137; and Furuseth, 47–51, 71–72, 86, 95; and seamen-longshoremen conflict, 83–84; and injunctions, 97, 187; and World War I, 143–145; and League of Nations, 151, 153–154
Grade book, 13, 30, 31, 106, 167, 180
Grange, David, 198
Great Lakes Carriers' Association, 105–106, 121, 126, 147
Great Lakes seamen's unions, 51–52, 54–55, 56, 81–82, 105–106, 142, 147, 190, 211
Green, William, 153, 181
Greene, William S., 103, 116, 117
Griffin, Henry P., 198

Hagen, Charles, 33, 52, 53
Haist, John, 52
Hammond, A. B., 94–95
Hammond Lumber Co., 77, 78, 94
Hanson, Morris, 35
Hanson, Thomas A., 128, 190
Hardy, Rufus, 120
Harlan, John, 35
Haskell, Burnette G., 11, 13, 16–19, 50, 206, 207
Hearst, William Randolph, 67, 87
Heney, Francis J., 87, 93
Hoffmeyer, Volney, 29
Hopkins, Albert J., 33
Hours of work, 130, 179. *See also* Watches
Humphrey, William E., 116
Hunter, Ivan, 194, 198
Huntington, Collis P., 46
Hurley, Edward M., 150
Hutton, H. W., 35, 77

Immigration Act of 1924, 168
Industrial Workers of the World, 104–105, 160–163
Injunction issue, 51, 77, 95–98, 186–189
International Labor Organization, 151, 153, 177–182
International Seafarers' Federation, 150, 177–179
International seamen's conferences, 20, 98–100, 150–151, 177–179
International Seamen's Union, 142, 158, 168, 229; organization of, 56; jurisdictional disputes, 79–84; internal conflicts, 100–107, 160–162, 195–199; legislative program, 111 ff.; in World War I, 146–149; decline, 159–162, 190–191, 199
International Shipping Federation, 99, 134, 150
International Transport Workers' Federation, 82, 98–100, 115, 177, 179
International Workingmen's Association, 11, 12, 17–19

Jensdatter, Marthe, 2
Johnson, Hiram, 95
Jortall, Chris, 58
Jortall, Nicholas, 31, 57–59

Kahn, Julius, 192
Kalashi-Watch. *See* Watches
Kean, John, 58, 59
Kelner, Andrew, 77
Kern, John, 131

Index

La Follette, Robert M., 137; and Furuseth, 85, 87–88, 144–145, 189–190; and seamen's legislation, 103, 116, 117, 121–124, 128–132
La Follette, Robert M., Jr., 167
La Guardia, Fiorello, 167
Lamb, Charles, 72
Lane, Harry, 123
Larsen, George, 172, 186, 198, 199
League of Nations, 151–154, 179–180
Legislation, seamen's. *See* Deportation bills, Dingley Act, Maguire Act, Seamen's Act, Shipping Commissioners acts, and White Act
Livernash, Edward J., 87, 94, 109, 115
Lodge, Henry Cabot, 129
Longshoremen, 8, 60, 64, 75, 78–84, 138–139, 161, 162, 194–196
Low, Phillip D., 36
Lundeberg, Harry, 198
Lynch, George M., 31

Macarthur, Walter, 93, 94, 143, 206; union activities, 45, 48, 53, 58, 60, 82, 83; and Furuseth, 86, 91
McCarthy, P. H., 67, 93, 94
McDonald, Dave, 19
Machinists, 61–62, 70
Mackay, W. J. B., 32, 45
McKinley, William, 69
McNamara, John J., 93
Madsen, John A., 83
Maguire, James G., 32, 34, 40, 42, 87, 94
Maguire Act, 30–36
Manly, Basil M., 162
Mann, Tom, 104
Marine Engineers Beneficial Association, 158
Marine Transport Workers' Industrial Union, 160, 162
Martin, James J., 11
Martin, P. Ross, 11
Martinez, Juan, 102
Master's option, defined, 31. *See also* Wages, payment of
Merchant marine, American, 37, 39, 111, 134, 157, 166, 172–173, 174–175
Merchant Marine Act of 1920, 165
Merchant Marine Commission, 118
Metal polishers, 61
Michael, M. F., 61, 63, 67, 68
Miller, Paul, 99
Mooney, Tom, 139, 140
Morrison, Frank, 94

Municipal League, 63, 68

National Consumers' League, 123
NRA maritime code, 194
National Seamen's Union, 43, 52–56
Nelson, Knute, 122
Newhall, George W., 64, 65, 69
Nielsen, Andreas, 2
Nielsen, Rasmus, 11, 14
Nockles, Edward H., 127
Nolan, K. N., 190
Norris, George W., 123

O'Brien, Patrick, 191
Oceanic Steamship Co., 12–13
O'Keefe, Daniel, 81, 82
Olander, Victor, 85, 143, 172, 181, 198; and Furuseth, 86, 91, 95, 101, 185, 188; union activities, 106, 190–191, 194, 195; and seamen's bill, 116, 127, 128, 136; and injunctions, 188–189
Older, Fremont, 77, 87, 92, 93
Olsen, P. H., 35
"Oracle," defined, 159
Oriental issue, 111, 112–113, 133–135, 169–170, 230
Owen, Robert L., 131

Pacific Coast Steamship Co., 58, 62
Pacific Mail Steamship Co., 112
Page, Charles R., 149
Panama Canal, 138, 143
Paris Peace Conference, 150–151
Payne, Sereno E., 40
Penje, William, 54–55, 56, 81, 100, 101, 212
Perkins, Frances, 182
Peterson, Walter, 159
Phelan, James D., 61, 64–65, 67, 213
Pierce, Jefferson D., 60
Pilots, tugboat, 80
Pittsburgh Steamship Co., 105
Powderly, T. V., 32
Printers, 66
Pryor, Percy, 135, 139, 187

Red Record, 37–38
Redfield, William C., 122–125, 134–136
Renner, George, 70
Restaurant employees, 61, 80
Robertson, Robert, 35
Robertson, T. J., 53
Roe, Gilbert, 137
Rogers, William, 103
Rolph, James, 86, 93, 119

266   *Index*

Roney, Frank, 18, 45, 210
Roosevelt, Franklin D., 172, 195
Roosevelt, Theodore, 97
Root, Elihu, 129
Rosenberg, Ed, 58, 59, 68
Ruef, Abraham, 87, 92, 93
Ryan, Joseph P., 195

Safety issue, 112, 113, 119–130, 135–136, 166, 170, 181
Sailors' Union of the Pacific: formation of, 20; early history, 21–27; legislative programs, 30–44; and organization of national union, 52–56; internal conflicts, 58–60, 160–162, 195–199; and City Front Federation, 60 ff., 75; and longshoremen, 60, 80–84, 138–139, 195–196; first written contract, 72; expulsion from ISU, 199. For relations with shipowners, *see* Shipowners, Strikes
San Francisco Board of Supervisors, 68, 92
San Francisco Building Trades Council, 60, 67
San Francisco Central Labor Council, 60–69, 74, 92, 139–140, 197
San Francisco Draymen's Association, 63, 68, 70
San Francisco Employers' Association, 24, 26, 61–71
San Francisco Examiner, 67, 69
San Francisco Federated Trades Council, 13, 19, 23, 32, 45, 47, 48
San Francisco Industrial Association, 196
Scharrenberg, Paul, 165, 172, 183, 186, 191, 192, 217; and Furuseth, 86, 91, 95; union activities, 177, 179, 182, 199; conflict with "Communists," 197, 198
Schjotz, Jonas S., 2
Schmitz, Eugene E., 77–78, 93
Schneider, Martin, 11
Schwerin, R. P., 133, 134
Seamen's Act: development of the bill, 113–116; legislative history, 116–132; provisions of, 130–131; administration of, 135–137, 166; evaluation of, 137, 174–176; in the courts, 164–165; proposed legislation to close loopholes, 165–169
Sheraton, Charles H., 102–104
Shipowners: on Pacific Coast, 13, 22–27, 40, 55, 57–58, 61, 62, 72–78, 146, 156, 158, 159, 165, 190, 196; legislative activity, 29, 30, 170–173; opposition to seamen's bills, 33, 36, 38–39, 117–119,
126, 133–134; in World War I, 141, 146–147; postwar, 155–158, 164
Shipowners' Association, Pacific. *See* Shipowners
Shipping Commissioners acts, 29–30
Shipstead, Henrik, 187
Shipstead bill, 187–188
Silver, Selim, 91, 198, 215
Smith, Hoke, 130
Socialists, 17–19, 47, 50, 100
Southern Pacific Railroad Co., 74, 133
Spight, Thomas, 115, 116
Spreckles, John D., 12, 86
Spreckles, Rudolph, 119
Stanford, Leland, 32
Steamship Managers' Association, 63
Steamship sailors, 19–20, 57–58
Steffens, Lincoln, 193
Strasser, Adolph, 34, 211
Strikes: 1886, 12–13; 1893, 22–27; 1899, 57–58; 1901, 60–71; 1906, 74–78; 1916, 141; 1919, 155–156; 1921, 156–159; 1934, 195–196
Sullivan, Dan, 101, 102
Sutherland, George, 123, 165
Symmes, Frank, 69

Taft, William Howard, 94, 121, 122
Teamsters, 63, 67, 68, 70
Tennison, John H., 124, 149
Thomas, Albert M., 180
Thompson, George, 11
Thompson, John Vance, 59, 160, 161
Tobin, Daniel, 183

Uhler, George, 125, 128, 136
Union Labor party, 71, 92–94
United Fruit Co., 191
United Shipping and Transportation Association, 74, 75
United States Chamber of Commerce, 134, 170, 171, 195
United States Marine Inspection Service, 113, 136, 166
United States Sea Service Bureau, 148, 157, 158, 166
United States Shipping Board, 146–149, 154–158, 162, 166, 169, 191
United States Steel Corporation, 105–106

Vardaman, James K., 129
Vidal, James, 102, 104

Wages: amount of, 11, 12, 15, 20, 22, 57, 72, 75, 82, 109, 141, 147, 155, 190, 205;

Index

payment of, 31, 43, 115, 119, 130–131, 134, 170–171
Wahlstrom, A., 77
Walker, J. H., 153
Watches: legislation on, 31, 42, 115, 170; Kalashi-Watch defined, 111; administrative ruling on, 135; court decision on, 164–165
Waterfront Workers' Federation, 138
Waterhouse, Frank, 20, 31, 52
Wheeler, Benjamin Ide, 66
White, George W., 126
White, Stephen S., 41
White Act, 36–43
Williams, G. C., 24
Williams, John Sharp, 123
Wilson, J. Havelock, 20, 145, 217, 226; union activities, 53–54, 100, 102, 178, 179; and seamen's bill, 116, 150–151
Wilson, William B., 87, 125, 133, 146; and seamen's bill, 116–117, 120, 122, 123, 128, 137
Wilson, Woodrow, 87; and seamen's bill, 121, 123, 127, 128, 131–132, 134, 136, 220; and London conference on safety at sea, 124, 125; and World War I, 145, 146, 148, 149, 150; and League of Nations, 151, 154
Woll, Matthew, 153, 185, 188
Working conditions. *See* Conditions aboard ship
Workmen's compensation, 185–186

Yorke, Father Peter C., 67

www.ingramcontent.com/pod-product-compliance
Lightning Source LLC
Chambersburg PA
CBHW021658230426
43668CB00008B/663